XML for Catalogers and Metadata Librarians

Recent Titles in Libraries Unlimited
Third Millennium Cataloging Series

Susan Lazinger and Sheila Intner, Series Editors

Using the Open Archives Initiative Protocol for Metadata Harvesting
Timothy W. Cole and Muriel Foulonneau

Subject Access to a Multilingual Museum Database: A Step-by-Step Approach to the Digitization Process
Allison Siffre Guedalia Kupietzky

Moving Image Cataloging: How to Create and How to Use a Moving Image Catalog
Martha M. Yee

Collection-Level Cataloging: Bound-With Books
Jain Fletcher

Practical Strategies for Cataloging Departments
Rebecca L. Lubas, Editor

Demystifying FRAD: Functional Requirements for Authority Data
Qiang Jin

FRSAD: Conceptual Modeling of Aboutness
Maja Žumer, Marcia Lei Zeng, and Athena Salaba

Demystifying Serials Cataloging: A Book of Examples
Fang Huang Gao, Heather Tennison, and Janet A. Weber

XML for Catalogers and Metadata Librarians

Timothy W. Cole and Myung-Ja K. Han

Third Millennium Cataloging
Susan Lazinger and Sheila Intner, Series Editors

AN IMPRINT OF ABC-CLIO, LLC
Santa Barbara, California • Denver, Colorado • Oxford, England

Library of Congress Cataloging-in-Publication Data

Cole, Timothy W.
XML for catalogers and metadata librarians / Timothy W. Cole and Myung-Ja K. Han.
pages cm. — (Third millennium cataloging)
Includes bibliographical references and index.
ISBN 978-1-59884-519-8 (pbk.) — ISBN 978-1-61069-291-5 (ebook)
1. XML (Document markup language) 2. Cataloging—Data processing. 3. Metadata. I. Han, Myung-Ja K. II. Title.
Z678.93.X54C65 2013
006.7′4—dc23 2013006978

ISBN: 978-1-59884-519-8
EISBN: 978-1-61069-291-5

17 16 15 14 13 1 2 3 4 5

This book is also available on the World Wide Web as an eBook.
Visit www.abc-clio.com for details.

Libraries Unlimited
An Imprint of ABC-CLIO, LLC

ABC-CLIO, LLC
130 Cremona Drive, P.O. Box 1911
Santa Barbara, California 93116-1911

This book is printed on acid-free paper ∞

Manufactured in the United States of America

Contents

Preface

Libraries have long been early adopters of new technologies. By the late 1930s, well before the first programmable digital computer was built and more than 40 years before the introduction of the first desktop personal computers, libraries were using punch card systems (developed originally as tools for accountants) to streamline library circulation workflows. The Library of Congress acquired its first digital computer in 1964, at a point in time when such systems were still a relative rarity even on university campuses; two years later, the MAchine-Readable Cataloging (MARC) format was born (Arms 1990, 14–17). The advent of MARC, still ubiquitous in libraries today, was truly a watershed moment for library cataloging and bibliographic control.

What initially drove many early experiments in library automation during the mid-twentieth century were the "twin realities of disproportionately rising costs and the growing disjuncture between the strengths and capabilities of the traditional library and the changing information habits and demands of its clientele" (Battin 1990, 2). These motivating forces still pertain today and still drive libraries to investigate and adopt new technologies. In addition, as librarians have continued to explore and develop computer-based technologies, they have come to appreciate that many of these technologies can facilitate interoperability and, in doing so, can enable a level of collaboration and shared cataloging work flow not feasible before. This added benefit has further encouraged experimentation with and early adoption of computer technologies in libraries.

Today, as catalogers and metadata librarians struggle to manage and describe ever increasing volumes of resources (both digital and print) from increasingly disparate and diverse sources using a growing number of distinct metadata standards and dialects, working knowledge of new and emerging technologies, such as the Extensible Markup Language (XML), are among the most commonly requested qualifications appearing in cataloger and metadata librarian job postings. XML is a useful and increasingly prevalent format for authoring and validating structured data. The use of XML in cataloging and metadata work flows helps enforce and ensure metadata quality, the consistency of cataloging work flows, and adherence to standards. The use of XML facilitates the reuse and repurposing of catalog and metadata records. XML and XML-related technologies can simplify cataloging and metadata work flows and can support more efficient batch creation and processing of metadata and catalog records. Needing to do more with less, library administrators look to leverage the efficiency and scalability that technologies like XML bring to traditional cataloging units and new digital library initiatives alike. This in turn mandates a workforce well versed in XML and XML-related technologies.

This book is aimed at helping current and would-be catalogers and metadata librarians progress beyond a bare surface-level acquaintance with XML. We assume that readers come to this book with some prior knowledge of descriptive cataloging traditions and/or descriptive metadata basics albeit not necessarily an extensive amount of knowledge on these topics. The catalog and metadata records used in our examples and case studies are drawn largely from library contexts, but they are basic enough to be recognizable to professionals and students working in other cultural heritage institutions, such as museums, archives, historical societies, or any of the myriad other entities and organizations charged with the curation of physical or digital information resources. We do not assume any prior knowledge of XML, though a level of comfort with generic computer applications, such as Web browsers and word processors, is helpful in order to fully follow and experiment with the illustrations provided. In order to get the most out of the examples and illustrations in this book, we encourage readers to install an XML editor of their choice on their work station (for suggestions, see the section "Tools for Creating, Viewing, and Editing XML Metadata" in Chapter 1).

We have organized this book in four parts. Part I introduces XML terminology and the basic concepts of XML (Chapters 1 and 3). We also include in this part of the book a more detailed discussion of why XML is relevant to current and prospective catalogers and metadata librarians (Chapter 2). Part II illustrates how XML can be used to express resource descriptions conforming to a broad range of cataloging and descriptive traditions. The chapters of Part II examine not only traditional library bibliographic descriptions (e.g., MARC records in Chapter 4) but also descriptive approaches to metadata and cataloging standards used by museums, archives, and publishers (Chapter 5) and how XML improves the metadata interoperability (Chapter 6). Part III (Chapters 7, 8, and 9) focuses on the authoring and validation of XML metadata records. The chapters of Part III describe options in XML for expressing metadata standards and formats in a machine-actionable way, such that XML metadata and catalog records can be computer validated against the requirements of a specific community standard. Part IV (Chapters 10, 11, 12, and 13) presents more advanced and complex XML-related technologies that support the reuse and repurposing of XML and logical reasoning and inference across an aggregation of resource descriptions. Although a few of the details of these more sophisticated facets of XML may be advanced for some readers, we include these examples and case studies in order to illustrate the power of XML.

Throughout this book, we focus on examples of XML in action, introducing specific facets and features of XML and demonstrating how these features are exploited in practical contexts to support particular cataloging and metadata workflows. Within each part of this book, illustrations and case studies drawn from practice show how XML can play a pivotal role in meeting a concrete need. Many of the case studies introduced in the book are from our own work at the University of Illinois at Urbana-Champaign Library, but we also draw examples and case studies from other libraries and from collaborative projects, including the *Academic Commons* at Columbia University Libraries, the *Aquifer/American History Online* project of the Digital Library Federation, the *IMLS Digital Collections and Content* project at the University of Illinois, and the *Emblematica Online* project, a collaboration between the University of Illinois and the Herzog August Bibliothek in Wolfenbüttel, Germany. We are grateful for the willingness of Melanie Wacker and Robert Hilliker at Columbia University Libraries and Mara Wade and Thomas Stäcker of the *Emblematica Online* project to share details and materials pertaining to their projects. We also wish to acknowledge the generous support of project sponsors, without whom we would have far fewer examples and without whom we might not have had license ourselves to experiment with and learn about XML. Some of the examples, illustrations, and case studies included in this book are based on work supported variously by the National Endowment for the Humanities, the Deutsche Forschungsgemeinschaft, the Andrew W. Mellon Foundation, and the Institute of Museum and Library Services; however, any opinions, findings, and conclusions or recommendations expressed in this publication are those of the authors and do not necessarily reflect the views of the aforementioned grant sponsors.

We also would like to thank the many people who enabled us more directly to complete this book. Our colleagues at the University of Illinois at Urbana-Champaign Library, including especially Thomas Habing, Michael Tang, Jordan Vannoy, Michael Norman, Janet Weber, and William Mischo, provided us invaluable support and advice regarding the technical and cataloging details of examples and illustrations. The book also includes many figures and tables that illustrate the use of particular tools or that are derived from external sources. We would like to thank the Library of Congress, the Dublin Core Metadata Initiative, and the Joint Information Systems Committee for allowing us to include samples of XML, schemas, and style sheets from their Websites. We also wish to acknowledge the creators of the Oxygen, MarcEdit, and CONTENTdm applications for permission to create and include in this book screen captures from their programs.

Finally, we owe huge thanks to the University of Illinois at Urbana-Champaign Library Research and Publication Committee; to Susan Lazinger and Sheila Intner, the editors of the Third Millennium Cataloging series, of which this volume is a part; to unofficial copy editors and test readers Christine Cho and Megean Osuchowski; and to the production and editorial support team at Libraries Unlimited for their support and patience.

REFERENCES

Arms, Caroline. 1990. "The Technological Context." In *Campus Strategies for Libraries and Electronic Information*, 11–35, edited by Caroline Arms. EDUCOM Strategies Series on Information Technology. Bedford, MA: Digital Press.

Battin, Patricia. 1990. "Introduction." In *Campus Strategies for Libraries and Electronic Information*, 1–10, edited by Caroline Arms. EDUCOM Strategies Series on Information Technology. Bedford, MA: Digital Press.

PART I

INTRODUCTION AND OVERVIEW

CHAPTER 1

XML: What Is It?

The authoritative document defining the Extensible Markup Language (XML)[1] is a standard created and promulgated by the World Wide Web Consortium (W3C). More precisely, it is a *W3C Recommendation*, a specification and set of guidelines that have been formally endorsed by the W3C Director and the Consortium membership. Printed in full, this one document is about 40 pages in length. However, in addition to the W3C Recommendation defining XML, the W3C XML Core Working Group, the group charged with the upkeep of the standard, also publishes a number of ancillary documents dealing with particular facets and extensions of XML (e.g., *Namespaces in XML*,[2] *XML Inclusions*,[3] *XML Information Set*,[4] *XML Base*,[5] and so on). Additional W3C working groups, such as the XSLT Working Group,[6] the XML Query Working Group,[7] and the XML Schema Working Group,[8] are responsible for publishing and maintaining other essential documents relating to XML and its use. The complete set of W3C documents describing and relating to the use of XML, many hundreds of pages in total, is extensive and a bit intimidating to implementers new to the technology.

Not surprisingly therefore, there have been many attempts to provide short, easy-to-digest definitions of what XML is. The better of these definitions offer characterizations that are concise, elegant, and even pithy, but keep in mind that any single, one- or two-sentence definition cannot capture the essence of XML in its entirety and will almost always tend to emphasize different characteristics and attributes of XML at the expense of other features. Considered broadly as a technology, XML is multifaceted, can be used for diverse purposes, and is implemented in a variety of contexts. Both practically and in theoretical terms, the scope of XML is quite extensive.

This chapter provides an introduction to and overview of XML, beginning with three one-sentence definitions of XML that collectively illustrate its multifaceted nature in practical contexts. Next is a brief discussion of a model of information that views texts, including metadata records, as Ordered Hierarchies of Content Objects (OHCO). While providing a comprehensive and rigorous account of the theoretical underpinnings of XML is beyond the scope of this book, this introduction to the OHCO model of texts is intended to provide a grounding in a core theoretical model of information with which XML aligns well. The chapter continues with an overview showing how XML syntax is used to expose the OHCO view of a text. (Additional facets of XML syntax are discussed in more detail in Chapter 3.) The chapter closes with a consideration of the strengths and limitations of the OHCO model of texts, a synopsis of how the rest of this book is organized, and a brief sampling of tools that can be used to create and view XML metadata records. Subsequent chapters focus on the facets and features of XML most germane to its use by library catalogers and metadata librarians.

MANY DEFINITIONS OF XML

Some definitions of XML try to tease out a simple meaning from the words the acronym represents.[9] Others define XML by what it is similar and dissimilar to. Such definitions help provide a perspective on XML and its origins and are helpful in understanding the place of XML relative to other specifications for marking up documents and data, but such definitions are of limited aid in learning how to use XML or how to design XML applications. Since the goal of this book is to highlight the utility of XML in a metadata and library cataloging context and to demonstrate this utility through examples and illustrations drawn from practice, we will rely on pragmatic, utilitarian definitions that focus on uses of XML for conveying and using information resource descriptions in the context of libraries and library services.

In practical terms, the XML specification provides standard rules and conventions for converting data and information into a form that can be used, stored, and transmitted by and between computer applications. In the computer science domain, this process of making information ready for computers is known generically as *serialization*. Broken down into their most rudimentary and detailed processes, almost all computer-based applications involve serialization. Consider, for example, how a computer might be used to process information on a printed page. Ultimately, before the information can be processed by the computer or stored on disk, it must be converted into an ordered *series* of ones and zeros (i.e., a binary representation that can be processed by a digital computer). XML works at a higher level of abstraction, but the principle is similar. For example, before a bibliographic description of a book can be used by an XML-based application designed to disseminate or display metadata records, the statements and assertions of the bibliographic description must be labeled and serialized according to XML rules and syntax (i.e., according to the underlying, foundational grammar of XML). The following basic definition emphasizes the potential of XML as a standard useful for the serialization of metadata: *XML is an open standard that is used to serialize, that is, to encode and describe structured data and to facilitate the maintenance, organization, sharing, and reuse of these data by computer applications.*

In this definition, "data" is meant to be understood broadly. XML can be and is used routinely to express simple numeric data values of all kinds (e.g., meteorological observations, financial transactions, and geospatial coordinates), but XML also is used routinely to organize and convey textual and mixed alphanumeric values (e.g., author names, book titles, Library of Congress Subject Headings, and Dewey Decimal call numbers). Using specialized markup semantics (such as those defined for Scalable Vector Graphics[10]) and encoding approaches (such as base-64 encoding of nontextual data[11]), XML also can be used to serialize and express nonnumeric, nontextual content, such as pictures, graphs, and drawings. More significantly, XML can and is used to express resources that have complex structure, such as journal articles, cataloging records, tabular text, spreadsheets, dynamically generated Web pages with embedded hyperlinks, and even entire books. This suggests a second definition: "[XML] is a simple text-based format for representing structured information: documents, data, configurations, books, transactions, invoices, and much more."[12]

The modifier "structured" in the preceding definitions is significant. It conveys that the intended scope (range) of XML is data that have order and discrete elements or subdivisions that are useful to distinguish, label, and/or address (access) individually. Structured data are ubiquitous in text documents and in library applications, so much so that some structural cues go unnoticed most of the time. A book that has front matter, chapters, and an index is obviously structured, but so is any text that simply has punctuation, paragraphing, indentation, and/or bulleted or numbered lists. White space and punctuation do delineate structure, even if human readers are so used to such formatting as to take the structures delineated for granted. Computers are not so smart. They need help in recognizing the intellectual structural cues that humans infer from context, punctuation, and formatting. In many instances, the degree to which the intellectual structure of a metadata record is made explicit for computers will determine what functionality a computer-mediated application or service can offer to users. This suggests an even more utilitarian definition: *By delineating unambiguously the extent (the boundaries) of semantic elements, labeling these elements, and exposing their hierarchical arrangement, XML helps to make explicit for the computer the intellectual structure of an information resource, which human readers infer intuitively from context, resource formatting, and training.*

We will offer additional definitions of XML as we progress through the topics covered in this book, but these initial three definitions provide an introduction and an initial orientation to the topic. What follows builds from these perspectives on XML.

XML ELEMENTS AS CONTENT OBJECTS

So how does XML work? How does it allow implementers to expose and exploit the intellectual structure of an information resource? XML 1.0 was first published as a formal Recommendation of the W3 Consortium in February 1998. It is a member of the family of descriptive markup languages that model structured data according to the OHCO model of documents (Coombs, Renear, and DeRose 1987; DeRose et al. 1990). *Content objects* are the implicitly or explicitly delineated chunks of content within an information resource that qualify the resource as structured data. An individual chapter in a book may be thought of as a content object. The chapter appears in sequence within a list of other chapters making up the book, so each chapter is an ordered content object. Each chapter in turn could contain an ordered set of paragraphs. These paragraphs are ordered content objects within their parent chapter, so in this manner a book can be represented as an ordered hierarchy of content objects.

There are various ways to represent an OHCO view of an information resource. The XML specification defines a foundational grammar for serializing structured information and expressing OHCO views of information resources. This basic XML grammar encompasses a base character set and encoding (Unicode and UTF-8 or UTF-16[13]), special delimiter characters (<, >, &, ;, -, ', ", :, and !), and a basic markup morphology and syntax, including basic rules for declaring and serializing the content objects and markup components of XML, that is, *elements*, *attributes*, *entity references*, *comments*, and *processing instructions*.

From these rules and this basic, foundational XML grammar, application-specific grammars can be defined for specific classes of information resources through the creation of *Document Type Definitions* (DTDs) or *XML schema* (discussed in Chapters 7, 8, and 9). In this way, XML is inherently extensible. DTDs and schemas are used to declare the explicit names of allowed elements and attributes (i.e., the vocabulary of the application-specific grammar) and to define allowed roles and uses within the application-specific grammar for these elements and attributes. An analogy is the family of Western European languages, such as Italian, French, Spanish, English, German, and so on. The grammars of these languages share overlapping alphabets, punctuation symbols, and closely related concepts of words, sentences, and parts of speech, yet each language's grammar has different specific rules for putting these building blocks together (e.g., rules for word order), and each language has its own vocabulary of words and word forms that can be used within its grammar.

The content objects of an information resource are *elements* in XML parlance. XML elements must be named and may be elaborated using various markup features as defined in the XML specification (and discussed in more detail in Chapter 3). The XML specification provides rules for composing element names used in an application-specific grammar. Most alphanumeric characters and some punctuation characters (e.g., hyphen, underscore, and period) can be used when composing XML element names, but XML names cannot start with a numeral, period, or hyphen. The colon (:) has a reserved meaning in XML names and may be used only for that purpose (see Chapter 6). Names starting with "xml" (regardless of case) are also reserved. XML names may not contain spaces. XML names are accent and case sensitive (so in XML, an element labeled "word" is not the same as one labeled "WORD").

Unlike HyperText Markup Language (HTML) and some other markup languages, the XML specification does not define element names or other labels (with very few special exceptions); it simply requires that every structural element of a resource that the implementer wishes to delineate distinctly be labeled explicitly. Nor does XML on its own define element *content models* (the substructure allowed within an element). This is an important distinction. The foundational grammar of XML specifies basic *syntax* but does not specify *semantics* or specific content structures, leaving these details to be tailored by implementers to fit specific contexts and needs. XML is extensible because it allows implementers to define their own semantic labels and content models, that is, their own formal, application-specific vocabularies and grammars for labeling structure and content objects and for defining allowed relationships between content objects. In the formal parlance of linguists and computer scientists, XML-conformant grammars are *context-free* grammars, level 2 in the *Chomsky hierarchy* of computer-recognizable grammars. (Formally, the Chomsky hierarchy dates to a 1959 article [Chomsky 1959], though the hierarchy was foreshadowed in earlier work [e.g., Chomsky 1956], and the terminology of the hierarchy has evolved and been considerably elaborated by Noam Chomsky and others since 1959.)

Because XML is extensible and because it can be used to construct multiple distinct and different formal grammars for use in specific applications, XML is often termed a meta-markup language. It defines markup rules and syntax but not semantic labels or hierarchy. An information resource or data object that is serialized as an ordered hierarchy of content objects is also an *XML document instance* if it expresses its ordered hierarchy of content objects in a manner that conforms to the syntax and markup rules defined in the W3C XML recommendation. (See also the discussion in Chapter 3 of *well-formed* versus *valid* XML document instances.)

THE BASIC MARKUP RULES OF XML

Elements and Tags

The markup rules of XML require that the semantics and other markup (i.e., *attributes*, *processing instructions*, *declarations*, *CDATA*, and *comments* in XML terminology) used to label and describe elements (content objects) be differentiated from contained content (i.e., *character data*, including *parsed character data*, *entities*, and *character references* in XML terminology). This differentiation is accomplished by enclosing markup within matched pairs of left and right angle brackets, that is, "<" and ">". In XML, explicit markup must be used to delineate both the start and the end of each content-containing element, with the markup delineating the end of a content-containing element always

FIGURE 1.1 A very simple XML document.

```
<sentence>My entire content is this single string.</sentence>
```

starting with an angle bracket and a slash, that is, "</". A very simple example of an XML document instance is shown in Figure 1.1.

In this XML document instance, the string "`<sentence>`" is part of the markup and is an example of an element start-tag. A XML start-tag names and delineates the start of an element in a XML document instance. A matching bit of markup, an element end-tag, "`</sentence>`", is used to delineate the end of the element in our example. Note that the name of the element is repeated in the end-tag. The element name in the end-tag must match the element name in the start-tag exactly, even as to the case of the letters in the name. Thus, "`</Sentence>`" would not be a correct end-tag since the case of the letter "S" in the end-tag does not match the case of the letter "s" in the start-tag. Everything in between the start-tag and the end-tag is the content of the element, that is, the content object called "sentence."

Note that it is also possible in XML to have elements (i.e., content objects) that do not contain any text content, though this seems counterintuitive at first. These are called empty elements and are most often used as placeholders, such as to indicate a page or section break in an XML serialization of a digitized text or to locate an image embedded within a digitized text. (The latter example is analogous to the use of the `<img>` element in a Web page serialized in HTML.) Empty elements may be indicated in an XML document instance by a start-tag immediately followed by an end-tag. Alternatively, a special form of markup (called an empty-element-tag) may be used. An empty-element-tag starts with a left angle bracket and element name and ends with the two-character sequence "/>". Thus, `<pageBreak/>` is an example of an empty-element-tag.

A slightly—but only slightly—more complicated XML document instance is shown in Figure 1.2. This second example contains two elements (content objects), the second nested inside the first: `sentence` and `name`. Note that the end-tag for `name` appears before the end-tag for `sentence`. In XML, all tags opened within a parent element must be closed before the start of any sibling element and also must be closed within the parent element, that is, before the parent element can be closed. This makes clear the hierarchy of elements and is called proper nesting of elements. Thus, the example shown in Figure 1.3 would be incorrect because `<sentence>` is closed before `<name>`, contrary to the order in which these elements were opened.

FIGURE 1.2 An XML document containing a nested content object.

```
<sentence>One author of this book is <name>Myung-Ja Han</name>.</sentence>
```

FIGURE 1.3 Incorrectly nested elements.

```
<sentence>One author of this book is <name>Myung-Ja Han.</sentence></name>
```

Nodes: A Tree View of Hierarchical Elements

The hierarchical elements (content objects) of an XML document instance are often depicted as a tree, with each element being a *node* (i.e., a branch) of the tree. Some nodes in the tree will have child nodes (subsidiary branches). Others will have parent nodes (from which they branch). Some nodes will have *sibling nodes*. Others will have both *child* and *parent nodes* and so on. Terminal nodes are sometimes called *leaf nodes* of the tree. As discussed in Chapter 3, tree views of an XML document may include constructs other than elements. All elements in an XML document instance appear as nodes in the tree view of that document instance, but not all nodes in an XML tree view represent elements in the corresponding XML document instance.

Every XML document instance is allowed one and only one *root node* at the base of the document tree from which all other nodes in the tree ultimately stem. The root node represents the element (content object) at the top of the document's hierarchy. The root node is the very first element to be opened in an XML document instance (and, of course, the very last element to be closed at the end of an XML document). All other elements appearing in the XML document are directly or indirectly a child of the root element. In both the above illustrations (Figures 1.1 and 1.2), the root node of the tree view is the element labeled `sentence`.

Figure 1.4 illustrates how an element-only tree view of a book might be depicted. The corresponding XML is shown in Figure 1.5. Note that the indentation of the text shown in Figure 1.5 is not required; it is provided only to enhance human readability.

Tree views of XML documents are sometimes thought of as being synonymous with a *Document Object Model* (DOM) view of an HTML Web page. Although a reasonable (and reasonably useful) analogy, strictly speaking this is not true, at least not in all cases; there are

FIGURE 1.4 Illustration of a possible node tree for a book serialized as XML.

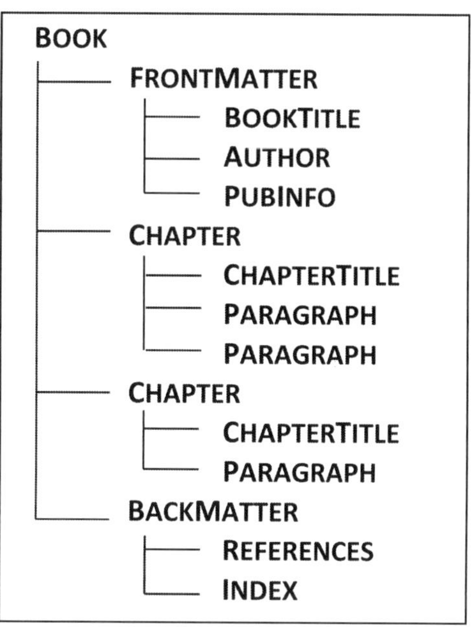

FIGURE 1.5 XML consistent with the node tree shown in Figure 1.4.

```
<Book>
  <FrontMatter>
    <BookTitle>My Book Title</BookTitle>
    <Author>John Smith</Author>
    <PubInfo>My University Press: Urbana, IL, 2012</PubInfo>
  </FrontMatter>
  <Chapter>
  <ChapterTitle>...content...</ChapterTitle>
    <Paragraph>...content...</Paragraph>
    <Paragraph>...content</Paragraph>
  </Chapter>
  <Chapter>
    <ChapterTitle>...content...</ChapterTitle>
    <Paragraph>...content...</Paragraph>
  </Chapter>
  <BackMatter>
    <References>...content...</References>
    <Index>...content...</Index>
  </BackMatter>
</Book>
```

important small differences in the details. There is indeed such a thing as a DOM view of an XML document instance, but this view, while useful when writing programs or scripts to manipulate an XML document instance, is only one treelike view of the information contained in a document instance. Other tree-based views may be useful for other purposes, such as when creating style sheets written in the Extensible Stylesheet Language for Transformations (XSLT style sheets; see Chapter 11). Two important non-DOM tree view data models of XML are the *XML Information Set*[14] and the *XPath Data Model*.[15] These tree-based models of XML are similar to each other and to various levels of the W3C DOM specifications but differ in small details of how they are implemented. The power of the XPath Data Model is illustrated in Chapters 10 and 11.

OHCO: PRACTICAL CONSIDERATIONS

As described in Chapter 3, in addition to naming and delineating the beginning and end of the elements (content objects) contained in an XML document, other kinds of XML markup can be used to describe and elaborate elements, to provide other information and comments useful for processing and using an XML document instance, and even to augment the content of an XML document. However, first and foremost, markup in XML discloses the structure of an information resource by naming and delineating the ordered hierarchy of content objects that make up the resource. Thus, before discussing additional features of XML syntax, the practical strengths and limitations of the OHCO model of information must be examined further.

Scope and Limitations of OHCO Markup Languages

The OHCO model underlying many markup languages exposes a rich view of the intellectual structure of an information resource and fits well with common intuitions about information, particularly textual information. In many contexts, this model is a useful way to represent and think about structured texts, metadata, and other kinds of data. Cogent arguments can be made that the OHCO model of text aligns well not only with computer processing practice but also with theories of philosophy dealing with scientific explanation, ontology, and interpretation (Renear 1995). As compared to common alternative approaches, such as unstructured plain-text serialization and bitmapped page images, the OHCO model for representing text provides a superior way to support abstraction and reuse of the individual intellectual components of a resource, such as for analyzing just the subject headings appearing in a group of library catalog records encoded in XML, for extracting and referencing cohesive segments of text contained in a larger text, or for performing philological or statistical analysis of a textual work or across a corpus of textual works. Serializing OHCO views of texts and other forms of data and information as XML can facilitate the management of a collection of information resources, the consideration of an individual resource in comparison to other resources, or the integration of an individual resource into a collection of resources.

Nonetheless, as Sperberg-McQueen (1991) notes, "Markup reflects a theory of the text. A markup language reflects a theory of texts in general" (35). It is important to recognize that how an implementer chooses to serialize metadata and other kinds of information informs the implementer's thinking about such information albeit in subtle and nuanced ways.

For the most part, the OHCO model of information matured and came to prominence after the creation of Standard Generalized Markup Language (SGML),[16] effectively the parent to XML and an early example of another meta-markup language that models information as OHCO. (XML is formally described in the W3C Recommendation defining XML as a restricted form or subset of SGML.) It has been argued that as a paradigm for texts and similar classes of information resources, the OHCO model is too much an ex post facto rationalization for SGML; is overly reliant on pragmatic, intuitive decisions made by programmers needing to address immediate problems of text processing; and is underdeveloped as a first-principle analysis of the textual form in the abstract (Golumbia 2009). Although not on their own a compelling rebuttal of the utility of the OHCO model in many contexts, these concerns continue to stimulate debate about the correctness of relying on OHCO-based models in some settings (e.g., Schmidt 2010).

Indeed, there are generally accepted, well-known limitations to the basic OHCO model. To begin with, a structured information object may have greater complexity than what can be modeled by a single hierarchy view.

FIGURE 1.6 Improperly nested elements (overlapping hierarchies) for a poem fragment.

```
<PoemFragment>
  <Stanza>
    <Line>The third approached the animal,</Line>
    <Line>And, happening to take</Line>
    <Line>The squirming trunk within his hands,</Line>
    <Line>Thus boldly up he spoke:</Line>
    <Line><Quote>"I see,"</Quote> quoth he, <Quote>"the elephant</Line>
    <Line>Is very like a snake!"<Quote></Line>
  </Stanza>
</PoemFragment>
```

Content objects may be discontinuous, such as a sentence in an article interrupted by a figure or table or a character's speech in a play script interrupted by a stage direction. There may be multiple, equally valid (albeit for different purposes) but overlapping OHCO views of an information resource. Thus, in a brief snippet of a poem (Figure 1.6), it is not always possible in a single XML representation to use XML syntax in the normal way to simultaneously delineate the start and end points of both lines of poetry and quoted text; the snippet, as shown in Figure 1.6, is not well-formed XML (i.e., it contains incorrectly nested elements).

These issues are well known, and various workarounds have been implemented or proposed to address XML limitations as regards representation of discontinuous content objects and overlapping hierarchies (e.g., Renear, Mylonas, and Durand 1996). Such workarounds hold up well in certain contexts and for certain purposes, but most involve assigning nonstandard interpretations to at least some XML constructs. To date, a wholly satisfactory, universal solution to the overlapping markup problem remains elusive. When using XML to mark up an information resource, an implementer must choose which structures to delineate and how, taking into account anticipated use cases. Markup choices must anticipate the use(s) to which the XML serializations being created will be put and must recognize the limitations that XML and the underlying OHCO model of information impose on the potential uses of the XML serializations.

Nor is the OHCO representation of an information resource something that can be thought of as wholly intrinsic to the resource in isolation. The best hierarchy to use is not always obvious from inspection of the information resource alone (i.e., without additional context and without considering likely use). This recognizes that syntax and semantic meaning are related but often in complex, multifaceted ways. Implementers of XML need to understand the nature of the information they are serializing, the context surrounding this information, and the purpose for which the information is being serialized.

While in some cases semantic meaning can inform the application of syntax and in particular may influence the way an information resource is best broken down into an ordered hierarchy of content objects, it is not a fully deterministic process. Reversing the process is even more difficult; our understanding of meaning from syntax is at best incomplete. As Chomsky (1957) notes, "In proposing that syntactic structure can provide a certain insight into problems of meaning and understanding we have entered onto dangerous ground" (93). Implementers have to be mindful of the distinction between syntax and semantics, and when deciding how best to serialize a metadata record, catalogers and metadata librarians have to be prepared to look beyond the resource being described on its own.

Consider the sentence "They are flying planes." For the purposes of linguistic analysis, it might be useful to serialize this sentence in XML as consisting of a `<nounPhrase>` and a `<verbPhrase>` (after Chomsky [1956, 118], from which this illustration of a "constructional homonymity" text is borrowed). This is easily done without knowing anything more about the sentence beyond the fact that it is in English. The difficulty with this particular sentence considered out of context comes in trying to further identify the discrete content objects of the `<verbPhrase>`. Figures 1.7 and 1.8 show two different OHCO views (serialized in XML) of the sentence "They are flying planes." Both views conform to the rules of XML; however, it is not possible to know which more effectively preserves the intent of the author without knowing more about the context in which the sentence is used and the semantic meaning intended by the speaker or writer of the sentence. (The ambiguity here is the antecedent of "they"; is the antecedent the pilots or the airplanes?) This illustrates that the utility of any OHCO serialization of an information resource may be dependent not only on the intended use to which the serialization is to be put but also on the meaning and context of the information resource being serialized.

The salient observation is that the OHCO model of information is not about discovering the one intrinsic content object hierarchy of an information resource. Rather, OHCO is about imposing an order and hierarchy on an information resource in order to make it easier to serialize for use in computer applications. The ordered hierarchy to impose should be consistent with intended semantic meaning and should reflect intended use. At the same time, any OHCO view of an information resource (and therefore any XML

FIGURE 1.7 One OHCO view of "They are flying planes."

```
<sentence>
  <nounPhrase>They</nounPhrase>
  <verbPhrase>
    <verb>are</verb>
    <nounPhrase>flying planes</nounPhrase>
  </verbPhrase>
</sentence>
```

FIGURE 1.8 An alternative OHCO view of "They are flying planes."

```
<sentence>
  <nounPhrase>They</nounPhrase>
  <verbPhrase>
    <verb>are flying</verb>
    <nounPhrase>planes</nounPhrase>
  </verbPhrase>
</sentence>
```

serialization that expresses an OHCO view of the resource) must be recognized as only one of multiple ways the information resource can be represented as an ordered hierarchy of content objects. There is rarely an absolute "best" XML markup of an information resource; markup quality should always be measured relative to how well it preserves meaning and relative to its usefulness for an intended range of anticipated use.

Creating Machine-Readable Documents

The OHCO approach to representing structured data as implemented in XML can seem overly verbose for some use cases. This is because XML was designed assuming that most consumers of XML documents would be computers. Consider the encoding of a chapter of a novel in XML. Human readers rely on punctuation, capitalization, and white space to recognize the intellectual structure of a text as they read. In English, a sentence is delineated by an initial capital letter for the first word of the sentence and a period punctuation mark immediately following the last word of the sentence. Punctuation and white space are forms of presentational markup that must be interpreted in order to glean implications regarding intellectual structure. Humans make such interpretations as they read, but initial capital letters are also used for proper names, titles, and acronyms, and period punctuation marks are also used for abbreviations and in writing decimal numbers. Some (but not all) four-digit numbers are years. This creates potential ambiguities that human readers resolve easily but that computer applications find hard to resolve reliably. (Hard but not impossible, as evidenced by the ever-increasing quality of natural language processing.) Consider the simple sentence shown in Figure 1.9.

Starting with the recognition that the above text comprises a single, complete sentence, a human reader instantly recognizes intellectual structure and multiple subdivisions of information implicit in this sentence, for example, the individual words that make up the sentence, a name (Muriel Foulonneau), a year (2007), and a book title (*Using the Open Archives Initiative Protocol for*

FIGURE 1.9 A human-readable sentence.

```
In 2007 Muriel Foulonneau co-authored a book entitled Using the Open Archives Initiative
Protocol for Metadata Harvesting.
```

FIGURE 1.10 Sentence from Figure 1.9 represented in XML.

```
<sentence>In <date>2007</date> <authorName>Muriel Foulonneau</authorName>
co-authored a book entitled <bookTitle>Using the Open Archives Initiative Protocol
for Metadata Harvesting</bookTitle>.</sentence>
```

Metadata Harvesting). A computer has a harder time extracting the same information from the sentence as quickly and with as much confidence; however, all of this structure can be delineated using XML, as shown in Figure 1.10.

The author of the XML shown in Figure 1.10 did not have to include the sentence-terminal period punctuation mark in creating an XML representation of this sentence. Nor did he or she have to capitalize the "I" in "In" or the initial character of author's name or the book title words. Since the sentence and other elements have been explicitly labeled in the XML, the period and most capitals could be inferred and added by the consuming computer application at the time of presentation based on rules for presentation for each kind of content object. In practice, however, capitalization and punctuation are typically retained when encoding content in XML if it simplifies subsequent processing and reuse and if it is not expected to interfere with why the content is being serialized in XML.

Having the subelements of this sentence exposed facilitates machine processing. If returned as part of a user's search result, a computer application could automatically look for related books by author name. If an item in a list of sentences, an application could use the markup substructure to colocate this sentence with other sentences by date, by name, or by the kind of information contained in the sentence. While such exercises with individual sentences are of limited practical use, when entire articles or books are marked up this way or when comprehensive and structured metadata records are represented this way, applications that act across collections of XML documents can be quite powerful.

However, the OHCO approach is useful and practical only if the implementer uses it appropriately and judiciously. Human resources are typically involved in the initial markup of an information resource, such as the initial creation of a metadata record in XML. It is not necessary to delineate every possible content object. Use markup only to label and describe the elements and properties likely to be used and useful for the content being marked up and in the context of the XML-based application(s) you are implementing or can readily anticipate. Select what structure to expose carefully so as to avoid hierarchy overlaps or unnecessary markup. Frequently when marking up a book-length digital object, it is sufficient to mark up the bulk of the text only to the granularity of paragraphs or possibly even just chapters. In combination with strategic markup of names, places, topics, and temporal entities, this may reveal enough about the intellectual structure of the work for most anticipated uses. On the other hand, when marking up a well-studied literary work, it may be useful to label and describe the part of speech of each word or phrase in the novel. Do not be put off by the verbosity of XML when it is needed. Since XML is intended mostly for machine consumption and given the relatively low cost of computer disks and the relatively high performance of computer networks, such verbosity is generally not a significant impediment practically speaking.

Finally, keep in mind that XML serialization is only part of what is required to manipulate, exploit, and reuse structured data. The XML specification defines a foundational grammar, a markup vocabulary, a syntax, and a set of markup rules for encoding structured data. It allows implementers to define application-specific grammars—rules for exactly how to label and structure texts or data information objects for a specific application. However, while XML allows implementers to employ application-specific semantics and content models, it does not directly provide mechanisms to describe the meaning of these application-specific semantics and content models. From a syntactical standpoint, it does not matter if the start-tags of the preceding small XML examples are `<sentence>` or `<foobar>`. As long as the end-tag name matches the start-tag name, it is correct XML. And while an implementer can specify that `<sentence>` should be used in preference to `<foobar>` for a particular class of XML documents, XML does not provide a way to express directly what the meaning and interpretation of a `<sentence>` content object should be. Such semantic refinements are outside the scope of XML.

HOW THE REST OF THIS BOOK IS ORGANIZED

This book is divided into four parts. This chapter and Chapters 2 and 3 are an introduction to and an overview of the topic. Chapter 2 examines the changing work flows and requirements of catalogers and metadata librarians involved in descriptive cataloging and bibliographic control and looks at how XML can help make new work flows more efficient and conformant with new requirements. Chapter 3 explores the syntax of XML metadata records in more detail. The intent is not to be comprehensive but rather to create a shared foundation of terminology and common concepts for the examples and illustrations that follow in subsequent chapters and to provide context for these examples and illustrations.

The rest of the book, Parts II, III, and IV, describes and examines a range of specific use cases and applications that exploit the core XML standard and the related standards mentioned above, that is, those that define and describe XML schema languages, XML namespaces, XPath, and XSLT. The applications examined range from the relatively simple to the more complex. Part II of this book, Chapters 4, 5, and 6, looks at how commonly used metadata semantics and structures are serialized using XML and explores real-world case studies involving the use of XML serialized metadata in libraries. Chapter 6 also introduces XML Namespaces, a powerful and very practical feature of XML. Part III of this book, Chapters 7, 8, and 9, delves further into the details of XML DTDs and XML Schemas and examines how XML validating parsers and related tools can be used to facilitate metadata record creation, enhance metadata quality control, and support applications dependent on metadata records conforming to specific standards in whole or in part. Part IV of this book, Chapters 10, 11, 12, and 13, illustrates the power of XPath and XSLT, discusses the distinctions between RDF and XML, and considers the utility of XML for library-based Web services and applications. Chapter 13 also provides a capstone and summary of material covered in earlier chapters.

TOOLS FOR CREATING, VIEWING, AND EDITING XML METADATA

Readers are encouraged to delve deeper into the examples and illustrations provided as they read. There is no substitute for a certain amount of hands-on work with XML when trying to learn and appreciate its nuances and functionality. There are a number of excellent tutorial and reference resources in the literature and online (e.g., Van der Vlist 2001; Walsh 1998)[17,18] that can be used to expand on and elaborate the basic discussion of XML syntax provided in this chapter and in Chapter 3. In terms of XML tools for viewing XML document instances, editing document instances, creating schemas, and applying XSLTs, there are a number of good options available.

To create a simple XML document, any good plain-text editor will do. If special characters are needed, a text editor that can save in compliance with the UTF-8 serialization of Unicode is recommended. (Beware of word processors that use non-Unicode character encodings, such as for word processor–specific quote marks, dashes, and the like.) Figure 1.11 shows an abridged MARCXML record, MAchine-Readable Cataloging (MARC) records serialized in XML, created using *Microsoft Windows Notepad.* (More about this record, its syntax, and MARCXML can be found in Chapters 3 and 4.) Figure 1.12 shows this same file as viewed on an Apple Mac using the *Emacs/Carbon* plain-text editor. Figure 1.13 shows this file in *gedit* (running under the *Linux* operating system).

Web browsers are a ubiquitous tool for viewing XML documents. Figure 1.14 shows the same abridged MARCXML record viewed using *Firefox.* As discussed in Chapter 11, most Web browsers also can be used to test out and perfect XSLT style sheets that convert XML metadata records into XHTML. As discussed in Chapter 3, most Web browsers do not *validate* XML but most typically do check that an XML document instance is *well formed.*

FIGURE 1.11 An abridged MARCXML record as created in *Microsoft Notepad* (Windows).

```
File Edit Format View Help
<?xml version="1.0" encoding="UTF-8"?>
<?xml-stylesheet type="text/xsl" href="displayRecord_marc.xsl"?>
<record  xmlns="http://www.loc.gov/MARC21/slim"
        xmlns:xsi="http://www.w3.org/2001/XMLSchema-instance"
        xsi:schemaLocation="http://www.loc.gov/MARC21/slim
                         http://www.loc.gov/standards/marcxml/schema/MARC21slim.xsd">
    <leader>01698cam  22003614a 4500</leader>
    <controlfield tag="001">5439928</controlfield>
    <controlfield tag="005">20080104135038.0</controlfield>
    <controlfield tag="008">070313s2007    ctua     b    001 0 eng  </controlfield>
    <datafield tag="010" ind1=" " ind2=" ">
        <subfield code="a">  2007009006</subfield>
    </datafield>
    <datafield tag="035" ind1=" " ind2=" ">
        <subfield code="a">(OCoLC)ocn105428765</subfield>
    </datafield>
    <datafield tag="100" ind1="1" ind2=" ">
        <subfield code="a">Cole, Timothy W.</subfield>
    </datafield>
    <datafield tag="245" ind1="1" ind2="0">
        <subfield code="a">Using the Open Archives Initiative protocol
                         for metadata harvesting /</subfield>
        <subfield code="c">Timothy W. Cole and Muriel Foulonneau.</subfield>
    </datafield>
    <datafield tag="260" ind1=" " ind2=" ">
        <subfield code="a">Westport, Conn. :</subfield>
        <subfield code="b">Libraries Unlimited,</subfield>
        <subfield code="c">&#xA9; 2007.</subfield>
    </datafield>
    <datafield tag="300" ind1=" " ind2=" ">
        <subfield code="a">xv, 208 p. :</subfield>
        <subfield code="b">ill. ;</subfield>
        <subfield code="c">26 cm.</subfield>
    </datafield>
    <datafield tag="440" ind1=" " ind2="0">
        <subfield code="a">Third millennium cataloging</subfield>
    </datafield>
    <datafield tag="650" ind1=" " ind2="0">
        <subfield code="a">Metadata harvesting.</subfield>
    </datafield>
    <datafield tag="610" ind1="2" ind2="0">
        <subfield code="a">Open Archives Initiative.</subfield>
    </datafield>
    <datafield tag="700" ind1="1" ind2=" ">
        <subfield code="a">Foulonneau, Muriel.</subfield>
    </datafield>
</record>
```

FIGURE 1.12 Same abridged MARCXML record in *Emacs/Carbon* (running under Mac OS X).

```
Emacs@mobile-253-116.near.uiuc.edu
<?xml version="1.0" encoding="UTF-8"?>
<?xml-stylesheet type="text/xsl" href="displayRecord_marc.xsl"?>
<record  xmlns="http://www.loc.gov/MARC21/slim"
        xmlns:xsi="http://www.w3.org/2001/XMLSchema-instance"
        xsi:schemaLocation="http://www.loc.gov/MARC21/slim
                         http://www.loc.gov/standards/marcxml/schema/MARC21slim.xsd">
    <leader>01698cam  22003614a 4500</leader>
    <controlfield tag="001">5439928</controlfield>
    <controlfield tag="005">20080104135038.0</controlfield>
    <controlfield tag="008">070313s2007    ctua     b    001 0 eng  </controlfield>
    <datafield tag="010" ind1=" " ind2=" ">
        <subfield code="a">  2007009006</subfield>
    </datafield>
    <datafield tag="035" ind1=" " ind2=" ">
        <subfield code="a">(OCoLC)ocn105428765</subfield>
    </datafield>
    <datafield tag="100" ind1="1" ind2=" ">
        <subfield code="a">Cole, Timothy W.</subfield>
    </datafield>
    <datafield tag="245" ind1="1" ind2="0">
        <subfield code="a">Using the Open Archives Initiative protocol
                         for metadata harvesting /</subfield>
        <subfield code="c">Timothy W. Cole and Muriel Foulonneau.</subfield>
    </datafield>
    <datafield tag="260" ind1=" " ind2=" ">
        <subfield code="a">Westport, Conn. :</subfield>
        <subfield code="b">Libraries Unlimited,</subfield>
        <subfield code="c">&#xA9; 2007.</subfield>
    </datafield>
    <datafield tag="300" ind1=" " ind2=" ">
        <subfield code="a">xv, 208 p. :</subfield>
        <subfield code="b">ill. ;</subfield>
        <subfield code="c">26 cm.</subfield>
    </datafield>
    <datafield tag="440" ind1=" " ind2="0">
        <subfield code="a">Third millennium cataloging</subfield>
    </datafield>
    <datafield tag="650" ind1=" " ind2="0">
        <subfield code="a">Metadata harvesting.</subfield>
    </datafield>
    <datafield tag="610" ind1="2" ind2="0">
        <subfield code="a">Open Archives Initiative.</subfield>
-u(DOS)--  BibRec-short-ColeFoulonneau.xml   Top L42   (XML)------------------
```

FIGURE 1.13 Same abridged MARCXML record in *gedit* (running under Linux).

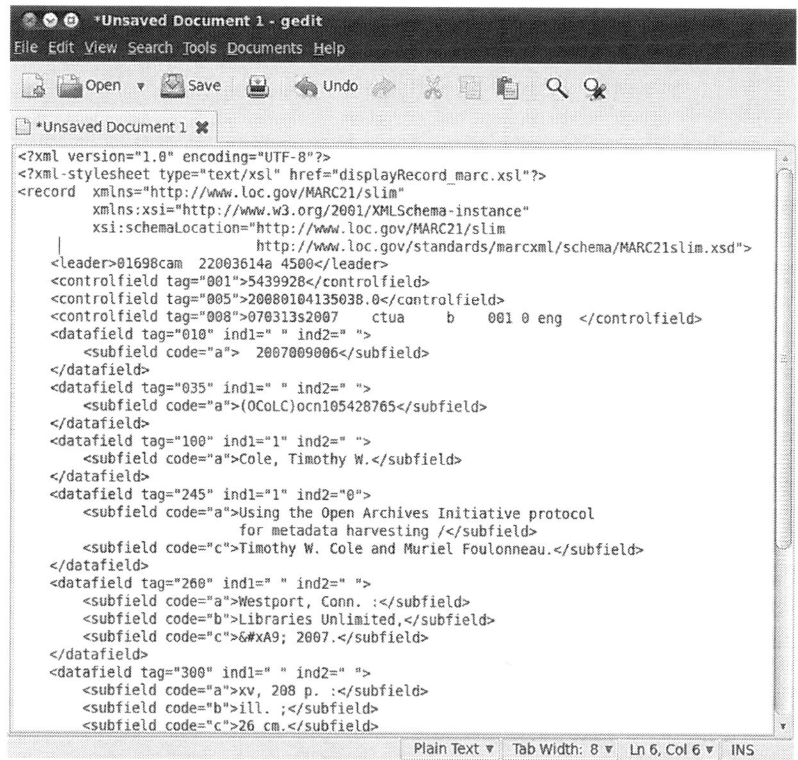


```
<?xml version="1.0" encoding="UTF-8"?>
<?xml-stylesheet type="text/xsl" href="displayRecord_marc.xsl"?>
<record  xmlns="http://www.loc.gov/MARC21/slim"
        xmlns:xsi="http://www.w3.org/2001/XMLSchema-instance"
        xsi:schemaLocation="http://www.loc.gov/MARC21/slim
                           http://www.loc.gov/standards/marcxml/schema/MARC21slim.xsd">
    <leader>01698cam  22003614a 4500</leader>
    <controlfield tag="001">5439928</controlfield>
    <controlfield tag="005">20080104135038.0</controlfield>
    <controlfield tag="008">070313s2007    ctua     b    001 0 eng  </controlfield>
    <datafield tag="010" ind1=" " ind2=" ">
        <subfield code="a">  2007009006</subfield>
    </datafield>
    <datafield tag="035" ind1=" " ind2=" ">
        <subfield code="a">(OCoLC)ocn105428765</subfield>
    </datafield>
    <datafield tag="100" ind1="1" ind2=" ">
        <subfield code="a">Cole, Timothy W.</subfield>
    </datafield>
    <datafield tag="245" ind1="1" ind2="0">
        <subfield code="a">Using the Open Archives Initiative protocol
                          for metadata harvesting /</subfield>
        <subfield code="c">Timothy W. Cole and Muriel Foulonneau.</subfield>
    </datafield>
    <datafield tag="260" ind1=" " ind2=" ">
        <subfield code="a">Westport, Conn. :</subfield>
        <subfield code="b">Libraries Unlimited,</subfield>
        <subfield code="c">&#xA9; 2007.</subfield>
    </datafield>
    <datafield tag="300" ind1=" " ind2=" ">
        <subfield code="a">xv, 208 p. :</subfield>
        <subfield code="b">ill. ;</subfield>
        <subfield code="c">26 cm.</subfield>
```


FIGURE 1.14 Same abridged MARCXML record rendered in *Firefox*.

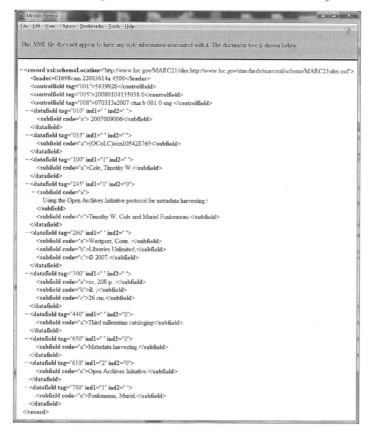

Mozilla Firefox

File Edit View History Bookmarks Tools Help

This XML file does not appear to have any style information associated with it. The document tree is shown below.

```
- <record xsi:schemaLocation="http://www.loc.gov/MARC21/slim http://www.loc.gov/standards/marcxml/schema/MARC21slim.xsd">
    <leader>01698cam 22003614a 4500</leader>
    <controlfield tag="001">5439928</controlfield>
    <controlfield tag="005">20080104135038.0</controlfield>
    <controlfield tag="008">070313s2007 ctua b 001 0 eng </controlfield>
  - <datafield tag="010" ind1=" " ind2=" ">
      <subfield code="a"> 2007009006</subfield>
    </datafield>
  - <datafield tag="035" ind1=" " ind2=" ">
      <subfield code="a">(OCoLC)ocn105428765</subfield>
    </datafield>
  - <datafield tag="100" ind1="1" ind2=" ">
      <subfield code="a">Cole, Timothy W.</subfield>
    </datafield>
  - <datafield tag="245" ind1="1" ind2="0">
    - <subfield code="a">
        Using the Open Archives Initiative protocol for metadata harvesting /
      </subfield>
      <subfield code="c">Timothy W. Cole and Muriel Foulonneau.</subfield>
    </datafield>
  - <datafield tag="260" ind1=" " ind2=" ">
      <subfield code="a">Westport, Conn. :</subfield>
      <subfield code="b">Libraries Unlimited,</subfield>
      <subfield code="c">© 2007.</subfield>
    </datafield>
  - <datafield tag="300" ind1=" " ind2=" ">
      <subfield code="a">xv, 208 p. :</subfield>
      <subfield code="b">ill. ;</subfield>
      <subfield code="c">26 cm.</subfield>
    </datafield>
  - <datafield tag="440" ind1=" " ind2="0">
      <subfield code="a">Third millennium cataloging</subfield>
    </datafield>
  - <datafield tag="650" ind1=" " ind2="0">
      <subfield code="a">Metadata harvesting.</subfield>
    </datafield>
  - <datafield tag="610" ind1="2" ind2="0">
      <subfield code="a">Open Archives Initiative.</subfield>
    </datafield>
  - <datafield tag="700" ind1="1" ind2=" ">
      <subfield code="a">Foulonneau, Muriel.</subfield>
    </datafield>
  </record>
```

For more complex tasks involving XML, a good editor that includes support for schema and/or DTD creation and for document validation is desirable. Some of these editors incorporate XSLT debugging as well, or there are separate stand-alone XSLT authoring and debugging environments available for creating XSLT style sheets that convert from one application-specific XML grammar to another. Many of the examples in this book were created and validated using the Oxygen XML editing application marketed by *SyncRO Soft Ltd.* This commercially available tool is implemented for both PCs and Macs and is currently the XML editing tool of choice for most classes involving XML taught at the University of Illinois Graduate School of Library and Information Science. Oxygen includes document and schema editing and authoring functionality and an XSLT debugger perspective along with a number of other

FIGURE 1.15 Same abridged MARCXML record displayed in Oxygen. Screen shot was made using Oxygen XML Editor (http://www.oxygenxml.com).

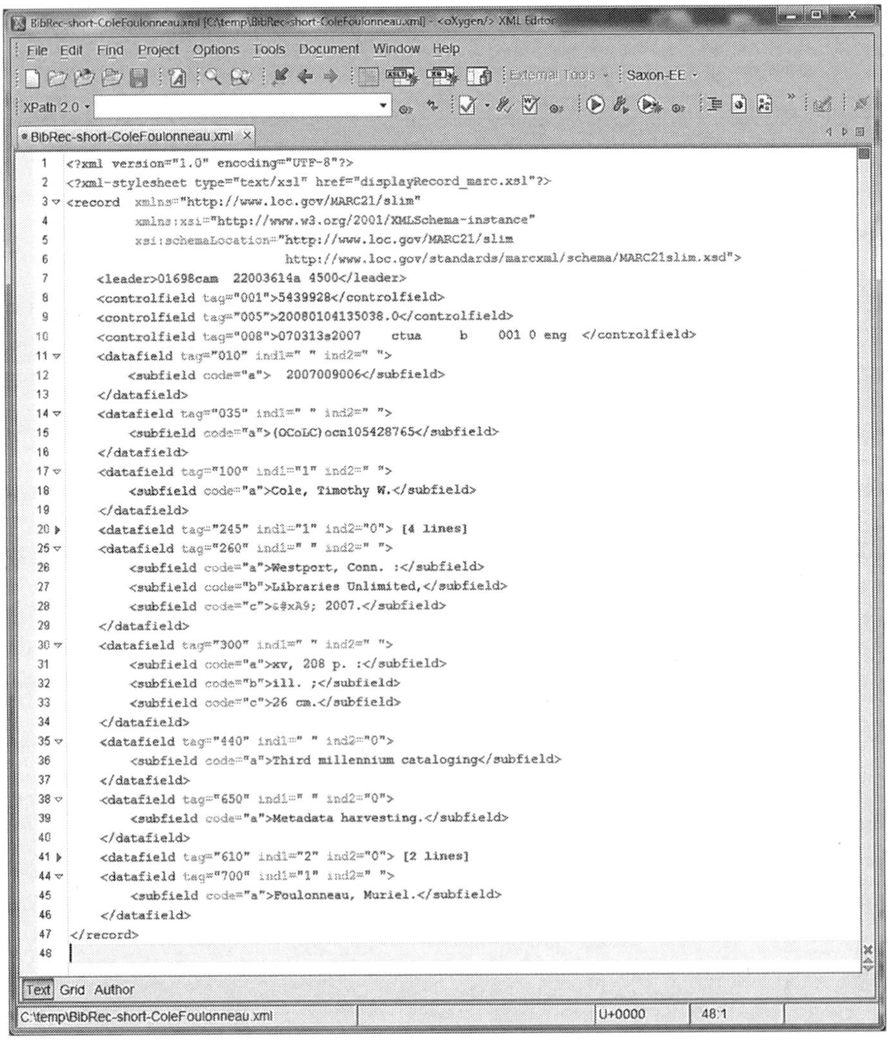

```
<?xml version="1.0" encoding="UTF-8"?>
<?xml-stylesheet type="text/xsl" href="displayRecord_marc.xsl"?>
<record  xmlns="http://www.loc.gov/MARC21/slim"
         xmlns:xsi="http://www.w3.org/2001/XMLSchema-instance"
         xsi:schemaLocation="http://www.loc.gov/MARC21/slim
                  http://www.loc.gov/standards/marcxml/schema/MARC21slim.xsd">
    <leader>01698cam  22003614a 4500</leader>
    <controlfield tag="001">5439928</controlfield>
    <controlfield tag="005">20080104135038.0</controlfield>
    <controlfield tag="008">070313s2007    ctua     b    001 0 eng  </controlfield>
    <datafield tag="010" ind1=" " ind2=" ">
        <subfield code="a">  2007009006</subfield>
    </datafield>
    <datafield tag="035" ind1=" " ind2=" ">
        <subfield code="a">(OCoLC)ocn105428765</subfield>
    </datafield>
    <datafield tag="100" ind1="1" ind2=" ">
        <subfield code="a">Cole, Timothy W.</subfield>
    </datafield>
    <datafield tag="245" ind1="1" ind2="0"> [4 lines]
    <datafield tag="260" ind1=" " ind2=" ">
        <subfield code="a">Westport, Conn. :</subfield>
        <subfield code="b">Libraries Unlimited,</subfield>
        <subfield code="c">&#xA9; 2007.</subfield>
    </datafield>
    <datafield tag="300" ind1=" " ind2=" ">
        <subfield code="a">xv, 208 p. :</subfield>
        <subfield code="b">ill. ;</subfield>
        <subfield code="c">26 cm.</subfield>
    </datafield>
    <datafield tag="440" ind1=" " ind2="0">
        <subfield code="a">Third millennium cataloging</subfield>
    </datafield>
    <datafield tag="650" ind1=" " ind2="0">
        <subfield code="a">Metadata harvesting.</subfield>
    </datafield>
    <datafield tag="610" ind1="2" ind2="0"> [2 lines]
    <datafield tag="700" ind1="1" ind2=" ">
        <subfield code="a">Foulonneau, Muriel.</subfield>
    </datafield>
</record>
```

FIGURE 1.16 The MarcEdit (©Terry Reese) MARC Tools dialog for converting MARC21XML into traditional MARC.

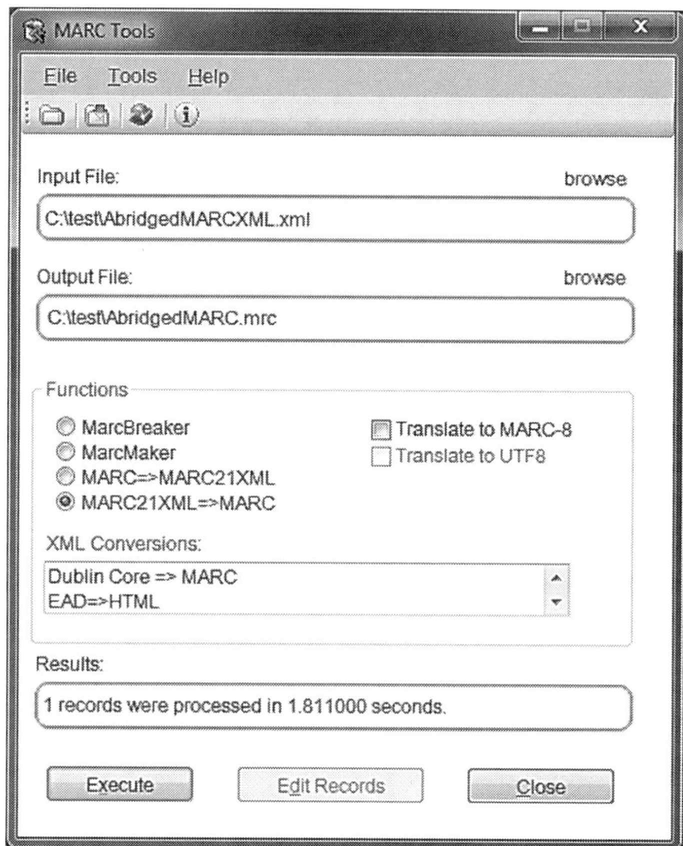

useful features and functionalities. Figure 1.15 shows the abridged MARCXML record from Figure 1.11 as displayed in Oxygen. Markup and character data are distinguished through the use of color, and Oxygen provides a customizable authoring and validation environment for creating XML documents conforming to a DTD or schema. Another popular XML editor is XML Spy, marketed by Altova. Similar to Oxygen, XML Spy supports validation against XML DTDs and other forms of XML schemas, supports editing and debugging of XSLT and cascading style sheets, and includes several built-in XML document templates. Other XML editors, some free and open source, are available as well. Selection of editors is often a matter of personal or institutional preference.

Domain-specific tools can be used to ingest (convert) and/or export XML records from and into domain-specific formats. For example, MarcEdit, a freely available (i.e., open source) software application created by Terry Reese while at Oregon State University,[19] can both export and read XML. It can convert properly serialized XML back into the traditional MARC format. Such tools can be useful for converting between non-XML, domain-specific metadata record serializations and XML. Figure 1.16 illustrates the MarcEdit tool dialog used (in this instance) to convert the abridged XML metadata record shown in Figure 1.11 into traditional MARC. Which tool to use when is a matter of context and personal preference. Regardless of tool used, readers should spend some time exploring XML by trial and error, learning what is allowed and what is not and what can be done and what cannot be done.

QUESTIONS AND TOPICS FOR DISCUSSION

1. What are the possible benefits of having bibliographic records in XML format?
2. In order to create metadata in XML, one should use tools that support XML. Compare the functions of one of the XML editors mentioned in this chapter to other XML editors you learn about through your own research. What are the most important features you would like to have in an XML editor?
3. Search online for an example of an XML document. How can the data in the document be serialized in XML differently (such as with more or fewer kinds of content objects)? What uses can you imagine for this XML document in a computer application?

SUGGESTIONS FOR EXERCISES

1. Create an XML document representing a chapter (or part of a chapter) from this textbook. Start by defining and naming the content objects of interest for the ways that you envision that such an XML representation might be used.
2. In Oxygen (or your own favorite XML editor), try to use different capitalization in start-tag and end-tag for the same element. What does the resulting error message say?
3. MarcEdit is open source software. Download MarcEdit to your work station and experiment with MarcEdit Tools, both *Functions* and *XML Conversions*, using a bibliographic record in MARC format.
4. Pick a couple of functions from MarcEdit that are useful to staff in a cataloging unit and create a document titled "How to Use MarcEdit" that can be used as instruction material.

NOTES

1. The original 1998 release of the XML 1.0 is available at http://www.w3.org/TR/1998/REC-xml-19980210. The latest edition (2008 as of this writing) of the XML 1.0 specification can always be found at http://www.w3.org/TR/xml. The latest edition (2006 as of this writing) of the XML version 1.1 specification can always be found at http://www.w3.org/TR/xml11.
2. http://www.w3.org/TR/REC-xml-names.
3. http://www.w3.org/TR/xinclude.
4. http://www.w3.org/TR/xml-infoset.
5. http://www.w3.org/TR/xmlbase.
6. http://www.w3.org/XML/2010/10/xsl-charter.html.
7. http://www.w3.org/2003/09/xmlap/xml-query-wg-charter.html.
8. http://www.w3.org/2003/09/xmlap/xml-schema-wg-charter.html.

9. See, for example, http://articles.sitepoint.com/article/really-good-introduction-xml.

10. http://en.wikipedia.org/wiki/Scalable_Vector_Graphics.

11. http://en.wikipedia.org/wiki/Base64.

12. http://www.w3.org/standards/xml/core.

13. The Unicode Consortium, *The Unicode Standard, Version 5.0.0*, defined by The Unicode Standard, Version 5.0 (Boston: Addison-Wesley, 2007) (ISBN 0-321-48091-0).

14. http://www.w3.org/TR/xml-infoset. Note that the DOM Level 3 core specification, http://www.w3.org/TR/DOM-Level-3-Core, completes the mapping between the DOM and the XML Information Set.

15. http://www.w3.org/TR/xpath/#data-model, the XPath 1.0 Data Model. See also http://www.w3.org/TR/xpath-datamodel, the XQuery 1.0 and XPath 2.0 Data Model.

16. http://www.iso.org/iso/catalogue_detail.htm?csnumber=16387.

17. W3 Schools.com XML Tutorial: http://www.w3schools.com/xml/default.asp.

18. ZVON.org XML basics quick start: http://www.zvon.org/comp/m/xml.html.

19. http://people.oregonstate.edu/~reeset/marcedit/html.

REFERENCES

Chomsky, Noam. 1956. "Three Models for the Description of Language." *IRE Transactions on Information Theory* 2: 113–24.

Chomsky, Noam. 1957. *Syntactic Structures*. The Hague: Mouton & Co.

Chomsky, Noam. 1959. "On Certain Formal Properties of Grammars." *Information and Control* 2: 137–67.

Coombs, James H., Allen Renear, and Steven J. DeRose. 1987. "Markup Systems and the Future of Scholarly Text Processing." *Communications of the ACM* 30, no. 11, 933–47. DOI: 10.1145/32206.32209

DeRose, Steven J., David G. Durand, Elli Mylonas, and Allen H. Renear. 1990. "What Is Text, Really?" *Journal of Computing in Higher Education* 1, no. 2: 3–26. DOI: 10.1007/BF02941632

Golumbia, David. 2009. *The Cultural Logic of Computation*. Cambridge, MA: Harvard University Press.

Renear, Allen H. 1995. "Theory and Metatheory in the Development of Text Encoding." Available at: http://homepages.rpi.edu/~brings/renear.target

Renear, Allen H., Elli Mylonas, and David Durand. 1996. "Refining Our Notion of What Text Really Is: The Problem of Overlapping Hierarchies." In *Research in Humanities Computing*, edited by N. Ide and S. Hockey. Oxford: Oxford University Press. A postprint version of this paper is available online at http://www.ideals.illinois.edu/handle/2142/9407.

Schmidt, Desmond. 2010. "The Inadequacy of Embedded Markup for Cultural Heritage Texts." *Literary and Linguistic Computing* 25, no. 3: 337–56.

Sperberg-McQueen, C. M. 1991. "Text in the Electronic Age: Textual Study and Text Encoding, with Examples from Medieval Texts." *Literary and Linguistic Computing* 6, no. 1: 34–46.

Van der Vlist, Eric. 2001. "Using W3C XML Schema." Available at: http://www.xml.com/pub/a/2000/11/29/schemas/part1.html

Walsh, Norman. 1998. "A Technical Introduction to XML." Available at: http://www.xml.com/pub/a/98/10/guide0.html

CHAPTER 2

XML: Why It Is Important to Catalogers and Metadata Librarians

In response to changes in the nature and scope of the information resources that libraries collect and curate, descriptive cataloging practices in libraries are evolving. As annual print acquisitions by libraries reduce in volume, as the availability of publisher-supplied cataloging records and Library of Congress cataloging-in-publication records grows, and as other sources for copy cataloging continue to expand, the time spent at most libraries on the original cataloging of print monographs and serials declines. However, this should not be interpreted to mean that the need for bibliographic control and descriptive cataloging is on the wane.

As the hours spent on original cataloging of print materials have been trending fewer, library cataloging units are doing more original cataloging of digital resources (often in collaboration with noncataloging units). And while the MAchine-Readable Cataloging (MARC) standard remains the dominant cataloging standard in most libraries, concurrent with the growth in digital resources being processed by libraries, cataloging units have been adding more expertise in non-MARC descriptive metadata standards. Surveys of catalogers and metadata librarians (e.g., Veve and Feltner-Reichert 2010) suggest that the increased integration of non-MARC metadata standards into library cataloging work flows is being driven both by the rapidly increasing volume of nonprint, digital resources needing to be cataloged and by the increased demands from users for improved and enhanced virtual access to information over a broader range of formats and granularities.

The magnitude and centrality of these issues was highlighted in the May 2011 announcement from the Library of Congress of a new initiative, *Transforming Our Bibliographic Framework*, which noted that many institutions are "being asked to broaden their services, especially in terms of the availability of digital data. Efficiencies in the creation and sharing of cataloging metadata are therefore imperative."[1] Part of the solution suggested by the Library of Congress is to look beyond the dominant MARC cataloging format at new and emerging metadata standards that can better exploit the semantic web, foster catalog record and metadata reuse, facilitate end-user navigation of information resource entities, and enable the use of new and emerging bibliographic systems.

The proliferation of non-MARC metadata standards now in wide use means that catalogers and metadata librarians spend more time crosswalking catalog records and metadata from one standard to another. In turn, as library cataloging units continue to work with a wider variety of digital formats and incorporate non-MARC metadata standards into their production work flows, catalogers and metadata librarians are increasingly finding it necessary to make use of and add expertise in XML technologies and/or tools that make use of XML.

This chapter discusses some of the changes in cataloging and metadata work flows happening in libraries today and examines how these new and still evolving work flow changes are impacting the job descriptions and expected competencies of catalogers and metadata librarians in regard to XML and related technologies.

TRENDS IN BIBLIOGRAPHIC CONTROL AND DESCRIPTIVE CATALOGING

A Diversity of Resources

The volume of information resources in digital format cataloged and actively curated by libraries continues to grow. Many traditional resources formerly disseminated almost exclusively in print format, including both serials and books, are now available also or only in digital form. Libraries are increasingly purchasing e-books and e-journal subscriptions in lieu of printed materials for reasons of economy and to meet user expectations in regard to convenience and rapidity of access. The range of other kinds of digitized and born-digital resources that libraries process and to which they provide access has expanded as well, as scanning technologies have become less expensive, easier to use, and of higher quality; as academic and scholarly institutions generate more born-digital resources; and as the Web and other information creation and delivery technologies continue to evolve.

Almost all sizes and types of libraries now deal with multiple types of digital resources alongside their print books and journals. Larger libraries have increasingly been choosing to participate in mass digitization projects, such as the Google Books Library Project[2] and the Internet Archive–sponsored Open Content Alliance digitization initiative,[3] as well as to initiate their own institution-based digitization projects for both books and special collections. Many universities now mandate that their graduate students submit theses and dissertations in electronic format,[4] with the electronic publication being considered the deposit of record. As a result of these and similar initiatives, more and more libraries find themselves needing to provide bibliographic control for a growing influx of born-digital and retrospectively digitized information.

In order to deal with the scale and breadth of this influx, tools and services available to catalogers and metadata librarians (as well as to the end users of library resources) have evolved and become more efficient to use and more ubiquitous. A public view of the complete Online Computer Library Center (OCLC) bibliographic and holdings database (i.e., WorldCat[5]) can be searched today from nearly any Web-enabled device. Web interfaces are available as well for some more specialized OCLC cataloging tools (though typically with limited functionality as compared to dedicated desktop clients still provided by OCLC). The entirety of the Library of Congress Subject Headings (LCSH), the LC Name Authority File, the MARC Code List for Countries, and the MARC Code List for Geographic Areas can be accessed via the Web,[6] and every LCSH term now has its own unique persistent Uniform Resource Identifier. Powerful cataloging tools created at individual institutions can be shared widely and easily (e.g., MarcEdit[7] created by Terry Reese while at Oregon State University).

XML supports requirements for scalability, interoperability, and flexibility and is often relied on by these tools and services, sometimes behind the scenes, sometimes in more obvious and visible ways. In some instances, the underlying XML records are made available for export, viewing, or download through a tool or service. Thus, the popular MarcEdit tool can both import and export XML records conforming to the MARC 21 XML Schema.[8] (See Chapter 4 for a discussion of MARC records serialized as XML according to this schema.)

As another example, registry records for several of the major authorities and vocabularies are now available to be viewed as XML. Figure 2.1 shows the Library of Congress registry record for the LCSH topical term "metadata harvesting" serialized in XML. Because it shows an advanced real-world application, the XML document instance depicted in Figure 2.1 illustrates several features of XML not yet discussed, including examples of *attributes* and an *XML declaration* (specialized kinds of XML markup described in Chapter 3) and the use of *XML namespaces* (discussed in Chapter 6). Figure 2.1 also illustrates the use of the Resource Description Framework (RDF),[9] a framework and data model developed by the World Wide Web Consortium (W3C) for representing information about resources in the World Wide Web (e.g., for creating and structuring descriptive metadata). RDF can be used in conjunction with XML or with select other serialization formats. RDF is discussed in more detail in Chapter 12. Figure 2.1 also illustrates the use of Simple Knowledge Organization System (SKOS) semantic labels that have been defined by the W3C Semantic Web Deployment Working Group.[10] LCSH registry record examples are discussed in greater detail in Chapters 6 and 11. For now, this example is provided simply to illustrate the increasing use of XML by mainstream library institutions (e.g., the Library of Congress).

FIGURE 2.1 Registry record in RDF/XML for LCSH term "metadata harvesting." (Source: Library of Congress)[11].


```
<?xml version="1.0" encoding="UTF-8"?>
  <rdf:RDF
    xmlns:dcterms="http://purl.org/dc/terms/"
    xmlns:owl="http://www.w3.org/2002/07/owl#"
    xmlns:rdf="http://www.w3.org/1999/02/22-rdf-syntax-ns#"
    xmlns:skos="http://www.w3.org/2004/02/skos/core#">
    <rdf:Description rdf:about="http://id.loc.gov/authorities/sh2007001751#concept">
      <dcterms:modified rdf:datatype="http://www.w3.org/2001/XMLSchema#dateTime">
        2009-12-15T13:52:15-04:00</dcterms:modified>
      <owl:sameAs rdf:resource="info:lc/authorities/sh2007001751"/>
      <dcterms:created rdf:datatype="http://www.w3.org/2001/XMLSchema#dateTime">
        2007-04-12T00:00:00-04:00</dcterms:created>
      <skos:related rdf:resource="http://id.loc.gov/authorities/sh2009009406#concept"/>
      <skos:altLabel xml:lang="en">Harvesting, Metadata</skos:altLabel>
      <skos:inScheme rdf:resource="http://id.loc.gov/authorities#topicalTerms"/>
      <skos:inScheme rdf:resource="http://id.loc.gov/authorities#conceptScheme"/>
      <rdf:type rdf:resource="http://www.w3.org/2004/02/skos/core#Concept"/>
      <dcterms:source xml:lang="en">Work cat.: 2007009006: Cole, Timothy W. Using the
      Open Archives Initiative protocol for metadata harvesting, c2007.
      </dcterms:source>
      <skos:prefLabel xml:lang="en">Metadata harvesting</skos:prefLabel>
      <skos:broader rdf:resource="http://id.loc.gov/authorities/sh85066148#concept"/>
      </rdf:Description>
      <rdf:Description rdf:about="http://id.loc.gov/authorities/sh85066148#concept">
      <skos:prefLabel xml:lang="en">Information retrieval</skos:prefLabel>
      </rdf:Description>
   <rdf:Description rdf:about="http://id.loc.gov/authorities/sh2009009406#concept">
```

The Impact of XML

The power and ready availability of these resources and tools, the ways in which they rely on and use XML, the inherent flexibility and power of XML, and its foundational Ordered Hierarchy of Content Objects model of text have an impact on how catalogers and metadata librarians create, manipulate, update, and exploit descriptions of information resources. Writing more than two decades ago on library bibliographic control and descriptive cataloging, Michael Gorman (1990) offered the following definition of "descriptive cataloging" in a library context:

> The term *descriptive cataloguing* is somewhat ambiguous. It is often confused with *bibliographic description*, which is a significant part of descriptive cataloguing but not the whole. In this chapter *descriptive cataloguing* signifies the activities connected with the bibliographic description of library materials, assigning of access points (previously called *headings*) to those descriptions, the construction of authority records containing access points and references to these access points, and the MARC tagging and coding of bibliographic descriptive data and authority records. This definition goes beyond the traditional because it deliberately embraces the effects of computer technology on descriptive cataloguing rather than, as is mostly the practice, assuming that cataloguing is essentially unaffected by, and separate from, the major change in the medium through which cataloguing data is transmitted and stored. The truth of the matter is that one cannot think about any aspect of cataloguing, except at the most rarified and abstract level, without taking the effects of the MARC record into account. (63)

Twenty years on, it remains true that the nature and character of the technologies used by library catalogers and metadata librarians affect substantively the descriptive cataloging work done and the way information curated by the library is organized and presented to users. No discussion of current library cataloging practice is complete without attention to the features and nuances of the MARC record, but now also, in many contexts, no discussion of cataloging and metadata authoring is complete without taking into account the features and nuances of XML and how the assumptions, functionalities, and capabilities of XML (and any missing capabilities) impact on how catalogers and metadata librarians approach their work. The reduction in emphasis on MARC and *Anglo-American Cataloguing Rules* Second Edition (AACR2), which was anticipated by the Library of Congress in their *Transforming Our Bibliographic Framework* initiative (mentioned above), has implications not only for how catalogers and metadata librarians do their job but also for how they understand and think about descriptive cataloging. XML has emerged as a generally good choice for serializing structured data like bibliographic metadata in part because, properly used, it "makes library cataloging workflows more robust, more modular, more flexible, and more standards-based"

(Han 2011, 21). This can allow catalogers to work more efficiently and can help with scalability, but it also requires catalogers to account for and think about the implications of potentially easier sharing, reuse, and repurposing of their cataloging output. Such new thinking then can result in adjustments in cataloging decisions and practices.

As an example of the flexibility of XML and its implications, consider how library catalog information is presented to library users. By design, most metadata records or document instances serialized according to an application-specific XML-based grammar can be easily manipulated and transformed into XHTML, into XML conforming to alternate semantics, or even into other serializations altogether (e.g., into PDF or for ingest into a relational database). These transformed metadata records become available for use in other contexts beyond the Online Public Access Catalog (OPAC). Figure 2.2 shows the OPAC display of a catalog record for a book recently digitized from the University of Illinois Library's collection *War-songs for freemen*. The MARCXML for this catalog record is shown in Figure 2.3. (The syntax and semantics of MARCXML records like this one are discussed in more detail in Chapter 4.)

Through the application of a relatively simple style sheet written in the Extensible Stylesheet Language for Transformations (XSLT[12]), this same MARCXML record can be reused outside the OPAC and integrated library system context to form the basis for a "splash page" through which users can access different views of the digitized book. (XSLTs are discussed and illustrated in Chapter 11.) Splash pages work as a landing place from which Web users accessing digitized library resources can view a digitized work in different formats, such as a volume-length PDF, individual page images, or plain text derived from the photographed pages using optical character recognition. Figure 2.4 illustrates such a splash screen as implemented at the University of

FIGURE 2.2 An OPAC view (screen shot) of catalog record for *War-songs for freemen*.

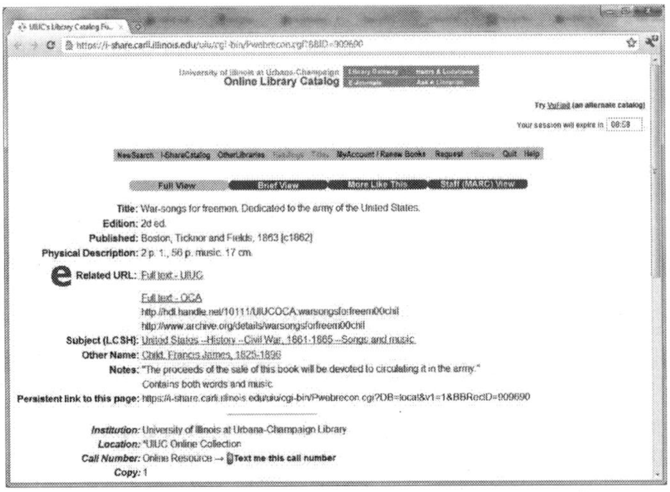

FIGURE 2.3 MARC XML record for *War-songs for freemen* (some text omitted for brevity).


```
<record xmlns="http://www.loc.gov/MARC21/slim">
  <leader>00767ccm a2200229 4500</leader>
  <controlfield tag="001">909690</controlfield>
  <controlfield tag="005">20020415161827.0</controlfield>
  <controlfield tag="008">800522c18631862mausgd n n 0 eng d</controlfield>
  <datafield tag="035" ind1=" " ind2=" ">
    <subfield code="a">(OCoLC)ocm06346108</subfield>
  </datafield>
  <datafield tag="035" ind1=" " ind2=" ">
    <subfield code="9">ADT-3548</subfield>
  </datafield>
  <datafield tag="040" ind1=" " ind2=" ">
    <subfield code="a">KBE</subfield>
    <subfield code="c">KBE</subfield>
    <subfield code="d">UIU</subfield>
  </datafield>
  <datafield tag="045" ind1=" " ind2=" ">
    <subfield code="a">w0w6</subfield>
  </datafield>
  <datafield tag="047" ind1=" " ind2=" ">
    <subfield code="a">sg</subfield>
  </datafield>
  <datafield tag="245" ind1="0" ind2="0">
    <subfield code="a">War-songs for freemen.</subfield>
    <subfield code="b">Dedicated to the army of the United States.</subfield>
  </datafield>
  <datafield tag="250" ind1=" " ind2=" ">
    <subfield code="a">2d ed.</subfield>
  </datafield>
```


(continued)

FIGURE 2.3 (Continued)


```
  <datafield tag="260" ind1="0" ind2=" ">
    <subfield code="a">Boston,</subfield>
    <subfield code="b">Ticknor and Fields,</subfield>
    <subfield code="c">1863 [c1862]</subfield>
  </datafield>
  <datafield tag="300" ind1=" " ind2=" ">
    <subfield code="a">2 p. 1., 56 p.</subfield>
    <subfield code="b">music.</subfield>
    <subfield code="c">17 cm.</subfield>
  </datafield>
  <datafield tag="500" ind1=" " ind2=" ">
    <subfield code="a">"The proceeds of the sale of this book...."</subfield>
  </datafield>
  <datafield tag="500" ind1=" " ind2=" ">
    <subfield code="a">Contains both words and music.</subfield>
  </datafield>
  <datafield tag="651" ind1=" " ind2="0">
    <subfield code="a">United States</subfield>
    <subfield code="x">History</subfield>
    <subfield code="y">Civil War, 1861-1865</subfield>
    <subfield code="v">Songs and music.</subfield>
  </datafield>
  <datafield tag="700" ind1="1" ind2="0">
    <subfield code="a">Child, Francis James,</subfield>
    ...
</record>
```

FIGURE 2.4 Splash page (HTML) for digitized copy of *War-songs for freemen*, generated dynamically from MARCXML record.

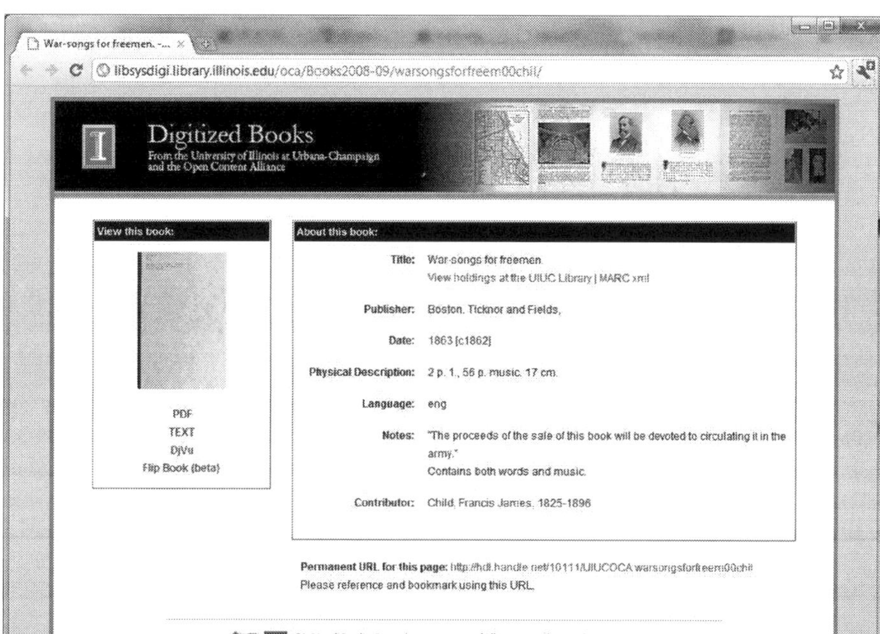

Illinois at Urbana-Champaign. The underlying MARCXML is the same for both Figure 2.2 and Figure 2.4, only the rules by which the MARCXML (Figure 2.3) is transformed to XHTML and prepared for presentation are different.

XML as a Foundation for New Cataloging Work Flows

Considered as a foundation for library cataloging work flows, the flexibility and versatility of XML yield additional advantages beyond the ability to facilitate the presentation of catalog records in multiple contexts. Until recently, most library cataloging units have focused mainly on what is physically held on the shelves of the library they serve. This has changed as the Web has altered user expectations and with the advent of large-scale digitization projects, increased licensing of digital resources (e.g., e-books and e-journals), the need to catalog digitized special collection items at highly granular levels, and the need for online institutional repositories to catalog and curate deposited content, such as electronic theses and dissertations, digital departmental and project research reports, journal article preprints, conference paper postprints, and so on. MARC is not always the most appropriate format for describing nonbook, nonserial digital content or for describing very granular resources, such as individual digitized photographs held by a special collections unit. This is especially true as digital library initiatives and projects continue to proliferate. A recent review of existing and in-progress digital library projects determined that across the range of projects reviewed, "no single standard or set of standards existed for the creation of digital library metadata objects . . . digital library metadata workflows and standards varied widely from project to project" (Valentino 2010, 542). The assumption of a single, monolithic library standard for cataloging is no longer viable, even to the admittedly limited extent it ever was.

Other formats, such as Simple and Qualified Dublin Core (see Chapter 5); specialized formats, such as CDWA-Lite[13] (based on *Categories for the Description of Works of Art* and the metadata value encoding practices outlined in *Cataloging Cultural Objects*[14]); and mixed semantics application profile formats, such as the Dublin Core Library Application Profile (Chapter 6), which draw from multiple metadata standards and guidelines, can be more cost effective, more scalable, or more appropriate for content and anticipated use. Because of its extensible nature, XML is well suited to and useful for a broad range of metadata schemes and standards and for mixing semantics from multiple standards. This allows a library cataloging unit to support a diversity of metadata standards while simultaneously maintaining a unified, XML-based technical infrastructure that leverages off-the-shelf tools (e.g., for authoring XML, transforming XML, and validating XML).

Beyond flexibility, scalability, and versatility, XML also offers advantages for collaborative metadata authoring and for interoperability in cataloging work flows. Catalogers in many libraries have long traditions of working across library units as a way to incorporate specialized knowledge of content into catalog records and as a way to glean insights into likely use and discipline-specific models of discovery (i.e., as a way to improve cataloging outcomes). Thus, rare book curators often work closely with cataloging unit librarians to enrich catalog records for items in special collections. Archivists collaborate with catalogers in central support units of the library to develop MARC records for manuscript archives. In the 1970s and 1980s, subject bibliographers collaborated routinely in the original cataloging of books at the University of Illinois at Urbana-Champaign, where for many years "holistic" librarianship was the norm.

Intellectually, these past traditions of working across the breadth of the library point the way now for collaborating with faculty and other experts outside the library on descriptive cataloging. Boydston and Leysen (2006), in an article discussing the role of academic library catalogers in the creation of descriptive metadata, note that some elements of descriptive metadata are increasingly being initially created by groups outside the library community using discipline or domain-specific standards. Often these metadata schemes and standards (e.g., for sequenced learning objects) go beyond the descriptive but overlap and include elements of bibliographic description of interest to and useful for library catalogers and metadata librarians.

Delegated cataloging of this sort requires tools and supporting services that can integrate a range of cataloging information resources, such as union catalog records, vendor/publisher provided cataloging, author-generated metadata, and subject expert annotation. This in turn has implications for tool design and architecture of XML, because it is a recognized standard and given its adherence to structure and inherent separation of semantics from syntax, is a good way to approach shared cataloging while still maintaining quality control and rigor. What XML does is to facilitate such interactions by facilitating crosswalks between different formats and schemes and by making it easy to validate and build up a descriptive metadata record piecemeal, that is, bit by bit from multiple sources and from multiple metadata authors working largely independent of one another.

These and other strengths of XML as a technology for supporting descriptive cataloging and other facets of digital library design and implementation were recognized early on (e.g., Cole et al. 2000). The capability to crosswalk between metadata schemes and formats offered by XML and the associated technologies for creating and using XSLT style sheets is seen as especially helpful for design and implementation of cataloging and metadata work flows. The Library of Congress maintains more than a dozen XSLT style sheets for transforming XML catalog records to/from MARCXML, Metadata Object Description Schema, Dublin Core, ONline Information Change (ONIX), and other metadata standards.[15] (Each of these formats mentioned are discussed in later chapters of this book.) OCLC, the worldwide member-owned library cataloging cooperative, has an ongoing Metadata Transformation Service Project[16] that includes a public metadata Crosswalk Web Service Demonstrator[17] providing automated transformations between several popular XML metadata standards and schemas.

XML is a technology supportive of the changing and evolving needs of library catalogers and metadata librarians. At the same time, the assumptions and models of information inherent in XML affect how catalogers and metadata librarians view descriptive cataloging and go about altering and improving cataloging work flows. These shifts are apparent both in the increasing attention paid to XML as a medium for sharing and maintaining metadata and in changing expectations and job requirements for both traditional library cataloger and newly minted metadata librarian positions.

CHANGING JOB DESCRIPTIONS

As libraries deal with many different types of resources from many different sources, developing the best work flows for this diversity of incoming content has become one of the major challenges they face. In regard to bibliographic control and management of digital resources and publications, including online serials, e-books, and retrospectively digitized special collections and databases, research has identified two common approaches that are routinely adopted by libraries separately or in concert to make users aware of such resources:

- Some libraries create a separate, database-driven Web page for electronic resources organized by an A-to-Z title list.
- Other libraries integrate MARC format records for these resources into the library OPAC.

Each method has its pros and cons in terms of user experiences, and some libraries have chosen to implement both approaches in parallel (Belanger 2007; Powell 2008). Although different in outcomes, both methods have one attribute in common: they require new work flows for records creation and/or records ingestion into the library OPAC or Web Content Management System database used to control the A-to-Z e-resource listing Web page. Regardless of the approach taken, librarians need to create metadata for these resources to assist users in searching and discovering electronic resources.

While metadata for electronic resources can be created via many different work flows, which work flow approach to use often depends on the way the resources being described are produced. The skill set involved in creating metadata for electronic resources differs in meaningful ways from that required to catalog print materials. In the case of born-digital resources available through information resource providers and aggregators, vendors and publishers often provide initial draft catalog records directly. Depending on the vendor, such starting point metadata records may be made available in MARC format, in ONIX, or even as rows in a spreadsheet. The cataloger or metadata librarian must then transform or convert these supplied records for ingestion into his or her local catalog environment. Each of these formats requires a different type of work flow to transform or convert records according to the local practice and standard. Cataloging of retrospectively digitized books, while more similar to traditional copy cataloging, requires a separate work flow as well. AACR2 and Library of Congress Rule Interpretations, as well as the Resource Description and Access treat digitized books as reproductions (or manifestations), so, for retrospectively digitized resources, the work flow often focuses on the transformation of existing print records into e-book records.

Local digitalization projects featuring digitized special collections materials also may require special skill sets and work flows to support metadata creation. These locally digitized resources are often maintained in and accessed via digital content resource management software other than the library's main integrated library system and OPAC. The special collections unit may have developed specialized local metadata schemes customized for the description of their unique collections. Catalogers and metadata librarians are charged to find ways to convert descriptions in such a local standard into another, more interoperable metadata standard that is supported by the content management software. This may require not only transforming existing descriptions but also augmenting and normalizing such descriptions to meet system requirements and/or the requirements of target metadata standards.

The need to work with different types of resources, metadata work flows, metadata standards, and many different units of the library (and sometimes units outside the library proper) has changed dramatically the nature of the cataloger's job at many institutions. As mentioned earlier, the increasing volume of digital content needing to be cataloged also is exerting pressure on traditional work flows and job responsibilities. A review of the library literature suggests that over the last decade, significant changes have occurred in work flows and job descriptions across several segments of the librarian profession, but changes in cataloging and metadata librarian roles, responsibilities, titles, qualifications, and organizational structures have been especially notable. These changes are not entirely new and to some degree were anticipated; more than a decade ago, Buttlar and Garcha (1998) suggested that library automation was changing the focus of cataloging librarians from primarily cataloging to a focus encompassing more managerial and technical duties, including database management and training. This trend has been accelerating in recent years.

These changes in required skill sets are reflected in job titles. Since 2000, there are fewer institutions looking for traditional catalogers. Han and Hswe (2010) surveyed library position announcements in *American Libraries*, *College and Research Libraries News*, and online sources. While the number of announcements for library "catalogers" decreased from 19 per year to four per year over the period 2000–2008, the number of jobs including the word "metadata" in the job title, either singly or in combination with "cataloger," increased from five per year to 19 per year over the same span (see Table 2.1, replicated from the Han and Hswe study). This research established that many

TABLE 2.1 Number of job postings for metadata librarian and cataloging librarian from 2000 to 2008 (Han and Hswe 2010, 132).

Year	Metadata Librarian	Cataloging Librarian
2000	5	19
2001	6	19
2002	7	10
2003	5	8
2004	2	10
2005	8	5
2006	10	7
2007	24	3
2008	19	4
Total	86	85

institutions are changing cataloging librarians' titles to new titles better suited for the changes in roles and responsibilities and/or are creating entirely new positions, such as digital collection librarian, coordinator of metadata services, and so on, whose responsibilities include metadata management and planning.

The study also found that libraries are changing their organizational structure as well. The paper noted that not every cataloging and metadata specialist belongs to a technical services division any more. The positions responsible for metadata creation and management today may belong to a digital library unit, to an archive, or to newly chartered units, such as so-called learning or scholarly commons units. This suggests the growing importance of providing metadata for digital resources and how libraries have been trying to accommodate changes in priorities and work flows dictated by the influx of digital content coming under their care.

Changes in the cataloging and metadata librarian roles and responsibilities are reflected in the qualifications, both required and desired, posted in job descriptions (Chaudhry and Komathi 2002; Khurshid 2003; Kwasik 2002). The literature suggests that catalogers need to know not only traditional cataloging rules and integrated library systems but also emerging metadata standards and related technology, such as XML, the Open Archives Initiative Protocol for Metadata Harvesting (OAI-PMH), and a variety of different metadata formats and schemas (Han and Hswe 2010; Park and Lu 2009). Figure 2.5 shows the range of metadata format knowledge being asked for in recent cataloging and metadata librarian position announcements, with knowledge of Dublin Core expected very nearly as often as knowledge of MARC.

Judging by position announcements, knowledge of XML also is seen as important in the current library environment. This is not surprising since many work flows now require librarians to transform and modify records using XML technologies and XML-based tools and/or to disseminate metadata records in XML format (e.g., to meet the requirements of the OAI-PMH standard). Table 2.2 tracks the increasing frequency with which a number of XML-related skills are requested in cataloging and metadata librarian position announcements.

Hall-Ellis (2008) pointed out that traditional library school cataloging courses focusing primarily or exclusively on MARC and AACR2 are no longer sufficient in and of themselves to prepare catalogers and metadata librarians for the current and future job market. Knowledge of multiple metadata standards, XML, and related technical skills and standards has become a valuable qualification for the profession, required more often than not when libraries look to hire.

FIGURE 2.5 Knowledge of metadata formats required for metadata librarian positions (Han and Hswe 2010, 138).

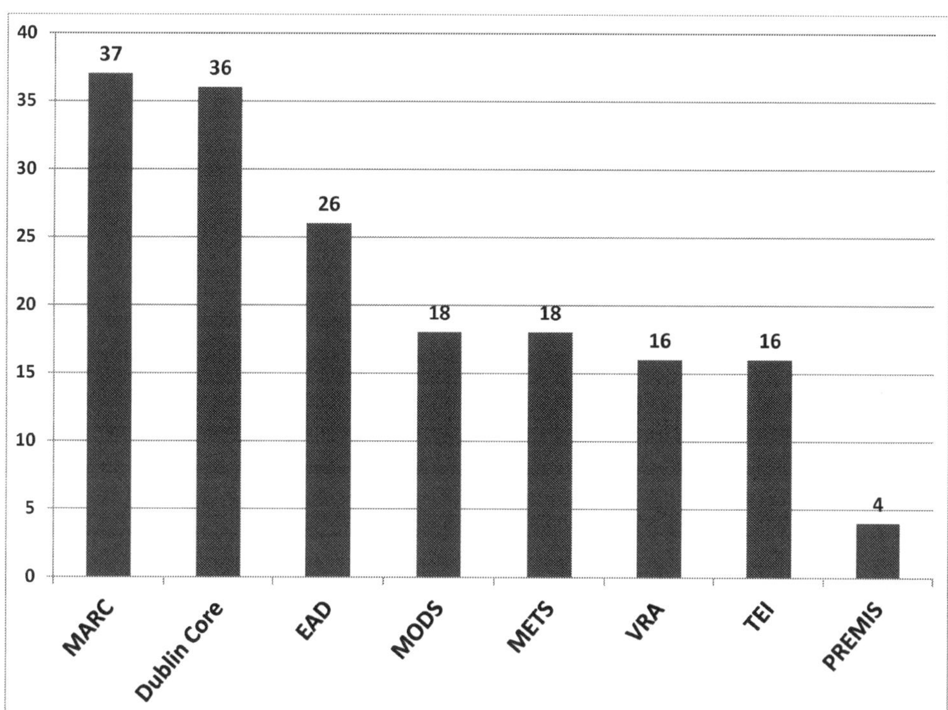

LOOKING AHEAD

In order to provide access to digital information resources in a timely and efficient manner, libraries must deal with two new challenges. First, they must decide on the approaches they will use to optimize the discoverability and utility of their digital resources. How do their users look for digital resources differently than print resources? How do they use digital resources differently than print resources? Second, libraries must decide how their work flows need to change and evolve in order to support access and user needs while effectively dealing with the huge influx of digital content. How can libraries scale up existing work flows to deal with the greater granularity and volume of content needing to be cataloged? What features of traditional work flows can be kept, and what new kinds of work flows are needed? Which emerging technologies

TABLE 2.2 Technical skills required for metadata librarian positions advertised from 2000 to 2008 (Han and Hswe 2010, 138).

	2000	2001	2002	2003	2004	2005	2006	2007	2008	Total
OAI			2	2			2	6	4	16
XML	1	1	3	3		2	4	7	2	23
RDF	1	2	1		1			1	1	7
XSL								1		1

can help librarians do their job better and more efficiently? How do libraries leverage new technologies to become more efficient at bibliographic control and descriptive cataloging?

To address these questions, library cataloging units must reexamine traditional work flows and look at the potential of available new technologies. Then catalogers and metadata librarians must implement the approaches and infrastructure designs developed, leveraging available tools and technologies. In doing so, they must thoroughly understand the technologies they adopt and recognize that the technologies adopted can have an impact on how librarians catalog and describe information resources.

As a routine part of their work, many librarians, archivists, museum curators, and others involved in managing and curating scientific data and cultural heritage materials spend much of their time ordering and organizing collections of unordered and disorganized information resources. They do this in part by creating catalogs of collections and populating these catalogs with structured information records (i.e., catalog records about each of the items counted as a member of a specific collection). These records include basic bibliographic information, such as the author and title of an item, the year it was published and by whom and where, the extent of an item, and so forth. For a digital resource, these records also contain information to facilitate locating and using the resource on the Web, information describing the relationship of the resource to other print and digital objects, information describing the source and provenance of the resource, and so on. By design, XML is capable of facilitating the creation, use, and sharing of structured information. As described in Chapter 1, XML is a serialization format well suited for transmitting and storing library cataloging records and metadata, not least because it facilitates the reuse and repurposing of metadata and the abstraction and recombination of individual metadata attributes from multiple sources.

Cataloging work flows have already changed dramatically and are continuing to evolve. Broader collaboration in the creation of metadata for digital information resources is becoming more common. The same metadata record is often ingested into multiple tools and made available to users in multiple ways. Dempsey et al. (2005) suggest that "supporting the creation, use and reuse of diverse complex resources, the creation of repository frameworks, the creation and merger of metadata and knowledge organization services, the provision of distributed disclosure, discovery and deposit services—these will all be difficult and interesting" (23). Dempsey and his colleagues go on to suggest that crucial to this objective is the ability to selectively extract and recombine elements of metadata.

Ultimately, the greatest motivation for studying XML may lie in the ways in which it has facilitated and even encouraged library catalogers to rethink their approach to descriptive cataloging and bibliographic control. XML makes it easy to selectively transform, reuse, and repurpose structured records and parts of structured records. This in turn supports models of information architecture that rely on the reuse and repurposing of information resource description both for efficiency and economy of scale and to allow us to rethink our understanding of information and view the same information in different ways. The trend toward applications featuring the recombination of catalog records and metadata has continued and has been gaining momentum in recent years. XML is particularly well suited to this model of metadata as recombinant.

QUESTIONS AND TOPICS FOR DISCUSSION

1. What cataloging work flow changes can the library community anticipate in the coming year? How do you imagine it may change further 10 years from now?
2. Why XML? What are the alternatives that catalogers can turn to for digital records, and why has XML become a de facto standard?
3. What are the main technical skill sets that new catalogers and metadata librarians should have and why?

SUGGESTIONS FOR EXERCISES

1. Create your job descriptions for a cataloging librarian and a metadata librarian, including required and desired qualifications.
2. Choose a library Web site and browse separately its digital resources and online catalog. Compare metadata records. How might the work flows be different for creating such records?
3. Choose a second library Web site and browse its digital resources and catalog. How do the services and descriptions compare to the library resources you previously viewed? What practices appear similar, and what practices appear different?

NOTES

1. http://www.loc.gov/marc/transition/news/framework-051311.html.
2. http://books.google.com/googlebooks/library.html.
3. http://www.opencontentalliance.org.

4. For example, as of July 2010, the Graduate College at the University of Illinois at Urbana-Champaign stopped accepting hard-copy theses and dissertations for review or deposit from candidates for master's or doctoral degrees (http://www.grad.illinois.edu/step-3-deposit). For more on the trend toward mandating electronic theses and dissertations, see the *ETD Census* at https://spreadsheets.google.com/ccc?key=0AtSglIhGWCkpdHJvOUNSZUZyRC04UXRUa0w3UmgtYWc&hl=en#gid=0, originated by Dorothea Salo of the University of Wisconsin–Madison.

5. OCLC WorldCat is available on the Web (http://www.worldcat.org) and on your iPhone or Google Android smart phone using downloadable apps optimized for your device (http://whatcounts.com/bin/archive_viewer?id=6FB64ED51A04512E6FD46729B6487C56).

6. http://id.loc.gov.

7. http://people.oregonstate.edu/~reeset/marcedit/html/index.php.
8. http://www.loc.gov/standards/marcxml.
9. http://www.w3.org/TR/rdf-primer.
10. http://www.w3.org/2004/02/skos.
11. http://id.loc.gov/authorities/subjects/sh2007001751.rdf.
12. http://www.w3.org/TR/xslt.
13. http://www.getty.edu/research/publications/electronic_publications/cdwa/cdwalite.html.
14. http://cco.vrafoundation.org.
15. http://www.loc.gov/standards/marcxml/#stylesheets.
16. http://www.oclc.org/research/activities/schematrans/default.htm.
17. http://www.oclc.org/research/activities/xwalk/default.htm.

REFERENCES

Belanger, Jacqueline. 2007. "Cataloguing e-Books in UK Higher Education Libraries: Report of a Survey." *Program: Electronic Library and Information Systems* 41, no. 3: 203–16.

Boydston, Jeanne M. K., and Joan M. Leysen. 2006. "Observations on the Catalogers' Role in Descriptive Metadata Creation in Academic Libraries." *Cataloging and Classification Quarterly* 43, no. 2: 3–17.

Buttlar, Lois, and Rajinder Garcha. 1998. "Catalogers in Academic Libraries: Their Evolving and Expanding Roles." *College and Research Libraries* 59, no. 4: 311–21.

Chaudhry, Abdus Sattar, and N. C. Komathi. 2002. "Requirements for Cataloguing Positions in the Electronic Environment." *Technical Services Quarterly* 19, no. 1: 1–23.

Cole, Timothy W., William H. Mischo, Robert Ferrer, Thomas G. Habing, and Donald H. Kraft. 2000. "Using XML, XSLT, and CSS in a Digital Library." *Knowledge Innovations: Celebrating Our Heritage, Designing Our Future. (Proceedings of the 63rd ASIS Annual Meeting)* 37: 430–39.

Dempsey, Lorcan, Eric Childress, Carol Jean Godby, Thomas B. Hickey, Andrew Houghton, Diane Vizine-Goetz, and Jeff Young. 2005. "Metadata Switch: Thinking About Some Metadata Management and Knowledge Organization Issues in the Changing Research and Learning Landscape." In *E-Scholarship: A LITA Guide*, edited by Debra Shapiro. Preprint available at: http://www.oclc.org/research/publications/library/2004/dempsey-mslitaguide.pdf

Gorman, Michael. 1990. "Descriptive Cataloguing: Its Past, Present, and Future." In *Technical Services Today and Tomorrow*, compiled by Michael Gorman. Englewood, CO: Libraries Unlimited, 63–73.

Hall-Ellis, Sylvia D. 2008. "Cataloger Competencies … What Do Employers Require?" *Cataloging and Classification Quarterly* 46, no. 3: 305–30.

Han, Myung-Ja. 2011. "Creating Metadata for Digitized Books: Implementing XML and OAI-PMH in Cataloging Workflow." *Journal of Library Metadata* 11, no. 1: 19–32.

Han, Myung-Ja, and Patricia Hswe. 2010. "The Evolving Role of the Metadata Librarian: Competencies Found in Job Descriptions." *Library Resources and Technical Services* 54, no. 3: 129–41.

Khurshid, Zahiruddin. 2003. "The Impact of Information Technology on Job Requirements and Qualifications for Catalogers." *Information Technology and Libraries* 22, no. 1: 18–21.

Kwasik, Hanna. 2002. "Qualifications for a Serials Librarian in an Electronic Environment." *Serials Review* 28, no. 1: 33–37.

Park, Jung-ran, and Caimei Lu. 2009. "Metadata Professionals: Roles and Competencies as Reflected in Job Announcements, 2003–2006." *Cataloging and Classification Quarterly* 47, no. 2: 145–60.

Powell, Christina K. 2008. "OPAC Integration in the Era of Mass Digitization: The MBooks Experience." *Library Hi Tech* 26, no. 1: 24–29.

Valentino, Maura L. 2010. "Integrating Metadata Creation into Catalog Workflow." *Cataloging and Classification Quarterly* 48, no. 6/7: 541–50.

Veve, Marielle, and Melanie Feltner-Reichert. 2010. "Integrating Non-MARC Metadata Duties into the Workflow of Traditional Catalogers: A Survey of Trends and Perceptions among Cataloger in Four Discussion Lists." *Technical Services Quarterly* 27, no. 2: 194–213.

CHAPTER 3

XML: Core Syntax and Grammar

XML-based grammars distinguish between *content* (the substantive information being serialized in XML) and *markup* (used to delineate, label, and otherwise describe the structure of the information being serialized). The XML standard introduces the concept of XML *elements*, delineated within document instances by paired start-tag and end-tag markup (or by empty-element-tags), as a way to provide an Ordered Hierarchy of Content Objects view of information (e.g., a metadata record). The name or semantic label of an element appears as part of its start-tag (or its empty-element-tag) and is repeated in its end-tag. The XML standard allows implementers to declare in an XML Document Type Definition (DTD) or XML schema the application-specific element names that are allowed for a particular class of document instances.

While elements are the basic building blocks of XML, the core grammar of XML also defines additional concepts and forms of markup to further describe, elaborate, constrain, and normalize XML serialized hierarchies of content objects. For example, in addition to elements, the XML standard defines other classes of markup entities, such as *attributes*, and introduces the concept of *element content models*. In XML document instances (e.g., XML metadata records) attributes are used to associate additional values with elements; typically, attribute values elaborate or augment the content of an element or refine the semantic meaning of an element. For instance, in an XML metadata record, an attribute on the element `<name>` might be used to differentiate corporate names from personal names. An element's content model describes what that element may contain, including the names and order of any child elements allowed. For instance, in an XML metadata record, the content model of the element `<name>` might allow two child elements, `<familyName>` and `<givenName>`. Element content models are declared and defined in XML DTDs and schemas as a way to constrain what may be contained in an element. This ability to declare application-specific semantic labels, attributes, and content models for a class of XML document instances—in other words, to define an application-specific grammar that builds on and extends the core grammar of XML—is what makes XML extensible.

This chapter discusses features and nuances of the core syntax and grammar of XML (beyond those already described in Chapter 1) and examines a few application-specific XML grammar illustrations that build on this core foundation. The additional details about XML grammar introduced in this chapter,

FIGURE 3.1 An abridged MARCXML record.

```xml
<?xml version="1.0" encoding="UTF-8"?>
<?xml-stylesheet type="text/xsl" href="displayRecord_marc.xsl"?>
<record xmlns="http://www.loc.gov/MARC21/slim"
        xmlns:xsi="http://www.w3.org/2001/XMLSchema-instance"
        xsi:schemaLocation="http://www.loc.gov/MARC21/slim http://www.loc.gov/standards/marcxml/schema/MARC21slim.xsd">
    <leader>01698cam 22003614a 4500</leader>
    <controlfield tag="001">5439928</controlfield>
    <controlfield tag="005">20080104135038.0</controlfield>
    <controlfield tag="008">070313s2007 ctua b 001 0 eng </controlfield>
    <datafield tag="010" ind1=" " ind2=" ">
        <subfield code="a"> 2007009006</subfield>
    </datafield>
    <datafield tag="035" ind1=" " ind2=" ">
        <subfield code="a">(OCoLC)ocn105428765</subfield>
    </datafield>
    <datafield tag="100" ind1="1" ind2=" ">
        <subfield code="a">Cole, Timothy W.</subfield>
    </datafield>
    <datafield tag="245" ind1="1" ind2="0">
        <subfield code="a">Using the Open Archives Initiative protocol
                           for metadata harvesting /</subfield>
        <subfield code="c">Timothy W. Cole and Muriel Foulonneau.</subfield>
    </datafield>
    <datafield tag="260" ind1=" " ind2=" ">
        <subfield code="a">Westport, Conn. :</subfield>
        <subfield code="b">Libraries Unlimited,</subfield>
        <subfield code="c">© 2007.</subfield>
    </datafield>
    <datafield tag="300" ind1=" " ind2=" ">
        <subfield code="a">xv, 208 p. :</subfield>
```

```
        <subfield code="b">ill. ;</subfield>
        <subfield code="c">26 cm.</subfield>
    </datafield>
    <datafield tag="440" ind1=" " ind2="0">
        <subfield code="a">Third millennium cataloging</subfield>
    </datafield>
    <datafield tag="650" ind1=" " ind2="0">
        <subfield code="a">Metadata harvesting.</subfield>
    </datafield>
    <datafield tag="610" ind1="2" ind2="0">
        <subfield code="a">Open Archives Initiative.</subfield>
    </datafield>
    <datafield tag="700" ind1="1" ind2=" ">
        <subfield code="a">Foulonneau, Muriel.</subfield>
    </datafield>
</record>
```

while not comprehensive, are intended to provide a solid foundation for further discussions of application-specific use cases and cases studies in subsequent chapters. Figure 3.1 (the same as Figure 1.11) is an abridged MARCXML record, that is, a MAchine-Readable Cataloging (MARC) record serialized in XML, derived from a bibliographic record contained in the University of Illinois at Urbana-Champaign library catalog. This abridged record is used to illustrate the syntax of the features and facets of XML markup discussed below. The complete version of this MARCXML record will be examined in more detail in Chapter 4 as part of a discussion of the semantics (rather than just the syntax) of MARCXML.

CHARACTER DATA, WHITE SPACE, AND ENTITIES

In an XML document instance, everything not markup is termed *character data* according to the W3C Recommendation defining XML. Typically, the bulk of the intellectual content of an XML document is represented as character data, though some intellectual content can be included instead, either directly or by reference, using special kinds of markup (e.g., general entities, character references, or attribute values, as described below). In a tree view of an XML document instance, blocks of character data will often be treated as special kinds of leaf nodes on the tree. For example, continuous segments of character data (i.e., segments of character data between a ">" end-of-markup delimiter and the next "<" start-of-markup delimiter) are termed *text nodes* in the XPath Data Model tree view of an XML document instance.

Markup and most character data contained in an XML document is parsed and normalized during the processing of an XML document in part to separate markup from character data. The subset of character data subject to this kind of processing is often referred to as *parsed character data*, abbreviated `#PCDATA`, a term inherited from Standard Generalized Markup Language (SGML). Some rules used in parsing an XML document instance have the effect of normalizing parsed character data, in part to mitigate differences in computer operating system conventions.

For example, the way a line of text is terminated in a computer file is often application and/or operating system specific. Most applications written to run under the Linux operating system use a single line-feed character as the end-of-line delimiter. Most applications written to run on Microsoft Windows platforms use a two-character sequence of carriage-return and line-feed to denote the end of a line of text. Some other (mostly older, now deprecated) systems and applications use only a carriage-return character to denote end of line. XML processors normalize all end-of-line delimiters in parsed character data to a single line-feed character. For most subsequent normalization and parsing, the line-feed character is then treated as a *white space* character, along with the tab character and the space character. Unless specifically instructed not to do so, most XML applications replace any multicharacter strings of

FIGURE 3.2 Data field 245, showing title proper (subfield a) and statement of responsibility (subfield c), from Figure 3.1.

```
<datafield tag="245" ind1="1" ind2="0">
    <subfield code="a">Using the Open Archives Initiative protocol
                       for metadata harvesting /</subfield>
    <subfield code="c">Timothy W. Cole and Muriel Foulonneau.</subfield>
</datafield>
```

consecutive white space characters with a single white space character. (The assumption is that in most cases, line breaks, tabs, and multispace character sequences are there for convenience or for human readability of the XML rather than to be processed as meaningful to an XML application.)

Thus, the end-of-line and extra white space that occurs in the middle of the book title in Figure 3.2 is all reduced to a single white space character between the words "protocol" and "for" when that book title is normalized during XML parsing. This normalization facilitates composition of record displays for the end user. Optionally, it is possible to tell the XML processor to preserve white space (i.e., preserve strings of consecutive white space characters); this can be important in certain instances, such as (as discussed in more detail in Chapter 4) in regard to certain MARC fields, for example, any MARC general information fixed-length data field that appears in MARCXML as a `<controlfield>` element (see Figure 3.3).

Parsed character data in XML can consist of any character or string of characters deemed legal according to the ISO/IEC 10646[1] and Unicode[2] standards with three notable exceptions. The characters "<" and ">" are two of these exceptions. Because these characters are used to delineate start-tags and end-tags of elements as well as the start or end of other kinds of XML markup, they cannot be used directly as part of content without creating potential ambiguities. The third exception is "&" for reasons that become clear below. Other characters, though legal to include as part of an XML document's character data content, can be problematic to input. The XML specification requires conforming applications to accept Unicode UTF-8 and UTF-16 character encoding, allowing for tens of thousands of possible characters, but in practice it can be difficult to enter some Unicode characters and symbols directly from the keyboard (e.g., there is no key on standard U.S. keyboards for the copyright symbol).

FIGURE 3.3 An example of a MARC fixed-length field, control field 008, from Figure 3.1 (white space preserved).

```
<controlfield tag="008">070313s2007  ctua  b  001 0 eng </controlfield>
```

FIGURE 3.4 Different ways to express “>” in XML document.

```
&gt; (pre-defined, intrinsic named entity)
&#62; (decimal character reference)
&#x3E; (hexadecimal character reference)
```

To deal with “<,” “>,” and “&” and to address difficulties of entering directly from the keyboard references to symbols and non-Latin characters, XML provides special constructs for use within document markup and embeddable in parsed character data called *parsed entities* and *character references*. Character references and parsed entities begin with an ampersand (“&”) and end with a semicolon (“;”) (hence the reason why the “&” character is reserved). Character references and parsed entities are used as references and placeholders for an individual character or string of characters. During processing of an XML document, these placeholders are for all intents and purposes replaced with the character or string they reference.

Between the “&” and the “;” is either a numeric reference to the code point for a character as defined in Unicode (character reference) or a name for the character or string being referenced (parsed entity). Unlike HyperText Markup Language (HTML), XML includes only a very small number of intrinsic, predefined parsed entities, specifically, `<` (<), `>` (>), `&` (&), `'` ('), and `"` (“). Names and replacement strings for all other parsed entities must be declared as part of a document type declaration (see Chapter 7) before they can be used. Usually, it is easier to use character references to reference single character Unicode code points. These can be referenced by either their decimal base-10 value (character reference starts “&#”) or by their hexadecimal base-16 value (character reference starts “&#x”). As illustration, any of the options shown in Figure 3.4 can be used in an XML document as a placeholder for the greater-than character (>).

A character frequently used in metadata records that is sometimes difficult to enter from the keyboard when authoring XML is “©,” the copyright symbol. To add this character to the illustrative sample catalog record shown in Figure 3.1, one option is to insert a character reference, either `©` or, in this case, `©` in the part of the record dealing with publication information (see Figure 3.5). Each of these XML character references resolves to the

FIGURE 3.5 Data field 260, publication details, from Figure 3.1 with an embedded character reference.

```
<datafield tag="260" ind1=" " ind2=" ">
    <subfield code="a">Westport, Conn. :</subfield>
    <subfield code="b">Libraries Unlimited,</subfield>
    <subfield code="c">&#xA9; 2007.</subfield>
</datafield>
```

copyright symbol, "©," when processed by an XML parser. Character references and parsed named entities can be embedded within parsed character data (content) as well as used, for example, in attribute values which are defined and discussed below in the subsection on Attributes.

Parsed entities as described above (i.e., that are meant to be embedded within the content of an XML metadata record) are defined in the XML specification as a subset of *general entities*. (Another kind of parsed entity, *parameter entities*, used only with DTDs, are discussed in Chapter 7.) Parsed entities can be useful for advanced XML authoring in instances when it is convenient to associate a string of text with a parsed entity name that can then referenced repeatedly in a document or group of documents. Simply by changing the parsed entity declaration, all references to that parsed entity (i.e., all occurrences of the parsed entity's replacement text in document instances) are updated.

The other kind of general entity is an unparsed entity. Unparsed entities are used in XML as one way to reference external, non-XML content, such as binary data not able to be conveniently included directly in the XML document. A GIF formatted image would be an example of external content that might be referenced in XML by an unparsed entity. Unparsed entities must be declared with reference to a *notation name* providing an XML processor with information about what will come back when the external unparsed named entity is resolved or dereferenced. However, the details of how to process unparsed entities are largely left up to the application; the XML specification does not levy extensive requirements regarding how unparsed entities should be processed. Often there are alternative ways to embed non-XML information in an XML document instance. CDATA (discussed later in this chapter) is one alternative.

ELEMENT TYPES

In XML, elements conform to type definitions that dictate what kinds of content and/or markup can occur within a particular element. There are four high-level classes of content types recognized in the XML specification: *Element Content*, *Character Data Content*, *Mixed Content*, and *Empty*. Consider Figure 3.2, the book title and statement of responsibility portion of the MARCXML catalog record shown in Figure 3.1. This snippet includes two elements, `<datafield>` and `<subfield>`, and illustrates the first two classes of content types listed above. There are two instances of `<subfield>`, and both share the single `<datafield>` element as parent. The type of `<datafield>` is element content; the content model of `<datafield>` allows as immediate children `<subfield>` elements. Conversely, the `<subfield>` element contains only parsed character data (#PCDATA), illustrating the content type of character data content. Alternatively (not illustrated), XML elements may contain a mix of element and character data (mixed content type) or may not be allowed to contain character data or element content at all (empty content type). Empty elements can be represented either by a start-tag immediately followed by an end-tag or by an empty-element-tag, which looks like and has essentially the same syntax as a start-tag except for the insertion of a "/" as the penultimate character of the tag (e.g., in `<myEmptyTag />`, the white space before the slash is not required).

While relatively obvious and intuitive, this formal classification of element content types allows implementers to specify and control how the semantics they define are used and how document hierarchies are constrained. As detailed in Chapters 7, 8, and 9, element and mixed content types can be elaborated (i.e., with content models) to define the order in which child elements are allowed to appear, the numbers of each child element allowed, the data type of character data allowed within an element, and so on. The formalism of the XML element type approach can be quite powerful.

ATTRIBUTES

XML allows implementers to expose the structure of metadata records. Using XML, implementers can give elements names and constrain an element's contents. In addition, XML allows implementers to express other properties of an element. This is accomplished through the use of another kind of XML markup called *attributes*. Attributes consist of an *attribute name* (rules for composing attribute names are similar to those for composing element names) and an *attribute value string* joined with an "=" (equals) symbol. Attribute values must be enclosed within quotes (either single or double quotes can be used); a value must always be provided, and the quotes must always be included (unlike in HTML). Attributes are a mechanism to associate name-value pairs with elements. Attributes can appear only within start-tags and empty-element-tags; attributes are separated from the element name and from other attributes within the tag by white space. In Figure 3.2, `tag`, `code`, `ind1`, and `ind2` are all examples of XML attribute names.

Attributes are used most often to refine or embellish the semantic meaning of an element, a bit like an adjective can be used to refine the meaning of a noun in everyday speech and writing. For example, an element used to delineate each author name in a descriptive metadata record could have an attribute named `order`, the value of which conveys author order; that is, the element containing the name of the first author might have a start-tag of `<authorName order="1st">`, the second author's name element would then have start-tag of `<authorName order="2nd">`, and so on.

In the snippet of MARCXML shown in Figure 3.2, the `tag` attribute is used to convey the identity of a `datafield` (i.e., which MARC field). Similarly, the `code` attribute is used to convey the identity of a `subfield`. Attributes can also be used to augment or elaborate element content. In Figure 3.2, the values of the ind1 and ind2 attributes represent the MARC field 245 indicator values that go with the book title information, which is the main content of the <datafield>. Effectively, these attribute values refine the content of the element. Some implementations of XML convey all or most element content through attribute values rather than through parsed character data external to the markup angle brackets.

An XML attribute can be declared to be required or implied (optional), may be assigned a default value, and/or may even be declared to have a fixed, constant value. Just like other components of the core XML grammar, attributes are given names and assigned semantic meaning by the implementer. For application-specific XML grammars, attribute names and characteristics are defined in a DTD or XML schema. In lieu of an element type or content model, an attribute can be assigned a specific role or function and may be restricted in what values it can have. An attribute is assigned a role by declaring it to be of a particular XML attribute type, that is, declaring it to have a particular purpose in the context of the XML markup. The most commonly used XML attribute type is "string." String type attributes are general purpose attributes and can take as a value any string, i.e., any arbitrary sequence of character data. Or an XML attribute can be declared to be of attribute type "enumerated" such that valid values for that attribute must be drawn from an enumerated list. Enumerated type attributes are useful, for instance, as a way to associate a role property with a name element, such as to differentiate the name of the author from the name of the illustrator in a book metadata record. A third option for attribute type is "tokenized." This option is used when declaring attributes for special purposes within the context of the XML markup itself. For example, attributes are frequently declared to be of an XML tokenized subtype called "ID." Attributes of this type convey unique identifiers for XML elements within the context of a specific XML document instance. This allows a specific element within an XML document to be referenced by the value of its ID type attribute precisely and uniquely according to the value of an XML ID identifier attribute.

PROCESSING INSTRUCTIONS, DECLARATIONS, CDATA, AND COMMENTS

The syntax rules for elements, character data, character references, general entities, and attributes described above provide ample expressiveness for most XML implementations and applications, but there is additional syntax defined in the core XML grammar to handle certain additional special functions.

Processing Instructions

For instance, all segments of markup that begin "<?" but not "<?xml" (regardless of the case of the characters "x," "m," and "l") and end "?>" are

FIGURE 3.6 A processing instruction invoking an XML style sheet.

```
<?xml-stylesheet type="text/xsl" href="displayRecord_marc.xsl"?>
```

called processing instructions. Processing instructions are not parsed like most character data and other markup but instead are passed through as is by XML parsers and processors for use by application-specific tools and services. The string immediately following the first "?" character is the `PITarget` and serves as the name or label by which a processing instruction can be recognized. The syntax and format of the rest of the processing instruction markup following the `PITarget` is largely processing instruction specific. Processing instructions are a means to provide special instructions to XML application(s) to facilitate an application's use of an XML document. Because processing instructions are application specific, they may safely be ignored by applications (and by you) when the `PITarget` is not recognized as relevant.

As alluded to above, markup that starts with "`<?xml`" is not necessarily a processing instruction; it may or may not be. Markup that starts with "`<?xml`" is reserved for XML standardization (including possible future standardization). Two instances of such markup from Figure 3.1 are discussed here, one instance in which the markup is a processing instruction and one instance in which it is not.

Figure 3.6 is an example of a standardized XML processing instruction. The `PITarget` is `xml-stylesheet`. This class of processing instruction specifies the location of a style sheet (`href=`) for use by those XML-aware applications that have the capacity to apply style sheets to XML document instances. The type of style sheet must also be specified (`type=`); currently, the type values commonly recognized by Web browsers and most other XML-aware applications are "`text/xsl`" (as illustrated) for use with style sheets written in the Extensible Stylesheet Language for Transformations (XSLT) and "`text/css`", for use with cascading style sheets (CSS). Most modern Web browsers, including current versions of Mozilla Firefox, Google Chrome, and Microsoft Internet Explorer, have the capacity to apply both CSS and XSLT, so this processing instruction will be recognized and exploited by such Web browsers. As described and illustrated in Chapter 11, XSLT style sheets are a good way to transform arbitrary XML into XHTML for presentation to end users. Figure 3.7 shows how Mozilla Firefox renders the XML from Figure 3.1 (with the addition of the copyright symbol character reference as discussed above) in the absence of the processing instruction shown in Figure 3.6. Figure 3.8 shows how Mozilla Firefox renders the same XML with the processing instruction included.

FIGURE 3.7 MARC record rendered in Firefox without XML style sheet processing instruction.

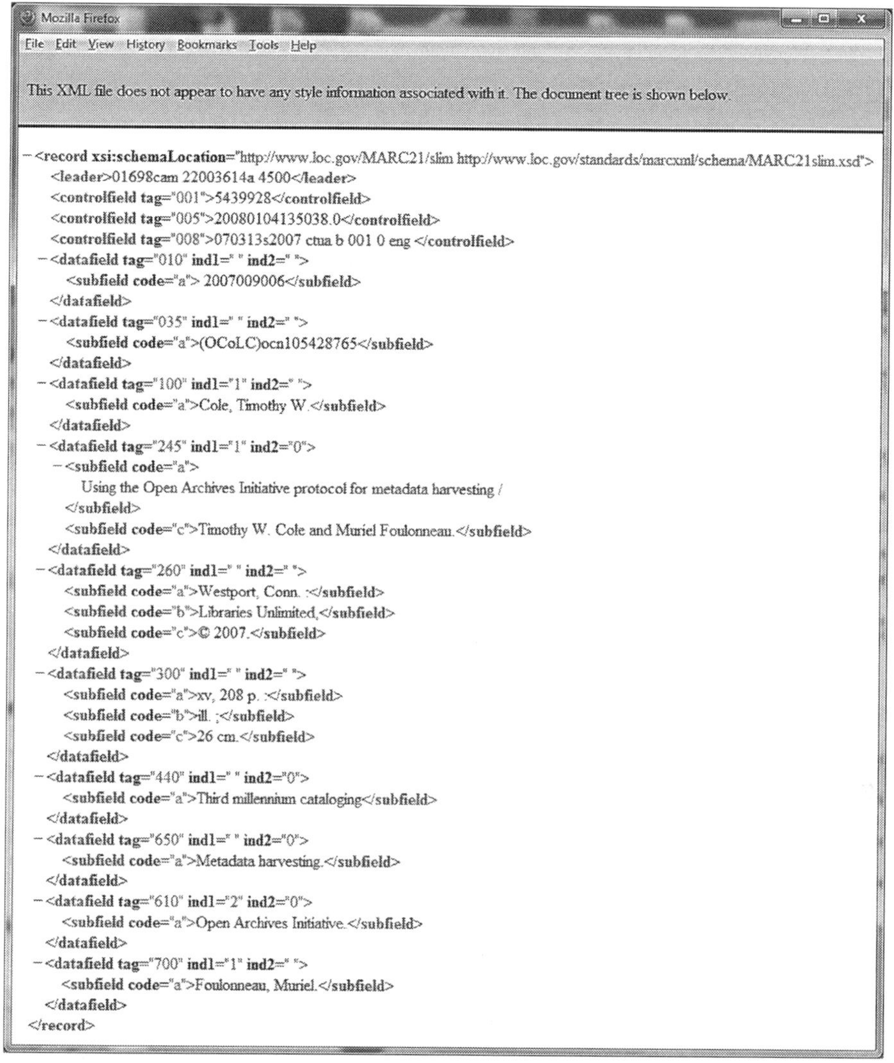


```
– <record xsi:schemaLocation="http://www.loc.gov/MARC21/slim http://www.loc.gov/standards/marcxml/schema/MARC21slim.xsd">
    <leader>01698cam 22003614a 4500</leader>
    <controlfield tag="001">5439928</controlfield>
    <controlfield tag="005">20080104135038.0</controlfield>
    <controlfield tag="008">070313s2007 ctua b 001 0 eng </controlfield>
  – <datafield tag="010" ind1=" " ind2=" ">
      <subfield code="a"> 2007009006</subfield>
    </datafield>
  – <datafield tag="035" ind1=" " ind2=" ">
      <subfield code="a">(OCoLC)ocn105428765</subfield>
    </datafield>
  – <datafield tag="100" ind1="1" ind2=" ">
      <subfield code="a">Cole, Timothy W.</subfield>
    </datafield>
  – <datafield tag="245" ind1="1" ind2="0">
    – <subfield code="a">
        Using the Open Archives Initiative protocol for metadata harvesting /
      </subfield>
      <subfield code="c">Timothy W. Cole and Muriel Foulonneau.</subfield>
    </datafield>
  – <datafield tag="260" ind1=" " ind2=" ">
      <subfield code="a">Westport, Conn. :</subfield>
      <subfield code="b">Libraries Unlimited,</subfield>
      <subfield code="c">© 2007.</subfield>
    </datafield>
  – <datafield tag="300" ind1=" " ind2=" ">
      <subfield code="a">xv, 208 p. :</subfield>
      <subfield code="b">ill. ;</subfield>
      <subfield code="c">26 cm.</subfield>
    </datafield>
  – <datafield tag="440" ind1=" " ind2="0">
      <subfield code="a">Third millennium cataloging</subfield>
    </datafield>
  – <datafield tag="650" ind1=" " ind2="0">
      <subfield code="a">Metadata harvesting.</subfield>
    </datafield>
  – <datafield tag="610" ind1="2" ind2="0">
      <subfield code="a">Open Archives Initiative.</subfield>
    </datafield>
  – <datafield tag="700" ind1="1" ind2=" ">
      <subfield code="a">Foulonneau, Muriel.</subfield>
    </datafield>
  </record>
```

XML Declaration

The markup shown in Figure 3.9, the first line from the abridged MARCXML record shown in Figure 3.1, is not a processing instruction. Instead, it is the *XML Declaration* for the MARCXML record. It serves as part of the XML document instance *Prolog*, which encompasses everything that goes before the start-tag of the root element in an XML document instance. Every XML document instance *should* start with an XML declaration. (Every XML version 1.1 document instance *must* start with an XML declaration.) When present, the XML declaration can appear only on the first line of an XML document. The XML Declaration always declares the version of the XML specification to which the XML document conforms (in this illustration,

FIGURE 3.8 MARC record rendered in Firefox with XML style sheet processing instruction.

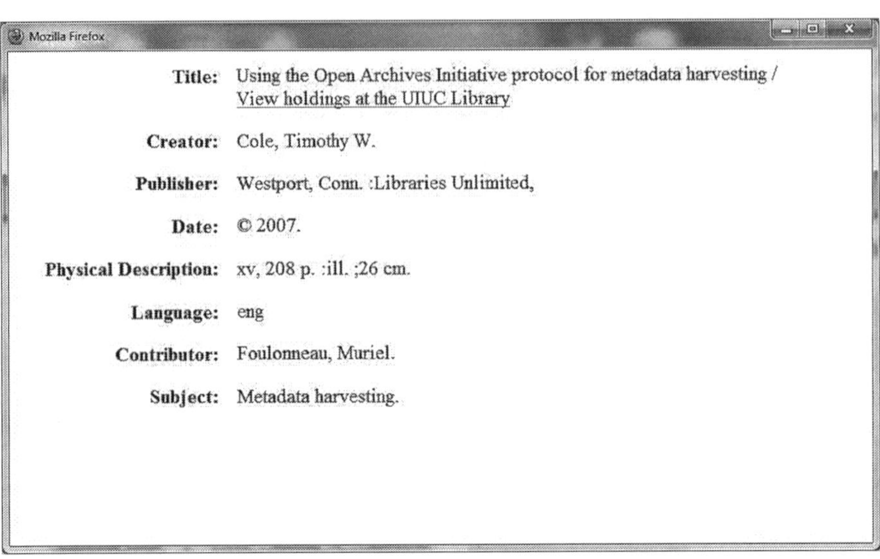

version 1.0). Optionally, the XML Declaration may also provide an *encoding declaration*. In the example shown, the encoding declaration is included (`encoding="UTF-8"`); this informs a consuming XML application that Unicode UTF-8 character encoding can be assumed for this XML document (this is the default for most XML applications). Other kinds of declarative information may be included. For example, inclusion of the string `standalone="yes"` tells the processor that there are no external entity references in this document instance. In all illustrations and case studies discussed in this book, a prolog XML declaration identical to the one in Figure 3.9 will suffice.

XML also recognizes other kinds of declarations, in particular the document type declaration that follows the XML declaration and must appear before the document root element start-tag (i.e., as part of the prolog). The document type declaration in turn includes and/or references one or more *markup declarations*, of which there are four kinds: element type declaration, entity declaration, notation declaration, attribute-list declaration. Collectively, the document type declaration and the markup declarations that the document type declaration contains or references comprise a DTD for a particular class of XML documents. DTDs and the use of DTDs are discussed in Chapter 7. For now, it is important only to mention that DTDs, which are required in SGML, are optional in XML. XML, unlike SGML, allows alternatives to

FIGURE 3.9 An XML declaration including version information and encoding declaration.

```
<?xml version="1.0" encoding="UTF-8"?>
```

DTDs, that is, schemas conforming to other semantics and syntax that can be used in lieu of DTDs to declare element names, attribute names, and other details of application-specific XML grammars to which a class of XML documents conform.

CDATA Delimiters and Comments

Two other important components of XML markup syntax not illustrated in the reference MARCXML metadata record depicted in Figure 3.1 are CDATA *delimiters* and *comments*. CDATA delimiters allow authors of XML documents to include character data that go mostly unparsed and are not normalized. The start of a segment of CDATA is delimited by the string "`<![CDATA[`". Any character data encountered by an XML parser after this delimiter, even character data that would normally be recognized as markup or would be subject to normalization (e.g., consecutive white space characters), are left unchanged and are not treated as markup. This behavior continues until the XML parser encounters the CDATA end-delimiter, "`]]>`". The raw character data enclosed between CDATA delimiters is treated as part of the XML document's content, just as much as parsed character data. When a CDATA delimited segment of character data appears within an element, it is treated as part of the content object delineated by the element start-tag and end-tag, albeit character data not normalized and not checked for characters and strings that would normally be considered XML markup. Such data appear as part of the element's content when rendered. The only character sequence that cannot be included in a CDATA segment is the string "`]]>`" since this is the sequence of characters used to delineate the end of a CDATA segment.

The text of an *XML comment*, on the other hand, is expected to be ignored by XML processors and applications. XML comments are designed to allow inclusion of human-readable notes and documentation in an XML document. Such text is explicitly not part of the XML document's character data, normalized or otherwise. As with CDATA segments, characters and strings included in the text of an XML comment that would normally be recognized as markup or entity references are not treated as such. Unlike with CDATA segments, XML parsers are not required to pass on the text of an XML comment to applications and services. The start of an XML comment is delimited by "`<!–`", and the end of an XML comment is delimited by "`–>`". The only character sequence that cannot be included in XML comments is consecutive hyphens since this is the first part of the sequence of characters used to delineate the end of the comment.

WELL-FORMED XML VERSUS VALID XML

As mentioned above, the XML declaration should always appear as the first line of an XML document instance. By contrast, other kinds of declarations and references to declarations, such as a document type declaration incorporating markup declarations or references to markup declarations, are optional. This is a key distinction between how XML is implemented and how other classes of SGML are implemented.

Generic SGML requires that all document instances include or reference a DTD. Having a DTD allows SGML tools and services to *validate* that a given document instance conforms not only to the core syntax and grammar of generic SGML but also to the constraints for the use of the semantic labels and content models as laid out in the DTD and associated markup declarations. Documents (SGML or XML) that meet all rules of the core grammar (SGML or XML, as appropriate) *and also* conform to the constraints expressed in a DTD (or other kind of XML schema), including all embedded or referenced markup declarations, are termed *valid* document instances. Effectively, the assumption for generic SGML is that without a DTD to declare allowed element names, attribute names, content models, and so on, SGML applications would not be able to properly make use of a SGML document instance.

By 1998, early experience with the Web was already sufficient to suggest that rigorous validation of DTD-enumerated constraints was not necessary for at least some purposes. Web browsers were (and still are) primarily presentation and hyperlinking applications; for the most part, they do not act on the descriptive semantics of the resources they display, except for enabling hyperlinks and resolving internal entity references. They do not need to know whether an XML document requested by the user conforms to an application-specific grammar in order to display it directly or display it after applying a style sheet (CSS or XSLT). Thus, the XML specification defines a new class of document instances: *well-formed* XML document instances. Well-formed XML document instances still need to conform to the core grammar and well-formedness constraints of the W3C XML Recommendation defining XML, but they do not need to conform to the constraints laid out in any DTD or other kind of schema. XML well-formedness constraints include a requirement that any parsed entities referenced are also well-formed fragments. (XML snippets that are well formed in all respects except for not having a single root element are termed "well-formed XML fragments" in the specification.)

For other use cases, however, validation against a set of markup declarations is still required. An XML metadata record author could misspell an element name, and as long as he or she did so consistently in both start-tag and end-tag, the XML document instance could still be well formed. Unfortunately in such a scenario, a computer application written to consume specific semantics would not recognize the misspelled element and so would not process the XML document correctly. To support such use cases, the XML specification inherits the SGML concept of document instance validity. Well-formed XML document instances that also conform to the constraints of a DTD or XML schema are valid XML document instances. XML-aware tools and services that require document validity rely on validating XML parsers. (Most users and authors of XML metadata records interact with XML parsers indirectly, through the XML tools and services they use. The XML editor Oxygen, for example, can be configured through menus to use any of several different XML parsers.) Other XML tools and services (e.g., Web browsers as mentioned above) that do not need to check for validity even when a DTD or XML schema reference is provided, rely on nonvalidating XML parsers, which still check for well-formedness. The conformance requirements for both validating and nonvalidating XML parsers are spelled out in the W3C XML Recommendation that defines XML.

SCHEMAS AND NAMESPACES

There is one more syntactical feature from the abridged MARCXML metadata record depicted in Figure 3.1 left to discuss, specifically the three attributes that appear in the document root element start-tag, which are repeated for convenience in Figure 3.10. These attributes have to do with XML schemas (the alternatives to DTDs mentioned above) and XML Namespaces. Neither schemas nor XML Namespaces are mentioned prominently in the XML W3C Recommendation. The term "schema" appears for the first time only in passing in the last appendix of the Specification. The term "namespace" is mentioned only three times in the XML W3C Recommendation. In practice, however, as illustrated in coming chapters, these are especially powerful features of XML.

XML schemas and XML Namespaces address additional perceived shortcomings of SGML in a Web context. DTDs and markup declarations, as inherited from SGML, use different syntax than are used throughout the rest of an XML document instance. The use of DTDs therefore requires consuming applications to be more complex; that is, they must be able to parse both XML document instances and XML DTD markup declarations. In XML, there are also limits on available options offered by DTDs for constraining the data types and other properties of parsed character data segments (text nodes) appearing within elements. The authors of the XML specification also wanted to facilitate reuse of markup declarations such that multiple document classes could inherit the subsets of needed element names, attribute names, and content models from several different sets of markup semantics simultaneously and more easily.

FIGURE 3.10 Root element start-tag of the abridged MARCXML record shown in Figure 3.1.

```
<record xmlns="http://www.loc.gov/MARC21/slim"
        xmlns:xsi="http://www.w3.org/2001/XMLSchema-instance"
        xsi:schemaLocation="http://www.loc.gov/MARC21/slim
                http://www.loc.gov/standards/marcxml/schema/MARC21slim.xsd">
```

Accordingly, XML schemas were introduced as an alternative means for describing markup constraints, managing markup declaration references, and validating XML document instances. XML schemas are themselves well-formed (and valid) XML document instances and so can be parsed and processed by applications that understand XML syntax rules for document instances (but may not understand rules for parsing and processing syntax used for DTD markup declarations). XML schemas declare the application-specific element names, attribute names, content models, and so on, necessary to define an application-specific grammar. As compared to DTDs, XML schemas can better specify the constraints on the type of data an element may contain. XML schemas provide semantics for defining types and declaring elements and attributes. These definitions and declarations, equivalent to DTD markup declarations, can then be used as constraints during authoring and to assess the validity of well-formed XML.

XML schemas have been implemented in multiple languages. The W3C XML Schema Definition Language[3] is the most widely supported schema language standard, but other languages, notably the RelaxNG schema language,[4] are also supported by many XML validating parsers. XML schemas are discussed in more detail in Chapters 8 and 9.

The key feature of XML schemas to mention here is that they are typically used to associate the set of markup constraints they define with a specific XML namespace. The *Namespaces in XML* specification[5] provides a simple method for qualifying element and attribute names used in XML documents in order to associate these names with a collective identity. Namespaces in XML are globally identified by a Uniform Resource Identifier (URI). (URIs look like the URLs used as Web site and Web page addresses, but URIs may or may not resolve; that is, when you put a URI in your Web browser as you would a URL, you may or may not get an information resource returned.)

Being able to associate a group of element and attribute names with a namespace, URI allows the use of names and content models from multiple sets of application-specific grammars within a single XML document without name collisions. A *qualified name* in XML (e.g., a qualified element name) is subject to namespace interpretation. In practical terms, qualified element and attribute names in XML consist of two parts: a namespace name and a local name. The namespace name serves as a prefix for the local name, enabling the mixing of semantic labels and content models from multiple metadata standards without fear of collisions because of common local names.

Within an XML document instance, rather than prefix each occurrence of a local name with the complete URI for its parent namespace, attributes are used to associate each namespace URI with a short prefix. This prefix is then used with the document instance to reference the namespace URI. One namespace URI in each XML document may be associated with no prefix, making it the default namespace prefix for that XML document. (As is addressed in Chapter 6, namespace declarations can be scoped to specific parts of a document, making it possible to have a different default namespace in select parts of a document.) Declared namespace prefixes are then prepended to element and attribute names, separated from the local name with a colon character. In the abridged MARCXML record shown in Figure 3.1, the default namespace URI is declared by the first `xmlns` attribute, `xmlns="http://www.loc.gov/MARC21/slim"`. A second namespace URI, `http://www.w3.org/2001/XMLSchema-instance`, is associated with the namespace prefix `xsi`. This namespace prefix is then used on the last attribute shown in Figure 3.10, `xsi:schemaLocation`, to provide the location of the XML schema for the document, `http://www.loc.gov/standards/marcxml/schema/MARC21slim.xsd`. As shown in Figure 3.10, the `xsi:schemaLocation` attribute value contains both the namespace URI and the location of the XML schema definition document. Additional nuances to do with the use of XML DTDs, schemas, and namespaces are illustrated in subsequent chapters.

SUMMARY

The core grammar of XML anticipates a wide range of use cases. As described in Chapter 1, the concept of elements (content objects) is core to XML, but the W3C Recommendation defining XML also anticipates the need for attributes to elaborate and refine the meaning and content of elements and as a way to support more complex use cases. Parsing and normalization rules are provided for both element content (character data) and markup as a way to mitigate low-level file serialization issues related to differences in operating systems and as a way to support special character references and the inclusion of named entities, including entity references to external, non-XML data. Anticipating other kinds of use cases, XML also allows for the inclusion of application-specific processing instructions, comments, and unparsed character data (i.e., CDATA).

Borrowing the concepts of DTDs and element types from generic SGML, XML provides the means to construct application-specific grammars that build on the core syntax of XML. Implementers are able to define their own element and attribute names (semantic labels), their own element types defining allowed element hierarchies and allowed element content data types, and their own parsed and unparsed named entities. When declaring attributes for use in an application-specific XML grammar, implementers can select from a range of predefined attribute types and can constrain allowed attribute values.

As compared to generic SGML, XML is more flexible and better optimized for integration in Web applications. For defining and declaring the components of application-specific grammars, XML schemas are provided as an alternative to DTDs, one that does not require implementers (or parsers) to understand a distinct markup declaration syntax. XML also introduces the concept of well-formedness, allowing applications to use XML document instances without having to deal with understanding a DTD or XML schema. In many contexts, this allows for a more lightweight implementation (technically speaking) as compared to SGML. For more complex scenarios that require document instance validation, XML namespaces facilitate the reuse and recombination in new contexts of markup declarations abstracted from multiple other application-specific XML grammars previously implemented.

The core syntax and grammar of XML is flexible, robust, and feature rich. Powerful, complex and extensive applications and application-specific grammars, involving multiple coordinated, potentially widely dispersed components, can be built on this foundation. Along with Chapter 1, this chapter has provided an introduction to the core grammar of XML. To construct real-world XML-based applications or even to simply make use of them, the reader will undoubtedly want to refer to ready-reference and tutorial Web sites that recap and extend this introductory summary of core XML features and syntax. There are number of excellent Web sites providing additional details and illustrations of XML grammar.[6]

QUESTIONS AND TOPICS FOR DISCUSSION

1. How might empty-element-tags be used as part of a workaround for the poetry fragment overlapping content object hierarchy illustration in Chapter 1 (Figure 1.6)? How satisfactory is this as a workaround for the overlapping hierarchy problem?
2. What are some advantages and disadvantages of using a DTD or a schema? In what instances might you prefer to use or not use one?
3. Examining either Figure 3.1 or Figure 3.7 (the MARCXML records), how does this compare to a non-XML (i.e., traditional version of the MARC record)? How is the syntax different? Do you think it is easier or more difficult to create? Would you change anything about the MARCXML syntax or structure?

SUGGESTIONS FOR EXERCISES

1. Create an XML document serializing a page from this textbook. Start by defining and naming the elements of interest for how you envision that such an XML representation will be used but feel free to employ attributes and other forms of XML markup as you see fit in addition to elements. Identify ways that attributes enhance the XML serialization.
2. Check the XML document that you just created. Describe the content types and content models of your elements.
3. Find an example of a valid XML document. Using your preferred XML editor, make alterations in the XML that result in an invalid document. What are the error messages?

NOTES

1. International Organization for Standardization (ISO), ISO/IEC 10646-1:2000, Information Technology—Universal Multiple-Octet Coded Character Set (UCS)—Parts 1 and 2, http://www.iso.org/iso/iso_catalogue/catalogue_tc/catalogue_detail.htm?csnumber=51273.

2. The Unicode Consortium, *The Unicode Standard, Version 5.0.0*, defined by The Unicode Standard, Version 5.0 (Boston: Addison-Wesley, 2007).

3. The W3C XML Schema Language specification is provided in three parts: http://www.w3.org/TR/xmlschema-0, XML Schema 1.0 Primer, Part 0; http://www.w3.org/TR/xmlschema-1, XML Schema 1.0 Structures, Part 1; and http://www.w3.org/TR/xmlschema-2, XML Schema 1.0 Data Types, Part 2. Version 1.1 of XML Schema parts 1 and 2 are currently available in draft.

4. http://www.relaxng.org/spec-20011203.html. See also the RelaxNG home page: http://www.relaxng.org.

5. http://www.w3.org/TR/REC-xml-names.

6. A sampling of tutorial and ready-reference Web sites providing more details and illustrations of core XML grammar:
   a. W3Schools XML Tutorials: http://www.w3schools.com/xml/default.asp
   b. Zvon.org: http://zvon.org/comp/m/xml_schema.html
   c. quackit XML Tutorial: http://www.quackit.com/xml/tutorial
   d. tizag.com XML Tutorial: http://www.tizag.com/xmlTutorial
   e. xmlfiles.com XML Tutorial: http://www.xmlfiles.com/xml
   f. A Gentle Instruction to XML: http://xmlzoo.net

PART II

STRUCTURED METADATA IN XML

CHAPTER 4

MARCXML: Library Catalog Records as Structured Data

Libraries have a long history of collecting, managing, and preserving information. The key to libraries being able to carry out these missions is the proper organization of the information resources they curate. *Bibliographic control* encompasses the methods and practices by which libraries organize the information they hold. The exact methods and practices of bibliographic control have changed over the years, reacting to and taking advantage of changes in the size of collections, formats of resources, scope of library services offered, and technologies available. When most libraries held relatively few books and the sharing of bibliographic information between libraries was uncommon, bibliographic control was relatively easy since everything could be described and tracked in a notebook or notebooks maintained by the librarian—an inventory more than a catalog. However, as the mass production of paper and print technology improved and produced more books at less cost and as requirements for user access and sharing between libraries evolved, the need for more advanced, structured systems to organize bibliographic information increased. The library card catalog model, which originated in the nineteenth century and was perfected in the twentieth, featured a main entry, added entry(ies), a call number, and classification information for each item in a library on a three-by-five-inch card. This proved a practical, effective, and long-lived approach for organizing bibliographic information in a systematic way. Card catalog records have their own structure that allows library staff (and users) to see quickly what information is available in a library and where each item is located.

In the mid-1960s as mainframe computing was becoming a viable option for larger academic and research institutions, the Library of Congress introduced MAchine-Readable Cataloging (MARC) as a way to facilitate computer-based catalog record creation and exchange. MARC inherited much from the catalog card format and was created in part to further facilitate the printing of cards for library catalogs, but it also was a way for libraries to leverage and exploit emerging technologies. Since it features a clear, structured format for sharing information, the MARC standard also facilitated information exchange between libraries, initially via magnetic tape.

The underlying design of the MARC record as a framework for bibliographic description has survived even as computing technologies have become more powerful and ubiquitous; however, magnetic tape as a media for storage and dissemination of MARC records has become increasingly marginalized and deprecated. The development of the Internet and attendant new digital library and information technologies has prompted libraries to look for other, more efficient and flexible ways to make bibliographic information available in the networked environment. MARC bibliographic records serialized in XML (MARCXML) represent a newer way of creating, delivering, and sharing bibliographic metadata and providing access to library-managed resources. This chapter will discuss the design of *MARCXML* as an extension of the original MARC framework for bibliographic description, noting the differences and similarities in how the framework is implemented in traditional MARC versus MARCXML and how these formats are now often used alongside each other.

TRADITIONAL MARC

In the United States and Canada and in many other parts of the world, MARC is regarded as the standard bibliographic record format in the library community. Since it was developed and introduced, MARC has been widely used in creating, sharing, and managing bibliographic records throughout the library community. Due to its central importance in library bibliographic control strategies, the development of MARC is often referred to as a "revolutionary event" (Tennant 2002, 2004). Originally developed to aid the distribution of bibliographic card catalog records from Library of Congress to other libraries, MARC has also become a tool for sharing bibliographic records between libraries because of its clear semantics and structured data approach (Avram 2003).

Over the years, MARC has had several names and variants, including many nation-specific variants. Currently, ever since *USMARC* and *CAN/MARC* were harmonized as one in the late 1990s, MARC as used in North America is known as *MARC 21* (McCallum 2002). For this discussion of MARCXML, the distinctions between the different national variants of MARC are of secondary importance. In this chapter, we will address MARC 21 and other national variants of the traditional tape-based MARC format simply as MARC. There also are different subformats of MARC for different kinds of information (e.g., bibliographic descriptions, holding records, and authority); this chapter will focus primarily on the MARC Bibliographic Format.

The Structure of MARC

MARC implements national and international standards, including the International Organization for Standardization's ISO 2709 *Format for Bibliographic Information Interchange on Magnetic Tape*[1] and ANSI/NISO Z39.2 *Information Interchange Format*[2] promulgated by the American National Standards Institute and the National Information Standards Organization. Since it was originally designed to be serialized and recorded on a magnetic tape, a raw MARC record is simply one long string of coded characters. Delineated in that stream are three major kinds of substructures: a MARC record leader, a MARC record directory, and some number of MARC "variable" fields. Variable fields, which vary record to record in number, length, and contents, are further subdivided into control fields and data fields. In an XML metadata record, special markup characters such as left- and right-angle brackets ("<" and ">") are used to delineate the structural elements of the record. In a traditional (i.e., raw) MARC record, structure is delineated by character position in the record, sometimes referred to as character offset or byte offset (e.g., relative to the start of the record or the end of the MARC record directory). The Library of Congress maintains the MARC 21 standard and provides extensive documentation of MARC semantics and structures, which the reader is encouraged to browse.[3] The components and main features of MARC are described here first in order to explain the way machines process MARC records and to provide context for subsequent discussions of MARCXML.[4] (Most of the MARC examples in this chapter are borrowed or derived from Library of Congress documentation.[5])

The MARC Record Leader

The first part of a MARC record is called the leader. An example of a MARC record leader is shown in Figure 4.1. A MARC leader is always composed of exactly 24 characters (character positions 00 to 23) including spaces (white space). The value found in each character position of the leader has a specific meaning. The leader describes the record itself, not the resource being described by the rest of the record. The leader is designed to provide information needed by computer applications to efficiently process a MARC bibliographic record.

Among these 24 characters, the first five (positions 00 to 04) give the length of the record in bytes (i.e., in characters). The record from which the leader shown in Figure 4.1 is taken is 1,329 bytes long (note the inclusion of the leading zero). Character coding scheme description (position 09), encoding level (position 17), and type of record description (position 06) are also included in the leader. Values in these subfields of the leader are especially helpful for processing a tape full of MARC records; for example, records of a type not of interest for a particular work flow can be skipped, knowing the length of a record allows an application to quickly and precisely move forward on the tape to the start of the next record, and so on.

FIGURE 4.1 The leader part of a MARC record (from *Understanding MARC* 1998).

```
01329cam  2200313 a 4500
```

FIGURE 4.2 Directory in traditional MARC (from *Understanding MARC* 1998).

01329cam 2200313 a 4500**001**002000000000**005**001700008**008**004100025**035**0021
00066**906**004500087**955**012500132**010**001700257**020**002500274**020**004400299**04**
0001800343**042**000900361**050**002400370**082**001800394**100**003200412**245**008700
444**250**001200531**260**003700543**300**002900580**500**004200609**520**022000651**740**0
03600916**650**003300871**650**001200763^3873627^19911106082810.9^891101s19

The MARC Record Directory

The directory portion of the MARC record comes after the leader. Figure 4.2 is an example of the directory for a MARC record. The directory tells the machine what MARC variable fields are used in this record and where each field's information is located in the record.

Each segment of the directory is 12 characters long. The first three characters of each 12-character-long segment in the directory (the bolded characters in Figure 4.2) identify a MARC variable field contained in the record. (In the MARC standard, every variable field is assigned a three-character numeric code or "tag." These three-character numeric codes are then used in a MARC record directory to label the semantic elements, that is, to label the top-level content objects contained in that MARC record.) The next four positions of each segment in the directory show the length of the associated MARC field on the tape (in bytes). The next five positions of the segment indicate the starting point (byte offset) for this field within the string of data that follows the directory. From the MARC record directory shown in Figure 4.2, an application can understand that the first field of the record is the 001 field (Record Control Number) and the last field is 650 (Subject Added Entry-Topical Term). The length of the 001 field is 20 bytes (0020), and the information for the 001 field will start immediately after the directory (00000).

Variable Fields

MARC and ISO 2709 define three different kinds of variable fields: record identifier field (001), reserved fields (002 to 009), and data fields (010 to 999). The identifier field and any reserved fields present are also referred to collectively as the control fields of a record. Data fields may include indicators and subfields.

The bibliographic information included in a MARC record consists of "a description of the item, main entry and added entries, subject headings, and the classification or call number" (*Understanding MARC* 1998). In MARC formatted cataloging records, each component of bibliographic information appears in a specific data field. For example, the main title information belongs in the data field 245, physical description in the data field 300, and so on.

Each data field may have up to two indicators, each indicator having its own meaning. In addition, data fields are made up of subfields. The meaning of indicators and subfields is contextual. In other words, the meaning of indicators and the number of and meaning of subfields can vary by bibliographic field; thus, for bibliographic format MARC records, subfield $c of the data field 245 (title statement) is for the statement of responsibility, while subfield $c of the data field 260 (imprint) is for the date of publication. Indicators are used for a variety of purposes; for example, for bibliographic format MARC records, the second indicator of the data field 245 tells the number of nonfiling characters that appear at the start of the item's title. The information contained in each field and subfield is constructed according to a content standard, such as *Anglo-American Cataloguing Rules* Second Edition (AACR2) or the newer Resource Description and Access standard.

Since the starting and ending positions of each field are already recorded in the directory, all the bibliographic information contained in a traditional MARC record is displayed in one string without human-readable delimiters. This information can be extracted because machines can parse the directory information by data field code and determine the location of the data field of interest. Figure 4.3 is an example of several data fields concatenated in a MARC record (i.e., as these data fields would appear on magnetic tape). The last entry in the directory (the string **650**001200763 in Figure 4.2 and grayed out in Figure 4.3) tells an application that the last data field used in the MARC record is the 650 field, which is 12 characters long and starts at location 763 relative to the end of the directory. The directory and each data field end with a field terminator ("^"). Each empty space in the record is preserved as is, and any field, including fixed, variable, and indicators, with no value is marked with an octothorpe ("#"). A record is ended with a terminator ("\"), as shown in Figure 4.3.

FIGURE 4.3 Data fields in MARC (from *Understanding MARC* 1998).

```
650003300871650001200763^3873627^19911106082810.9^891101s1990####maua#
j###000 0#eng#^##$-9(DLC) 89048230^##$-a7-$bcbc-$corignew-$d1-$eocip$-f19$-gy-gen
catlg^##$apc14 to he00 11-01-89; he06 11-01-89; he00 11-03-89; fa00 11-06
-89; fa05 11-22-89; he03 11-28-89; CIP ver. he06 08-08-90^#-#$a 89048230^#
#$-a0316107514 : $c$12.95^##$-a0316107506 (pbk.) :$c$5.95 ($6.95 Can.)^##$aD
LC$-cDLC$-dDLC^##$-alcac^00$aGV943.25$-b.B74 1990^00$a796.334/2220^1#$aBrenner,
Richard J.,$-d1941-^10$aMake the team.$-pSoccer :$-ba heads up guide to super
soccer! /$-cRichard J. Brenner.^##$-a1st ed.^##$aBoston :-$bLittle, Brown,-
$cc1990.^##$a127 p. :-$bill. ;$c19 cm.^##$a"A Sports illustrated for kids
book."^##$aInstructions for improving soccer skills. Discusses dribbling,
heading, playmaking, defense, conditioning, mental attitude, how to handle
problems with coaches, parents, and other players, and the history of so
ccer. ^#0$aHeads up guide to super soccer.^#0$-aSoccer-$xJuvenile
literature.^#0$-aSoccer.\
```

Character Encoding in Traditional MARC

When MARC was first introduced, the ubiquitous standard for character encoding was *7-bit US-ASCII* (American Standard Code for Information Interchange). This standard, still widely used today, represents printable numerals and characters commonly used in the English language as 7-bit binary numbers with equivalent decimal values between 33 and 127. Spaces, tabs, carriage returns, line feeds, and other special control characters are represented by 7-bit numbers less than 33. However, 7-bit US-ASCII encoding is insufficient to represent accented characters, mathematical symbols, and other non-Latin alphabets used in foreign languages. Some schemes for meeting these needs had been proposed by the time MARC was created, but all had some limitations. Most of these schemes involved making use of an eighth binary bit to double the number of character code points available (i.e., 0 to 255 instead of 0 to 127); however, this was still not enough codes for all the characters needed. As a result, multiple sets of characters or "code pages" were introduced for the upper range of binary values from 128 to 255. One code page might support the encoding of Greek characters, another the Slavic alphabet, and another specialized mathematics symbols. MARC-8 (Library of Congress n.d.) defines a scheme by which the code pages necessary to encode the characters needed for a particular MARC record are invoked. MARC and MARC-8 also support combining characters (e.g., diacritics combined with a base character as a way to form characters such as the character Ä) and options for specifying text directionality (reading left to right versus right to left).

When MARC was created, it was required to use MARC-8 for character encoding. Over the years, the MARC-8 encoding character set has been extended in order to work with a wider range of languages and alphabets, such as Arabic, Chinese, Cyrillic, Greek, Japanese, and Korean. However, the functionality of MARC-8 is not wholly satisfactory. Eventually, entirely new approaches to character encoding were created, such as Unicode and its associated UTF-8 and UTF-16 encoding standards. These approaches can support many times the number of characters supportable by MARC-8 and do so much more easily and efficiently. UTF-8 has been supported in MARC records as an alternative to MARC-8 since 1998. New characters are no longer being added to MARC-8. The UTF-8 encoding scheme is used in MARC records when the characters needed for the bibliographic data are not included in MARC-8. UTF-8 is supported by all commonly used Web browsers. MARC-8 is a scheme parochial to libraries, and support for MARC-8 is limited mostly to integrated library systems. As a result, MARC-8 characters (other than the basic 94 characters of 7-bit ASCII) are usually unrecognizable when MARC records are viewed in Web-based applications. This hinders interoperability of traditional MARC format records in the Web environment. All else being equal, when interoperability is a desired outcome, UTF-8 encoding should be used.

MARC SGML

Since the advent of the Web, libraries acquiring and providing access to digital resources have sought a more flexible and extensible MARC data serialization approach that would facilitate exchange of catalog records in the Internet environment, that is, an approach that would support exchange via the Web rather than via magnetic tape. Digital resource management tools, the increasing number of born-digital and digitized resources, and emerging new metadata standards other than MARC also contributed to the need for a new MARC data serialization method. In the 1990s, the Library of Congress first introduced MARC SGML as a way to serialize MARC data in an extensible markup language in order to provide more flexibility in how MARC data are created, used, and shared.

As implied by its name, this first attempt at a more flexible way to serialize and disseminate MARC format records made use of the *Standard Generalized Markup Language* (SGML) specification (McCallum n.d.). The Library of Congress drafted a MARC Document Type Definition (DTD) for SGML (Network Development and MARC Standards Office, Library of Congress n.d.) to define MARC elements in an SGML serialization. This was done to ensure that the transformation of a MARC bibliographic record into the MARC SGML format could be done without data loss. That is, a MARC record can be transformed to MARC SGML and then back to traditional, tape-based MARC without any loss of information.[6] At the time this was done, SGML was used widely as a text encoding and serialization strategy for electronic documents, and the Library of Congress hoped that SGML would be able to handle the complexity of MARC format records. However, librarians quickly realized that the infrastructure of SGML was too complex and heavyweight for it to be effective as a Web-based dissemination option or a means to facilitate interoperability with other metadata standards. Additionally, the strategy taken in implementing MARC in SGML and the nature of how SGML handles white space and manages data type requirements resulted in very verbose records (by nature, SGML is a verbose format, even more so than XML). Figure 4.4 illustrates sample MARC 008 control field information as serialized in SGML to show how verbose and complex MARC SGML can be. Notice how each byte position within the 008 control field is treated as its own content object (element), with the value of the byte serialized as an attribute value.

Contrast this with how the same information appears in a traditional MARC record and in MARCXML, as shown in Figure 4.5. Notice also in Figure 4.5 that for the 008 control field, MARCXML uses white space rather than "#" characters (traditional MARC) or the string "`blank`" (MARC SGML) to indicate null or blank bytes in the 008 field. (To allow this behavior, the data type of the character data allowed as content for the MARCXML `<leader>` and `<controlfield>` elements must be declared so as to preserve white space.

FIGURE 4.4 MARC 008 field shown in MARC SGML.

```
<mrcb008-bk>
<mrcb008-bk-00-05 value="920811"/>
<mrcb008-bk-06 value="s"/>
<mrcb008-bk-07-10 value="1991"/>
<mrcb008-bk-11-14 value="blank"/>
<mrcb008-bk-15-17 value="ch"/>
<mrcb008-bk-18-21 value="blank"/>
<mrcb008-bk-22 value="blank"/>
<mrcb008-bk-23 value="blank"/>
<mrcb008-bk-24-27 value="b "/>
<mrcb008-bk-28 value="blank"/>
<mrcb008-bk-29 value="0"/>
<mrcb008-bk-30 value="0"/>
<mrcb008-bk-31 value="0"/>
<mrcb008-bk-32 value="blank"/>
<mrcb008-bk-33 value="0"/>
<mrcb008-bk-34 value="blank"/>
<mrcb008-bk-35-37 value="chi"/>
<mrcb008-bk-38 value="blank"/>
<mrcb008-bk-39 value="d"/>
</mrcb008-bk>
```

FIGURE 4.5 The same MARC 008 field shown in traditional MARC and MARCXML.

```
920811s1911####ch#######b####000#0#chi#d
<controlfield tag="008">920811s1991    ch     b   000  0 chi d</controlfield>
```

Validating XML parsers will respect this requirement; however, nonvalidating parsers, such as Web browsers, may normalize white space when displaying these MARCXML fields.) Because of the verbosity and complexity of MARC in SGML and because of the advent of XML in 1998, MARC SGML never really caught on as an alternative to traditional, tape-based MARC serialization.

MARCXML

XML was introduced by the World Wide Web Consortium in 1998. As described in Chapter 1, a main objective of the XML initiative was to create a new extensible markup language format that preserved much of the power and best features of SGML but that did so in a more Web-friendly way. When XML was introduced, the Library of Congress converted the MARC DTD for SGML to XML because it was recognized that XML-based MARC would be simpler and easier to use in the Web environment than SGML (Guenther 2004; McCallum 2002). The Library of Congress also learned from their experience with SGML and was able to create a MARCXML that is more straightforward in design ("MARC XML Architecture" n.d.).

MARCXML Root Elements

The design chosen by the Library of Congress for serializing MARC in XML is a clear improvement over the approach taken with SGML. MARCXML defines two possible root elements: `<record>` or `<collection>`. The `<record>` element is a container element for the leader, control field, and variable field elements that make up a single MARCXML record. (As described later in this chapter, there is no need for a MARC record directory in MARCXML.) The alternative root element `<collection>` is simply a means of including multiple MARC records in a single XML document instance; the only allowed child of `<collection>` is `<record>`. There is no limit specified to the number of `<record>` elements that can be contained within a single `<collection>` element, though practical constraints of the typical PC and XML application set the limit in the low hundreds of thousands of records in most instances. The only attribute allowed for the `<collection>` element is the optional "`id`" attribute (which is used to provide identity within the XML document instance and has no particular meaning relative to traditional MARC). The `<record>` element as well is allowed an "`id`" attribute; however, the `<record>` element also may have a "`type`" attribute. The values for `<record> type` attribute are constrained to "Bibliographic," "Authority," "Holdings," "Classification," or "Community," corresponding to the current formats of MARC Records defined by the Library of Congress and the existing MARC 21 specification.

Figure 4.6 shows an example of a single, complete MARC bibliographic record serialized in XML. This is the full version of the abridged MARC record referenced in Chapters 1 and 3 (Figures 1.11 and 3.1) to illustrate XML syntax and grammar. Following here is a complementary discussion focusing on the semantics of this record.

The Child Elements of `<record>`

A MARCXML `<record>` element must have as children, in order, exactly one `<leader>` element, at least one `<controlfield>` element, and at least one `<datafield>` element. No other elements are allowed as immediate children of a `<record>` element. Note that a subset of the first few variable fields, specifically the traditional MARC record control number fields (00X), are distinguished from other variable fields of a MARCXML record and collectively called control fields. These fields do not have indicators or subfields; hence, their structure (content type) from an XML standpoint is different (e.g., no child elements and fewer attributes allowed). To facilitate how MARCXML records are created and validated, it is useful to segregate the identifier field and reserved fields. For this reason, the `<controlfield>` element is declared as distinct from the `<datafield>` element.

FIGURE 4.6 Example of MARCXML record.


```
<?xml version="1.0" encoding="UTF-8"?>
<record xsi:schemaLocation=http://www.loc.gov/MARC21/slim http://www.loc.gov/standards/marcxml/schema/MARC21slim.xsd
      xmlns="http://www.loc.gov/MARC21/slim" xmlns:xsi="http://www.w3.org/2001/XMLSchema-instance">
  <leader>01698cam 22003614a 4500</leader>
  <controlfield tag="001">5439928</controlfield>
  <controlfield tag="005">20080104135038.0</controlfield>
  <controlfield tag="008">070313s2007    ctua     b    001 0 eng </controlfield>
  <datafield tag="010" ind1=" " ind2=" ">
      <subfield code="a">2007009006</subfield>
  </datafield>
  <datafield tag="035" ind1=" " ind2=" ">
      <subfield code="a">(OCoLC)ocn105428765</subfield>
  </datafield>
  <datafield tag="040" ind1=" " ind2=" ">
      <subfield code="a">DLC</subfield>
      <subfield code="c">DLC</subfield>
      <subfield code="d">BAKER</subfield>
      <subfield code="d">BTCTA</subfield>
      <subfield code="d">C#P</subfield>
  </datafield>
  <datafield tag="020" ind1=" " ind2=" ">
      <subfield code="a">9781591582809 (alk. paper)</subfield>
  </datafield>
      <datafield tag="020" ind1=" " ind2=" ">
      <subfield code="a">1591582806 (alk. paper)</subfield>
  </datafield>
      <datafield tag="029" ind1="1" ind2=" ">
      <subfield code="a">NLGGC</subfield>
      <subfield code="b">302541152</subfield>
```

```
</datafield>
<datafield tag="042" ind1=" " ind2=" ">
    <subfield code="a">pcc</subfield>
</datafield>
<datafield tag="050" ind1="0" ind2="0">
    <subfield code="a">Z666.7</subfield>
    <subfield code="b">.C65 2007</subfield>
</datafield>
<datafield tag="082" ind1="0" ind2="0">
    <subfield code="a">025.3</subfield>
    <subfield code="2">22</subfield>
</datafield>
<datafield tag="049" ind1=" " ind2=" ">
    <subfield code="a">UIUU</subfield>
    </datafield>
<datafield tag="100" ind1="1" ind2=" ">
    <subfield code="a">Cole, Timothy W.</subfield>
</datafield>
<datafield tag="245" ind1="1" ind2="0">
    <subfield code="a">Using the Open Archives Initiative protocol for metadata harvesting /</subfield>
    <subfield code="c">Timothy W. Cole and Muriel Foulonneau.</subfield>
</datafield>
<datafield tag="260" ind1=" " ind2=" ">
    <subfield code="a">Westport, Conn. :</subfield>
    <subfield code="b">Libraries Unlimited,</subfield>
    <subfield code="c">c2007.</subfield>
</datafield>
<datafield tag="300" ind1=" " ind2=" ">
    <subfield code="a">xv, 208 p. :</subfield>
    <subfield code="b">ill. ;</subfield>
    <subfield code="c">26 cm.</subfield>
```


(continued)

FIGURE 4.6 (Continued)


```
    </datafield>
    <datafield tag="440" ind1=" " ind2="0">
        <subfield code="a">Third millennium cataloging</subfield>
    </datafield>
    <datafield tag="504" ind1=" " ind2=" ">
        <subfield code="a">Includes bibliographical references and index.</subfield>
    </datafield>
    <datafield tag="505" ind1="0" ind2=" ">
        <subfield code="a">Definition and origins of OAI-PMH -- Underlying technologies and the technical development of OAI-PMH -- Context
for OAI-PMH : eprints, institutional repositories, and open access -- Technical details of the protocol -- Implementing an OAI data provider --
Creating metadata to share -- Post-harvest metadata normalization &amp; augmentation -- Using aggregated metadata to build digital library
services -- Concluding thoughts.
        </subfield>
    </datafield>
    <datafield tag="650" ind1=" " ind2="0">
        <subfield code="a">Metadata harvesting.</subfield>
    </datafield>
    <datafield tag="610" ind1="2" ind2="0">
        <subfield code="a">Open Archives Initiative.</subfield>
    </datafield>
    <datafield tag="700" ind1="1" ind2=" ">
        <subfield code="a">Foulonneau, Muriel.</subfield>
    </datafield>
    <datafield tag="856" ind1="4" ind2="1">
        <subfield code="3">Table of contents only</subfield>
        <subfield code="u">http://www.loc.gov/catdir/toc/ecip0714/2007009006.html</subfield>
    </datafield>
</record>
```

Note also that there is no analog for the traditional MARC record directory component. The MARC directory was needed to facilitate processing of MARC records on magnetic tape. Because tape is a sequentially read media (i.e., a sequential access media) and a relatively slow medium to read, it was desirable for performance reasons to know exactly where in a given MARC record each bit of information was. This is less a concern with XML-based applications today. XML files are typically stored on disk and often loaded in their entirety in computer memory for processing. Both disks and modern computer memory support random access (i.e., are random-access media). While some XML parsers (computer applications that read and process XML files) do treat XML documents as sequential streams of characters, many others treat XML documents as tree structures (as described in Chapter 1). Even when dealing with sequential stream XML parsers, for documents the size of MARC records, the performance differences between treating the `<record>` as a stream of characters or as a tree of element and attribute nodes is modest, so knowing in advance the byte offset for each control field and data field is insignificant. For these reasons, the directory component of the traditional MARC record is not carried over into MARCXML. As a result, MARCXML implementers do not need to worry about how changes in record contents (e.g., a change in bibliographic information) might affect the overall length of the record or other information traditionally stored in the MARC directory. Nor do MARCXML applications need to deal with how changes to the start and end location of data fields within a record might require an update to a record's directory.

The construction of the `<leader>` element in a MARCXML record has some minor nuances. Typically, a MARCXML `<leader>` element takes, as content, the leader string unchanged from the way it would appear in a traditional MARC record serialization for magnetic tape, including any spaces. However, implementers should recognize, especially when creating MARCXML records from scratch rather than transforming existing MARC records, that a few character positions of the `<leader>` element are ambiguous in a MARCXML serialization. In traditional MARC, the first five characters of the leader string (character positions 0 to 4) are meant to hold the length of the record. They can be used for this purpose in MARCXML, but XML-applications processing MARCXML records do not use this information; they have other (more reliable) options to determine the length of an XML-serialized MARC record or to move on to the next `<record>` element in a MARCXML `<collection>` instance. If transformed from a traditional MARC record, these first five characters often are left as is (i.e., representing the length of the record when it was serialized according to the tape-based traditional MARC record format). In other instances, these first five characters of the leader may be set to all zeros in the MARCXML record (the authors' personal preference). Similar logic is applied to leader character positions 12 to 16, which are designed to hold the base address for a traditionally serialized MARC record on tape. Finally, leader character positions 20 to 23 make up the entry map for the MARC record directory. Since directory entries are not relevant to the MARCXML serialization of the record, these character positions are either left as they would appear in the traditional MARC serialization (always "4500") or left blank (i.e., four spaces).

Each <controlfield> has one required attribute, "tag", and each <datafield> element has three required attributes: "tag", "ind1", and "ind2 ". The tag attribute for both the <controlfield> element and the <datafield> element conveys the three-character numeric MARC code for the <controlfield> or <datafield>, for example, "001", "245", "260", and so on. As in traditional MARC, tag attribute values for <controlfield> elements will always start "00". For obvious reasons, a value for all tag attributes is required. The ind1 and ind2 attributes convey the first and the second indicator for each <datafield> element. Allowable values and interpretation of the values for these attributes depends on the value of the tag attribute since indicators are context sensitive; however, regardless of the tag attribute value, a value (a string of exactly one character) must be supplied for each and every ind1 and ind2 attribute in a MARCXML serialized record, even if the value is simply a single space (white space). MARCXML applications understand that a single white space as the value for an indicator attribute is intended to mean a blank or empty indicator, that is, the equivalent a "#" indicator value in traditional MARC serialization.

Each <datafield> is required to have at least one <subfield> element. Whereas <controlfield> elements contain string content directly, the content of a <datafield> element is contained within one or more child <subfield> elements. In other words, <controlfield> elements have a character data content type, while <datafield> elements have an element content type. In MARC, subfields are used to break data values into more granular components. Thus, using subfields, it is possible to separately label components of the 245 data field (title statement) as main title, rest of title, statement of responsibility, number or name of part/section, and so on.

In the MARCXML scheme, each and every <subfield> element is required to have a "code" attribute. The value of the code attribute is the semantically meaningful label (albeit typically coded as a single letter) for the <subfield> element, much as the value of the tag attribute is the semantic label (coded as a three-digit number) of the <datafield> or <controlfield> element. The <subfield> element code attribute values are the same as the subfield labels used in traditional MARC serialization, except without the delimiter "$".

Figure 4.7 is a close-up view of the leader, control field 008, and data fields 245 and 300 and shows the preserved white space for the leader and control field 008 and for blank indicator values in the MARCXML record. Per specifications for the MARC bibliographic format, both indicators for data field 300 (physical description) are undefined (not used). However, as mentioned, the MARCXML specification requires attributes ind1 and ind2 for all

FIGURE 4.7 Close up view of MARCXML leader, control field 008, and data fields 245 and 300.

```
<leader>01698cam 22003614a 4500</leader>
...
<controlfield tag="008">070313s2007 ctua b 001 0 eng </controlfield>
...
<datafield tag="245" ind1="1" ind2="0">
        <subfield code="a">Using the Open Archives Initiative protocol for metadata
harvesting/</subfield>
        <subfield code="c">Timothy W. Cole and Muriel Foulonneau.</subfield>
</datafield>
<datafield tag="300" ind1=" " ind2=" ">
        <subfield code="a">xv, 208 p. :</subfield>
        <subfield code="b">ill. ;</subfield>
        <subfield code="c">26 cm.</subfield>
</datafield>
```

`<datafield>` elements; that is, it declares all `<datafield>` elements to have these attributes and declares them as required. Additionally, these attributes are required to always have attribute-value strings that are at least one character long. Accordingly, for data field 300, the value of these two attributes is always a single space. MARCXML applications understand that the meaning of this is no value for these indicators.

Uses of MARCXML

The bibliographic information converted from MARC to MARCXML is lossless; however, if the character encoding of the original MARC record being transformed is MARC-8, it must be changed from MARC-8 to UTF-8. (As noted above, UTF-8 is more broadly supported. It is also the default character encoding for XML.) As a bibliographic record serialization format, MARCXML has several recognized advantages that traditional, tape-based MARC does not have. These advantages can be categorized as having to do with "transformation, presentation and analysis," as discussed in the Library of Congress's *MARCXML Architecture*[7] documents and briefly recapped here.

Transformation and Reusability

Most retrospective digitization initiatives involving library collections, such as the mass book digitization projects by Google and the Open Content Alliance (OCA), make use of MARC-compatible bibliographic catalog records provided by libraries participating in these projects. Sometimes these records need to be transformed to other metadata standards, such as to Dublin Core or to the Metadata Object Description Schema (MODS), to facilitate resource sharing and to increase resource access and discoverability. MARC-based metadata are also utilized when these projects build their own index of digitized content. If the records are already in MARCXML format, then all the transformations

FIGURE 4.8 MARCXML transformed into Simple Dublin Core.

```
<datafield tag="260" ind1=" " ind2=" ">
      <subfield code="a">Westport, Conn. :</subfield>
      <subfield code="b">Libraries Unlimited,</subfield>
      <subfield code="c">c2007.</subfield>
</datafield>
```

```
<dc:publisher> Westport, Conn. : Libraries Unlimited</dc:publisher>
<dc:date>c2007.</dc:date>
```

can be easily done using style sheets written in the Extensible Stylesheet Language for Transformations (XSLT). The open source MARC editing utility MarcEdit, developed by Terry Reese,[8] can convert records from MARC to MARCXML and back again. This tool also can transform between MARCXML and other XML metadata formats, such as MODS, Dublin Core, and Encoded Archival Description, using XSLT style sheets. In addition, if the records are in MARCXML format, the metadata can be easily embedded into JPEG 2000 page images created during book digitization (the JPEG 2000 standard supports the inclusion of arbitrary XML) or transformed to a locally defined XML-based metadata standard used for institutional digital asset management software. Figure 4.8 illustrates how the publication information element of a MARCXML record might be transformed to Dublin Core.

MARCXML also makes MARC format metadata more shareable. Although a library may own an invaluable collection of resources, due to the limited number of applications that can use metadata serialized in traditional, tape-based MARC directly, these resources are discoverable and used by only a limited user community when described solely in traditional MARC. Users cannot find or search these resources from more heavily used or specialized community nonlibrary search portals. However, if the records are in MARCXML format, they can more easily be harvested or transformed and indexed by other portals, which will ultimately increase access as well as use of these resources.

Presentation and Validation

Serializing catalog records in MARCXML makes it especially easy to transform and present these records in XHTML format. Transformed via an XSLT style sheet to XHTML, records can be displayed in a broad range of Web applications, enhancing access and discoverability. A more detailed discussion of XML transformations to XHTML is provided in Chapter 11. For now, the sequence of displays depicted in Figures 4.9, 4.10, and 4.11 illustrate in practical terms how the same bibliographic information, shared as MARCXML, can be presented in additional venues beyond the library online public access catalog and spanning multiple contexts.

FIGURE 4.9 MARC information as displayed in University of Illinois Library's OPAC interface, VuFind.

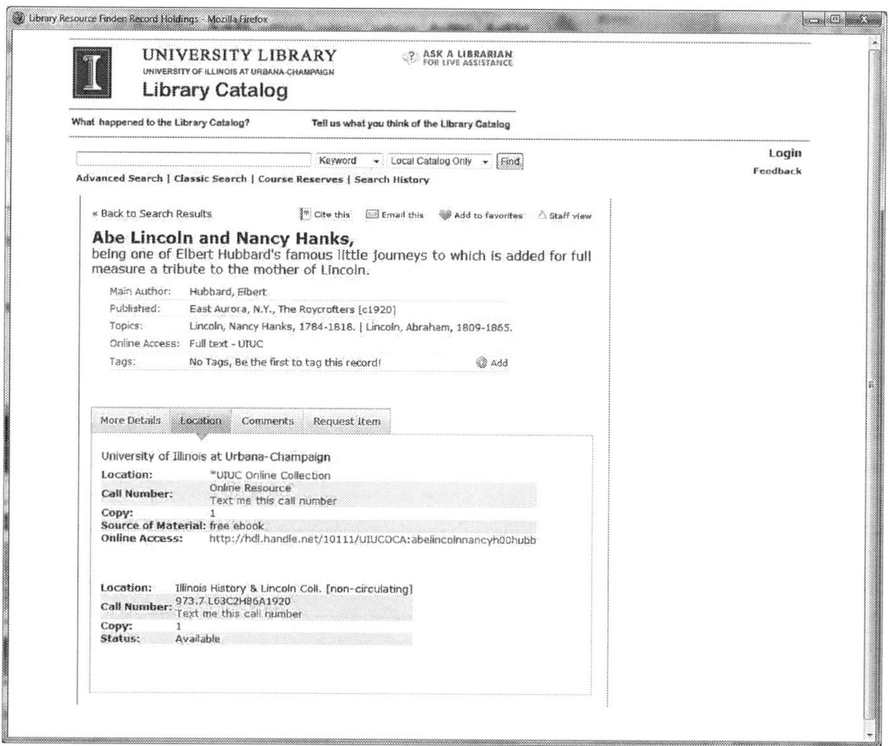

Figure 4.9 shows a bibliographic catalog record as displayed in the University of Illinois Library VuFind online public access catalog. Because VuFind is a specialized library application, the display shown in Figure 4.9 was generated after internal conversion of a bibliographic record serialized in traditional, tape-based MARC. This bibliographic record describes a book from the University of Illinois collection that has now been digitized by the OCA. The University of Illinois loaned the print book from its collection to the OCA for scanning, at the same time generating and providing the OCA and the Internet Archive with a copy of the library's bibliographic record. This record was then transformed into MARXML and ingested into their indexing system as part of their automated digitization work flow. (Their system, being general purpose and designed to deal with more than just library content, cannot ingest tape-based MARC serializations directly.) The digital copy of this book is now discoverable not only through Illinois Library online catalog (i.e., through the Illinois local VuFind online public access catalog application, as shown in Figure 4.9) but also through the more broadly based Internet Archive search portal. Figure 4.10 is the display of the bibliographic record in the Internet Archive portal. This view was created not directly from a traditional, tape-based MARC serialization of the information but rather from the MARCXML serialized bibliographic record derived from the record supplied to the OCA by the University of Illinois Library at the time of digitization.

FIGURE 4.10 Internet Archive display of bibliographic information derived from University of Illinois Library MARC record.

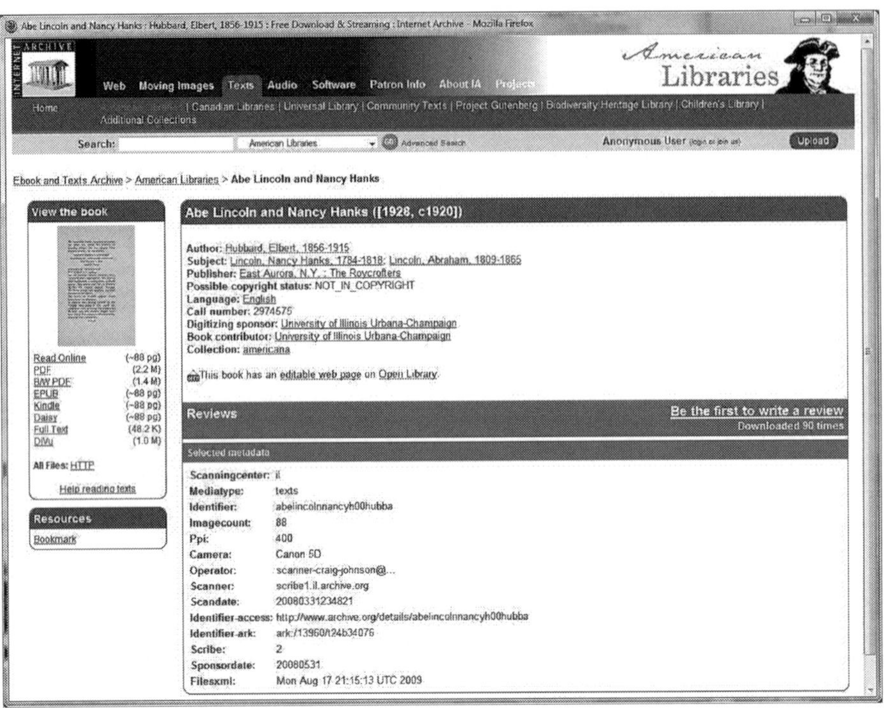

After digitization by the OCA, the University of Illinois Library retrieved the digital files created by the OCA. These files, along with the MARCXML record, now augmented and updated with information about the digitized copy of this print manifestation, were then made available from a metadata-based portal application hosted on one of the University of Illinois Library's Web servers. The Illinois Harvest Portal display shown in Figure 4.11 is generated dynamically on the fly from the augmented MARCXML record by a style sheet. Thus, even within the University of Illinois Library, having MARCXML serialized records facilitates making information more discoverable from more applications. The style sheet used to dynamically generate the view shown in Figure 4.11 is explored in Case Study 11.1 in Chapter 11.

Finally, MARCXML also provides an easy way to validate bibliographic records using off-the-shelf, standard and unmodified validating XML parsers. This is possible because the specifics and requirements of MARC semantics are captured not in an application or specialized tool but rather in an XML DTD or, alternatively, in the declarations and definitions of an XML schema maintained by the Library of Congress. When the University of Illinois Library converts its traditionally serialized MARC records to MARCXML, catalogers at the library use tools that can automatically validate the records created according to appropriate DTD or schema. Most incorrect usage of

FIGURE 4.11 Illinois Harvest portal display of bibliographic information dynamically derived from MARCXML record.

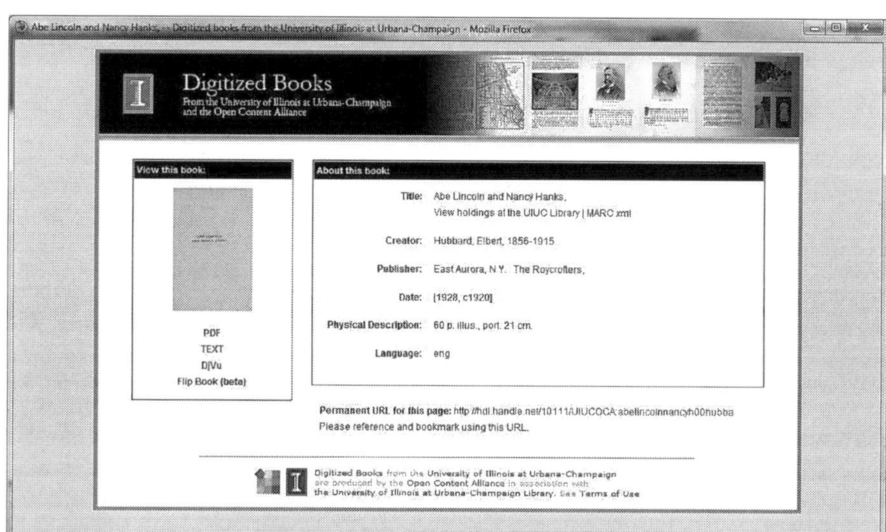

data fields or indicators and most incorrect content data typing are identified by standard XML validating parsers. A MARC-specific application is not required. As is discussed in more detail in Chapters 8 and 9, this facilitates ongoing record maintenance and cleanup.

CASE STUDY 4.1
Creating an XML Snapshot of a Library Catalog for Google

Synopsis: As a participant in the Google Books Library Project, the University of Illinois Library is one of many libraries making its books available to Google for digitization. In order to more efficiently identify and select books for digitization, Google requested complete bibliographic and volume-level holding and item information from participating libraries in MARCXML format. Individual holding and item information, such as the item bar code, call number, item location, item type, item record ID, enumeration, and chronology information (e.g., volume number and issue year) are added to bibliographic records according to a Google-specified scheme utilizing data fields in the MARC format reserved for local extension. The reason Google wants the records in MARCXML format is obvious: the MARCXML format provides a scalable means to obtain, manage, and integrate metadata from a range of different online catalog systems describing literally tens of millions of volumes from some of the largest academic research libraries in the world.

Illustrates: Using XML to combine shared manifestation-level bibliographic descriptions with associated local item-level holdings metadata; interoperability of metadata in XML format; MARC-to-MARCXML conversion.

FIGURE 4.12 Snippet of tab delimited file prepared for Google work flow.

```
BIB_ID OCLC Symbol  ITEM_BARCODE  ITEM_ID  LOCATION_NAMECALL_NO  COPY_NUMBER
       BIB_FORMAT  ENUMERATION  CHRONOLOGY
       955 subfield a  955 subfield b  955 subfield c  955 subfield d  955 subfield e  955
       subfield f  955 subfield g  955 subfield h  955 subfield i
267407 UIU  30112084119822  9284758  stx  025.3  C676u  1  am
```

At the University of Illinois Library, the Content Access Management Unit (formally the Cataloging Unit) in the Technical Services Division was responsible for preparing MARCXML records for Google. The first step in doing so was to gather all the bibliographic and item-level holdings records from the Library's catalog, excluding (of course) bibliographic and holding records describing resources available in electronic format only. The University of Illinois Library uses the Voyager integrated library system (with a VuFind end-user interface). Illinois librarians began by creating a query for the Voyager Report system that generated a tab-delimited file format listing all volume-level holdings information, one record per line. A tiny bit of this tab-delimited report file is shown in Figure 4.12.

Illinois then used a locally built tool, BibCultivator (written in Perl), to read through this file and separately retrieve the bibliographic MARC records associated with these holding records. BibCultivator relies on an open source code library called VBZoom,[9] developed at the University of Illinois Library several years previously. This code library allowed BibCultivator to retrieve the bibliographic MARC records from Voyager one by one using the Z39.50 information retrieval protocol. As it retrieved each bibliographic MARC record from Voyager, BibCultivator added the item-level holdings information from the tab-delimited file to each corresponding MARC record in a 955 field, using the library's local bibliographic identifier number as a matching point. A separate MARC record was created for each volume owned; that is, if the library owned 10 bound volumes of a given serial, 10 MARC records were created, one for each volume, all records identical except for the contents of the 955 field.

These raw MARC records were then batch converted to MARCXML using MarcEdit. Per Google's request, the individual MARCXML record files created were combined into several MARCXML `<collection>` records. Practical considerations limited the size of any one MARCXML collection catalog to about 1 million MARCXML records. (The collection of the University of Illinois Library includes approximately 11 million physical volumes.) Note that the format that Google requested for augmenting bibliographic MARC records with holdings and item-level information was nonstandard (Figure 4.13).

Two other standard approaches could have been taken to incorporate these data. The first option would have exploited the fact that the Z39.50 protocol can be used to grab not only bibliographic records but also holdings and

FIGURE 4.13 MARCXML data field 955 for Google.

```
<datafield tag="955" ind1=" " ind2=" ">
  <subfield code="a">UIU</subfield>
  <subfield code="b">30112084119822</subfield>
  <subfield code="c">9284758</subfield>
  <subfield code="d">stx</subfield>
  <subfield code="e">025.3 C676u</subfield>
  <subfield code="f">1</subfield>
  <subfield code="g">am</subfield>
</datafield>
```

item-level records from compliant cataloging systems. The Z39.50 OPAC Record Syntax as defined in Z39.50-1995 describes a format for holding and circulation (i.e., item) records. One of the benefits of using this OPAC Record Syntax[10] is that it maps well to XML (see Figure 4.14). This format can be used to create virtual union cataloging applications. Had catalogers at Illinois the option to exploit the OPAC Record Syntax, the MARCXML records for Google would have been generated more efficiently, and the resulting records would have been more amenable for reuse (since they would have conformed to an established and well-documented standard), though to include this information in the library's MARCXML, records would still have required reliance on use of the MARC 955 local extension data field.

The other option would have been to make use of the MARC holdings record format.[11] As described in MARC21 Format for Holdings Data, the holdings data format can capture detailed information relating to local holdings data requested by Google

FIGURE 4.14 Holdings and item information in OPAC record format.

```
<holdingsData>
    <holdingsAndCirc>
         <typeOfRecord>x</typeOfRecord>
         <encodingLevel>4</encodingLevel>
         <receiptAcqStatus>0</receiptAcqStatus>
         <generalRetention>8</generalRetention>
         <completeness>1</completeness>
         <dateOfReport>000000</dateOfReport>
         <nucCode>stx</nucCode>
         <localLocation>Main Stacks</localLocation>
         <callNumber>025.3; C676u</callNumber>
         <copyNumber>1</copyNumber>
    <circulationData>
         <availableNow>0</availableNow>
         <availablityDate>2010-10-13 23:00:00</availablityDate>
         <itemId>9284758</itemId>
         <renewable>0</renewable>
         <onHold>0</onHold>
    </circulationData>
    </holdingsAndCirc>
 </holdingsData>
```

FIGURE 4.15 MARC holdings data in XML format.

```
<?xml version="1.0" encoding="UTF-8"?>
<record xsi:schemaLocation="http://www.loc.gov/MARC21/slim
http://www.loc.gov/standards/marcxml/schema/MARC21slim.xsd"
xmlns="http://www.loc.gov/MARC21/slim" xmlns:xsi="http://www.w3.org/2001/
XMLSchema-instance">
    <leader>00177cx a22000854 4500</leader>
    <controlfield tag="001">62886820</controlfield>
    <controlfield tag="004">5439928</controlfield>
    <controlfield tag="005">20090518214818.0</controlfield>
    <controlfield tag="008">071220 0 p____8___1 001 u u___0 000000</controlfield>
    <datafield tag="852" ind1="1" ind2=" ">
        <subfield code="b">stx</subfield>
        <subfield code="h">025.3</subfield>
        <subfield code="i">C676u</subfield>
        <subfield code="t">1</subfield>
    </datafield>
    <datafield tag="876" ind1=" " ind2=" ">
        <subfield code="a">9284758</subfield>
        <subfield code="p">30112084119822</subfield>
        <subfield code="t">1</subfield>
        <subfield code="j">charged</subfield>
    </datafield>
```

and store these data in MARC data fields 852 and 876, as shown in Figure 4.15. (Note that subfield elements with attribute `code = "t"` appear in both 852 and 876 data fields, binding holding and item information together for a given volume.)

CASE STUDY 4.2
Creating MARCXML Records for the HathiTrust

***Synopsis*:** The HathiTrust[12] was originally founded as a "collaboration between thirteen universities on the Committee on Institutional Cooperation (CIC) and the University of California system to establish a repository for these universities to archive and share their digitized collections" (CIC eNews 2009). As one of the CIC university libraries, the University of Illinois Library decided to add some of its retrospectively digitized book collections to the HathiTrust. The HathiTrust has specific requirements for bibliographic metadata. As a first step toward ingesting retrospectively digitized content, the HathiTrust requires a record serialized as MARCXML describing the print object that was digitized and providing identifiers that can be used to retrieve the digital objects required for ingestion, such as from the Open Content Alliance (OCA). Once MARCXML records have been processed by HathiTrust staff, they initiate a process to ingest the digital resources using the link to the resource found in these metadata records. For OCA-digitized resources, bibliographic information required by the HathiTrust includes the record's enumeration/chronology, the OCA/Internet Archive digitized volume identifier, and the ARK Identifier in the MARC 955 field.

(*continued*)

Illustrates: Creating a new MARCXML metadata from different XML metadata; enhancing interoperability using XML metadata; extracting and adding information from and to XML metadata.

To prepare the metadata for OCA-digitized content that the University of Illinois Library wished to contribute to the HathiTrust, librarians at Illinois began with the MARCXML records created by the OCA at the time of the book digitization. These records were augmented as part of the postdigitization work flow at Illinois with the addition of enumeration/chronology information in data field 245 subfield $n as well as the addition of OCA/Internet Archive identifiers (in the data field 856) and CNRI Handle System handles in another 856 data field. The CNRI handles added resolve to local Illinois copies of the digital files. (The display shown in Figure 4.11 is generated from these augmented MARC records; the same records are also used as a basis for creating e-book records, which are subsequently added to OCLC.)

As requested by the HathiTrust, ARK identifiers assigned by the OCA were retrieved and added to Illinois MARCXML records before forwarding to HathiTrust staff. (The ARK identifier scheme was developed by the California Digital Library.[13] ARK identifiers are not used at Illinois, which favors the more established and generally more Web-friendly CNRI-style handles.[14] CNRI-style handles are the foundation for the immensely successful Digital Object Identifiers used by commercial journal publishers and supported by the American Association of Publishers.) The ARK identifiers were retrieved from the OCA from their custom-format "meta" XML files (Figure 4.16), which in large part derived from the MARCXML files that Illinois provides at the time of book digitization but also contain additional metadata generated locally by the OCA during the digitization process. The ARK identifiers retrieved were added to MARCXML data field 955 subfield $b per HathiTrust instructions. In addition, the separate OCA/Internet Archive identifier in the 856 field was copied to data field 955 subfield $q (stripped of the leading protocol and server part of the http URL), and the enumeration/chronology information recorded in data field 245 subfield $n was copied to data field 955 subfield $v when applicable. See Figure 4.17 for an illustration of the custom HathiTrust data field 955.

Of interest in both of these case studies is the contradiction of requiring MARCXML records for bibliographic information as a way to achieve interoperability and standards-based information exchange while simultaneously disregarding standards-based ways to exchange holdings and item information and actionable identifiers in favor of one-time application-specific methods for sharing this information. This illustrates how much further along and accepted standards for descriptive metadata interoperability are at this point in time as compared to the acceptance of standards for expressing identifiers and local holdings and item metadata.

FIGURE 4.16 MetaXML record created by Internet Archive.


```
<metadata>
    <title>Early history and pioneers of Champaign County : illustrated by one
hundred and fifteen superb engravings by Melville : containing biographical sketches
of the early settlers, the early history of the county obtained from the most
reliable sources and many graphic scenes and incidents from the bright and shady
sides of pioneer life
    </title>
    <creator>Mathews, Milton W</creator>
    <creator>McLean, Lewis A., b.1843</creator>
    <subject>Champaign County (Ill.) -- Biography</subject>
    <subject>Champaign County (Ill.) -- History</subject>
    <publisher>Urbana, Ill. : Champaign County Herald</publisher>
    <date>[1891]</date>
    <language>eng</language>
    <possible-copyright-status>NOT_IN_COPYRIGHT</possible-copyright-status>
    <sponsor>University of Illinois Urbana-Champaign</sponsor>
    <contributor>University of Illinois Urbana-Champaign</contributor>
    <scanningcenter>il</scanningcenter>
    <mediatype>texts</mediatype>
    <collection>americana</collection>
    <call_number>4180416</call_number>
    <repub_state>4</repub_state>
    <updatedate>2008-04-29 13:27:16</updatedate>
    <updater>chris.jones@archive.org</updater>
    <identifier>earlyhistorypion00math</identifier>
    <uploader>chris.jones@archive.org</uploader>
    <addeddate>2008-04-29 13:26:30</addeddate>
    <publicdate>2008-04-29 13:26:35</publicdate>
    <imagecount>182</imagecount>
    <ppi>400</ppi>
    <lcamid/>
    <rcamid/>
    <camera>Canon 5D</camera>
    <operator>scanner-craig-johnson@archive.org</operator>
    <scanner>scribe1.il.archive.org
    </scanner>
    <missingpages/>
    <scandate>20080430023744</scandate>
    <foldoutcount>0</foldoutcount>
    <identifier-access>
    http://www.archive.org/details/earlyhistorypion00math
    </identifier-access>
    <identifier-ark>ark:/13960/t7mp53p28</identifier-ark>
    <notes>On+page+129%2C+the+book+changes+numbering+order.</notes>
    <curation>
[curator]jae@archive.org[/curator][date]20080527222313[/date][state]approved
[/state]
    </curation>
    <sponsordate>20080531</sponsordate>
    <filesxml>Tue Aug 18 16:45:23 UTC 2009</filesxml>
</metadata>
```

FIGURE 4.17 MARCXML data field 955 for the HathiTrust.

```
<datafield tag="955 ind1=" " ind2=" ">
        <subfield code="b">ark:/13960/t7mp53p28</subfield>
        <subfield code="q">earlyhistorypion00mah</subfield>
</datafield>
```

SUMMARY

Libraries have been using MARC to organize and describe their collections since the 1960s. MARC made it possible for libraries to leverage computers in new ways and to begin sharing bibliographic records with each other on a larger scale and more efficiently. This in turn helped to reduce duplicative efforts in creating catalog records.

Today, libraries find themselves needing to process and manage a growing influx of digitized and born-digital resources and to share their cataloging records with entities outside the mainstream library community. The traditional MARC serialization, developed for use with magnetic tape, is not optimal for this task. In practice, MARCXML is making it possible to leverage the Web more effectively to share catalog records. MARCXML is proving more robust, especially for sharing library catalog records with Web portals such as Google, the Internet Archive, the HathiTrust, and Daum. (Daum, a Web portal based in South Korea, now includes in searches MARCXML records made available by the National Library of Korea.) MARCXML is also proving helpful to members of the library community (not to mention abstracting and indexing services like Medline) wanting to engage and align with initiatives such as the Open Knowledge Foundation's Open Bibliographic Data Initiative.[15] Providing an XML-based serialization of MARC has proven a good way to extend the viability of MARC and protect the investment that libraries have made in MARC cataloging over the decades.

This acceptance is not to minimize the importance of the decisions made as to how to serialize MARC in XML. As early experimentation with MARC in SGML at the Library of Congress demonstrated, there are less (MARC SGML) and more (MARCXML) effective and efficient application-specific grammars that can be used to migrate traditional MARC into modern markup language syntax. The success of MARCXML as compared to MARC SGML suggests that the Library of Congress did much better on its second try.

Nor does the success of MARCXML mean that MARC will continue as the nearly singular semantics for descriptive cataloging in the library community. As the tangible and virtual holdings of libraries continue to diversify, so will the metadata formats used for descriptive cataloging. XML implementations of several of these alternative metadata formats are described in the next two chapters. Nonetheless, as a tool to extend and facilitate the evolution of library cataloging work flows and as a structured data syntax for the library community's legacy of rich bibliographic records and still significant output of new print and e-book catalog records, the potential role of MARCXML in today's library technical service units is far from insignificant.

QUESTIONS AND TOPICS FOR DISCUSSION

1. MARC has been used as the bibliographic standard in libraries since the late 1960s. What is the main reason that MARC has been used in the library community for so long?
2. What kinds of significant changes occurred in the late 1990s that impacted bibliographic control?
3. Google, the Internet Archive, and the HathiTrust all keep records for their digitized books in MARCXML format. What could be the benefits of having bibliographic records in XML format for records management?
4. Having bibliographic metadata in XML format will have many benefits in resource sharing that will increase access to resources. What kinds of things can you do with XML format records that you cannot do with traditional tape-based MARC format records?

SUGGESTIONS FOR EXERCISES

1. Create a simple book record in MARC format.
2. Find a freely available tool that can convert MARC records to MARCXML, make the conversion, and compare the two records in readability and modularity.
3. Try to extract the title information from your MARC record and your MARCXML record.

NOTES

1. http://www.iso.org/iso/iso_catalogue/catalogue_ics/catalogue_detail_ics.htm?csnumber=7674.
2. http://www.niso.org/standards/z39-2-1994R2001.
3. http://www.loc.gov/marc.
4. http://www.loc.gov/marc/marcxml.html.
5. http://www.loc.gov/marc/umb/um01to06.html.
6. http://www.loc.gov/marc/marcsgmlarchive.html.
7. http://www.loc.gov/standards/marcxml/marcxml-architecture.html.
8. http://people.oregonstate.edu/~reeset/marcedit/html/index.php.
9. http://vb-zoom.sourceforge.net.
10. http://www.biblio-tech.com/html/z39_50_record_syntaxes.html#opac.
11. http://www.loc.gov/marc/holdings/echdhome.html.
12. http://www.hathitrust.org.
13. https://wiki.ucop.edu/display/Curation/ARK.

14. http://www.handle.net.
15. http://openbiblio.net.

REFERENCES

Avram, Henriette D. 2003. "Machine-Readable Cataloging (MARC) Program." In *Encyclopedia of Library and Information Science*, 1712–30, edited by Miriam Drake. Washington, DC: Library of Congress. DOI: 10.1081/E-ELIS-120008993

CIC eNews. 2009. "HathiTrust Develops Search Interface." Available at: http://info.cic.net/eNews/CLI/Article.aspx?List=e2b6f931%2D966b%2D48a1%2Da375%2D36f2c6a5860d&ID=23

Guenther, Rebecca. 2004. "New and Traditional Descriptive Formats in the Library Environment." Presentation, DC2004: IFLA session, Shanghai, China, October 11–14.

Library of Congress. N.d. "Character Sets and Encoding Options: Part 2 MARC-8 Encoding Environment." Available at: http://www.loc.gov/marc/specifications/speccharmarc8.html

"MARC XML Architecture." N.d. Available at: http://www.loc.gov/standards/marcxml/marcxml-architecture.html

McCallum, Sally H. 2002. "International MARC: Past, Present, and Future." *Advances in Librarianship* 26: 127–48.

McCallum, Sally H. N.d. "MARC Data in an SGML Structure." Available at: http://xml.coverpages.org/McCallumMARC.html

Network Development and MARC Standards Office, Library of Congress. N.d. "MARC DTDs (Document Type Definitions): Background and Development." Available at: http://www.loc.gov/marc/marcdtd/marcdtdback.html

Tennant, Roy. 2002. "MARC Must Die." *Library Journal* 127, no. 17: 26.

Tennant, Roy. 2004. "A Bibliographic Metadata Infrastructure for the Twenty-First Century." *Library Hi Tech* 22, no. 2: 175–81.

CHAPTER 5

Other Metadata Standards in XML: Dublin Core, MODS, and ONIX

Growth in the scope and complexity of digital libraries and a seemingly ever-increasing influx of newly digitized and born-digital resources are creating new challenges for libraries. Libraries now curate an increasingly diverse and heterogeneous body of information resources not only in terms of format but also in terms of granularity and descriptive requirements. Special collections acquisitions have always placed extra demands on technical services staff, but more than ever catalogers and metadata librarians today are routinely called on to catalog retrospectively digitized texts, photos, posters, manuscript archives, and multimedia resources as well as born-digital databases, Web pages, Web sites, dissertations, data archives, reports, and blogs. While the MAchine-Readable Cataloging (MARC) standard is well suited as a model for describing books, serials and several other more specialized formats, and while MARCXML is a logical serialization of this standard for use in digital library applications, it is not always practical to describe one by one the growing volume of items curated by today's digital libraries using MARCXML alone. (Consider the cataloger resources that would be required to create a full MARCXML record for every unique digitized photograph held today by a large academic library.) Nor is every digital resource held by libraries best described using the MARC standard (Tennant 2004).

Today many alternative, XML-compatible metadata standards are available. As complementary alternatives to MARCXML, these standards allow the cataloger or metadata librarian greater flexibility to create more succinct descriptions when necessary (e.g., to save time and assets) or to create descriptions that focus on attributes more germane to the discovery and use of specific classes of digital resources. Serialized as XML, these alternative metadata standards become distinctive XML metadata grammars and allow the cataloger to work more efficiently and effectively than if required to use MARCXML exclusively to describe each and every information resource in a digital library.

Currently, many libraries routinely work with both *Simple* and *Qualified Dublin Core*,[1] the *Metadata Object Description Schema* (MODS),[2] the *Encoded Archival Description* (EAD),[3] and the *Visual Resources Association* (VRA) *Core*[4] (Ma 2007). Although not yet as ubiquitous in libraries, the *ONline Information eXchange for Books* (ONIX) standard in XML[5] is another metadata grammar of potential interest to libraries. A number of publishers and content vendors now provide bibliographic data in ONIX XML instead of in MARCXML because the ONIX XML metadata grammar includes semantics relevant to the sale and distribution of content as well as semantics for describing bibliographic features of a resource. Fortunately, ONIX XML records can be transformed to MARCXML records programmatically by using technologies such as the *Extensible Stylesheet Language for Transformations* (XSLT). Using XSLT style sheets, libraries can implement efficient computer-based batch work flows that make direct use of vendor-provided ONIX XML records to update their MARC-based online public access catalog (OPAC).

This chapter describes XML metadata grammars based on the Dublin Core, MODS, and ONIX for Books metadata standards as representative of alternatives to MARCXML. Illustrated more briefly at the end of the chapter are facets of XML serializations of other metadata standards, specifically selected features of VRA Core, EAD, and *Categories for the Description of Works of Arts* (CDWA)[6] as serialized in XML. The illustrations of this chapter are just a sampling. According to the *Metadata Map* created by Jenn Riley (2010), there are over a hundred community-recognized metadata standards from which to choose (most, though not all, well suited to serialization in XML). Additional metadata standards will continue to emerge as new classes of digital resources are created and as new user needs are identified. Comprehensively treating all current and emerging alternatives to MARCXML is beyond the scope of this book, but the following introduction to frequently used alternatives to MARCXML suggests the range of options available and demonstrates how MARC-alternative, XML-compatible metadata standards can be approached and utilized in a digital library context.

WORKING WITH OTHER METADATA STANDARDS

The role in the library of description and metadata has become more fluid in recent years. Traditionally, bibliographic records (i.e., library catalog records) were designed to help users identify and locate physical books in a library. Secondarily, the traditional library catalog as a whole served as an inventory of physical holdings. Seymour Lubetzky (1953) defined the objectives of cataloging as, first, the *identification* of individual bibliographic materials and, second, the *collocation* or bringing together of related works in the catalog. With the advent of digital libraries, there has been a transition to more distributed (albeit interconnected) models of content and collections. This in turn has broadened the role of bibliographic records.

The *Functional Requirements for Bibliographic Records* (FRBR) *Final Report*, published by the International Federation of Library Associations and Institutions Study Group on the FRBR (1998), went a step further than Lubetzky, listing *find*, *identify*, *select*, and *obtain* as four user tasks illustrating "the importance of relationships [between bibliographic entities] in assisting the user to 'navigate' in the bibliographic universe." Other research has included "navigate" explicitly as a fifth "metadata mediated task" (Svenonius 2000, 20). Indeed, in the hypertextual world of the Web, the significance to the end user of being able to obtain, navigate, *utilize*, and *repurpose* resources is reinforced. Among these tasks, "the navigate task is reliant on an understanding of how resources correlate one to another" (Cole and Foulonneau 2007, 163). Efficient navigation of digital resources has become much of what descriptive metadata (e.g., as contained in bibliographic records) must facilitate in the context of digital libraries.

In the context of digital libraries, beyond the ultimate end user, there is another metadata user group to consider: librarians, information specialists, archivists, and curators. These individuals increasingly make use of metadata created, assembled, managed, and disseminated by colleagues. As libraries create and share more digital collections, the role of metadata has expanded to support not only resource discovery but also resource organization, administration, and management, especially through virtual collocation of disparate and widely distributed digital resource holdings.

Simultaneously, as discussed in Chapter 2, collaborative metadata authoring becomes more viable for digital resources, not only metadata authoring involving multiple librarians but also metadata authoring involving nonlibrarians. Machines and end users now participate in creating various parts of metadata records. For example, computers, digital cameras, scanners, and format-conversion software now routinely record certain events in the life cycle of a digital resource. Such information summarized in metadata is used not only for description but also for preservation and resource management and to provide provenance, which is increasingly important in a digital environment. Authors or other users with specialized expertise may contribute metadata element values (see Case Study 5.2). Increasingly in today's environment, libraries need to deal with metadata created by nonlibrarian entities.

Such factors drive the need to understand and learn how to utilize alternative metadata standards. Like MARC, many of these alternative metadata standards have roots in library and book publishing descriptive traditions. In other words, like MARC, many alternative descriptive metadata standards, such as Dublin Core, MODS, and ONIX for Books, each described in more detail below, are optimized to describe *document-like objects* and are used primarily to record bibliographic descriptions. However, unlike MARC, these schemes were invented after the advent of the World Wide Web. Accordingly, they were designed to describe a wider range of information resources in varying formats and of varying granularities. Other metadata standards, such as VRA Core, EAD, and CDWA Lite, have emerged post-Web out of different descriptive traditions, often based in the archival, slide library, or museum communities. These standards, while also cognizant of the new realities of the Web, tend to describe resources as intellectual aggregates rather than singly or in series.

For example, VRA Core is most often used to describe a work and its multiple digital instantiations or image representations. There is considerable overlap with library-derived bibliographic standards, but there are also important distinctions. Some of these distinctions are illustrated briefly at the end of this chapter. We begin, however, with closer looks at Dublin Core, MODS, and ONIX for Books.

DUBLIN CORE IN XML

After MARC, Dublin Core is by far the most used descriptive metadata standard in the library domain (Ma 2007, 21). Dublin Core was first introduced in 1995 as an everyman metadata standard for the Web. It was hoped that many (if not most) Web page authors would adopt Dublin Core to describe the persistent Web-based information resources they created. Originally published as a draft for comment in 1995, Dublin Core initially consisted of only 13 properties (called *elements* or *fields* in Dublin Core documentation). These fields were designed to capture what the authors of the standard felt to be the essential descriptive attributes of Web-based information resources. The model embraced by the authors of Dublin Core was consciously bibliographic in scope and viewed Web-based information resources as being document-like (Lagoze 2001). Two more elements were added prior to the formal 1.0 release of Dublin Core in 1998.

The number of elements was constrained in part to make the standard more accessible to nonlibrarians. However, in spite of these and other efforts to keep it simple and easy to use, uptake by the Web community at large was limited, and when implemented by nonlibrarians, the quality and usefulness of the records created varied greatly (Lagoze et al. 2006). As a result, for a majority of practical purposes, Dublin Core remains the provenance primarily of librarians and other metadata specialists.

Today, there are two Dublin Core metadata record standards: Simple (unqualified) Dublin Core and Qualified Dublin Core. ("Dublin Core" not proceeded by "Simple" or "Qualified" can be assumed to mean Simple Dublin Core.) Consisting of 15 elements (Table 5.1, column 1), Simple Dublin Core includes the initial elements proposed in 1995 plus two additional elements accepted prior to the release of version 1.0 of the standard. A minor update in Simple Dublin Core element definitions was made in 1999 (version 1.1), and documentation has been updated subsequently; however, no new elements have been added to Simple Dublin Core since 1998. The elements of Simple Dublin Core are now fixed and will not change.

Qualified Dublin Core includes all the elements of Simple Dublin Core and adds three classes of entities: additional top-level elements (designed to capture descriptive properties not captured by the 15-element set of Simple Dublin Core), element refinements, and element encoding schemes. Element refinements and element encoding schemes are defined in terms of Simple Dublin Core elements and are listed in columns 2 and 3 of Table 5.1 (for the

TABLE 5.1 Simple Dublin Core elements, encoding schemes and element refinements (*Source:* The Dublin Core Metadata Initiative[7]).

Simple Dublin Core Elements	Element Refinements	Encoding Schemes
<title>	<alternative>	
<creator>		
<contributor>		
<coverage>	<spatial>	DCMI Point ISO 3166 DCMI Box TGN
	<temporal>	DCMI Period W3C-DTF
<date>	<created> <valid> <available> <issued> <modified>	DCMI Period W3C-DTF
<description>	<tableOfContents> <abstract>	
<format>	<extent>	
	<medium>	IMT
<identifier>		URI
<language>		ISO 639-2 RFC 1766
<publisher>		
<rights>		
<relation>	<isVersionOf> <hasVersion> <isReplacedBy> <replaces> <isRequiredBy> <requires> <isPartOf> <hasPart> <isReferencedBy> <references> <isFormatOf> <hasFormat>	URI

(*continued*)

TABLE 5.1 (Continued)

Simple Dublin Core Elements	Element Refinements	Encoding Schemes
<source>		URI
<subject>		LCSH MeSH DDC LCC UDC
<type>		DCMI Type Vocabulary

original 15 top-level elements). These elements can (and in a few instances do) have their own refinement or encoding qualifiers. Qualified Dublin Core, as commonly understood in the library community and as discussed here, includes top-level elements only because of the historical decision by the Dublin Core Metadata Initiative (DCMI) to fix in name and number the elements of Simple Dublin Core (i.e., to define Simple Dublin Core as corresponding to the version 1.1 element set). As a result, over time, as the need has arisen for additional top-level elements, the names "Simple Dublin Core" and "Qualified Dublin Core" have become increasingly misleading. More recent updates to DCMI documents now talk about *Classic* Dublin Core and the *legacy* element set of version 1.1 rather than Simple Dublin Core. Similarly, the name "Qualified Dublin Core" has fallen out of favor in many DCMI documents, replaced by the name "DCMI Metadata Terms" with additional elements (terms) including `<accrualMethod>`, `<accrualPeriodicity>`, `<accrualPolicy>`, `<audience>`, `<instructionalMethod>`, `<provenance>`, and `<rightsHolder>`. However, the names "Simple Dublin Core" and "Qualified Dublin Core" are entrenched in the library metadata community and so are used throughout this chapter.

As described in "Dublin Core Qualifiers" (2000), Dublin Core element refinements "make the definitions of Simple [and other top-level] Dublin Core elements narrower and more specific." Each refined element shares a base definition with one top-level Dublin Core element but with a more restricted scope. The element `<spatial>` shares a base definition with the element `<coverage>` but is narrower in scope; that is, it is limited to containing values describing the geographic coverage of an information resource. Similarly, `<hasVersion>` is more restrictive than `<relation>`, the top-level Simple Dublin Core element it refines. When using Qualified Dublin Core, it is recommended that the qualifiers not extend the semantic scope of an element. By definition, all values contained by refinement elements in Qualified Dublin Core records are valid as values for the corresponding Simple or other top-level Dublin Core element as well. This is a facet of what is known as the Dublin Core "dumb-down principle" (Hillmann 2005).

Encoding schemes, another category of Qualified Dublin Core entities, are used to convey information about the source or rules used in creating element values. By exposing the encoding schemes used in making a metadata record, a metadata author can convey that a `<subject>` value is a Library of Congress Subject Heading (an example of a Dublin Core *vocabulary encoding scheme*) or that the string in a `<date>` element is formatted in accordance with the formal date notation specified by the World Wide Web Consortium's Date-Time Format[8] (an example of a Dublin Core *syntax encoding scheme*). The inclusion of encoding scheme qualifiers in Qualified Dublin Core records can make the values of these metadata records more reliably machine actionable. Again, when "dumbed down" to Simple Dublin Core, the value (content) of the element remains unchanged (i.e., only the encoding scheme reference is removed).

Another feature that sets apart Simple Dublin Core from Qualified Dublin Core is extensibility. Qualified Dublin Core is designed to be extensible in both encoding schemes and refinements when necessary for a specific project, although in an XML context, this requires developing a project-specific version of the *XML Schema* or *Document Type Definition* (DTD) used to validate metadata records (see Chapters 7, 8, and 9). Today, Simple and Qualified Dublin Core are used not only for describing Web pages but also for describing digitized images, such as photographs and slides, and many other kinds of digital resources for which MARC is not well suited. There are an increasing number of instances where Simple or Qualified Dublin Core is used to describe document-like digital text resources as well, especially when extended with locally developed qualifiers or constrained by a project-specific *metadata application profile* (discussed in Chapter 6). These uses trade off the rigor, precision, and completeness of a MARC record against the shorter time required to create a Simple or Qualified Dublin Core record for the same resource.

There are four primary reasons why libraries use Dublin Core more than most other non-MARC metadata standards. First, it is relatively easy to use. It is semantically simple, especially in the case of Simple Dublin Core, which has only 15 natural language-labeled elements compared with almost 2,000 alphanumeric-labeled fields and subfields available in MARC. Second, there are many digital content management tools that support Dublin Core as their default metadata standard, such as CONTENTdm,[9] a heavily used digital content management tool for digitized images (Ma 2007), and DSpace,[10] a software application widely used for institutional repositories. Third, the Open Archives Initiative Protocol for Metadata Harvesting (OAI-PMH),[11] which supports metadata sharing and interoperability, mandates the use of Simple Dublin Core as its lingua franca, or lowest-common-denominator XML metadata grammar. Although data providers can additionally use other metadata standards with OAI-PMH, a majority of data providers choose to provide their metadata in Simple Dublin Core only, even when dumbed down from semantically richer standards. Fourth, the semantics of Simple Dublin

Core and Qualified Dublin Core lend themselves to use in metadata application profiles. As discussed in the next chapter, metadata application profiles are a way that metadata application implementers can mix and match semantics and other grammatical features from multiple different metadata schemes in order to create a more customized and optimized metadata solution for their application, content, and audience.

The intrinsic bibliographic-property-as-element model of Dublin Core generally aligns well with the content object model of XML. However, Dublin Core is not specified as a complete, self-contained grammar; for example, for XML serialization, no root node is provided. Additionally, Dublin Core semantics are carefully designed to be serialization agnostic. This makes Dublin Core semantics compatible with multiple serialization technologies. In practical terms, this means that Dublin Core elements (the content objects of Dublin Core) are intended to be contained within other, non-Dublin Core content objects, such as within an HTML `<meta>` element, within a Resource Description Framework (RDF)[12] document instance, or within a separately defined and declared XML document instance root node. This complicates XML implementation of Dublin Core slightly and mandates the use of XML Namespaces (also discussed in Chapter 6).

In practical terms, this also means that there is more than one way to serialize Dublin Core semantics in XML. The DCMI provides multiple recommendations for implementers regarding XML serialization of Dublin Core metadata semantics, including the following:

1. *Guidelines for Implementing Dublin Core in XML*[13]
2. *Expressing Dublin Core Description Sets Using XML*[14]
3. *Expressing Dublin Core Metadata Using the Resource Description Framework (RDF)*[15]

The last is not strictly speaking a recommendation for serializing Dublin Core in XML (since RDF itself can be serialized in multiple formats), but in combination with *Expressing Dublin Core Description Sets Using XML*, which includes an appendix illustrating Dublin Core-RDF serialized as XML, it provides useful guidance for would-be implementers wanting to serialize Dublin Core semantics in RDF XML.

Documents 2 and 3 in the above list are newer (2008 versus 2003) and hew closer to the relatively new Dublin Core Abstract Model,[16] but the *Guidelines for Implementing Dublin Core in XML* has broad acceptance and is more representative of current practice in the library community. The broader acceptance also is explained in part by the fact that the *Guidelines for Implementing Dublin Core in XML* document links to a set of *XML Schema Definition Language* schemas that facilitate XML validation. A separate, related DCMI document, *Notes on the W3C XML Schemas for Qualified Dublin Core*,[17] provides help on how to use these schemas to validate Dublin Core serialized in XML. Practice also has been heavily influenced by OAI-PMH. OAI-PMH provides an additional XML schema and, in concert with the XML schemas mentioned above, facilitates the serialization of Dublin Core in XML. The examples of Dublin Core in XML used for this book follow the guidance of the *Guidelines for Implementing Dublin Core in XML* document. The following list summarizes four of the high-level recommendations from this document:

1. When expressed in XML, all Simple and Qualified Dublin Core element names (i.e., property names) should start with lowercase characters. If the property names start with uppercase characters, the resulting XML record is not valid.
2. All elements are repeatable. If, for example, two subject headings apply to a resource, then each heading value should be expressed in its own `<subject>` element, resulting in the record containing two `<subject>` elements. This recommendation has been borne out in practice. For example, repeating elements for each value works better for service providers who often need to modify or normalize the metadata for their users or search environments.
3. According to DCMI guidelines generally, all elements are optional. However, some systems that use Dublin Core may enforce requirements for selected elements. For example, CONTENTdm requires a `<title>` element in every record. Service providers that harvest Dublin Core metadata may levy their own requirements of this sort.
4. For Qualified Dublin Core implementations, if local extensions in refinements or encoding schemes are to be used, it is critical to provide a local XML schema capturing these extensions. Such local schemas may import schema(s) referenced in the *Guidelines for Implementing Dublin Core in XML* or may simply be a revised version of the canonical DCMI schemas.

Figure 5.1 shows a Simple Dublin Core record serialized in XML. Some of the attributes of the root node in this example have to do with XML Namespaces, which will be introduced in the next chapter; for now, these can be ignored.

The record describes the book titled *Using the Open Archives Initiative Protocol for Metadata Harvesting*. The root node of this metadata record, `<oai_dc:dc>`, is not a part of the Dublin Core semantics. Rather, it is a component of the OAI-PMH XML grammar (hence the need for XML Namespaces). It is required here as a container for the remaining XML elements in this example, all of which are defined as part of the Dublin Core semantic set. Note that formatting and punctuation tends to be retained in the value strings of Dublin Core elements since the semantics of Dublin Core does not make it easy for such information to be inferred.

FIGURE 5.1 Contents of the metadata node of an OAI-PMH record (Simple Dublin Core format).


```
<?xml version="1.0" encoding="UTF-8"?>
<oai_dc:dc
  xmlns:oai_dc="http://www.openarchives.org/OAI/2.0/oai_dc/"
  xmlns="http://purl.org/dc/elements/1.1/"
  xmlns:xsi="http://www.w3.org/2001/XMLSchema-instance"
  xsi:schemaLocation="http://www.openarchives.org/OAI/2.0/oai_dc/
http://www.openarchives.org/OAI/2.0/oai_dc.xsd">
  <title>Using the Open Archives Initiative protocol for metadata harvesting</title>
  <creator> Cole, Timothy W</creator>
  <creator>Foulonneau, Muriel</creator>
  <publisher>Westport, Conn. : Libraries Unlimited</publisher>
  <date>2007</date>
  <format>xv, 208 p. : ill. ; 26 cm. </format>
  <language>eng</language>
  <description>Includes bibliographical references and index.</description>
  <description>Definition and origins of OAI-PMH --
    Underlying technologies and the technical development of OAI-PMH --
    Context for OAI-PMH : eprints, institutional repositories, and open access
-- Technical details of the protocol -- Implementing an OAI data provider -- Creating
metadata to share -- Post-harvest metadata normalization &amp; augmentation -- Using
aggregated metadata to build digital library services --
 Concluding thoughts</description>
   <subject>Open Archives Initiative</subject>
   <subject>Metadata harvesting</subject>
  <identifier>http://www.loc.gov/catdir/toc/ecip0714/2007009006.html</identifier>
  </oai_dc:dc>
```


CASE STUDY 5.1

Dublin Core Metadata in CONTENTdm

Synopsis: In the University of Illinois Library, Dublin Core is used as the baseline metadata scheme for all digital collections made accessible through the digital collection management Software CONTENTdm®. Simple Dublin Core is the default metadata format for CONTENTdm. The Library acquired CONTENTdm in 2003 for its digital resource management functionality and collaborative metadata authoring features. Since then, the number of collections hosted in the Illinois CONTENTdm implementation has grown to 35; among these, 26 collections are either open to the public or available to on-campus users only. (The remaining collections are experimental or in an early stage development.) Although CONTENTdm defaults to Simple Dublin Core, it allows local extensions and refinements. It also supports XML metadata export, including export of OAI-PMH XML for metadata sharing and interoperability. Catalogers and metadata librarians at Illinois have used this flexibility to good effect. As illustrated below, the CONTENTdm interface makes it easy to exploit Simple Dublin Core and XML, all while still allowing considerable local customization.
Illustrates: Creation of Dublin Core metadata using CONTENTdm; export of metadata serialized as XML from CONTENTdm; local extension/refinements of Dublin Core elements in CONTENTdm.

FIGURE 5.2 CONTENTdm field properties (CONTENTdm screen capture used with permission from the Online Computing Library Center [OCLC]).

Collection field properties

View, add, edit and delete fields. Enable full text searching and controlled vocabulary. After you have added, changed, or deleted fields, index the collection to update changes.

	Field name	DC map	Data type	Large	Search	Hide	Required	Vocab		add field
1	ID Number	Identifier	Text	No	Yes	No	No	No	move to	edit | delete
2	Title	Title	Text	No	Yes	No	Yes	No	move to	edit | delete
3	Date	Date-Created	Date	No	No	No	No	No	move to	edit | delete
4	Role	Description	Text	No	Yes	No	No	Yes	move to	edit | delete
5	Play	Title-Alternative	Text	No	Yes	No	No	Yes	move to	edit | delete
6	Subject	Subject	Text	No	Yes	No	No	Yes	move to	edit | delete
7	Type	Type	Text	No	Yes	No	No	Yes	move to	edit | delete
8	Dimensions	Format-Extent	Text	No	No	No	No	No	move to	edit | delete
9	Technique	Subject	Text	No	Yes	No	No	Yes	move to	edit | delete
10	Creator	Creator	Text	No	Yes	No	No	Yes	move to	edit | delete
11	Publisher	Publisher	Text	No	Yes	No	No	No	move to	edit | delete
12	Description	Description	Text	Yes	Yes	No	No	No	move to	edit | delete
13	Rights	Rights	Text	No	No	No	No	No	move to	edit | delete
14	Collection	Relation-Is Part Of	Text	No	Yes	No	No	No	move to	edit | delete
15	Repository	Source	Text	No	Yes	No	No	No	move to	edit | delete
	Field name	DC map	Data type	Large	Search	Hide	Required	Vocab		add field

There are two particularly noteworthy strengths of CONTENTdm with regard to metadata. First, the system allows collection curators to extend Dublin Core semantics by defining additional metadata elements. Extension elements can be collection specific or can be borrowed from other XML metadata grammars. Collection curators routinely use elements from MARC, EAD, and VRA Core as well as locally created field names in their CONTENTdm implementations (Han et al. 2009). A second strength of CONTENTdm is the ease of metadata sharing. The metadata in CONTENTdm can be disseminated via OAI-PMH as well as via Z39.50,[18] another standard for metadata sharing between client and server. CONTENTdm metadata also can be directly exported into WorldCat[19] (where it is transformed into MARC); inclusion in WorldCat can increase the visibility of the collection and expand the collection's user base.

CONTENTdm makes it possible to support metadata grammar customizations for use within a local instance of the application while still making metadata records harvestable in Dublin Core (both Simple and Qualified). To exploit this feature, collection curators simply map any local extension field they have defined for a collection to the most appropriate Dublin Core element. (It is allowed to have local metadata fields, such as for collection administrative purposes, that do not map to any Dublin Core field; these values then are simply not exported.) Figure 5.2 illustrates the metadata element mapping for the *Portraits of Actors* image collection made available through CONTENTdm by the University of Illinois Library. The custom item-level metadata semantics for

FIGURE 5.3 CONTENTdm end-user view of metadata and item (CONTENTdm screen capture used with permission from the Online Computing Library Center [OCLC]).

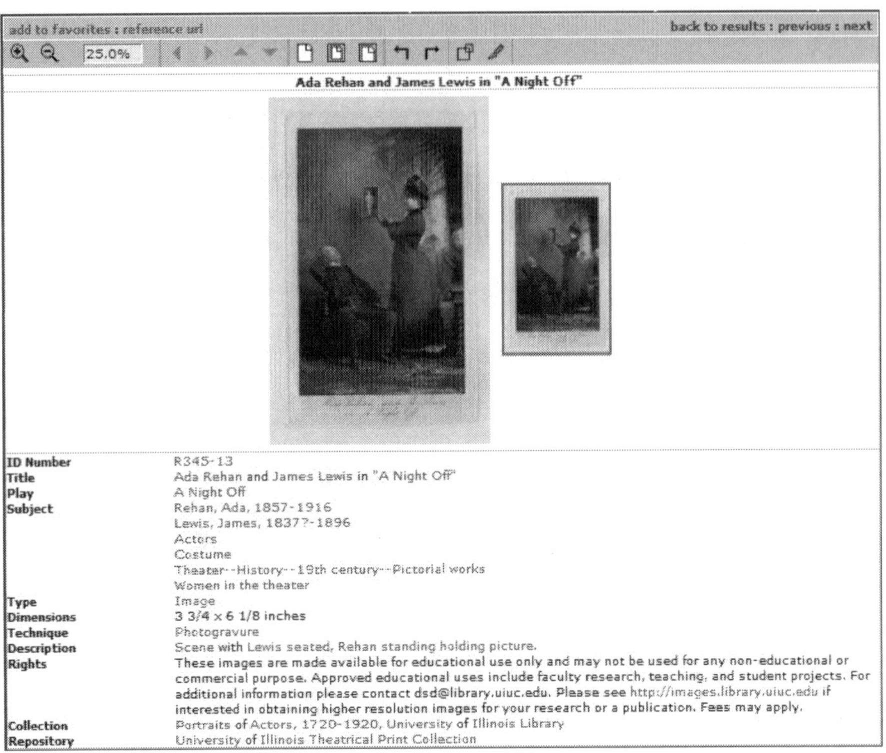

this collection includes *ID Number*, *Role*, *Play*, *Dimensions*, *Technique*, *Collection*, and *Repository* as locally defined fields. As shown in Figure 5.2, these fields are refinements of or synonyms for Simple or Qualified Dublin Core elements. Note that one other field in the *Portraits of Actors* custom metadata grammar, *Date*, is mapped not directly to `<date>` in Simple Dublin Core but rather to the Qualified Dublin Core element `<created>`, a refinement of the Simple Dublin Core element `<date>`. (This illustrates that when mapping between XML metadata grammars, it is not safe to assume that elements of the same name are necessarily synonymous.) With this mapping, the metadata record then can be harvested by service providers in Simple or Qualified Dublin Core serialized as XML via OAI-PMH. In addition, both local fields and Dublin Core elements defined as part of the metadata scheme for a CONTENTdm collection can be mapped to MARC for WorldCat ingestion using a new feature of CONTENTdm called Digital Collection Gateway.[20]

Figure 5.3 shows the end-user view of a metadata record in CONTENTdm for an item in the *Portraits of Actors* collection. Note the mix of Dublin Core and local names. The metadata in CONTENTdm are created or edited item by item in a Web editor (see Figure 5.4) or using a desktop application called CONTENTdm Project Client (which can also be used to create or edit metadata in batch mode or for a compound object, such as a set of digitized maps from

FIGURE 5.4 Metadata created in CONTENTdm Web editor (CONTENTdm screen capture used with permission from the Online Computing Library Center [OCLC]).

view this item

ID Number	R345-13	
Title *	Ada Rehan and James Lewis in "A Night Off"	
Date		
Role		controlled vocabulary
Play	A Night Off	controlled vocabulary
Subject	Rehan, Ada, 1857-1916; Lewis, James, 1837?-1896;	controlled vocabulary
Type	Image	controlled vocabulary
Dimensions	3 3/4 x 6 1/8 inches	
Technique	Photogravure	controlled vocabulary
Creator		controlled vocabulary
Publisher		
Description	Scene with Lewis seated, Rehan standing holding picture.	
Rights	These images are made available for educational use on	
Collection	Portraits of Actors, 1720-1920, University of Illinois Li	
Repository	University of Illinois Theatrical Print Collection	
Permissions		edit
OCLC number		
Date created	2007-03-16	
Date modified	2007-06-22	
CONTENTdm number	2490	
CONTENTdm file name	2491.jpg	

delete save changes

a single atlas volume). Once ingested into CONTENTdm, metadata records can be converted and exported in multiple different semantics and serializations, for example, as tab-delineated plain text (for ingestion into a spreadsheet application such as Microsoft Excel), as Dublin Core XML, and as custom XML. Figure 5.5 shows CONTENTdm export options.

The CONTENTdm standard XML export format option creates well-formed (rather than valid) XML and keeps all the local field names in the exported metadata. This preserves refinements and contextual information potentially lost in mapping local metadata fields to Dublin Core. Figure 5.6 shows an XML record in the CONTENTdm standard XML output. Exporting metadata in the CONTENTdm standard XML export format can be a good option when migrating existing digital collections to another instance of CONTENTdm or to a different repository. Exported XML records have all the local field names that were created for the collection, including for URLs, such as URLs for thumbnails as well as for views of the image with metadata. In addition,

FIGURE 5.5 Metadata export options in CONTENTdm (CONTENTdm screen capture used with permission from the Online Computing Library Center [OCLC]).

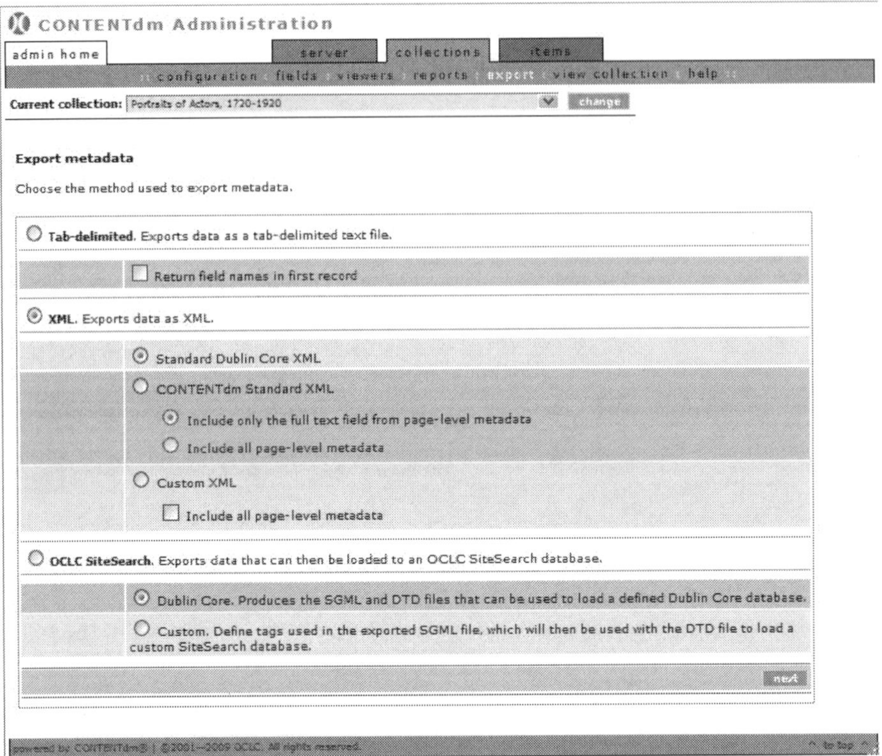

data automatically generated by the system at item ingestion, such as `<created date>`, `<modified date>`, and `<CONTENTdm local id>`, are included in the CONTENTdm standard XML export format.

A "Standard Dublin Core XML" export option is also available from CONTENTdm and provides metadata in a Dublin Core-RDF XML serialization. This export option gives CONTENTdm administrators and collection curators a chance to preview the metadata that will be disseminated via OAI-PMH, allowing them, for example, to confirm the values that will appear in various Dublin Core elements and the general mapping to Dublin Core. Research has shown that service providers (metadata harvesters) want to have rich descriptive metadata but not the administrative metadata that are important for local metadata and resource management (Han et al. 2009). By reviewing the Dublin Core metadata export, one can check the mapping to determine whether the mapping is correct or whether administrative information was inadvertently mapped to the Dublin Core format. By comparing the Standard XML CONTENTdm export to the Dublin Core XML CONTENTdm export, collection curators can also see what information they might have neglected to map to Simple or Qualified Dublin Core and confirm that only unneeded information has not been mapped to the output Dublin Core formats.

FIGURE 5.6 CONTENTdm Standard metadata format serialized as XML.

```
<?xml version="1.0" encoding="UTF-8"?>
  <metadata>
    <record>
      <unmapped>R345-13</unmapped>
      <title>Ada Rehan and James Lewis in &quot;A Night Off&quot;</title>
      <created></created>
      <unmapped></unmapped>
      <unmapped>A Night Off</unmapped>
      <subject>Rehan, Ada, 1857-1916; Lewis, James, 1837?-1896; Actors; Costume;
Theater--History--19th century--Pictorial works; Women in the theater</subject>
      <type>Image</type>
      <extent>3 3/4 x 6 1/8 inches</extent>
      <subject>Photogravure</subject>
      <creator></creator>
      <publisher></publisher>
      <description>Scene with Lewis seated, Rehan standing holding picture.
</description>
      <rights>These images are made available for educational use only and may not be used
for any non-educational or commercial purpose. Approved educational uses include faculty
research, teaching, and student projects. For additional information please contact
dsd@library.uiuc.edu. Please see http://images.library.uiuc.edu if interested in
obtaining higher resolution images for your research or a publication. Fees may
apply.</rights>
      <isPartOf>Portraits of Actors, 1720-1920, University of Illinois Library</isPartOf>
      <source>University of Illinois Theatrical Print Collection</source>
      <fullResolution></fullResolution>
      <cdmid>2490</cdmid>
      <cdmaccess></cdmaccess>
      <cdmcreated>2007-03-16</cdmcreated>
      <cdmmodified>2007-06-22</cdmmodified>
      <thumbnailURL>http://images.library.uiuc.edu:8081/cgi-
bin/thumbnail.exe?CISOROOT=/actors&amp;CISOPTR=2490</thumbnailURL>
      <viewerURL>http://images.library.uiuc.edu:8081/u?/actors,2490</viewerURL>
      <structure>http://images.library.uiuc.edu:8081/cgi-
bin/showfile.exe?CISOROOT=/actors&amp;CISOPTR=2490</structure>
    </record>
  </metadata>
```

MODS IN XML

Known as a simpler and more Web-friendly version of MARCXML, MODS was first introduced in 2002 by the Library of Congress. As described in Sally H. McCallum's "An Introduction to the Metadata Object Description Schema (MODS)," MODS was developed to meet the need for a new metadata standard that "gives special support to cataloging electronic resources, is less detailed, and is compatible with MARC21" (McCallum 2004, 82). Although MODS has close ties to MARCXML, it is not simply an alternate serialization of MARC21. The two are intended as separate and independent standards; MODS is not a long-term replacement for MARC, and MARC cannot do everything MODS can do. There is overlap in semantics, but they are certainly not synonymous. For example, as discussed in McCallum's paper, MODS can accommodate the entity data structures introduced in FRBR, especially group 1 entities: *work*, *expression*, *manifestation*, and *item*. These are harder to describe and properly relate in MARCXML. Also, with the introduction of the Metadata Authority Description Schema,[21] MODS can be used more effectively with the Functional Requirements for Authority Data (FRAD)[22] along with the new data content standard *Resource Description and Access*,[23] which is based on FRBR and FRAD data models.

Since it was first introduced in 2002, MODS has evolved, gradually adding new elements and attributes. The latest version of MODS as of this writing, version 3.5, was published in February 2013. Rather than rely on the three-digit number tags of MARCXML, MODS semantic labels are human readable and better suited for describing digital resources, including relationships with print or original source resources. Because MODS was built from the ground up with XML serialization in mind, the length of a record can be flexible and easily altered, and MODS supports Unicode and UTF-8/16, making it easy to encode special characters and display MODS records in standard Web applications, such as Web browsers (McCallum 2004).

Since MODS does not have the same subfield structure as MARC, it is not required to rigorously follow the International Standard Bibliographic Description (ISBD)[24] punctuations to distinguish one subfield to another. However, because there is a possibility that MODS records may be converted to other metadata standards that follow the ISBD punctuation rules, the *Digital Library Federation* (DLF)/*Aquifer Project Implementation Guidelines for Shareable MODS Records*[25] recommends that the "punctuation should be retained if it occurs within an element."

For XML serializations, like MARCXML, the MODS grammar allows two different root elements: `<mods>`, when the MODS document contains only a single MODS record, and `<modsCollection>`, when one MODS document contains multiple MODS records. (The only allowed child of the `<modsCollection>` element is the `<mods>` element, which can appear one or more times inside the `<modsCollection>` element.) Below the `<mods>` element, MODS defines 20 top-level elements (see Table 5.2) and numerous subelements and attributes. The availability of subelements and the hierarchical structure of MODS (features missing from Dublin Core) allow the descriptive values contained in MODS records to include fine-grained substructure and provide specific and detailed information. For example, `<namePart>`, which occurs under MODS top-level element `<name>`, allows a metadata author to label named entity components, that is, to delineate family name from given name. MODS goes further and actually allows a certain amount of recursion. For example, all MODS elements (below the level of `<mods>`) may appear within MODS `<relatedItem>` content. This means that a MODS description of the second edition of a book can contain the

TABLE 5.2 MODS top-level elements (Source: Library of Congress[26]).

titleInfo	note
name	subject
typeOfResource	classification
genre	relatedItem
originInfo	identifier
language	location
physicalDescription	accessCondition
abstract	part
tableOfContents	extension
targetAudience	recordInfo

complete MODS description of the first edition of the book as a `<relatedItem>`. This structural flexibility allows MODS to describe relationships between FRBR entities. Another notable feature of MODS (Versions 3.3 and subsequent) is the option to include subelements for holdings information under the top-level element `<location>`. This accommodates application-specific requirements to have holding-specific information bound within bibliographic records.

Common properties, such as the language of an element value and the encoding schemes and controlled vocabularies used in creating element values, are conveyed using general purpose attributes available for use with all MODS elements. All top-level elements are optional and repeatable, as are most subelements. Like MARCXML, MODS serialized as XML yields a complex, expressive XML grammar. The pre-XML legacy of MARC record sharing and the standard's close association with the *Anglo-American Cataloging Rules* Second Edition (AACR2) ensure relatively good consistency across any collection of MARCXML records. MODS records from different institutions and different projects tend to be less consistent at this time. In order to encourage more consistent, interoperable MODS records, several MODS-based profiles have been published, defining rules and best-practice guidelines for implementers to follow for specific projects or initiatives. The Web-published DLF/*Aquifer Implementation Guidelines for Shareable MODS Records* is a good example of such guidelines. Developed to guide the creation of MODS metadata records intended for contribution to the DLF/Aquifer initiative, the *Guidelines* detail required and recommended MODS elements most useful for interoperability (Table 5.3). The *Guidelines* also define levels of conformance as a way to normalize expectations. These *Guidelines* are now maintained by the Library of Congress and have in part been incorporated into its *MODS User Guidelines*.[27]

TABLE 5.3 Required and recommended MODS elements (Source: DLF/*Aquifer Implementation Guidelines for Shareable MODS Records*).

Required MODS Elements	Recommended MODS Elements
<titleInfo><title>	<name<namePart>
<typeOfResource>	<genre>
<originInfo>	<abstract>
<language>	<tableOfContents>*
<physicalDescription><digitalOrigin>	<targetAudience>*
<physicalDescription><internetMediaType>	<note>*
<subject>*	<relatedItem>*
<location><uri usage="primary display">	<identifier>
<accessCondition type="use and reproduction">	<part>*
<recordInfo><languageOfCataloging>	
<recordInfo><languageTerm>	

**Recommended if applicable*

Since 2008, the Library of Congress has provided catalog records in both MARC and MODS to encourage the use of MODS. However, creating MODS records from scratch is not easy for many catalogers since easy-to-use, stand-alone MODS editors are still few and not yet well known to many practitioners. Nor are there MODS-specific integrated library system cataloging modules available to facilitate MODS record creation. To help address the former lack, the Library of Congress now maintains a Web page[28] linking to several Web-based MODS authoring tools that are freely available to anyone. These Web-based MODS authoring tools typically provide fill-in templates to facilitate MODS record creation, though they still require users to understand generally the semantics of MODS elements and relevant content standards, such as controlled vocabularies, MARC relater codes, and encoding schemes. When all values have been entered via the tool's Web templates, the user can view and save the resultant MODS metadata record in XML format. Figure 5.7

FIGURE 5.7 MODS XML metadata created from a Web-based authoring tool.

```
<titleInfo>
  <title>Using the Open Archives Initiative protocol for metadata
          harvesting</title>
  </titleInfo>
  <name type="personal" authority="LCNAF">
    <namePart type="family">Cole</namePart>
    <namePart type="given">Timothy W.</namePart>
  <role>
    <roleTerm authority="marcrelator" type="text">Author</roleTerm>
  </role>
  </name>
  <name type="personal">
    <namePart type="family">Foulonneau</namePart>
    <namePart type="given">Muriel</namePart>
```

FIGURE 5.7 (Continued)

```
<role>
  <roleTerm authority="marcrelator" type="text">Author</roleTerm>
</role>
</name>
```

depicts a partial view of a MODS record created using the University of Tennessee's MODS Workbook Version 1.2.[29] (The XML Namespace prefixes have been removed for readability.)

CASE STUDY 5.2
Hypatia: A MODS Record Creation and Ingest Tool

***Synopsis*:** When the Columbia University Libraries' institutional repository, Academic Commons,[30] was migrated from DSpace to Fedora[31] in the fall of 2009, the Columbia University Libraries/Information Service Team developed a new application called Hypatia, a MODS cataloging and Fedora ingestion tool. Hypatia includes a number of predefined templates to be used according to the type of resource being described, such as serial, monograph, thesis/dissertation, or article. The tool is also used by scholars and students to deposit their works using the *Academic Commons Self-Deposit Form*. This form allows scholar authors to provide values for selected metadata fields themselves. The staff at the Center for Digital Research and Scholarship then review submitted information and add any additional information required by the template. For each template, certain fields are prepopulated with fixed values based on resource type. The completed template is used to generate a MODS XML record for ingestion with the item into Fedora. When Hypatia is used wholly within the cataloging unit's work flow to facilitate MODS record creation, repository support staff select the template appropriate for describing items associated with a specific project or collection. Repository support staff then fill in the template as necessary to generate MODS metadata that are then serialized as XML for ingestion into Fedora. The MODS XML records in Academic Commons can be viewed directly from the institutional repository's user interface.
***Illustrates*:** Metadata authoring tools and templates; integration of user provided information to facilitate MODS records creation.

Metadata and cataloging specialists at Columbia University Libraries use MODS as the descriptive metadata standard for digital resources because of its rich semantics and hierarchical structure, allowing digital and original resources to be described in a single record. When the Columbia University Libraries' institutional repository, Academic Commons, was migrated from DSpace to Fedora, the metadata standard was changed from Dublin Core to MODS. Figure 5.8 shows a typical MODS record for an item in Columbia's Academic Commons. However, creating such MODS records from scratch was a challenge. As mentioned above, easy-to-use tools for authoring MODS records are not yet ubiquitous, nor are those that do exist well known to the whole community. In addition, the Academic Commons wanted scholars and

FIGURE 5.8 A sample MODS XML record from Academic Commons (some text deleted for brevity).


```
<?xml version="1.0" encoding="ISO-8859-1"?>
<mods xmlns="http://www.loc.gov/mods/v3" xmlns:xlink="http://www.w3.org/1999/xlink"
xmlns:xsi="http://www.w3.org/2001/XMLSchema-instance"
xsi:schemaLocation="http://www.loc.gov/mods/v3
http://www.loc.gov/standards/mods/v3/mods-3-4.xsd">
   <titleInfo>
      <title>Automatic access level cataloging for Internet resources...</title>
   </titleInfo>
   <name type="personal" ID="kh33">
    <namePart type="family">Harcourt</namePart>
    <namePart type="given">Kathryn</namePart>
    <role><roleTerm type="text">author</roleTerm></role>
    <affiliation>Columbia University. Libraries Bibliographic Control...</affiliation>
   </name>
   <name type="personal" ID="mw2064">
    <namePart type="family">Wacker</namePart>
    <namePart type="given">Melanie</namePart>
    <role><roleTerm type="text">author</roleTerm></role>
    <affiliation>Columbia University. Libraries Bibliographic Control...</affiliation>
   </name>
   <name type="personal">
    <namePart type="family">Wolley</namePart>
    <namePart type="given">Iris</namePart>
    <role><roleTerm type="text">author</roleTerm></role>
   </name>
   <name type="corporate">
    <namePart>Columbia University. Libraries and Information Services</namePart>
    <role><roleTerm type="text">originator</roleTerm></role>
   </name>
   <typeOfResource>text</typeOfResource>
   <genre>Articles</genre>
   <originInfo><dateIssued encoding="w3cdtf"
   keyDate="yes">2007</dateIssued>     </originInfo>
   <language><languageTerm type="text">English</languageTerm></language>
   <abstract>The explosive growth of remote access electronic resources
(e-resources) has added to the workload of libraries' cataloging departments....
   </abstract>
   <subject><topic>Library science</topic></subject>
   <relatedItem type="host">
    <titleInfo><title>Library Resources & Technical Services</title>
    </titleInfo>
    <part>
       <detail type="volume"><number>51</number></detail>
       <detail type="issue"><number>3</number></detail>
       <date>2007</date>
    </part>
    <identifier type="issn">2159-9610</identifier>
   </relatedItem>
   <identifier type="hdl">http://hdl.handle.net/10022/AC:P:9892</identifier>
   <location>
```

FIGURE 5.8 (Continued)

```
      <physicalLocation authority="marcorg">NNC</physicalLocation>
      </location>
      <recordInfo>
      <recordContentSource authority="marcorg">NNC</recordContentSource>
      <recordCreationDate encoding="w3cdtf">2011-03-03 22:04:32 UTC</record
CreationDate>
      <recordChangeDate encoding="w3cdtf">2011-05-19 20:11:32 UTC</record
ChangeDate>
      <recordIdentifier>2997</recordIdentifier>
      <languageOfCataloging>
         <languageTerm authority="iso639-2b">eng</languageTerm>
      </languageOfCataloging>
      </recordInfo>
</mods>
```

students depositing their works into the repository to provide certain descriptive metadata values at the time of deposit.

The approach taken to solve these issues was to develop a Web-based application featuring collection-specific templates for inputting the resource metadata necessary to generate the MODS metadata records required by the Academic Commons to support digital asset management and resource discovery and dissemination. Since different types of resources require different kinds of information, Hypatia provides different templates developed according to document type from which repository support staff can choose. Views of these templates are made available for use in concert with deposit process such that scholars and students can provide the descriptive information they know best, including department affiliation at the institution; description of the work; names of any coauthors, editors, or advisers; and special file formats. Depositors also indicate what software is required to open and access contents of the files deposited. The staff at the Center for Digital Research and Scholarship review and augment this information as they complete the appropriate template. During this process, additional information, such as `<identifier>`, `<location>/<physicalLocation>`, `<recordInfo>/<recordCreationDate>`, and `<recordInfo>/<recordChangeDate>`, is autogenerated and added to metadata records.

As illustrated in this case study, metadata today are created not only by a single cataloger or metadata librarian but also through semiautomated means and sometimes in collaboration with scholars and students both inside and outside of the library. Information provided by a scholar or nonlibrarian through templates can serve as a starting point for metadata record creation. XML-based work flows can allow user inputs to be reviewed and modified as necessary for consistency, completeness, and quality and then augmented by both metadata librarians and automated processes. The MODS XML metadata record shown in Figure 5.8 is representative of the resulting records that are created and stored in Academic Commons and used to support discoverability and management of resources. Because these MODS records are created from a template, the metadata are more consistent in quality and scope, improving interoperability both internally and with libraries outside of Columbia.

ONIX FOR BOOKS IN XML

ONIX for Books is a metadata standard used in the publishing industry to distribute its book production information in electronic format. First introduced (version 1.0) in 2000 by the Association of American Publishers, ONIX for Books was based on a preexisting standard called *EPICS* (*EDItEUR Product Information Communication Standards*). ONIX for Books is a semantically rich metadata standard designed to be serialized in XML. It supports publisher needs for a metadata standard that can include commercial product-related metadata as well as bibliographic descriptive information.

Version 2.1 of ONIX for Books consists of over 200 elements organized into 38 groups. As defined in the standard, 25 of these groups make up the *Product Record*, six groups the *Main Series Record*, and seven groups the *Subseries Record*. The bibliographic property values that map to MARCXML are found primarily in the Product Record segment of an ONIX for Books XML record.

Version 3.0 of ONIX for Books was recently introduced. Version 3.0, though retaining much of the semantics of version 2.1, is not fully backward compatible. Given the investment to date by the industry in version 2.1, *EDItEUR*, the international standards infrastructure group charged with maintaining ONIX for Books, has committed to support both version 2.1 and version 3.0 for the immediate future, giving time for implementers and users of ONIX for Books to update tools and transition to the new version of the standard.

While ONIX for Books XML metadata records do contain bibliographic details about the print book or e-book described, the bulk of an ONIX for Books XML metadata record is devoted to administrative and commercial information (e.g., target audience, territorial rights, pricing information, and Web links for end users). As a result, libraries generally do not create ONIX for Books records. However, many libraries benefit from being able to process and work with ONIX for Books records in being able to transform bibliographic portions of ONIX for Books XML metadata records to XML metadata grammars that are more compatible with library work flows, such as MARCXML. As libraries purchase access to more e-books from vendors and publishers, many libraries want to add MARC records for these e-books into their local cataloging systems so as to maintain the inventory functions of the catalog and make purchased e-books more easily findable by local users. To make e-books accessible in a timely manner, libraries need to find efficient ways of creating and ingesting MARC records for e-books into their OPACs. Converting ONIX XML records to MARCXML through automated batch processing can greatly facilitate and speed the creation and ingestion of MARC e-book records into a library's OPAC system. The Library of Congress Cataloging-in-Publishing Program's pilot project with ONIX for Books records[32] and the recent release of the OCLC Mapping Table for ONIX to MARC (Godby 2010) reflect the library community's growing effort to work with different metadata standards to provide better and faster access to e-books and other kinds of digital resources. The use of XML as a serialization format for metadata conforming to these various standards facilitates this effort.

CASE STUDY 5.3
Integrating ONIX Records into the OPAC

Synopsis: As libraries purchase more e-books, creating MARC format catalog records for e-books and integrating them into OPACs in order to provide access to these books has become one of the standard work flows at the library. The University of Illinois Library is testing work flows that include automatic transformations of ONIX for Books XML records to MARCXML records. Such a work flow can allow e-book records to appear in the library's OPAC even before the records for these resources become available in OCLC WorldCat. The Library of Congress has published a style sheet for transforming ONIX XML to MARCXML XSLT, and more recently OCLC has made available a detailed ONIX-to-MARC crosswalk. These resources facilitate new work flows for transforming ONIX XML to MARCXML.
Illustrates: Descriptive features of the ONIX for Books metadata standard; use of ONIX for Books XML metadata records in a library context.

After reviewing the ONIX records provided by several different vendors and publishers, the University of Illinois Library realized that there are two distinct XML serializations of ONIX in current use. One uses the ONIX *reference names* as XML element names (Figure 5.9). The other uses ONIX numeric

FIGURE 5.9 Part of an ONIX record with reference names.

```
<?xml version="1.0" encoding="UTF-8"?>
<!DOCTYPE ONIXMessage SYSTEM "http://www.editeur.org/onix/2.1/03/reference/
onix-international.dtd">
<ONIXMessage>
    <Header>
        <FromCompany>Elsevier Science and Technology</FromCompany>
        <FromPerson>Paula Daily, 619-699-6547</FromPerson>
        <SentDate>20100416</SentDate>
    </Header>
    <Product>
        <RecordReference>1092621:10872792</RecordReference>
        <NotificationType>03</NotificationType>
```

(*continued*)

FIGURE 5.9 (Continued)

```
        <ProductIdentifier>
            <ProductIDType>03</ProductIDType>
            <IDValue>9780123757289</IDValue>
        </ProductIdentifier>
        <ProductIdentifier>
            <ProductIDType>15</ProductIDType>
            <IDValue>9780123757289</IDValue>
        </ProductIdentifier>
        <Barcode>02</Barcode>
        <ProductForm>BB</ProductForm>
        <Title>
            <TitleType>01</TitleType>
            <TitleText>Crime Scene Photography</TitleText>
        </Title>
        <Website>
            <WebsiteLink>
    http://www.engineeringvillage.com/controller/servlet/OpenURL?genre=
book&amp;isbn=9780123757289
            </WebsiteLink>
        </Website>
        ...
    </Product>
</ONIXMessage>
```

tags (*short tags*) for most XML element names in the content object hierarchy (Figure 5.10). There is no difference in the information conveyed, simply differences in the semantic labels used to convey the information.

The transforming XSLT style sheet made available by the Library of Congress assumes the semantic labels illustrated in Figure 5.10. ONIX XML records with reference names rather than numeric tags for XML element names

FIGURE 5.10 Part of an ONIX record with code tags.

```
<?xml version="1.0" encoding="UTF-8"?>
<!DOCTYPE ONIXMessage SYSTEM "http://www.editeur.org/onix/2.1/03/reference/
onix-international.dtd">
<ONIXMessage>
    <Header>
        <m174>Elsevier Science and Technology</m174>
        <m175>Paula Daily, 619-699-6547</m175>
        <m182>20100416</m182>
    </Header>
    <Product>
        <a001>1092621:10872792</a001>
        <a002>03</a002>
    <ProductIdentifier>
        <b221>03</b221>
        <b224>9780123757289</b224>
    </ProductIdentifier>
```

FIGURE 5.10 (Continued)

```
    <ProductIdentifier>
        <b221>15</b221>
        <b224>9780123757289</b224>
    </ProductIdentifier>
    <b246>02</b246>
    <b012>BB</b012>
    <Title>
        <b202>01</b202>
        <b203>Crime Scene Photography</b203>
    </Title>
    <Website>
        <b295>
http://www.engineeringvillage.com/controller/servlet/OpenURL?genre=book&amp;
isbn=9780123757289
        </b295>
    </Website>
    ...
    </Product>
</ONIXMessage>
```

(e.g., Figure 5.9) must first be transformed to the other ONIX serialization before transformation to MARC using the Library of Congress XSLT style sheet is possible. Fortunately, a good, relatively simple and freely available XSLT style sheet to transform between the two ONIX XML serializations can be found at the EDItEUR site.[33] (The semantics and mechanics of XSLT style sheets are discussed in Chapter 11.) The EDItEUR XSLT style sheet transforms ONIX XML records with reference names to ONIX XML records with numeric code tags as XML element names. Once transformed to this point, MARCXML can then be generated by using the Library of Congress's XSLT style sheet for transforming ONIX XML records to MARCXML.[34] The MARCXML records can then be converted to traditional MARC format (e.g., using the MarcEdit tool discussed in Chapters 1 and 4) and ingested into a library OPAC, ultimately allowing these records to be displayed to OPAC users, as shown in Figure 5.11.

OTHER METADATA STANDARDS

As mentioned above, EAD, VRA Core, and CDWA-Lite are other metadata standards used heavily in the library community. All are XML compatible. In discussing how libraries use XML, these standards are notable because of their capacity to support descriptions of multiple related information resources within a single XML hierarchy. For example, using VRA Core, one can, in the same metadata record, describe a physical oil painting (the work) and one or more digitized photographs of that painting (the digital representations of or surrogates for the painting). As one way to express internal linkages between such related objects, EAD and VRA Core, when serialized as XML, allow for the use of special, XML-intrinsic ID and IDREF/IDREFS attribute types.

FIGURE 5.11 MARC format record (derived from ONIX XML) displayed in OPAC.

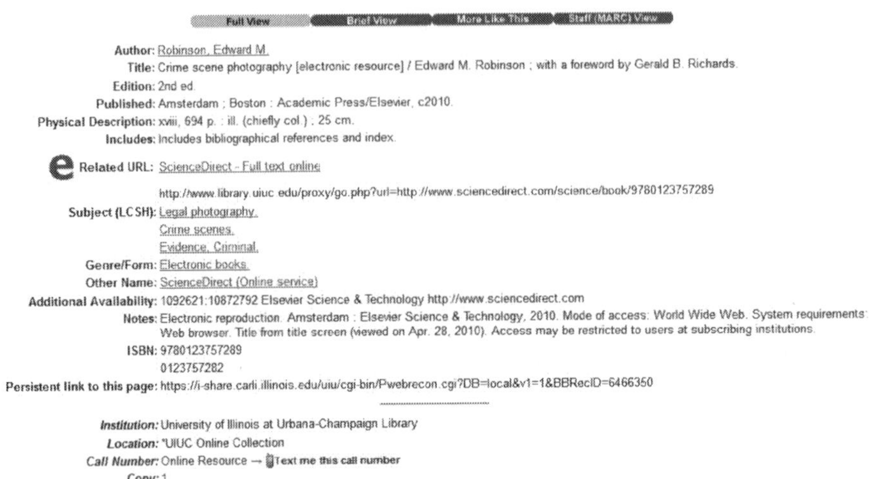

Full View | Brief View | More Like This | Staff (MARC) View

Author: Robinson, Edward M.
Title: Crime scene photography [electronic resource] / Edward M. Robinson ; with a foreword by Gerald B. Richards.
Edition: 2nd ed.
Published: Amsterdam ; Boston : Academic Press/Elsevier, c2010.
Physical Description: xviii, 694 p. : ill. (chiefly col.) ; 25 cm.
Includes: Includes bibliographical references and index.
Related URL: ScienceDirect - Full text online
http://www.library.uiuc.edu/proxy/go.php?url=http://www.sciencedirect.com/science/book/9780123757289
Subject (LCSH): Legal photography.
Crime scenes.
Evidence, Criminal.
Genre/Form: Electronic books.
Other Name: ScienceDirect (Online service)
Additional Availability: 1092621:10872792 Elsevier Science & Technology http://www.sciencedirect.com
Notes: Electronic reproduction. Amsterdam : Elsevier Science & Technology, 2010. Mode of access: World Wide Web. System requirements: Web browser. Title from title screen (viewed on Apr. 28, 2010). Access may be restricted to users at subscribing institutions.
ISBN: 9780123757289
0123757282
Persistent link to this page: https://i-share.carli.illinois.edu/uiu/cgi-bin/Pwebrecon.cgi?DB=local&v1=1&BBRecID=6466350

Institution: University of Illinois at Urbana-Champaign Library
Location: *UIUC Online Collection
Call Number: Online Resource → **Text me this call number**
Copy: 1
Note: Accessible anywhere on campus or with UIUC NetID

An example of how these special classes of XML attributes are implemented in EAD is described below. Additionally (in the case of EAD and VRA Core), all three standards provide their own idiosyncratic ways to internally reference and link related descriptions (e.g., to link the description of the digitized photograph of a painting to the description of physical painting).

EAD

EAD is a standard for encoding (making digital versions of) archival finding aids and is used in the management of archival resources. Since archival resources are organized based around concepts of archival collections, fonds, records, provenance, and the original order of the acquired resources, EAD incorporates these concepts into its semantic structure.[35] EAD is well suited, for example, for describing an archive consisting of letters, photographs, and papers to do with one individual or one organization. Such archives may include hundreds or even thousands of individual information resources (with only some, if any, available to view online). EAD intellectually links and organizes these by their chronology and their relationship to the individual or an organization.

Developed by the University of California at Berkeley in 1993, EAD was initially implemented in *Standard Generalized Markup Language*. XML *Schemas* for EAD were introduced in 2002; EAD 2002 Schemas are available in two syntaxes: *Relax NG Schema Language* and *W3C Schema Language*. An XML DTD for EAD is also available. (XML DTDs and Schemas are discussed in depth in Chapters 7, 8, and 9.) As of this writing, work on a revised and updated replacement for EAD is under way.

The semantics of the EAD XML metadata grammar focus on archival collection arrangement and description. An EAD record typically provides (as appropriate to the collection being described) administrative information about the EAD record itself, the acquisition and processing history of the archive, the extent and general arrangement of the archive, scope and content notes, biographical/historical notes, and an inventory/box/folder listing. When serialized as XML, the information about the EAD record itself appears in the `<eadheader>` element. All (or at least most) of the rest of the record, the description of the archive itself, appears in the `<archdesc>` element, with the inventory/box/folder listing appearing within the `<dsc>` element (a child of the `<archdesc>` element). The `<dsc>` element content model is hierarchical (up to 12 levels), with child element names indicative of their depth in the hierarchy (e.g., `<c01>, <c02>, <c03>, ..., <c12>)`. All together, EAD, when serialized as XML, provides a set of about 150 elements that can be used for encoding archival finding aids. EAD-encoded finding aids greatly facilitate the sharing of archival collection descriptions, enhancing discovery, searching, and management of such collections.

However, the granularity of an EAD XML metadata record is much different than that of a Dublin Core XML record. And although MARCXML can be used to describe archival collections and individual components of archival collections, it is not well suited to describing both simultaneously in a single MARCXML record. Since most EAD records describe a collection as a whole (as well as its components), the standard crosswalk from EAD to Dublin Core[36] converts only the EAD description of the archival collection as a whole to Dublin Core. Inventory details and descriptions of individual items contained in the archival collection are ignored. Similar transforms to MARC are also possible, though such transforms are complicated by the fact that MARC records are based on AACR2 as a content standard, while EAD records are based on the *Describing Archives: A Content Standard* (DACS) (Elings and Waibel 2007). DACS[37] was officially approved by the Society of American Archivists (SAA) as an SAA standard in 2004.

Another noteworthy feature of EAD serialized as XML is its use of ID and IDREF/IDREFS attributes. As mentioned in Chapter 3, ID and IDREF/IDREFS attributes are "*tokenized*" attributes according to the attribute type class hierarchy defined in the XML standard. Attributes of type ID are recognized by XML parsers and applications as denoting end points for links and cross-references between nodes within an XML EAD document instance that cannot be inferred from the EAD hierarchy. The value assigned to an ID type attribute associated with an XML element in an XML document instance must be unique within that document instance. The same value cannot be reused as a value for any other ID type attribute associated with any other XML element in the same document instance. This guarantees ID value uniqueness within the XML document instance scope and allows unambiguous reference to any element within a given XML document instance that has an ID attribute. IDREF type attributes are then used throughout a document instance to link other XML nodes to the single XML element having an ID attribute of matching value. (IDREFS type attributes take a list of IDs as their value, thus supporting one-to-many linkages.)

FIGURE 5.12 Portion of an EAD-encoded finding aid illustrating the use of ID attribute (*Source:* Library of Congress).

```
...
<c02 level="file">
<did>
<container type="box">135</container>
<unittitle encodinganalog="245$a">Hart, Lorenz <ref target="rodgers176"
show="replace" actuate="onrequest"><emph render="italic">See Container
176</emph>, Rodgers, Richard</ref></unittitle>
</did>
</c02>
...
<c02 level="file">
<did>
<container type="box">176</container>
<unittitle id="rodgers176" encodinganalog="245$a">Rodgers, Richard, and
Lorenz Hart, <title render="italic">I Married an Angel</title>,
<unitdate encodinganalog="245$f" normal="1938" type="inclusive">
[1938]</unitdate>
</unittitle>
</did>
</c02>
...
```

Figure 5.12 is a portion of an EAD-encoded finding aid[38] illustrating the use of ID and IDREF attributes. The finding aid includes descriptions of materials to do with composers Lorenz Hart and Richard Rodgers. In EAD, the attribute `id` appearing in Figure 5.12 as an attribute of the element `<unittitle>` is an XML ID attribute. In this illustration, it takes as its value the string "rodgers176." The attribute `target` appearing in Figure 5.12 as an attribute of the element `<ref>` is an XML IDREF attribute. Its value is the same string. In this way, the EAD author is able to express a link between box 135 of the archive, containing material to do with Hart, and box 176 of the archive, containing material to do with Rodgers and Hart and the song "I Married an Angel." This use of XML ID and IDREF attributes makes machine-actionable the human readable "See" cross-reference expressed in words in the finding aid.

VRA Core

As its name implies, the main user groups for VRA Core are visual resource professionals, slide librarians, and art historians. For these professionals, there is often the need in a single metadata record to describe precisely both the attributes of a work (e.g., a physical painting or sculpture) and the attributes of digitized images of that work (or of other digital surrogates). Dublin Core and MARC are not well suited to such compound descriptions. Efforts in Dublin Core to conflate the description of a physical object and its digital surrogate lead to violations of the Dublin Core "one-to-one principle," creating descriptive ambiguities. The one-to-one principle is discussed in section 1.2

of the online *Using Dublin Core* guide (Hillmann 2005). MODS is better suited to compound descriptions that include metadata about both a physical resource and its digital surrogate(s) but only to a degree. When it comes to describing both a work and its digital surrogates in a single record, VRA Core is the more natural projection into the digital realm of the descriptive traditions of slide libraries and similar organizations.

The current version of VRA Core as of this writing is version 4.0.[39] VRA Core and related ancillary documentation, including XML Schemas for VRA Core, are managed and maintained by the VRA Data Standards Committee. The VRA Core has elements and structure that allow metadata librarians to describe the relationships between work and images, such as to describe an original work and also image(s) rendered from that work, in one record.

Figure 5.13 is an excerpt from a VRA Core record created by the authors describing a locomotive exhibited at the National Museum of American History as part of the *America on the Move* Exhibition. This excerpt illustrates how VRA Core is used to describe both the physical locomotive (within the element `<work>`) and a digital surrogate for the work (element `<image>`). The URL from which the digital image described can be obtained is the value of the `href` attribute of the `<image>` element. The `<relationSet>` element within the `<image>` element is used to bind the image description to work description.

Using another layer of hierarchy, VRA Core also can be used to describe collections of works and their individual digital surrogates. In addition, notice

FIGURE 5.13 Excerpts from a VRA Core XML metadata record.

```
<vra>
 <work id="w_01234" refid="252681" source='America on the Move Exhibition at the
National Museum of American History'>
  <agentSet>
     <display>Baldwin Locomotive Works</display>
     <agent>
     <name type="corporate" vocab="LCNAF">Baldwin Locomotive Works</name>
     <culture>American</culture>
     <role vocab="AAT" refid="300077527">manufacturing</role>
     </agent>
  </agentSet>
  <dateSet>
     <display>In service from 1876 - 1960</display>
     <date type="creation">
       <earliestDate>1876</earliestDate>
       <latestDate>1876</latestDate>
     </date>
  </dateSet>
...
  </work>
```

(continued)

FIGURE 5.13 (Continued)

```
  <image id="i_01234" refid='3482070642' source="Richard's Flickr Photo Stream"
        href=' http://farm4.staticflickr.com/3643/3482070642_1acc29fca4_b.jpg'>
...
  <dateSet>
     <display>Photographed on April 25, 2009; Posted to Flickr on April 27, 2009
     </display>
     <date type="creation">
       <earliestDate>2009-04-25</earliestDate>
       <latestDate>2009-04-25</latestDate>
     </date>
     <date type="publication">
       <earliestDate>2009-04-27</earliestDate>
       <latestDate>2009-04-27</latestDate>
      </date>
  </dateSet>
...
  <relationSet>
     <relation type="imageOf" relids="w_01234">Steam locomotive Jupiter</relation>
  </relationSet>
...
  </image>
</vra>
```

how in Figure 5.13 VRA Core relies on XML hierarchy to differentiate display information from indexing data while still binding such related information together. Thus, the `<dateSet>` element contains in its child element `<display>` the relevant date information as a human-readable string while simultaneously providing in the substructure of other child elements (`<date>`) the earliest and latest date information. This approach facilitates both presentation and indexing. Finally, notice how the attributes on the `<role>` element of `<agent>` can be used to locate (link to) a description of the `<agent>` entity's role in an authoritative controlled vocabulary. Additional VRA Core examples[40] are maintained by the University of California San Diego Libraries.

CDWA

CDWA is another metadata standard developed to support the cultural heritage community, especially museum and visual resources professionals. CDWA Lite is an XML schema based on the CDWA metadata model and the metadata content guidelines titled *Cataloging Cultural Objects: A Guide to Describing Cultural Works and Their Images* (CCO).[41] The CCO is also used as a data content standard for the VRA Core. CDWA evolved out of art museum descriptive traditions. Not surprisingly, there are a number of similarities between the VRA Core schema and CDWA Lite. Documentation for CDWA Lite is maintained by the Getty Research Institute, a part of the J. Paul Getty Trust.

While CDWA is representative of metadata standards emerging from the museum community, it is not alone in that regard. Currently, there is an effort to reconcile multiple museum-oriented metadata standards. A new schema called the Lightweight Information Describing Object (LIDO) is emerging from that effort. LIDO[42] encompasses most of the semantics of CDWA Lite. First introduced in November 2010, the LIDO also borrows semantics and grammatical structures from Museumdat[43] and is informed by the SPECTRUM museum documentation standard[44] developed in the United Kingdom and by the *Conceptual Reference Model*[45] created by the Committee on Documentation of the International Council of Museums.

QUESTIONS AND TOPICS FOR DISCUSSION

1. What could be the pros and cons of using a metadata standard?
2. What motivates each user domain or community to develop its own metadata standard? What are the drawbacks of this approach?
3. What would you consider if you needed to create a new metadata standard?

SUGGESTIONS FOR EXERCISES

1. Find an image, a newspaper article, and a book and create records for them with Dublin Core, MODS, and MARC.
2. Compare the records based on resource types and metadata standards.
   a. Which metadata standard works best to describe an image?
   b. Which metadata standard works best to describe an article?
   c. Which metadata standard works best to describe a book?
3. Discuss the pros and cons of integrating user-generated metadata into the metadata creation work flow.

NOTES

1. http://dublincore.org.
2. http://www.loc.gov/standards/mods.
3. http://www.loc.gov/ead.
4. http://www.vraweb.org/projects/vracore4/index.html.
5. http://www.editeur.org/15/Previous-Releases.
6. http://www.getty.edu/research/publications/electronic_publications/cdwa.
7. http://dublincore.org/documents/2000/07/11/dcmes-qualifiers.
8. http://www.w3.org/TR/NOTE-datetime.html.
9. http://www.contentdm.org.
10. http://www.dspace.org.
11. http://www.openarchives.org/pmh.
12. http://www.w3.org/RDF.
13. http://dublincore.org/documents/dc-xml-guidelines.
14. http://dublincore.org/documents/dc-ds-xml.
15. http://dublincore.org/documents/dc-rdf.
16. http://dublincore.org/documents/abstract-model.
17. http://dublincore.org/schemas/xmls/qdc/2008/02/11/notes.

18. http://www.niso.org/standards/resources/Z39.50_Resources.
19. http://www.worldcat.org.
20. http://www.oclc.org/gateway.
21. http://www.loc.gov/standards/mads.
22. http://www.ifla.org/publications/functional-requirements-for-authority-data.
23. http://www.rdatoolkit.org.
24. http://www.ifla.org/en/isbd-rg.
25. https://wiki.dlib.indiana.edu/download/attachments/24288/DLFMODS_ImplementationGuidelines.pdf.
26. http://www.loc.gov/standards/mods.
27. http://www.loc.gov/standards/mods/userguide.
28. http://www.loc.gov/standards/mods/tools_for_mods.php.
29. http://dlc.lib.utk.edu/~cdeane/UTK_LIB_DLC/WB4/workbook.htm.
30. http://academiccommons.columbia.edu.
31. http://fedora-commons.org.
32. http://www.loc.gov/marc/onix2marc.html.
33. http://www.editeur.org/files/ONIX%203/switch-onix-tagnames-1.1.xsl.
34. http://www.loc.gov/standards/marcxml/xslt/ONIX2MARC21slim.xsl.
35. http://www.loc.gov/ead/tglib/element_index.html.
36. http://www.loc.gov/ead/ag/agappb.html.
37. http://www.archivists.org/governance/standards/dacs.asp.
38. http://www.loc.gov/rr/ead/lcp/lcp_links.html#p7.2a.
39. http://www.vraweb.org/projects/vracore4.
40. http://aal.ucsd.edu/vracore4/example026.html.
41. http://cco.vrafoundation.org.
42. http://cidoc.icom.museum/WG_Data_Harvesting%28en%29%28E1%29.xml.
43. http://www.museumdat.org/index.php?ln=en.
44. http://www.collectionslink.org.uk/programmes/spectrum.
45. http://www.cidoc-crm.org.

REFERENCES

Cole, Timothy W., and Muriel Foulonneau. 2007. *Using the Open Archives Initiative Protocol for Metadata Harvesting*. Westport, CT: Libraries Unlimited.

"Dublin Core Qualifiers." 2000. Available at: http://dublincore.org/documents/2000/07/11/dcmes-qualifiers

Elings, Mary W., and Günter Waibel. 2007. "Metadata for All: Descriptive Standards and Metadata Sharing across Libraries, Archives and Museums." *First Monday* 12, no. 3 (2007). Available at: http://firstmonday.org/article/view/1628/1543

Godby, Carol J. 2010. "Mapping ONIX to MARC." *New OCLC Research Report*. Available at: http://www.oclc.org/research/news/2010-04-09.htm

Han, Myung-Ja, Christine Cho, Timothy W. Cole, and Amy S. Jackson. 2009. "Metadata for Special Collections in CONTENTdm: How to Improve Interoperability of Unique Fields through OAI-PMH." *Journal of Library Metadata* 9, no. 3: 213–38.

Hillmann, Diane. 2005. "Using Dublin Core." Available at: http://dublincore.org/documents/usageguide

International Federation of Library Associations and Institutions Study Group on the Functional Requirements for Bibliographic Records. 1998. *Functional Requirements for Bibliographic Records*. Munich: K. G. Saur. Available at: http://www.ifla.org/en/publications/functional-requirements-for-bibliographic-records

Lagoze, Carl. 2001. "Keeping Dublin Core Simple." *D-Lib Magazine*. Available at: http://www.dlib.org/dlib/january01/lagoze/01lagoze.html

Lagoze, Carl, Dean Krafft, Tim Cornwell, Naomi Dushay, Dean Eckstrom, and John Saylor. 2006. "Metadata Aggregation and 'Automated Digital Libraries': A Retrospective on the NSDL Experience." In *JCDL '06 Proceedings of the 6th ACM/IEEE-CS Joint Conference on Digital Libraries*. New York: Association for Computing Machinery. Available at: http://dx.doi.org/10.1145/1141753.1141804

Lubetzky, Seymour, and American Library Association. 1953. *Cataloging Rules and Principles: A Critique of the A. L. A. Rules for Entry and a Proposed Design for Their Revision*. Washington, DC: Processing Department, Library of Congress.

Ma, Jin. 2007. *Metadata*. Washington, DC: Association of Research Libraries.

McCallum, Sally H. 2004. "An Introduction to the Metadata Object Description Schema (MODS)." *Library Hi Tech* 22, no. 1: 82–88.

Riley, Jenn. 2010. "Seeing Standards: A Visualization of the Metadata Universe." Available at: http://www.dlib.indiana.edu/~jenlrile/metadatamap/seeingstandards_glossary_pamphlet.pdf

Svenouis, Elaine. 2000. *The Intellectual Foundation of Information Organization*. Cambridge, MA: MIT Press, 2000.

Tennant, Roy. 2004. "A Bibliographic Metadata Infrastructure for the Twenty-First Century." *Library Hi Tech* 22, no. 2: 175–81.

CHAPTER 6

Interoperable XML: Namespaces, Shareable Metadata, and Application Profiles

For many years, the predominant mode of sharing catalog records between and among libraries has been via specialized services and tools dedicated to this purpose, such as among libraries within a statewide or regional consortium using shared cataloging utilities maintained and managed by the consortium or between a library's integrated library system (ILS) and the utilities and services administered by the Online Computer Library Center (OCLC). The traditional MAchine-Readable Cataloging (MARC) record is well suited for such library-centric applications. A library can create MARC records in its ILS and upload them to OCLC or can download MARC records from OCLC into its ILS. Such sharing is straightforward and simple once configured but does not leverage generic technologies efficiently and entails considerable up-front and ongoing dedicated resources to set up and maintain. This approach also is limited in scope and flexibility, especially when it comes to sharing non-MARC metadata records.

An early attempt to improve metadata interoperability was introduced in the late 1980s. The National Information Standards Organization Z39.50 protocol,[1] a standard for metadata sharing, opened up a few additional avenues for descriptive cataloging interoperability, but this is still a library-specific approach and requires both the data provider and the harvester to implement relatively complicated and specialized technical protocols. It does not leverage established and well-vetted Web technologies, although it does make some use of generic data serialization techniques, such as XML.

Otherwise, until recently, sharing MARC catalog records and especially other formats of metadata on a more ad hoc basis across the Internet between two libraries or between libraries and nonlibrary entities had been largely neglected. Yet the potential for labor savings and other benefits by doing so is clear. By leveraging ubiquitous technologies such as the World Wide Web and XML to facilitate broader sharing, reuse, and repurposing of metadata and descriptive cataloging, libraries can expand the shared community model of cataloging and bring more resources to the attention of their users. Simpler, more flexible ways to share metadata are a means to expand access, especially to the growing body of born-digital and retrospectively digitized resources now being curated by libraries.

Web- and XML-based approaches introduced since 2000 for disseminating catalog records and other metadata are opening up many new avenues for metadata sharing and interoperability, using both library-centric protocols—such as the Search/Retrieval via URL protocol (SRU),[2] a Z39.50-successor protocol, and the Open Archives Initiative-Protocol for Metadata Harvesting (OAI-PMH)[3]—and more generic Web-centric protocols (e.g., Really Simple Syndication [RSS][4] and the related Atom Syndication protocol[5]). Work with these newer protocols, while confirming their efficacies and the intuition that broader, more flexible metadata sharing can improve the visibility and use of collections (Shreeves 2007), also has highlighted the need to create quality *shareable metadata*, that is, quality metadata optimized and specifically intended for sharing and interoperability. Additionally, the broader dissemination of metadata in recent years has highlighted the need for high-quality collection descriptions as a way to help preserve the original context when catalogers interpret constituent item-level metadata records aggregated or reused in other contexts.

Moving beyond MARC-based metadata sharing has raised challenges. In particular, there is the challenge of how to encourage the design and deployment of metadata standards optimized for specific purposes and communities without engendering an unwieldy plethora of custom, limited-scope metadata schemes. Since each digital library application and target community can require specific semantic element sets and content standards to best describe their unique digital assets, promoting a single, universal metadata standard is unrealistic. This understanding has been borne out by experience. On the other hand, too many unique metadata standards can actually reduce interoperability (Chan and Zeng 2006; Park and Tosaka 2010).

One solution to this tension is to employ *metadata application profiles*. When implemented in XML, metadata application profiles amount to custom XML metadata grammars created by mixing together semantics and structures drawn from multiple metadata standards. Metadata application profiles allow implementers to tailor and optimize metadata as required for a particular application or use while still leveraging recognizable, community-based semantics and grammars (Coyle and Baker 2009; Heery and Patel 2000). Doing this in XML is facilitated by the use of *XML Namespaces*. First introduced as a W3C Proposed Recommendation in 1998,[6] XML Namespaces is an approach to interoperability and modular grammar design borrowed from the computer science domain (and not inherited from Standard Generalized Markup Languages).

This chapter introduces XML Namespaces, examining both the foundation and the rationale for this powerful feature of XML and looking at how XML

Namespaces are implemented in practice. Some of the implications of lessons learned for catalogers and metadata librarians from recent projects that focused on metadata sharing and interoperability (e.g., lessons about shareable metadata quality and ways XML metadata grammars facilitate interoperability) are then examined. Metadata application profiles are, in part, a response to some of these lessons, so this chapter closes with an introduction to metadata application profiles, illustrating, among other things, how the design of XML Namespaces aligns well with this still relatively new and innovative approach to metadata interoperability. The compatibility of XML Namespaces with metadata application profiles makes XML especially well suited for implementing this approach, which in turn can facilitate sophisticated metadata system architectures and robust metadata sharing and interoperability.

XML NAMESPACES

Interoperability and sharing imply goals of reuse, repurposing, and modularity as ways to take advantage of shared effort and avoid wasteful redundancy. These goals in turn imply a requirement to disambiguate (avoid *collisions*) between the semantic labels used by different agents involved in creating and sharing metadata and catalog records. In XML, potential semantic collisions spanning boundaries between XML metadata grammars can be avoided through the use of XML Namespaces.

Foundation and Rationale for XML Namespaces

In computer science, *namespaces* are generally used as a way to bind together a logical grouping of entity identifiers (i.e., names). In the abstract, a namespace is said to *contain* entity identifiers. Functionally, a namespace can be thought of as a modifier that qualifies a set of names as belonging to a specific logical grouping or class, such as a specific function or subroutine. The goal is to facilitate modularity and reuse. If a subroutine that can navigate a certain kind of data structure has already been written for an earlier project, reusing this subroutine in a new program that will deal with similar data structures is a way to conserve time and effort. Namespaces provide a way to keep names and labels in the reused subroutine from being confused with similar names and labels being used elsewhere in the new program. Namespaces disambiguate.

The same approach can disambiguate semantic labels. Consider that automobiles and books can both have components called "parts." This book has four parts. A car has parts of a different kind, such as an engine, seats, doors, and so on. When using the term "parts" in natural language, humans automatically (and typically without consciously considering the matter) comprehend from context the difference between a reference to a car part and a reference to a book part, even when the word "part" is not directly modified by car or book. This disambiguation is more difficult for computers to do, so it makes sense when working with computers to explicitly label each instance of "part" as to whether it is a kind of part pertaining to cars or a kind pertaining to books. This distinction avoids ambiguity, improves efficiency, and facilitates the reuse and evolution of names over time.

Similar semantic collisions can occur across metadata standards. For example, both Metadata Object Description Schema (MODS) and Simple Dublin Core include in their semantic schemes the label *subject*. In both standards, the value of this element conveys what the resource is about. In MODS, the semantic meaning of subject is broad, and the element is subdivided to distinguish topical subjects from geographic and temporal subjects; all three categories of subject fall under the single broad heading of MODS subject. In Simple Dublin Core, on the other hand, the meaning of subject is more limited and is focused exclusively on the topical (encompassing proper names and occupations as topical subjects). Simple Dublin Core provides a different element, *coverage*, to describe the spatial and temporal scope of the resource being described. Although overlapping, the meanings of MODS subject and Simple Dublin Core subject are different, and these differences must be recognized by metadata applications dealing with both grammars simultaneously. In practice, this requirement is met by leveraging XML Namespaces.

When the first edition of XML 1.0 was released as a World Wide Web Consortium (W3C) Recommendation in early 1998, *Namespaces in XML* was still just a W3C Working Draft. XML can be and is used without namespaces; however, it quickly became apparent that the inclusion of namespaces as an optional feature of XML was a prescient decision. *Namespaces in XML* became a W3C Recommendation in January 1999,[7] less than a year after the initial release of XML as a W3C Recommendation. The motivation for the use of XML namespaces was provided in this initial release and has been repeated in subsequent editions of *Namespaces in XML* version 1.0[8] and *Namespaces in XML* version 1.1:[9]

> We envision applications of Extensible Markup Language (XML) where a single XML document may contain elements and attributes (here referred to as a "markup vocabulary") that are defined for and used by multiple software modules. One motivation for this is modularity: if such a markup vocabulary exists which is well-understood and for which there is useful software available, it is better to re-use this markup rather than re-invent it.
>
> Such documents, containing multiple markup vocabularies, pose problems of recognition and collision. Software modules need to be able to recognize the elements and attributes which they are designed to process, even in the face of "collisions" occurring when markup intended for some other software package uses the same element name or attribute name.

> These considerations require that document constructs should have names constructed so as to avoid clashes between names from different markup vocabularies. This specification describes a mechanism, XML Namespaces, which accomplishes this by assigning expanded names to elements and attributes. (*Namespaces in XML* 1.1)

Over time, the XML Namespace approach has proven robust, powerful, and well suited for metadata applications. Metadata vocabularies and metadata-based applications evolve. Because XML Namespaces support modularity, it is relatively easy to use XML Namespaces to swap out or add new vocabulary components as an application evolves. Thus, there are metadata solutions that originally serialized author names in plain text in Dublin Core creator elements but now use more fine-grained *Friend-of-a-Friend* semantics (FOAF)[10] for this purpose.

Namespaces in XML also facilitate metadata work flows that reuse modular components. For instance, namespace-specific style sheets can be written and used in work flows to transform elements recognized from one namespace while simply copying and leaving unchanged elements from other namespaces not known to the style sheet. These style sheets can then be used across multiple work flows. (XML style sheets are discussed in Chapter 11.)

Some complexity unavoidably ensues from a decision to use XML Namespaces. One challenge is validation. As discussed in the next chapter, XML Document Type Definitions (DTDs), special files used to help validate XML document instances, do not really support the XML Namespaces approach. Validation of XML document instances containing element and attribute names drawn from multiple namespaces can be accomplished using DTDs but only by creating a custom DTD that includes every element used (i.e., from all namespaces) and sets in the DTD the namespace prefixes that will be used. This method defeats the purpose of namespaces. Fortunately, the potential of XML Namespaces was recognized early enough in the development of XML that most languages defined for creating XML schema alternatives to XML DTDs, are designed to work well with XML Namespaces. Validating parsers that rely on non-DTD schemas can invoke and process multiple schemas (e.g., one for each namespace used) in order to rigorously validate an XML document instance that contains semantics and grammatical components drawn from more than one namespace (as discussed in Chapter 9).

XML Namespace Implementation

Throughout the rest of this chapter and in subsequent chapters, XML Namespaces will be used in examples and case studies. Per the *Namespaces in XML* specification, an XML Namespace must be identified (named) within an XML document instance by a Uniform Resource Identifier (URI)[11] reference. URI references used for namespace identifiers should be chosen so as to be globally unique; that is, they should be minted so as to include strings that the namespace creator has registered on the Web and thereby claimed ownership over, such as a domain name or Web server address. Thus, *http://purl.org/dc/elements/1.1/* is the identifier for the namespace containing the core 15 elements of Simple Dublin Core,[12] and *http://purl.org/dc/terms/* is the identifier for the larger superset of Dublin Core terms, the namespace containing all of the elements of Simple Dublin Core plus the refinement and encoding scheme extensions that make up Qualified Dublin Core. Both these namespace URIs start with the string "http://purl.org/dc/," which is registered uniquely to the Dublin Core Metadata Initiative. The URI *http://www.loc.gov/MARC21/slim* (which incorporates the URL of the Web server of the Library of Congress) is the identifier for the MARCXML namespace as maintained by the Library of Congress. The same root is used for many other metadata schemas.

To implement namespaces within XML documents, the *Namespaces in XML* specification defines the concepts of *local names*, *qualified names*, *namespace names*, and *namespace prefixes*. Local names are the names (i.e., strings of characters) given by XML implementers to specific elements, attributes, and certain attribute values within a particular XML metadata grammar. Thus, for Simple Dublin Core, the local names of the elements are `title`, `creator`, `description`, `subject`, and so on. The local names for MARCXML are `collection`, `record`, `controlfield`, `datafield`, and so on.

Namespace names are simply the URIs (as illustrated above) used to identify the semantics of a particular XML metadata grammar (e.g., the URIs for Simple Dublin Core and MARCXML as given above). But because URIs can be long and awkward to use repeatedly within an XML document, namespace names are bound (within the scope of an XML document instance or part of an XML document instance) to *namespace prefixes*, usually short strings of characters. This binding is implemented through special attributes that can appear on almost any XML element. Thus, the following attribute appearing in an element's start tag binds the namespace prefix "*dc*" to the namespace URI for Simple Dublin Core: `xmlns:dc="http://purl.org/dc/elements/1.1/"`. This binding of the namespace prefix "dc" to the Simple Dublin Core namespace URI applies to the element on which the attribute appears and to all children of that element unless overridden in a subsequent child object by a different binding of "dc" to some other namespace name. Typically, most attributes binding namespace prefixes to namespace URIs occur in the root element of an XML document, but this practice is convention, not a requirement, and sometimes it is not the optimal option.

Note also that a *default namespace* or no-namespace prefix can be bound to a specific namespace URI. Thus, `xmlns="http://www.loc.gov/MARC21/slim"` binds the default namespace prefix (i.e., no-namespace prefix) to the MARCXML namespace. This is interpreted as meaning that elements and attributes without namespace prefixes should be assumed by default to be in the MARCXML namespace. Often, for the purposes of validation, it is useful to bind a namespace URI to the default namespace prefix in an XML document instance even when only elements from a single namespace are being used in that document instance.

Finally, qualified names are element, attribute, and sometimes attribute value names occurring within an XML document instance that are subject to namespace interpretation. In practical terms, qualified names are strings consisting of a local name prefixed by a properly bound namespace prefix. The delimiter between the namespace prefix and the local name is the colon (":") character. Thus, assuming the binding between "dc" and the Simple Dublin Core namespace URI given above, the element `<dc:title>` indicates that the content object "title" should be recognized as being in the namespace of Simple Dublin Core.

Namespace references have become ubiquitous in the domain of XML Web applications. Because namespace names (URI references) are globally unique, applications can be written to recognize specific namespace names and perform certain functions based on such recognitions. There are, for instance, well-established namespace names (URIs) for many W3C protocols and grammars, such as HTML, XHTML, and RSS.

Figure 6.1 shows a Web page resulting from a keyword search of the Illinois Researcher Information Service, a subscription-based current awareness service for grant opportunities managed by the University of Illinois Library. Users interested in keeping up with new grant opportunities in their domain of interest can subscribe to an RSS feed of this search result. Figure 6.2 shows part of the XML returned for this search by the RSS subscription service (viewed in the Oxygen XML editor). Notice the use of two namespace URIs in this document, one pointing to the Atom namespace and one to the namespace for XHTML (the XML version of HTML). Most Web browsers today are able to manipulate documents containing references to both the Atom namespace name and the XHTML namespace name so as to make the most of both the presentational features of XHTML and the current-awareness features of RSS.

Note that elements without a prefix are still bound to a namespace URI when within the scope of a default namespace binding, such as in Figure 6.2. Although no explicit prefix is present, the root element and all children down to the level of the `<summary>` element are bound to *http://www.w3.org/2005/Atom*, the Atom namespace URI. Elements `<div>` and lower in the XML hierarchy shown in Figure 6.2 are bound to *http://www.w3.org/1999/xhtml*, the XHTML namespace URI. As illustrated in Figure 6.1, Mozilla Firefox recognized both of these namespace URIs and so was able to properly format and display the information contained in this XML document.

FIGURE 6.1 Search results from the Illinois Research Information Services (IRIS).

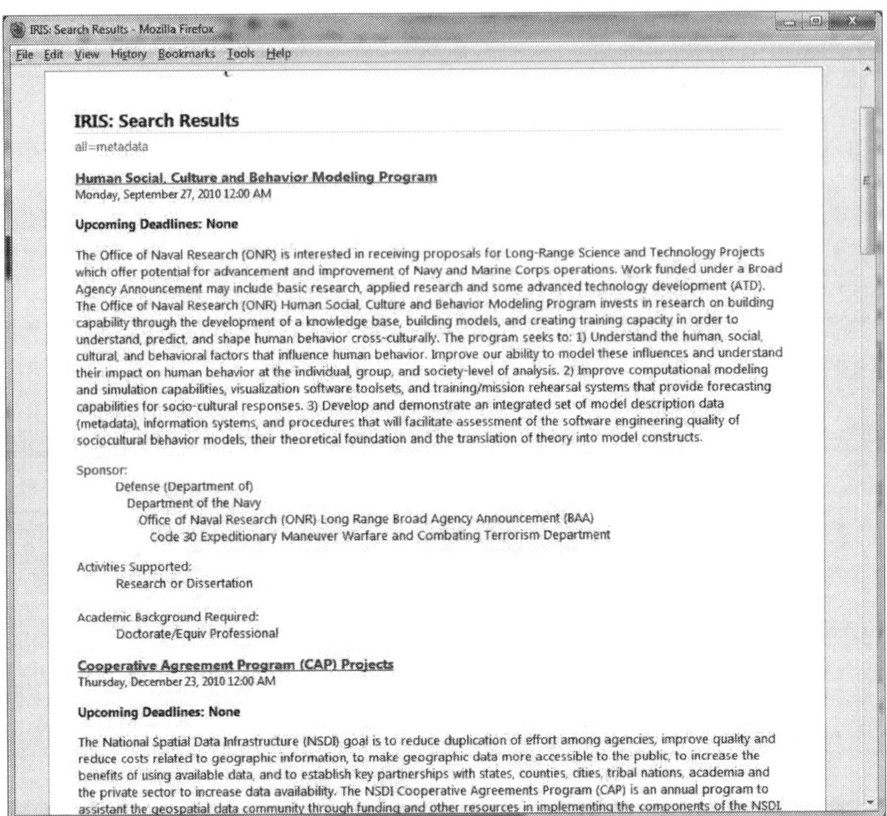

IRIS: Search Results - Mozilla Firefox

File Edit View History Bookmarks Tools Help

IRIS: Search Results

all=metadata

Human Social, Culture and Behavior Modeling Program

Monday, September 27, 2010 12:00 AM

Upcoming Deadlines: None

The Office of Naval Research (ONR) is interested in receiving proposals for Long-Range Science and Technology Projects which offer potential for advancement and improvement of Navy and Marine Corps operations. Work funded under a Broad Agency Announcement may include basic research, applied research and some advanced technology development (ATD). The Office of Naval Research (ONR) Human Social, Culture and Behavior Modeling Program invests in research on building capability through the development of a knowledge base, building models, and creating training capacity in order to understand, predict, and shape human behavior cross-culturally. The program seeks to: 1) Understand the human, social, cultural, and behavioral factors that influence human behavior. Improve our ability to model these influences and understand their impact on human behavior at the individual, group, and society-level of analysis. 2) Improve computational modeling and simulation capabilities, visualization software toolsets, and training/mission rehearsal systems that provide forecasting capabilities for socio-cultural responses. 3) Develop and demonstrate an integrated set of model description data (metadata), information systems, and procedures that will facilitate assessment of the software engineering quality of sociocultural behavior models, their theoretical foundation and the translation of theory into model constructs.

Sponsor:
Defense (Department of)
Department of the Navy
Office of Naval Research (ONR) Long Range Broad Agency Announcement (BAA)
Code 30 Expeditionary Maneuver Warfare and Combating Terrorism Department

Activities Supported:
Research or Dissertation

Academic Background Required:
Doctorate/Equiv Professional

Cooperative Agreement Program (CAP) Projects

Thursday, December 23, 2010 12:00 AM

Upcoming Deadlines: None

The National Spatial Data Infrastructure (NSDI) goal is to reduce duplication of effort among agencies, improve quality and reduce costs related to geographic information, to make geographic data more accessible to the public, to increase the benefits of using available data, and to establish key partnerships with states, counties, cities, tribal nations, academia and the private sector to increase data availability. The NSDI Cooperative Agreements Program (CAP) is an annual program to assistant the geospatial data community through funding and other resources in implementing the components of the NSDI.

As another illustration of how XML namespaces are used, consider the XML document instance shown in Figure 6.3. This is the Library of Congress Subject Heading (LCSH) authority record that was included in Chapter 2 as Figure 2.1. This XML document provides a description of the LCSH term "metadata harvesting." This description draws on the semantics of Qualified Dublin Core, the semantics of the Resource Description Framework (RDF) and the Web Ontology Language, and the semantics of the Simple Knowledge Organization System initiative. The use of semantics drawn from these four metadata grammars creates an LCSH description in XML that is rich and machine actionable; for example, it allows applications to collocate and sort resources described using LCSH according to the thesaurus hierarchy.

In Figure 6.3, four namespace prefixes—*dcterms*, *owl*, *rdf*, and *skos*—are bound by the XML namespace attributes appearing as part of the root element of this document. With the exception mentioned below, there is nothing magical about the namespace prefix strings that are used within any XML document; what matters is the URI to which the prefixes are bound. The authors of the XML document in Figure 6.3 could just as easily have used *foo*, *bar*, *over*, and *out* as namespace prefixes. Bound to the same namespace URIs, the

FIGURE 6.2 The RSS feed for the IRIS search shown in Figure 6.1. Screen shot was made using Oxygen XML Editor (http://www.oxygenxml.com).

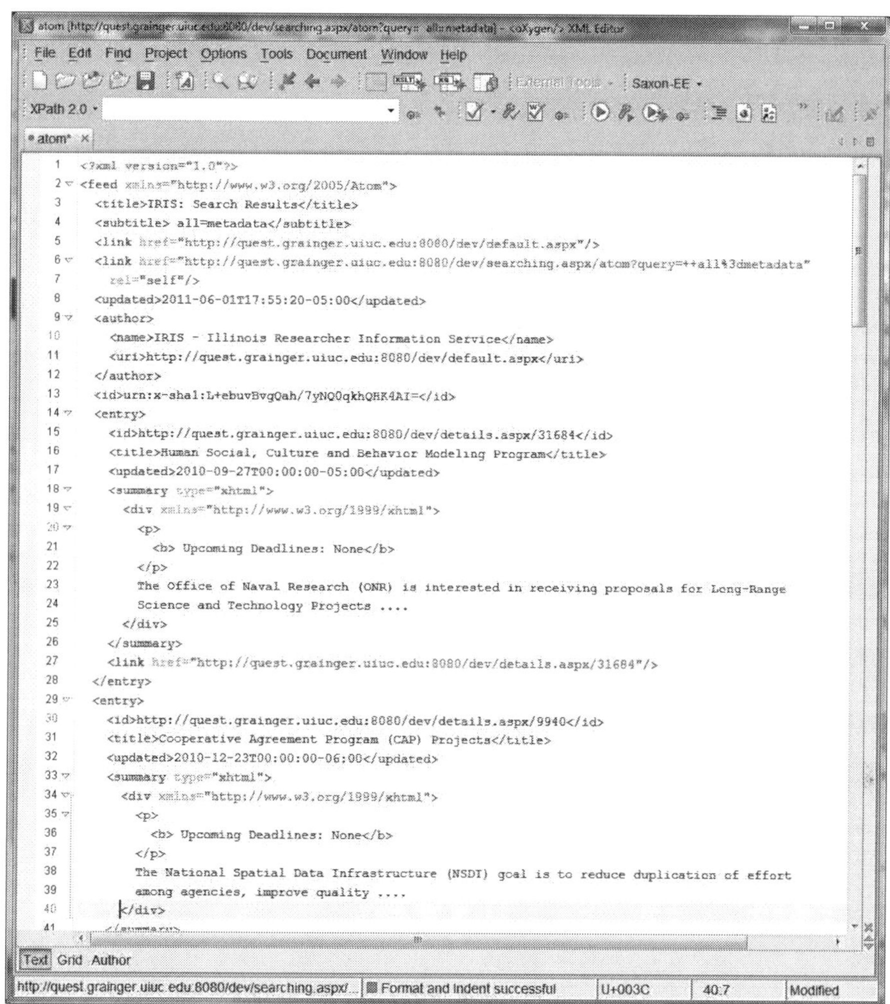

```
<?xml version="1.0"?>
<feed xmlns="http://www.w3.org/2005/Atom">
  <title>IRIS: Search Results</title>
  <subtitle> all=metadata</subtitle>
  <link href="http://quest.grainger.uiuc.edu:8080/dev/default.aspx"/>
  <link href="http://quest.grainger.uiuc.edu:8080/dev/searching.aspx/atom?query=++all%3dmetadata"
    rel="self"/>
  <updated>2011-06-01T17:55:20-05:00</updated>
  <author>
    <name>IRIS - Illinois Researcher Information Service</name>
    <uri>http://quest.grainger.uiuc.edu:8080/dev/default.aspx</uri>
  </author>
  <id>urn:x-sha1:L+ebuvBvgQah/7yNQ0qkhQHK4AI=</id>
  <entry>
    <id>http://quest.grainger.uiuc.edu:8080/dev/details.aspx/31684</id>
    <title>Human Social, Culture and Behavior Modeling Program</title>
    <updated>2010-09-27T00:00:00-05:00</updated>
    <summary type="xhtml">
      <div xmlns="http://www.w3.org/1999/xhtml">
        <p>
          <b> Upcoming Deadlines: None</b>
        </p>
        The Office of Naval Research (ONR) is interested in receiving proposals for Long-Range
        Science and Technology Projects ....
      </div>
    </summary>
    <link href="http://quest.grainger.uiuc.edu:8080/dev/details.aspx/31684"/>
  </entry>
  <entry>
    <id>http://quest.grainger.uiuc.edu:8080/dev/details.aspx/9940</id>
    <title>Cooperative Agreement Program (CAP) Projects</title>
    <updated>2010-12-23T00:00:00-06:00</updated>
    <summary type="xhtml">
      <div xmlns="http://www.w3.org/1999/xhtml">
        <p>
          <b> Upcoming Deadlines: None</b>
        </p>
        The National Spatial Data Infrastructure (NSDI) goal is to reduce duplication of effort
        among agencies, improve quality ....
      </div>
```

semantic meaning would be unchanged. Although by convention implementers try to use mnemonic strings for namespace prefixes, namespace prefixes have no meaning outside the context of the document in which they are used. Only namespace URIs can be relied on to be globally unique and meaningful. Thinking otherwise is a common error of beginners working with XML Namespaces.

The one exception to these principles is the namespace prefix "*xml*," which is reserved for special entities defined in the XML specification itself. This namespace prefix is by definition always bound to the namespace URI, http://www.w3.org/XML/1998/namespace, and does not have to be declared. It will always be recognized by properly conformant XML parsers. It cannot be bound to any other namespace URI. Thus, in Figure 6.3 the language of

FIGURE 6.3 Registry record in RDF/XML for the LCSH term "metadata harvesting" (*Source:* Library of Congress[13]).

```
<?xml version="1.0" encoding="UTF-8"?>
<rdf:RDF
  xmlns:dcterms="http://purl.org/dc/terms/"
  xmlns:owl="http://www.w3.org/2002/07/owl#"
  xmlns:rdf="http://www.w3.org/1999/02/22-rdf-syntax-ns#"
  xmlns:skos="http://www.w3.org/2004/02/skos/core#">
<rdf:Description
      rdf:about="http://id.loc.gov/authorities/sh2007001751#concept">
  <dcterms:modified rdf:datatype="http://www.w3.org/2001/XMLSchema#dateTime">
     2009-12-15T13:52:15-04:00</dcterms:modified>
  <owl:sameAs rdf:resource="info:lc/authorities/sh2007001751"/>
  <dcterms:created rdf:datatype="http://www.w3.org/2001/XMLSchema#dateTime">
     2007-04-12T00:00:00-04:00</dcterms:created>
  <skos:related
       rdf:resource="http://id.loc.gov/authorities/sh2009009406#concept"/>
  <skos:altLabel xml:lang="en">Harvesting, Metadata</skos:altLabel>
  <skos:inScheme rdf:resource="http://id.loc.gov/authorities#topicalTerms"/>
  <skos:inScheme rdf:resource="http://id.loc.gov/authorities#conceptScheme"/>
  <rdf:type rdf:resource="http://www.w3.org/2004/02/skos/core#Concept"/>
  <dcterms:source xml:lang="en">Work cat.: 2007009006: Cole, Timothy W. Using
         the Open Archives Initiative protocol for metadata harvesting, c2007.
  </dcterms:source>
  <skos:prefLabel xml:lang="en">Metadata harvesting</skos:prefLabel>
  <skos:broader
       rdf:resource="http://id.loc.gov/authorities/sh85066148#concept"/>
</rdf:Description>
<rdf:Description rdf:about="http://id.loc.gov/authorities/sh85066148#concept">
  <skos:prefLabel xml:lang="en">Information retrieval</skos:prefLabel>
</rdf:Description>
<rdf:Description
      rdf:about="http://id.loc.gov/authorities/sh2009009406#concept">
  <skos:prefLabel xml:lang="en">Microformats</skos:prefLabel>
</rdf:Description>
</rdf:RDF>
```

several elements is declared as English using the specially reserved `xml:lang` attribute and the attribute value `en` (the token for English as defined in ISO 639-1[14]).

The example shown in Figure 6.3 illustrates just how easily XML namespace references can be mixed and matched, even to the point of elements being from one namespace while attributes of those elements come from an entirely different namespace. While there are other approaches for referencing semantics from multiple distinct XML metadata grammars from within a single XML metadata record (e.g., using the RDF as described in Chapter 12), the *Namespaces in XML* approach has proven at once powerful and easy to implement, a compelling combination.

SHAREABLE METADATA

Sharing metadata can enhance visibility of collections and resources, which invariably leads to the reuse of digital content in new contexts. Sharing metadata also supports interoperability across collections and enables the repurposing of metadata to support new services. In addition, interoperability facilitates the discovery of new linkages and relationships between and among content objects, metadata, and services that ultimately support building new aggregated digital libraries (Cole and Shreeves 2004; Shreeves and Riley 2008; Shreeves et al., 2006).

Sharing metadata can benefit both users and collection developers / content providers (Shreeves 2007; Shreeves et al. 2006; Stvilia et al. 2004). For collection developers, "[sharing metadata] increases exposure of collection, which broadens user base, and potentially adds collaboration opportunities." For users, quality shareable metadata can "bring together distributed collections with the same topic or in the same format in one place, so users can do one-stop searching. Additionally, users can create their own mash-ups of metadata from different sources" (Shreeves 2007). One impact of the Web has been to diversify the ways that users discover and learn about collections and content. In this environment, the visibility of a digital collection depends more than ever on quality, shareable metadata. The creation of high-quality shareable metadata has become a priority goal for digital collection developers.

Sharing in the Library Domain

According to Karen Snow (2010), the sharing of bibliographic records in the library domain goes back at least as far as 1877, when libraries standardized the size of catalog cards. Eventually, nearly every library used the same size of card. The mid- to late nineteenth century was also when many of the antecedents to today's English-language cataloging rules were first published. The *British Museum Cataloging Rules* (Sir Anthony Panizzi) were first published in 1841. Charles Ammi Cutter's *Rules for a Dictionary Catalog* was first published in 1876. The American Library Association's *Condensed Rules for an Author & Title Catalog* first appeared in 1883. These rules emerged from and formalized a foundation for ongoing community agreements on descriptive cataloging, a prerequisite to useful metadata sharing (Joint Steering Committee for Development of RDA 2009).

In 1901, the Library of Congress initiated its card distribution program to libraries. This had a direct effect on library catalog record sharing and homogenization. As more and more libraries started using Library of Congress catalog cards, the institution became the leader in setting cataloging practices and rules (Snow 2010). The development of MARC in the mid-1960s completely changed bibliographic record sharing yet again. As discussed earlier, libraries routinely share MARC bibliographic records with OCLC, which acts in many respects like a trusted broker for library catalog records. The development of MARC was called "revolutionary" (Tennant 2004) because it helped libraries save money and time in creating and sharing records in an easier way. MARC further formalized catalog record sharing and helped give birth to collaborative, community-based cataloging utilities, such as OCLC.

However, metadata sharing in this model suffers from limitations. Copies of catalog records must be maintained in multiple locations (i.e., in each holding library's ILS and at OCLC). Updates to a record must be either made in both locations simultaneously or made first in OCLC with updated records subsequently exported to the local ILS manually or as part of a scheduled batch update. Arguably more important in the current two-way system between ILS and OCLC, resource descriptions are available only to users of OCLC or local users of the library's online catalog. Historically, there has been no easy way to export or import these records from or to other systems or to the Web more broadly. The advent of worldcat.org has been one response to this issue; however, as discussed above, the reliance on MARC is itself limiting. Non-MARC metadata records created for digitized special collection items are not easily shared using the MARC-based OCLC-ILS paradigm.

The XML-based OAI-PMH model was introduced in 2001 to help online preprint repositories share their (mostly) non-MARC, non-ILS metadata records. Over time, the use cases supported by OAI-PMH broadened, and now many applications, including some traditional library cataloging tools and services (e.g., OCLC and selected ILS implementations) make use of OAI-PMH. To take the maximum advantage of available technologies (i.e., in the spirit of reuse and modularity), the developers of OAI-PMH mandated the use of XML and HTTP (the protocol underlying the Web). OAI-PMH is a good illustration of the utility of the Web and XML for library metadata interoperability.

OAI-PMH has increased the discoverability and use of locally created digital resources, especially locally digitized special collections resources held by libraries and other cultural heritage institutions. Although OAI-PMH requires data providers to disseminate Simple Dublin Core (serialized as XML) as a lowest-common-denominator metadata format, it also allows data providers to share other formats of metadata, as long as metadata records are in XML and can be validated using an XML Schema written in the W3C XML Schema Definition Language.[15] (XML schemas are discussed in Chapters 8 and 9.)

Figure 6.4 illustrates a metadata record disseminated using OAI-PMH. In this case, the descriptive metadata standard is MODS, and the record describes the digital derivative of a book digitized from the print collections of the University of Illinois at Urbana-Champaign. Notice that the default namespace (no-namespace prefix binding) changes partway through this XML document. The root element of the document and all of the elements in the hierarchy of

FIGURE 6.4 MODS XML record harvested from University of Illinois OAI-PMH server.

```
<?xml version="1.0" encoding="UTF-8"?>
<OAI-PMH xmlns="http://www.openarchives.org/OAI/2.0/"
          xsi:schemaLocation="http://www.openarchives.org/OAI/2.0/
          http://www.openarchives.org/OAI/2.0/OAI-PMH.xsd">
  <responseDate>2011-05-24T21:01:15Z</responseDate>
  <request verb="GetRecord" metadataPrefix="mods"
      identifier="oai:oca.ratri.grainger.uiuc.edu:emblemsdivinemor00qua_marc">
      http://ratri.grainger.illinois.edu/oca-oaiprovider/oai.asp</request>
  <GetRecord><record>
   <header>
    <identifier>oai:oca.ratri.grainger.uiuc.edu:emblemsdivinemor00qua_marc</identifier>
    <datestamp>2010-01-22</datestamp>
  </header>
  <metadata>
   <mods version="3.2" xmlns="http://www.loc.gov/mods/v3"
       xsi:schemaLocation="http://www.loc.gov/mods/v3
       http://www.loc.gov/standards/mods/v3/mods-3-2.xsd">
   <titleInfo><title>Emblems, divine and moral</title></titleInfo>
   <name type="personal">
    <namePart>Quarles, Francis</namePart><namePart type="date">1592-1644</namePart>
    <role><roleTerm authority="marcrelator" type="text">creator</roleTerm></role>
  </name>
  <typeOfResource>text</typeOfResource>
  <genre authority="">Emblem books, English-19th century.</genre>
  <originInfo>
    <place><placeTerm type="code" authority="marccountry">enk</placeTerm>
    <place><placeTerm>Great Britain England London </placeTerm></place>
    <publisher>Printed [by Bradbury and Evans] for Thomas Tegg, 73, Cheapside
    </publisher>
    <dateIssued>1845</dateIssued>
    <dateIssued encoding="marc" keyDate="yes">1845</dateIssued>
    <issuance>monographic</issuance></originInfo>
    <language><languageTerm authority="iso639-2b" type="code">eng</languageTerm>
    </language>
  <physicalDescription><form authority="marcform">print</form>
    <extent>vii, [5], 312 p. : ill. ; 14 cm.</extent></physicalDescription>
  <note displayLabel="statement of responsibility">By Francis Quarles.</note>
  <note>Printers' names from t.p. verso.</note>
  <note>Title vignette (author's port.).</note>
  <note>Edited by Samuel Weller Singer.</note>
  <note>Bound with: The school of the heart... 1845.</note>
  <subject authority="lcsh"><topic>Emblems</topic></subject>
  <classification authority="lcc">PR3652 .E3 1945</classification>
  <identifier type="lccn">16018662</identifier>
  <identifier type="uri">
      http://hdl.handle.net/10111/UIUCOCA:emblemsdivinemor00qua </identifier>
  <identifier type="uri">
      http://www.archive.org/details/emblemsdivinemor00qua </identifier>
  <location><url usage="primary display" displayLabel="Full text - UIUC">
      http://hdl.handle.net/10111/UIUCOCA:emblemsdivinemor00qua</url>
  </location>
```

(continued)

FIGURE 6.4 (Continued)

```
<location><url displayLabel="Full text - OCA">
          http://www.archive.org/details/emblemsdivinemor00qua </url>
</location>
<location><physicalLocation>University of Illinois at Urbana-Champaign
          stos</physicalLocation>
</location>
</mods></metadata>
</record></GetRecord>
</OAI-PMH>
```

the document through the element with the local name `<metadata>` are in an OAI-PMH namespace, while the remainder of the elements, from the `<mods>` element on down, are in the MODS namespace. Also notice that both namespaces include an element with the local name of `identifier`; however, as is clear from the values of these elements in this document, the meaning of `identifier` in the MODS XML metadata grammar (`identifier` is a unique string by which the resource being described is known) differs significantly from the meaning of `identifier` in the OAI-PMH XML metadata grammar (`identifier` is the string by which the metadata item is known and retrievable using OAI-PMH). Through the use of XML namespaces, this distinction is made clear to applications processing this metadata record.

Considerations When Creating Shareable Metadata

The advent of OAI-PMH has led to more frequent and interchange of metadata records (including especially non-MARC metadata records) between libraries and other content providers and service providers. Several large-scale projects have made extensive use of OAI-PMH over an extended period of time, such as the *National Science Digital Library*[16] funded by the National Science Foundation and the *Digital Content and Collections* (DCC) research project at Illinois funded by the Institute of Museum and Library Services (IMLS).[17] The success of OAI-PMH also has encouraged libraries to look to other options for sharing metadata more broadly (e.g., the RSS and Atom Syndication protocols). Collectively, this work has generated a significant base of experience with metadata sharing, which informs new metadata interoperability projects. A common finding of projects involving metadata sharing is that the creation of high-quality shareable metadata brings with it unique challenges and difficulties.

Although the community is still coming to grips with all of the distinctions between quality metadata considered in a local context only and quality shareable metadata suitable for reuse in a variety of contexts, considerable progress has been made over the past decade in understanding the most important features and attributes of high-quality shareable descriptive metadata (e.g., Shreeves et al. 2006). One recommendation gleaned from the literature suggests that to create quality, interoperable item-level metadata that can be used effectively outside of its original context, it is necessary to employ an appropriate standard not only for the item-level descriptive metadata but also for collection descriptions, that is, to provide needed context for item-level records (Foulonneau et al. 2005). Enumerated here are several other factors that implementers who want to share metadata need to consider based on the results of metadata sharing projects to date:

1. **Audience:** Who is going to use the resources being described? How do users find/search for these resources? What metadata-based services beyond search and discovery are required to meet the needs of this audience? The optimum elements, encoding schemes, and controlled vocabulary to be used when describing resources are dependent in large part on intended audience and anticipated use.
2. **Standard:** Is there an appropriate available metadata standard to use? Using an established standard improves interoperability and shareability. If there is a standard that is widely used in the community for describing resources similar to what you have, then it may be best to use this standard. If not, creating an application profile (discussed below) may be another option.
3. **Granularity:** What level of description must be supported? When the item is a compound object (e.g., a digitized book comprised of page images and transcripts), are metadata for each page necessary? Will having metadata at the collection level, archival unit, and/or item level help users? Granularity of description decisions should be based on the resource type as well as the cataloging staff available to create the metadata.
4. **Context:** Some information contained in a metadata record that is useful in a data provider's local context (e.g., metadata pertaining to local administration or management of resources) may not be useful for end users or aggregators. In developing metadata dissemination strategies, it is important to think about what information is most likely to be of value to end users and aggregators as distinct from information that is of use only in a data provider's local environment.

Beyond these considerations, there are other factors to consider when creating metadata for sharing. Shreeves et al. (2006) do a good job synthesizing results from multiple projects in their "Moving towards Shareable Metadata" article. This article focuses in particular on shareable metadata in the context of larger, multi-data provider digital libraries, where metadata can easily be reexposed in aggregated environments using OAI-PMH, SRU, or OpenSearch.[18] The article identifies content, consistency, coherence, context, communication, and conformance to standards as the six Cs that are essential to consider when creating and sharing high-quality shareable metadata. The first four Cs, content, consistency, coherence, and context, focus on work flows to create shareable metadata. The last two Cs, communication and conformance to standards, have more to do with the sharing process itself (including the use of metadata standards; interoperability standards, such as OAI–PMH, Z39.50, or SRU; and standard serialization techniques, such as XML). By bearing all six Cs in mind and considering questions of audience, standards, granularity, and context, metadata creators are better equipped to design and implement shareable metadata work flows and successfully share metadata with others.

APPLICATION PROFILES

There are several considerations that go into selecting metadata standards to use for specific digital collections and projects. The nature of the items being described, the content management systems being used, the intended consumers of the metadata, and the format(s) of the digital objects being described are all factors that must be considered. Since there is no one metadata standard that works for every system or that meets everyone's needs, there is often pressure to create a new metadata standard for each new collection or project. However, doing so brings with it added expense and can undercut interoperability; metadata harvesters cannot be expected to understand every one-off, project-specific metadata schema. A proliferation of metadata standards can create problems for large digital libraries that seek to deliver services over aggregations of metadata harvested from multiple sources.

This hazard of too many metadata standards has been a recognized concern for some years, and various approaches have been proposed to address the issue (Chan and Zeng 2006). One approach worthy of an implementer's consideration is the use of a metadata application profile as an alternative to creating an entirely new metadata standard from scratch. An application profile borrows semantics from multiple different but well-known existing metadata standards, refining the meaning of these semantics as necessary for planned use. Such a mix-and-match approach to metadata design provides many of the benefits of a customized metadata scheme while at the same time preserving interoperability and saving the cost of having to start entirely from scratch.

Definition of a Metadata Application Profile

Rachel Heery and Manjula Patel introduced the concept of the metadata application profile in their article titled "Application Profiles: Mixing and Matching Metadata Schemas." They presented application profiles as "a type of metadata schema which consists of data elements drawn from one or more namespaces, combined together by implementers, and optimized for a particular local application" (Heery and Patel 2000). The concept of the application profile also stems from the Warwick Framework, "a container architecture for diverse sets of metadata" (Lagoze 1996).

The *Guidelines for Dublin Core Application Profiles* (DCAP) created by Karen Coyle and Thomas Baker (2009)[19] describe the main components of the DCAP. According to these guidelines, an application profile "is a document (or a set of documents) that specifies and describes the metadata used in a particular application," and documents attributes of an application profile:

- describes what a community wants to accomplish with its application (Functional Requirements);
- characterizes the types of things described by the metadata and their relationships (Domain Model);
- enumerates the metadata terms to be used and the rules for their use (Description Set Profile and Usage Guidelines); and
- defines the machine syntax that will be used to encode the data (Syntax Guidelines and Data Formats). (Coyle and Baker 2009)

The reader is referred to the DCAP guidelines (Coyle and Baker 2009) for further details about each of these application profile components.

Creating an Application Profile

In defining and documenting the components of an application profile, implementers should consider the following:

1. **Object types:** In order to identify the domain, the types of items included in the collection of resources being described should be enumerated. Knowing the object types being described helps to identify the specific semantics that can be used to express type information as well as the most relevant metadata standards and content standards to borrow from for the application profile.
2. **Characteristics of resources:** This encompasses consideration of how users find and use the resources of the collection and a determination of the necessary metadata elements to support these informational needs. As with knowing the object types of the items being described, this is important in coming up with source metadata standards and content standards to consider. Consideration of use cases also helps in developing the set profile.
3. **Digital content management tools:** Not all digital content management tools support every metadata standard. This means that the metadata standard(s) used to describe items can be limited by the system that is used to enable discovery of and access to the items. Designers of application profiles must be careful to check whether a content management system allows locally created elements. For example, the default metadata standard for the digital collection management software CONTENTdm® is Dublin Core, but this system also allows the use of locally created elements. Validation against standards other than Dublin Core must be done outside of CONTENTdm (i.e., CONTENTdm does not validate other standards), but the flexibility to integrate non-Dublin Core metadata does allow the use of application profiles that go beyond Dublin Core.
4. **Metadata standards:** After identifying the object types, determining the characteristics of the resources being described, and deciding where they will reside, the designer of an application profile must then select which metadata standard(s) contain elements that can be used in creating the profile. It is critical to thoroughly research the standards to be used in order to know what elements (properties) can be borrowed from existing standards to create an application

profile suited to the project. As much as possible, the application profile designer should pick metadata standards that have broadly recognized namespace URIs.

5. **How to share metadata:** Finally, an application profile designer must consider the interoperability features of the content management system being used. Without the ability to share metadata records, there is not much point in developing an application profile to facilitate sharing and interoperability. Currently, there are many content management systems that support metadata sharing via OAI-PMH, including both CONTENTdm and Omeka.[20] Additionally, if metadata can be exported in XML format, sharing via other protocols (e.g., RSS or ATOM) may be possible.

Documentation for an application profile typically includes a table summarizing the element names and namespaces included in the profile. For example, the application profile developed for describing Scholarly Works (SWAP) uses namespaces from Simple and Qualified Dublin Core, MARC, and FOAF. In this instance, the implementers of SWAP decided to create from scratch several additional elements they felt were needed to fully describe scholarly objects of interest. These additional semantic labels were created and put into the SWAP (i.e., e-print) namespace, a namespace they controlled. Table 6.1 lists the elements and namespaces that comprise the SWAP application profile.

The Joint Information Systems Committee (JISC) in the United Kingdom, which developed an application profile for e-prints, makes two mappings from SWAP available in its wiki,[21] one to Simple Dublin Core and one to DSpace

TABLE 6.1 Namespaces and semantic labels used in the Scholarly Works Application Profile (SWAP) (*Source:* JISC).

Simple Dublin Core	Qualified Dublin Core	MARC	FOAF	SWAP
type	abstract	funder	name	grant number
title	dateAvailable	supervisor	family name	affiliated institution
subject	hasVersion	editor	given name	has adaption
creator	bibliographic-		workplace-	is expressed as status
description	Citation		homepage	version number/
identifier	references		mailbox	string
language	dateModified		homepage	copyright holder
format	accessRight			has translation
publisher	license			is manifested as
	isPartOf			is available as

metadata. These mappings further facilitate the interoperability of the SWAP application profile with other major metadata standards.

The *Dublin Core Metadata Initiative* (DCMI) Libraries Application Profile is another good illustration. In 2004, the DCMI Libraries Application Profile drafting committee, under the auspices of the DCMI Libraries Working Group (now the DCMI Libraries Community), developed an application profile for the library community. This profile is known by the rubric DC-Lib[22] and is built on a foundation of Dublin Core elements. The group identified five functional requirements for DC-Lib:

TABLE 6.2 Namespaces and semantic labels used in DC-Lib application profile (elements with * have encoding schemes as shown in Table 6.3) (Source: The Dublin Core Metadata Initiative).

Simple Dublin Core	Qualified Dublin Core	MODS
title	alternative	dateCaptured*
creator	abstract*	edition
contributor	tableOfContents*	location*
publisher*	created*	
subject*	valid*	
description*	available*	
date*	issued*	
type*	modified*	
format*	dateCopyrighted*	
identifier*	dateSubmitted*	
source*	dateAccepted*	
language*	extent	
relation*	medium*	
coverage*	bibliographicCitation	
rights*	isVersionOf*	
	isFormatOf*	
	hasFormat*	
	isReplacedBy*	
	replaces*	
	isPartOf*	
	hasPart*	
	requires*	
	isReferencedBy*	
	references*	
	spatial*	
	temporal*	
	audience	

- To serve as an interchange format between various systems using different metadata standards/formats.
- To use for harvesting metadata from data sources within and outside of the library domain.
- To support simple creation of library catalog records for resources within a variety of systems.
- To expose MARC data to other communities (through a conversion to Dublin Core).
- To allow for acquiring resource discovery metadata from nonlibrary creators using Dublin Core.

DC-Lib borrows semantics from the metadata standards listed in Table 6.2. Encoding schemes are used for each element as shown in Table 6.3. For example, the `spatial` element borrowed from Qualified Dublin Core should have values encoded in accord with DCMI Point (http://purl.org/dc/terms/Point), ISO 3166 (http://purl.org/dc/terms/ISO3166), DCMI Box (http://purl.org/dc/terms/Box), or Getty Thesaurus

TABLE 6.3 Encoding schemes used for elements in DC-Lib application profile (*Source*: The Dublin Core Metadata Initiative).

Element	Encoding Scheme(s)
publisher	Role list (http://www.loc.gov/. . .)
subject	Library of Congress Subject Headings Medical Subject Headings Dewey Decimal Classification Library of Congress Classification Universal Dewey Classification
description abstract tableOfContents	URI
date created valid available issued modified dateCopyrighted dateSubmitted dateAccepted datecaptured	ISO 8601(without hyphens) W3C-DTF (with hyphens)

(*continued*)

TABLE 6.3 (Continued)

Element	Encoding Scheme(s)
type	DCMIType MARC list of sources Art & Architecture thesaurus Thesaurus for graphic materials
format medium	IMT The Internet media of the resource
identifier source language relation isVersionOf isFormatOf hasFormat isReplacedBy replaces isPartOf hasPart requires isReferenced By references	URI Serial Item and Contribution Identifier (SICI) ISBN ISSN DOI
spatial	DCMI Point ISO 3166 DCMI Box TGN
temporal	DCMI Period W3D-DTF
rights	URI
location	MARC Code list for organizations

of Geographic Names (http://www.getty.edu/research/tools/vocabularies/tgn). Values for the temporal `element` can come from DCMI Period (http://purl.org/dc/terms/Period) or W3C-Date and Time Format (http://purl.org/dc/terms/W3CDTF).

As of this writing, the 2004 release of DC-Lib remains a *DCMI Working Draft*. In late 2006, the DCMI *Libraries Application Profile Task Group* was recharged with finalizing DC-Lib and submitting it to the DCMI Usage Board for review and registration. However, the advent of RDA has delayed and altered the parameters of this process. In response to the implementation of RDA, the DCMI formed a community Bibliographic Metadata Task

Group (formerly the DCMI/RCA Task Group) charged with defining components of current and emerging library, publishing and related bibliographic metadata standards appropriate as RDF vocabularies for use in developing Dublin Core application profiles and semantic mapping. This work will inform any further work by the Libraries Application Profile Task Group. Additional application profiles are illustrated in the following two case studies.

CASE STUDY 6.1
Creating a Project-Based Application Profile

***Synopsis*:** Many application profiles are created for use in multi-institutional, collaborative projects, but application profiles can also be created for more narrowly scoped, local projects. The University of Illinois Library has been experimenting with project-based application profiles that can help provide more explicit and rigorous, project-specific guidelines for element use, content standard deployment, and best practices for metadata authoring. Taking into account the specifics of the content management system being used to index metadata records and make items available to end users, such guidelines can help ensure that consistent and quality metadata are generated for the items in the collection.

***Illustrates*:** Example of project-based metadata application profile.

The *Amos Paul Kennedy, Jr., Collection*[23] is housed in the Rare Book and Manuscript Library at the University of Illinois at Urbana-Champaign. The collection consists of 71 objects that represent artist's books, postcards, and posters. After the digitization, the collection became 71 compound objects composed of 480 digital images. When creating an application profile for the collection, a major priority was to find an internally consistent way to describe the many different formats and types of resources contained in the collection and to create both compound object-level and image item-level metadata.

Before creating an application profile for the collection, the metadata librarian working on the project followed the process outlined above, beginning with consideration of intended audience, likely metadata standards, object granularities, and collection context. Then the metadata librarian met with the special collection curator most familiar with the collection to discuss object types, characteristics of items in the collection, whether a digital content management tool should be used, and how the metadata might be shared. Given a decision to host the digitized content in CONTENTdm, it made sense to build the metadata application profile on a foundation of Simple Dublin Core semantics (the default for CONTENTdm). Qualified Dublin Core elements (optional in CONTENTdm) were added to the profile to allow the use of element refinements and encoding schemes for elements that were to contain controlled vocabulary values. Each element was then categorized as required or optional, searchable or not, and repeatable or not. Elements requiring controlled vocabulary terms for values were also identified; based on these decisions, encoding scheme requirements for each element were determined. Some elements, such as `medium` and `publisher`, were constrained to take only local controlled vocabulary values. These vocabularies were created by a cataloger in consultation with a special collections curator. Because the application profile was to be implemented by graduate student assistant staff (i.e., graduate student assistants were to be given the job of authoring the metadata records), the last part of the application profile consisted of examples and commentary so that the metadata record authors could adhere to best practices for metadata creation.

The application profile helped to ensure consistent metadata in spite of staff turnover during the time necessary to complete the project. Although based solely on Simple and Qualified Dublin Core, the decisions on encoding schemes and the best practice guidelines reflect well the characteristics of the collection and proved useful in actual practice. The complete application profile contains 19 elements. Table 6.4 is an excerpt from the application profile detailing the use of five of these. Figure 6.5 shows a sample metadata record that conforms to the application profile.

TABLE 6.4 Portion of the application profile created for cataloging the digitized *Amos Paul Kennedy, Jr., Collection*.

1. dc:title

Term Name:	**dc:title**
Label:	Title
Definition:	the title of the resource being described
Encoding Scheme:	n/a
Obligation:	Required
Occurrence:	minimum: 1; maximum: 1
Refines:	n/a
Searchable:	Yes
Comments: (Example)	Most items already have titles assigned; for an item that does not have a title yet, use the text on the title page; or a descriptive title will be used if there is no text

2. dc:subject

Term Name:	**dc:subject**
Label:	Subject
Definition:	the terms that describe the topical content of the resource

(*continued*)

TABLE 6.4 (Continued)

Encoding Scheme:	Library of Congress Subject Headings
Obligation:	Required
Occurrence:	minimum: 1; maximum: unbounded
Refines:	n/a
Searchable:	Yes
Comments: (Example)	Subject terms on geographic and time coverage should go under "dcterms:spatial" and "dcterms:temporal."

3. dcterms:created

Term Name:	**dcterms:created**
Label:	Date of Creation
Definition:	date of creation of the resource
Encoding Scheme:	W3C-DTF
Obligation:	Optional
Occurrence:	minimum: 0; maximum: 1
Refines:	dc:date
Searchable:	no (*if more than half of the objects have this element, set to yes)
Comments: (Example)	Format: YYYY-MM 1994-01 Most of the items only have information of the year of creation. Record the month if applicable.

4. dcterms:medium

Term Name:	**dcterms:medium**
Label:	Material of Resource
Definition:	material(s) or physical carrier(s) of the resource
Encoding Scheme:	n/a
Obligation:	Optional
Occurrence:	minimum: 0; maximum: unbounded
Refines:	dc:format
Searchable:	Yes
Comments: (Example)	pen; oil; paper Will create a local controlled vocabulary for this element. Multiple media are separated by semicolons. Record names of the materials or physical carriers (e.g., ink, paper, wood); do not record more detailed information, such as colors or process of making the resource.

5. dcterms:isPartOf

Term Name:	**dcterms:isPartOf**
Label:	Collection Title

(continued)

TABLE 6.4 (Continued)

Definition:	the title of the collection to which the digital resources belong
Encoding Scheme:	n/a
Obligation:	required (with default value)
Occurrence:	minimum: 1; maximum: 1
Refines:	dc:relation
Searchable:	No
Comments: (Example)	Amos Kennedy Collection (University of Illinois at Urbana-Champaign) Use "dcterms:isPartOf" instead of "dc:relation" to describe the collection name. The institution name is from LC Authorities.

FIGURE 6.5 A sample metadata record based on the application profile for the *Amos Kennedy Collection* exported in CONTENTdm Standard XML format.

```
<?xml version="1.0"?>
<rdf:RDF xmlns:rdf="http://www.w3.org/1999/02/22-rdf-syntax-ns#"
  xmlns:dc="http://purl.org/dc/elements/1.1/">
  <rdf:Description
      about="https://anubis.grainger.illinois.edu/u?/kennedy,217">
    <dc:title>Bible as whipping stick </dc:title>
    <dc:creator>Kennedy, Amos Paul, Jr.</dc:creator>
    <dc:subject>Bible</dc:subject>
    <dc:description>Whipping stick made by shredded pages of the Bible.
        </dc:description>
    <dc:type>Paper arts</dc:type>
    <dc:format>image/jpeg</dc:format>
    <dcterms:medium>paper</dcterms:medium>
    <dc:identifier/>
    <dc:source>University of Illinois at Urbana-Champaign. Rare Book
      &amp; Manuscript Library
      http://www.library.uiuc.edu/rbx/</dc:source>
    <dc:language>English</dc:language>
    <dcterms:isPartOf>Amos Kennedy Collection (University of Illinois at
      Urbana-Champaign. Library)</dcterms:isPartOf>
    <dc:rights>Amos Paul Kennedy, Jr., has given the University of Illinois Library
permission to digitize and make publicly accessible his creative works held in the
Library's collection. Amos Kennedy applies the concept of &quot;copyleft&quot; to
his creative works. Under copyleft, anyone has the right to use, modify, and redis-
tribute his work or any work derived from his work but only if the distribution terms
are unchanged. This means that you are free to use these images for any purpose but
you may not restrict through copyright any resulting works that contain these images
or derivatives of these images. To learn more about Copyleft, visit http://
www.gnu.org/copyleft/copyleft.html. Anyone requesting a copy of one or more of
these images from the University of Illinois Library will not be charged use fees,
but will be charged reproduction costs.</dc:rights>
    </rdf:Description>
</rdf:RDF>
```

CASE STUDY 6.2

IMLS DCC Collection Description Application Profile[25]

Synopsis: In 2002, the University of Illinois at Urbana–Champaign received a National Leadership Grant (NLG) from the IMLS to create a collection registry and item-level metadata repository for digital collections and content created by other NLG projects (Shreeves and Cole 2003). In order to create a collection registry, the library developed an application profile for collection descriptions[24] based initially on the United Kingdom Office for Library and Information Networking Research Support Libraries Programme (UKOLN RSLP) Collection Description Metadata Schema[25] and an early (2003) version of the Dublin Core Collection Description Application Profile. (DCAP further developed its application profile until 2008, when it was confirmed in its current form.) A Web-based template for the collection description was then added to the collection registry application to facilitate the creation of conforming collection description metadata records by content providers and project staff. The collection registry records can be searched in concert with item-level metadata records. Having both levels of descriptive metadata has enhanced search and discovery across the resources described (Foulonneau et al. 2005).
Illustrates: Developing an application profile for collection description.

The first step in creating the IMLS DCC portal at Illinois was to develop a tool that could be used to describe the digital collections. At the time, there were only a few, mostly nascent metadata standards and application profiles for collection description, such as UKOLN RSLP Collection Description Metadata Schema, an early draft of the DCAP, and the Encoded Archival Description (EAD). Researchers at Illinois examined the unique needs of their project, beginning with anticipated use cases, likely audiences, and the need to integrate the collection registry with the planned item-level metadata repository. It was anticipated that between 30 and 50 percent of the collections described in the collection registry would have descriptions of constituent items in the item-level metadata repository. Additionally, it was understood that the collection registry would serve the IMLS community as a view into the digital output of the NLG program to date. This initial analysis of functional requirements and the domain model for the planned application profile highlighted two requirements:

1. It must be possible to express multiple kinds of relationships among collections and between collections and other entities. There are many different relationships between digital collections in the IMLS DCC collection registry and between collections and NLG projects. Some projects consisted of multiple digital collections, while others were just one large collection with multiple subcollections. It needed to be possible to describe all of these kinds of relationships in the collection-level descriptions.
2. While the goal was a collection registry, the scope of the registry required that project-related information be accommodated in the records. Since

> all of the digital collections were created from IMLS NLG-funded projects, it was important to record grant information, including grant number, institution, and responsible agents, alongside essential collection information.

An analysis of available application profiles suggested that although the RSLP profile was well documented and had been implemented to good effect in the United Kingdom to describe physical collections, there had been only limited use of the RSLP standard to describe digital collections. DCAP, on the other hand, though more focused on describing digital collections, was still early in development and did not anticipate many of the location, administrative, and agent attributes that were considered important parts of collection information for the IMLS DCC collection registry. As for EAD, it assumed a more limited model of collections, with a focus on museum and archival collections rather than digital library collections (which were a plurality in the IMLS DCC collection registry).

Based on these analyses, the researchers at Illinois decided that it was best to start with the RSLP schema. The new application profile for the IMLS DCC added a few elements: `<institution>` instead of RSLP's `<location>`, `<identifier>` for IMLS grant identification, `<audience>`, and `<institution.contributing>`. Certain RSLP semantic labels that were used exclusively for describing physical collections, such as `<hours of access>`, were ignored by the IMLS DCC profile. The IMLS DCC collection application profile has been updated over time, with the last major revision in 2008. RSLP elements have been mapped to Simple Dublin Core, Qualified Dublin Core, or DCAP. Currently, the IMLS DCC profile is also used for another metadata-based digital portal at the Illinois Harvest,[26] which aggregates and provides digital collections about Illinois, scholarly works produced by Illinois scholars, and newly digitized books by the University of Illinois Library. The IMLS DCC profile also was a foundation for the DLF Aquifer Collection Registry.[27] The current version of the IMLS DCC Collection Description Application profile uses namespaces from Simple and Qualified Dublin Core and DCAP. For the elements that are unique to the project, the library created an IMLS DCC specific namespace. Elements used from each namespace are shown in Table 6.5.

A sample collection-level metadata record from the IMLS DCC collection registry is shown in Figure 6.6. Note the use of Simple Dublin Core, Qualified Dublin Core, DCMI CAP, and IMLS DCC namespaces. Encoding schemes when used for an element are expressed using the `xsi:type` attribute. Values for this attribute include appropriate namespace prefixes, illustrating the use of attribute values contained in XML Namespaces.

TABLE 6.5 Namespaces and semantic labels used in IMLS DCC collection description application profile.

Simple Dublin Core	Qualified Dublin Core	DCMI CAP	IMLS DCC
title	alternative	itemType	interactivity
identifier	extent	itemFormat	supplement
type	accrualPeriodicity	isAccessedVia	metadataSchema
creator	audience	dateItemsCreated	notes
language	accessRights	isLocatedAt	project
rights	accrualPolicy		managedBy
subject	provenance		administratedBy
source	abstract		participatedBy
relation	spatial		
publisher	temporal		
contributor	isPartOf		
	hasPart		

OBSERVATIONS

In their chapter "The Continuum of Metadata Quality: Defining, Expressing, Exploiting," Bruce and Hillmann (2004) identify the metrics for measuring metadata quality as completeness, accuracy, provenance, conformance to expectations, logical consistency and coherence, timeliness, and accessibility. Although having an application profile can facilitate the creation of quality, shareable metadata, to a large extent the quality of metadata is still up to cataloging and metadata creators. Authors of metadata records, whether these records are destined to be shared or not, must first meet the requirements outlined by Bruce and Hillmann.

As more and more people become aware of the importance of sharing metadata, the community-wide effort for promoting the creation of shareable metadata is getting more attention. Additional quality requirements and best practices for shareable metadata are emerging. Metadata application profiles as alternatives to new, custom from-scratch metadata schemas are gaining wider acceptance. Metadata training, such as the *Metadata for You and Me*[28] project, and the publication of best practices for the user community, such as CONTENTdm metadata best practices[29] and the DLF/Aquifer Implementation Guidelines for Shareable MODS Records,[30] illustrate emerging, experience-based guidelines for documenting metadata application profiles and authoring metadata that are intended to be shared.

Nonetheless, the demonstrated value of metadata application profiles can be overstated. Application profiles that were created from the bottom up to meet

FIGURE 6.6 A collection description record from the IMLS DCC Collection Registry (some elements omitted for brevity).


```xml
<?xml version="1.0" encoding="UTF-8"?>
<imlsdccP:collectionDescription
  xmlns:dc="http://purl.org/dc/elements/1.1/" xmlns:dcterms="http://purl.org/dc/terms/"
  xmlns:cld="http://purl.org/cld/terms/"
  xmlns:imlsdccP="http://imlsdcc.grainger.uiuc.edu/profile#" xmlns:imlsdcc="http://imlsdcc.grainger.uiuc.edu/types#"
  xmlns:marcrel="http://www.loc.gov/marc.relators/" xmlns:xsi="http://www.w3.org/2001/XMLSchema-instance">
  <dc:identifier xsi:type="dcterms:URI">http://imlsdcc.grainger.uiuc.edu/Registry/Collection/?2424</dc:identifier>
  <dcterms:accessRights>Indiana University provides the information contained on this web....</dcterms:accessRights>
  <dcterms:accrualPeriodicity xsi:type="cld:DCCDAccrualPeriodicity">No longer adding</dcterms:accrualPeriodicity>
  <dcterms:audience xsi:type="imlsdcc:Audience">General public</dcterms:audience>
  <dcterms:audience xsi:type="imlsdcc:Audience">Scholars/Researchers/Graduate Students</dcterms:audience>
  <dcterms:spatial xsi:type="imlsdcc:GeographicName">Canada (nation)</dcterms:spatial>
  <dcterms:spatial xsi:type="imlsdcc:GeographicName">United States (nation)</dcterms:spatial>
  <dcterms:temporal xsi:type="imlsdcc:TimePeriod">1950-1969</dcterms:temporal>
  <dcterms:temporal xsi:type="imlsdcc:TimePeriod">1930-1949</dcterms:temporal>
  <dcterms:temporal xsi:type="imlsdcc:TimePeriod">Middle 20th Century (1934-1967)</dcterms:temporal>
  <imlsdcc:project>IMLS Grant: ND-00022, Seeing the color of America:...</imlsdcc:project>
  <dcterms:abstract>Charles Weever Cushman, amateur photographer....</dcterms:abstract>
  <cld:itemFormat xsi:type="dcterms:IMT">image/jpeg</cld:itemFormat>
  <cld:itemFormat xsi:type="dcterms:IMT">image/tiff</cld:itemFormat>
  <imlsdcc:interactivity xsi:type="imlsdcc:Interactivity">Search</imlsdcc:interactivity>
  <imlsdcc:interactivity xsi:type="imlsdcc:Interactivity">Browse</imlsdcc:interactivity>
  <cld:isAccessedVia>OAI data provider, baseURL http://.....</cld:isAccessedVia>
  <cld:isLocatedAt xsi:type="dcterms:URI">http://webapp1.dlib.indiana.edu/cushman/</cld:isLocatedAt>
  <imlsdcc:managedBy>XXXXXX XXXXXX, XXXXXX@indiana.edu....</imlsdcc:managedBy>
  <imlsdcc:metadataSchema xsi:type="imlsdcc:MetadataSchema">Locally Developed</imlsdcc:metadataSchema>
  <imlsdcc:metadataSchema>MODS</imlsdcc:metadataSchema>
  <dc:publisher>Indiana University. Library., Indiana</dc:publisher>
  <imlsdcc:supplement xsi:type="imlsdcc:Supplement">Biographical information</imlsdcc:supplement>
```


(*continued*)

FIGURE 6.6 (Continued)

```
  <imlsdcc:supplement>Timeline</imlsdcc:supplement>
  <dcterms:extent>14,500</dcterms:extent>
  <dc:subject xsi:type="imlsdcc:GEM">Arts-Photography</dc:subject>
  <dc:subject xsi:type="dcterms:LCSH">Photography - 20th century - Exhibitions</dc:subject>
  <dc:subject>American Culture</dc:subject>
  <dc:title>Charles W. Cushman Photograph Collection</dc:title>
  <dc:type>collection</dc:type>
  <cld:itemType xsi:type="imlsdcc:Type">Photographs / slides / negatives</cld:itemType>
</imlsdccP:collectionDescription>
```

a particular need (e.g., the DLF/Aquifer Implementation Guidelines for Shareable MODS Records) have generally been more widely adopted and implemented than application profiles created more from the top down (e.g., the DC-Lib application profile). Application profiles, facilitated by the availability of XML Namespaces, were developed as a response to practical problems and are most useful and effective when created in the context of a practical problem (i.e., in the context of a particular project or initiative). Unlike general metadata schemas, discussed in Chapters 8 and 9, application profiles are not as useful when developed in more abstract contexts.

QUESTIONS AND TOPICS FOR DISCUSSION

1. What are the two most important reasons to have an application profile for your local digital collection or specific user community?
2. Think about the ways users may find digital resources and how metadata can help users discover resources.
3. In what ways do XML namespaces promote metadata sharing and interoperability? Why are they useful for application profiles?

SUGGESTIONS FOR EXERCISES

For this thought experiment, first find a private collection of yours that you would like to create as a digital collection.

1. Think about the domain model for your collection.
2. Select a digital content management tool you would like to use for your collection.
3. Identify a set of elements that best describes the items in your collection.
4. Identify and find namespaces for established metadata standards relevant to how you want to describe the items in your collection.
5. Identify any unique metadata properties or elements that should be created for describing the items in your collection.
6. Think about the encoding scheme and vocabularies appropriate for each element.
7. Create documentation for your data set, use of content standards, and overall application profile.

NOTES

1. http://www.niso.org/standards/resources/Z39.50_Resources.
2. http://www.loc.gov/standards/sru.
3. http://www.openarchives.org.
4. http://www.rssboard.org.
5. http://www.atomenabled.org.
6. http://www.w3.org/TR/1998/PR-xml-names-19981117

7. http://www.w3.org/TR/1999/REC-xml-names-19990114.
8. http://www.w3.org/TR/REC-xml-names.
9. http://www.w3.org/TR/xml-names11.
10. http://www.foaf-project.org.
11. http://en.wikipedia.org/wiki/Uniform_Resource_Identifier.
12. http://dublincore.org/documents/dcmi-namespace.
13. http://id.loc.gov/authorities/subjects/sh2007001751.rdf.
14. http://www.infoterm.info/standardization/iso_639_1_2002.php.
15. http://www.w3.org/TR/xmlschema-0.
16. http://nsdl.org.
17. http://imlsdcc.grainger.illinois.edu.
18. http://www.opensearch.org/Home.
19. http://dublincore.org/documents/2008/11/03/profile-guidelines.
20. http://omeka.org.
21. http://www.ukoln.ac.uk/repositories/digirep/index/SWAP#Mappings
22. http://dublincore.org/documents/library-application-profile.
23. http://images.library.illinois.edu/projects/kennedy/index.asp.
24. http://imlsdcc.grainger.uiuc.edu/cdschema_elements.asp.
25. http://www.ukoln.ac.uk/metadata/rslp.
26. http://illinoisharvest.grainger.uiuc.edu.
27. http://dlf.grainger.uiuc.edu/dlfcollectionsregistry/browse.
28. http://images.library.uiuc.edu/projects/mym.
29. http://contentdmmwg.wikispaces.com/Best+Practices.
30. https://wiki.dlib.indiana.edu/download/attachments/24288/DLFMODS_ImplementationGuidelines.pdf.

REFERENCES

Bruce, Thomas R., and Dianne I. Hillmann. 2004. "The Continuum of Metadata Quality: Defining, Expressing, Exploiting." In *Metadata in Practice*, 238–56, edited by Dianne I. Hillmann and E. L. Westbrooks. Chicago: American Library Association.

Chan, Lois Mai, and Marcia Lei Zeng. 2006. "Metadata Interoperability and Standardization—A Study of Methodology Part I: Achieving Interoperability at the Schema Level." *D-Lib Magazine* 12, no. 6. Available at: http://www.dlib.org/dlib/june06/chan/06chan.html

Cole, Timothy W., and Sarah L. Shreeves. 2004. "Search and Discovery across Collections: The IMLS Digital Collections and Content Project." *Library Hi Tech* 22, no. 3 (August): 307–22.

Coyle, Karen, and Thomas Baker. 2009. "Guidelines for Dublin Core Application Profiles (Working Draft)." Available at: http://dublincore.org/documents/2008/11/03/profile-guidelines

Foulonneau, Muriel, Timothy W. Cole, Thomas G. Habing, and Sarah L. Shreeves. 2005. "Using Collection Descriptions to Enhance an Aggregation of Harvested Item-Level Metadata." In *Proceedings of the 5th ACM/IEEE-CS Joint Conference on Digital Libraries*, 32–41. DOI: 10.1145/1065385.1065393

Heery, Rachel, and Manjula Patel. 2000. "Application Profiles: Mixing and Matching Metadata Schemas." *Ariadne* 25. Available at: http://www.ariadne.ac.uk/issue25/app-profiles

Joint Steering Committee for Development of RDA. 2009. "A Brief History of AACR." Available at: http://www.rda-jsc.org/history.html

Lagoze, Carl. 1996. "The Warwick Framework." Available at: http://www.dlib.org/dlib/july96/lagoze/07lagoze.html

Park, Jung-ran, and Yuji Tosaka. 2010. "Metadata Creation Practices in Digital Repositories and Collections: Schemata, Selection Criteria, and Interoperability." *Information Technology and Libraries* 29, no. 3: 104–16.

Shreeves, Sarah. 2007. "The Dynamics of Sharing: An Introduction to Shareable Metadata and Interoperability." PowerPoint presentation. Available at: http://www.ideals.illinois.edu/handle/2142/2263

Shreeves, Sarah L., and Timothy W. Cole. 2003. "Developing a Collection Registry for IMLS NLG Digital Collections." *DC-2003: Proceedings of the International DCMI Metadata Conference and Workshop*, 241–42.

Shreeves, Sarah L., and Jenn Riley. 2008. "Metadata for You and Me: Current and Emerging Trends in Metadata and Content Sharing." *Digital Library Federation Fall Forum*, Providence, RI, November 13. Available at: http://hdl.handle.net/2142/9158

Shreeves, Sarah L., Jenn Riley, and Liz Milewicz. 2006. "Moving towards Shareable Metadata." *First Monday* 11, no. 8. Available at: http://firstmonday.org/issues/issue11_8/shreeves/index.html

Snow, Karen. 2010. "A Study of Catalogers' Perception of Cataloging Quality, Past & Present." Presentation at ALA Cataloging Norms Interest Group, Boston, MA., January 16.

Stvilia, Besiki, Les Gasser, Michael Twidale, Sarah L. Shreeves, and Timothy W. Cole. 2004. "Metadata Quality for Federated Collections." In *Proceedings of ICIQ04—9th International Conference on Information Quality*. Cambridge, MA, 111–25.

Tennant, Roy. 2004. "A Bibliographic Metadata Infrastructure for the Twenty-First Century." *Library Hi Tech* 22, no. 2: 175–81.

PART III

AUTHORING AND VALIDATING XML

CHAPTER 7

Valid XML (Part I): Document Type Definitions

Chapters 4, 5, and 6 illustrate the versatility of XML with respect to the serialization of structured metadata. XML can be used to serialize metadata conforming to a broad range of standards. Using XML Namespaces, XML also can be used to serialize metadata application profiles that borrow from multiple standard metadata grammars. XML is not a single grammar for expressing structured data; rather, it is a foundational meta-markup language, providing the means by which any number of application-specific grammars can be described and used to serialize structured data. In this regard, the syntax of XML is a bit like the Latin-1 character set[1] used in computing. This character set includes most characters used in Western European languages. French, English, and German have substantively different vocabularies and grammars, yet the three languages build on individualized alphabets drawn from a shared superset of characters tracing back to the classical Roman Latin alphabet.

XML supports the definition and use of distinct application-specific metadata grammars in a formal manner. This allows implementers to enumerate and define the rules and semantics of their specialized XML metadata grammar with sufficient rigor to support automated vetting (*validation*) of XML document instances expected to conform to that metadata grammar. In XML, schemas express the rules and declarations by which implementers describe the semantics and constraints of a logical structure associated with a specific XML metadata grammar. Schemas follow either the *XML Document Type Definition* (DTD) model, which is defined in the XML standard itself, or one of the several alternative XML schema language models available (alternatives to DTDs are discussed in the next two chapters).

Having standard ways to express the rules and semantics of an XML metadata grammar allows catalogers and metadata librarians to make use in their work of more advanced XML programs, such as *validating* XML parsers and editors. Such programs can analyze an XML document instance against a DTD or XML schema to determine not only if the document instance is *well-formed* (something that all XML parsers must be able to do by definition) but also if the document instance is *valid*. A well-formed XML document instance meets the core syntactical requirements of XML. A valid XML document instance is well-formed and also conforms to the rules and semantics of a specific XML metadata grammar as described in a DTD or XML schema.

As a practical matter, this validation is a powerful and compelling feature of XML. The availability of XML DTDs and schemas allow libraries to build modular, flexible work flows for metadata authoring and editing that incorporate automated validation. Such work flows can depend on generic XML parsers and editors rather than on custom tools tied to a specific metadata standard (e.g., not a MAchine-Readable Cataloging [MARC] editor but an XML editor that can read and apply the MARCXML DTD or schema). This freedom also means that it is easier and more economical to make adjustments in metadata semantics and local metadata authoring practices as needed. To enforce new record creation constraints and/or identify which of the records previously created need to be reviewed and modified to meet the newly defined requirements, simply update the DTD or schema for a class of metadata records. The software involved does not need to be modified, only the DTD or schema. Because the approach is more modular—divorcing the definition of metadata grammar from the application doing the validation—the same underlying metadata record creation work flow can be used for multiple projects relying on different metadata standards or metadata application profiles with only minimal adjustments. Simply ensure that the XML metadata record instances for a given project are associated with the correct DTD or XML schema.

This chapter looks more closely at the XML metadata record authoring process, beginning with an examination of some of the trade-offs between basing an application on well-formed XML versus basing it on valid XML. The ease with which simple, well-formed XML can be created and shared is not to be underestimated, but there are times when valid XML is called for. The chapter continues with a discussion of the origin and functional roles of XML DTDs. Inherited from *Standard Generalized Markup Language* (SGML), the DTD approach borrows from the domain of computer programming and is intended to help ensure the completeness and quality of communications involving XML documents. The chapter concludes with a summary of the basics of DTD syntax and semantics and consideration of an illustrative case study describing the creation and use of a DTD for metadata records conforming to the Simple Dublin Core Standard. Ways to validate XML that rely on alternatives to DTDs are discussed in the next two chapters.

WHEN WELL-FORMED XML IS NOT ENOUGH

As described in Chapters 1 and 3, XML document instances consist of markup, parsed and unparsed character data, and entities. Markup is structured according to content models and subsumes the concepts of XML elements and attributes as well as special classes of markup that deal with comments, processing instructions, declarations, and CDATA delimiters. Generally, the XML standard leaves semantics open-ended other than to constrain in a few ways the

FIGURE 7.1 A not well-formed XML document. Screen shot was made using Oxygen XML Editor (http://www.oxygenxml.com).

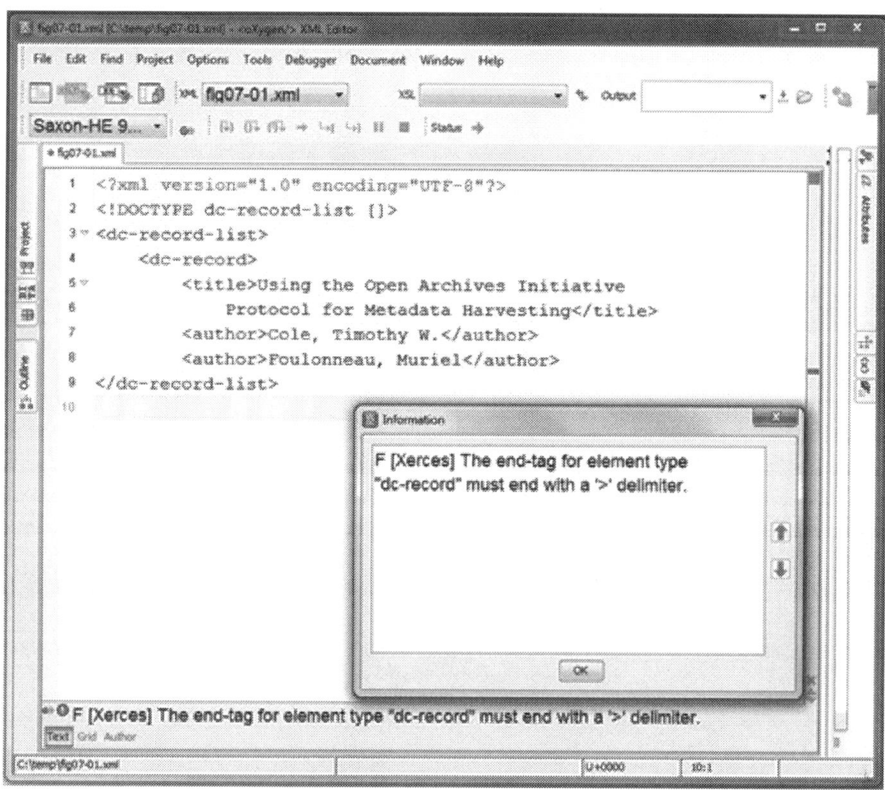

form of semantic labels used as element and attribute names. Instances of XML metadata records are said to be well-formed if they follow these constraints on element and attribute names and adhere to the syntactical rules for nesting element start-tags and end-tags, using attributes, referencing entities, delineating markup, integrating parsed character data, and so on. Figures 7.1 and 7.2 illustrate the difference between an XML document that is not well-formed (Figure 7.1) and one that is well-formed (Figure 7.2). The XML document instance used for this illustration is a brief, incomplete Simple Dublin Core metadata record serialized as XML. As the error message of Figure 7.1 indicates, this particular version of the metadata record is not well-formed because it is missing an end-tag for the `</dc-record>` element. When the end-tag is added, the metadata record becomes well-formed, as in Figure 7.2 (no error message and the small square in the upper right of the Oxygen document window turns from red to green.).

Well-formed XML metadata instances are easy and quick to create. As noted in Chapter 1, almost any plain-text editor can be used (e.g., *Emacs/Carbon*, *Microsoft Notepad*, *gEdit*, and so on). Well-formed XML metadata are useful for small-scale, ad hoc exchange and for small, tightly scoped applications where all the metadata records will be created over a short period of time

FIGURE 7.2 A well-formed XML document. Screen shot was made using Oxygen XML Editor (http://www.oxygenxml.com).

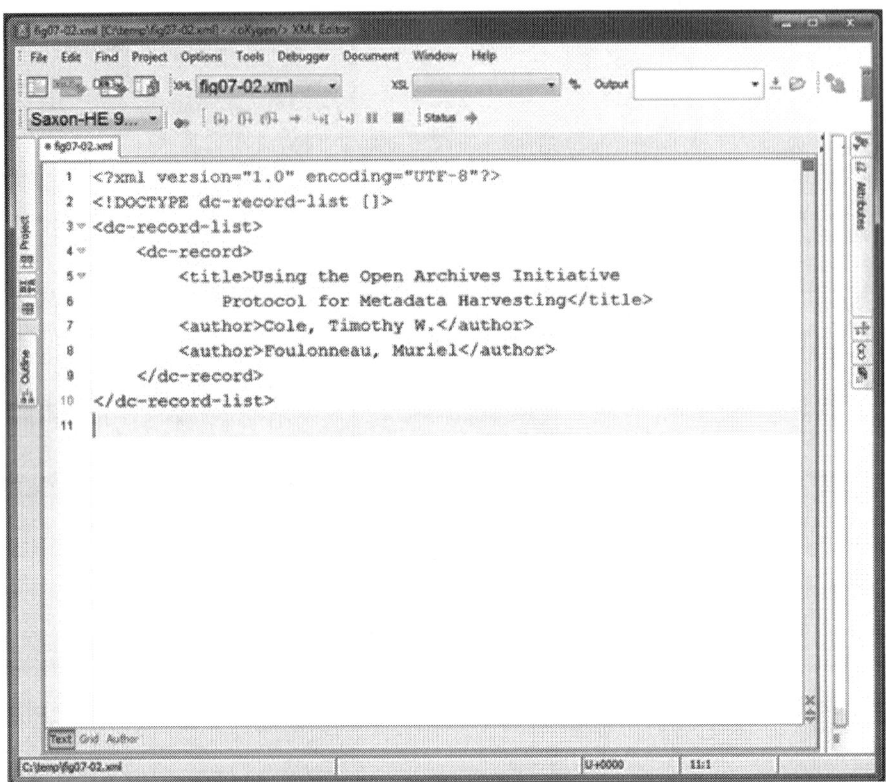

and by a single metadata record author. Semantics and rules to be used for creating metadata records in such a setting can be informal, ad hoc, and documented sparsely or not at all.

However, small and ad hoc metadata-based applications are of limited utility. Because of the dependency on one or two individuals (and their memories of how metadata records should be created for the application), the work flows underlying such applications are difficult to sustain over time. Because metadata strategy is ad hoc and poorly documented (if it is documented at all), such applications are difficult to expand and grow later. For the same reason, such applications also are difficult to enhance later with additional features or functionality. Interoperability is more difficult. What are the options when application scope and sustainability considerations demand more rigor, predictability, and consistency over time?

One approach to improving rigor and consistency for metadata-based applications that rely on XML is to have a computer program generate the XML metadata records required by the application rather than having a cataloger or metadata librarian directly author or edit XML metadata records. This approach works well when metadata for collection items are added not in the form of XML records but rather via a spreadsheet or into a database, either directly or mediated through a Web-based HTML form. In this model, conformity checking of metadata entry (and indirectly documentation of the metadata grammar) is accomplished through rules enforced in the database or spreadsheet or through checking the values entered into the Web-based form. Computer applications can be written to convert what has been stored in a database, index, or spreadsheet into XML metadata records programmatically, often on a just-in-time basis (i.e., dynamically as needed). If the database or form submittal rules are adequate and if the program generating the XML is well written, then the XML metadata generated will be well formed and will conform to the desired standard or application profile. In this approach, the rules and semantics of the metadata grammar being used are checked in the work flow before the XML is generated and used. A potential drawback of this approach is the need to integrate metadata grammar rules and semantics into application-specific database design and/or program code.

The XML alternative to this approach is XML *validation*. In the context of XML, validation begins by capturing the rules and semantics of the metadata standard or metadata application profile being used in an XML DTD or other recognized form of XML schema. The availability of a DTD or schema allows metadata grammar conformity checks (validation) to occur on the XML metadata records themselves. This in turn allows for direct ingestion by generic XML applications and/or direct human editing of the metadata records. This approach is more modular and can be used more effectively to isolate validation from application-specific database design and program code.

An XML document is valid if it conforms to the rules and semantics of an XML metadata grammar as described in a DTD or XML schema. The XML document shown in Figure 7.3 is not valid because the document uses an element `<author>`, which is not declared in its DTD. The DTD, which in this case is included with the XML document, has an element `<creator>` instead of `<author>`. So when the element name `<author>` is replaced with `<creator>` in the XML document instance, the document becomes valid, as shown in Figure 7.4.

Use of an XML DTD or schema is appropriate for work flows that require a cataloger or metadata librarian to create and/or edit metadata records in XML directly or using a generic XML authoring or editing application. Relying on a DTD or schema, generic XML authoring tools and editors can enforce the rules and semantics of the XML metadata grammar as the cataloger or metadata librarian works. An XML DTD or schema is also preferred (or required) when an application needs to ingest XML records directly (i.e., without an intermediate spreadsheet or database being used) or when a goal is to share XML metadata records with another application (e.g., a metadata harvester). Having access to an XML DTD or schema allows XML metadata records to be validated prior to ingestion and indexing by an application or as part of

FIGURE 7.3 Invalid XML document due to use of an element name not declared in DTD. Screen shot was made using Oxygen XML Editor (http://www.oxygenxml.com).

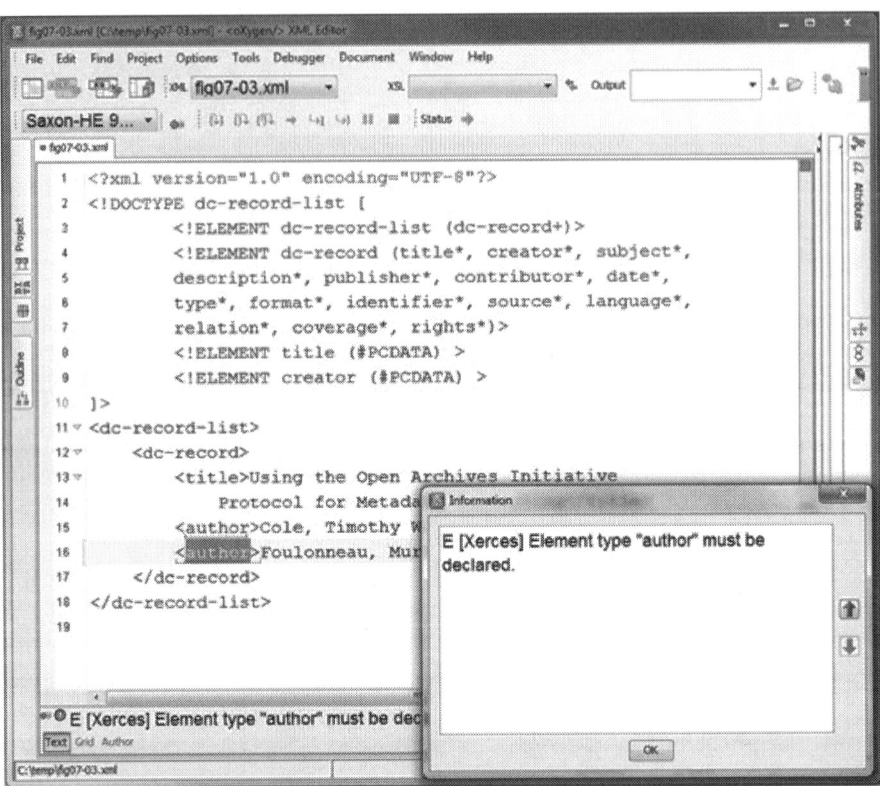

the initial acquisition and processing of XML metadata records requested by a harvester. This is why, for example, the *Open Archives Initiative Protocol for Metadata Harvesting* (OAI-PMH) mandates the use of the *XML Schema Definition Language* as a means to allow validation of XML metadata records as they are harvested.

Even for intra work flow exchange of metadata records within a stand-alone application—that is, the moving of metadata records between application modules or between the client and server components of a single application—the use of a DTD or XML schema can have advantages, among them the ability to validate XML metadata records by integrating generic, ubiquitous tools and parsers. XForms[2] is a *W3C Recommendation* (first issued in 2003) that provides an XML-based alternative to HTML-based forms on the Web. In an XForms application (running in the context of a Web browser), filling out the form generates XML, which can then be validated and, if valid, returned to the Web server. Validation and the ability to reuse off-the-shelf XML tools and established, well-described XML-based grammars are among the benefits of XForms.[3] For large, complex Web-based form applications, XML-based validation of data entered into the form can be easier to set up and maintain

FIGURE 7.4 A valid XML document. Screen shot was made using Oxygen XML Editor (http://www.oxygenxml.com).

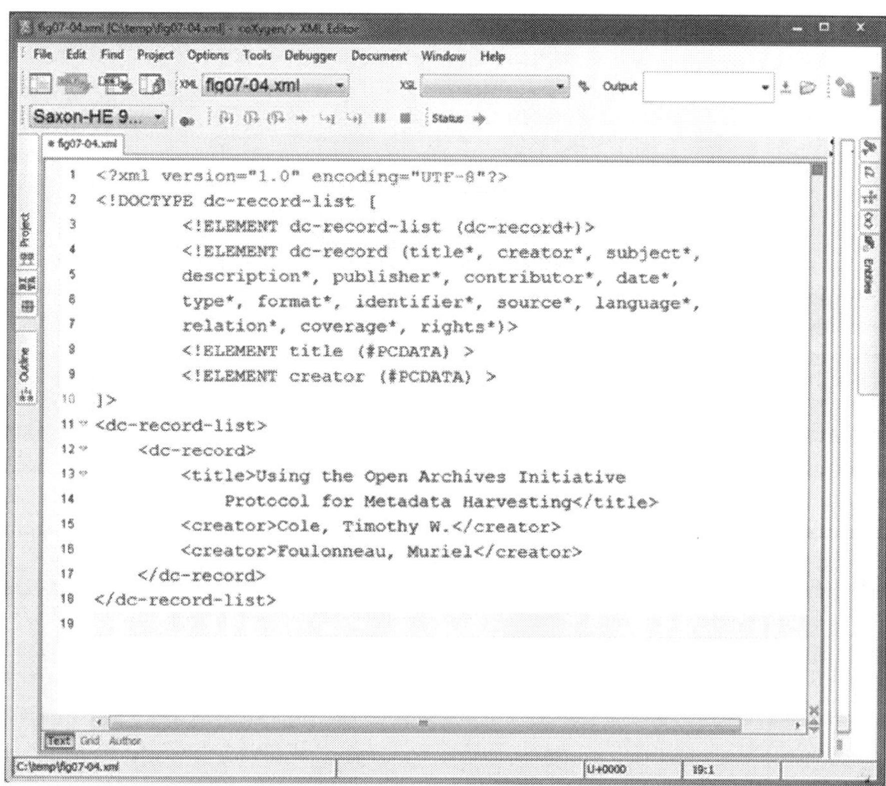

than other, more custom approaches to Web-based form input validation. As an illustration of an XForms-based metadata application, see the Web-based MODS authoring tool[4] created by the Center for Digital Initiatives at the Brown University Library (Salesky and Park 2008).

Valid XML and well-formed XML are not mutually exclusive within a single application. As mentioned in earlier chapters, some content management applications may support both local and community-shared XML metadata grammars. If metadata entry and updating is through a Web-based form connected to a back-end database or index, then the application may not maintain a DTD or XML schema for the custom local metadata grammar. In this scenario, XML metadata records conforming to the local grammar are well-formed but not valid. Simultaneously, the application may be able to export XML metadata records conforming to a community metadata standard as described in a ubiquitous DTD or schema. These exported XML records are both well-formed and valid.

Consider as an example of this model Case Study 5.1 in Chapter 5, which illustrates the ways the digital collection management software CONTENTdm® uses XML metadata. CONTENTdm allows implementers to create their own local metadata semantics (e.g., XML element names). These semantics are local to their instance of CONTENTdm. Descriptive metadata in CONTENTdm are entered through a Web form or through uploading a tab-separated plain-text file (typically converted from a spreadsheet) when working in batch mode. Metadata records in the local metadata grammar are stored and indexed by the CONTENTdm application in a proprietary format. While metadata records conforming to the local metadata grammar can be serialized as well-formed XML and exported for local use, the validation of metadata conformance to a local metadata grammar is done during ingestion into the CONTENTdm index, prior to serialization as XML. CONTENTdm does not generate a custom XML DTD or schema for the local metadata grammar; export of the records in the local metadata grammar generates well-formed but not valid XML. However, as illustrated in Case Study 5.1, CONTENTdm also allows local semantics to be mapped to Simple or Qualified Dublin Core. This mapping in turn supports the dissemination from CONTENTdm via OAI-PMH of valid XML conforming to either Simple or Qualified Dublin Core XML schemas.

DEFINING AN XML METADATA GRAMMAR IN A DTD

To understand the role and genesis of XML DTDs, it is necessary to dig deeper into the model of communication underlying XML. In any exchange of XML metadata records, communication is happening on two levels at once. On one level, the content of the metadata record is being communicated. Simultaneously on another level, information about this content and its structure is also being communicated, such as the division of record content into discrete content objects, what each content object is called, additional attributes associated with some content objects, and so on. This is not a new model of communication. XML inherits this model from SGML, and since well before SGML, typesetting systems used this model. HTML, the first language of the Web, also follows this paradigm. All Web browser applications recognize that text (a content object) contained within an HTML `<h2>` element (level 2 heading) is differentiated from and implicitly meant to be rendered differently than the text contained within an HTML `<sub>` element (subscript). While many information serialization approaches implement this two level communication model, there are two notable features of how XML implements it that are critical to the utility of XML as a serialization approach for metadata and that help explain the rationale for DTDs.

XML Is Descriptive and Extensible

First, markup in XML is meant to be *descriptive* rather than *procedural* or *presentational*. Word processing software and typesetting systems generally rely on procedural markup. (The distinction between procedural and presentational markup is nuanced and not important for this discussion; in this context, the two approaches are lumped together as *procedural markup*.) Procedural markup assumes that a document will be read as a stream of bytes and focuses on the instructions to be followed when processing this stream. For example, procedural markup might tell a system processing a document to render subsequent text in italics until markup is encountered instructing the processing system to resume rendering in a normal font. Such an approach does not distinguish between text that is rendered in italics because it is the title of a book and text that is rendered in italics because it is a term borrowed from a foreign language. In procedural markup, both segments of text are marked up in the same way.

By contrast, *descriptive markup* focuses on giving content objects semantically meaningful labels that explicitly reveal the logical and intellectual structure of a document instance. Descriptive markup distinguishes between content objects that are titles and content objects that are foreign language terms (or between topical subject headings and headings representing spatial or temporal coverage and so on). Descriptive markup does not give explicit instructions about processing or rendering, though systems will often infer rendering from content object definitions.

Thus, with its emphasis on descriptive markup, XML can be useful as a way to serialize structured metadata; however, implementers must be careful to use XML as a descriptive markup language. In practice, the distinction between descriptive and procedural markup can be blurred by how a markup language is used. Theoretically, HTML is a descriptive markup language; however, the elements of HTML were intentionally chosen to be closely tied to the way the content objects of an HTML document should be rendered. In practice, HTML today is typically used more like a procedural markup language than a descriptive markup language. (This is one consideration that makes HTML less useful than XML for serializing metadata.)

The second critical feature about how XML implements the model of simultaneously communicating both content and information about that content stems from the fact that XML is a meta-markup language. In HTML (as in most word processing and typesetting systems), the universe of markup semantic labels and the rules for using these semantic labels are fixed. In HTML, `<h2>` always signifies a second-level heading and `<sub>` a subscript. All element and attribute semantics are intrinsic to the HTML standard, and the semantics of HTML are not intended to be extensible. This is not the case for XML. The extensibility of XML, inherited (like DTDs) from SGML, makes it a meta-markup language and makes it useful for serializing a broad range of documents that conform to different metadata grammars.

Early on, the developers of SGML recognized the importance of emphasizing descriptive markup over procedural markup. This became one of the major ways that SGML (and now XML) differed at the outset from most typesetting systems and most prior document serialization standards. On the other hand, initially, the developers of SGML considered the possibility of defining for

SGML a single, universal, nonextensible set of fixed, machine-independent element names that would be invariant in semantic meaning across all SGML document instances (SoftQuad, Inc. 1991). The difficulties of doing this for the broad scope of documents for which SGML was meant to be used quickly became apparent. Moreover, even should it be possible to define a comprehensive set of element and attribute semantics for all documents, the overhead of requiring SGML parsing software to recognize such a comprehensive set of element and attribute names in order to validate document instances that typically would use only a small subset of these names was seen as unwieldy and a potential deterrent to adoption. Thus was born the vital (to our way of thinking) decision to create SGML and subsequently XML as meta-markup languages that intrinsically support extensibility.

DTDs as Header Files

The need for DTDs (or other kinds of schemas) is mainly a consequence of XML being a descriptive, extensible meta-markup language. DTDs describe (in the context of XML) the rules and semantics of an application-specific grammar. While some features of an application-specific XML grammar can be inferred by inspecting documents conforming to that grammar, to truly enhance the second level of communication described above—that is, to enhance the effectiveness with which authors can convey information about a document's content and its logical and intellectual structure—implementers need a way to describe the rules and enumerate the semantic labels of their particular XML metadata grammar. To enable a computer application to determine with certainty that a particular XML document instance conforms to a particular XML metadata grammar, the computer application needs access to a formal description of the rules of that grammar and the list of allowed semantic labels. While a DTD does not describe the meaning of application-specific semantic labels, a DTD does enumerate the semantic labels allowed in a particular XML-based metadata grammar and does describe the rules for nesting and using the semantic labels of that grammar in a way sufficient to support automated validation of document instances. How do DTDs do this?

The functional model for DTDs was inspired by the concept of *computer program header files*. Many programming languages (e.g., C++ and Java) require programmers to declare the names, types, and sometimes structure of identifiers, constants, object classes, subroutines, and the like before referencing these objects in their code. While these programming languages may allow such declarations to be embedded in the main code, it is common practice, both to facilitate modularity and reuse and to take advantage of preprocessing optimization features of these programming languages, to gather together declarations of this kind into special files, often called header files, that can then be referenced by any module of computer code that makes use of all or some subset of these identifiers, subroutines, and so on.

XML DTDs work in a similar fashion and fulfill an analogous role in applications involving XML documents. Declarations enumerating element, attribute, and entity names belonging to a specific XML metadata grammar are gathered together into a DTD. Integrated into these declarations are descriptions of the rules and structural requirements associated with the application-specific grammar, such as which attributes can be used with which elements, which element is the root element of the XML document hierarchy, which elements are allowed to appear in which places in a document instance hierarchy, which elements and attributes are required and which are optional, and so on. In other words, the first job of a DTD is to formalize the semantic labels (elements, attributes, and entities) that can be used in a conforming XML metadata instance. The second job is to describe element content models and attribute types. As can be seen in the next chapter, DTDs are not the only way to achieve this, but given the historical relationship of XML to SGML, it is understandable that XML would inherit DTDs from SGML as the first option for these functions.

SYNTAX AND SEMANTICS OF DTDS

Classes of Markup Declarations

XML DTDs contain or include by reference *markup declarations*. Markup declarations specify the semantic labels of a particular XML metadata grammar and define the rules for using these semantic labels within XML document instances that conform to the XML metadata grammar. As defined in the World Wide Web Consortium (W3C) XML Standard specifications (i.e., both version 1.0[5] and version 1.1[6]), there are exactly four classes of markup declarations:

- *Element type declarations*
- *Attribute-list declarations*
- *Entity declarations*
- *Notation declarations*

These classes of markup declarations are illustrated in Figure 7.5, and each class is discussed in detail below. In addition to markup declarations, DTDs are allowed to contain XML comments and processing instructions, which are covered in Chapter 3 and not discussed further here. To facilitate modular authoring of DTDs and the updating of DTDs over time, sections of a DTD may be designated *Conditional Sections*. These contain sets of markup declarations that are enforced or not according to whether the section is introduced by the keyword #IGNORE or #INCLUDE. Since this is primarily a matter of convenience, no example of this syntax is included here; the reader is instead referred to section 3.4 of the XML standard for more information about DTD Conditional Sections.

The first two classes of markup declarations mentioned above are straightforward. Element type declarations define the names of the elements included

FIGURE 7.5 Illustrations of markup declarations found in a DTD.

```
<?xml version="1.0" encoding="UTF-8"?>
<!ENTITY % commonAtts "id ID #IMPLIED
                      graphic ENTITY #IMPLIED">
<!ELEMENT metadata ( title, coverImage, creator*, copyright ) >
<!ELEMENT title ( #PCDATA ) >
<!ATTLIST title %commonAtts; >
<!ELEMENT coverImage EMPTY >
<!ATTLIST coverImage %commonAtts; >
<!ELEMENT creator ( #PCDATA ) >
<!ATTLIST creator firstAuthor (true | false) "false"
                  %commonAtts; >
<!ELEMENT copyright ( #PCDATA ) >
<!ATTLIST copyright %commonAtts; >
<!NOTATION GIF SYSTEM "image/gif">
```

in the XML metadata grammar (i.e., the names of the metadata grammar's content objects) and describe their associated *content models* (see Chapters 1 and 3). Attribute-list declarations give names to the attributes of the XML metadata grammar and are used to tie attributes to the elements they elaborate. Entity and notation declarations require a bit more context.

As described in Chapter 3, entities in XML essentially serve as shorthand references or placeholders. XML entities appearing within an XML document instance (but not within an XML DTD) are categorized as *parsed entities* (placeholders for XML content) and *unparsed entities* (entities that reference non-XML content, such as embedded images). Parsed entity names, like character references, can appear almost anywhere in an XML document instance. When processing an XML document instance, applications have the option to replace parsed entity occurrences by retrieving and parsing the parsed entity references as encountered. Unparsed entity names, on the other hand, can only appear as values for attributes of type *ENTITY* or *ENTITIES*. (Attributes of type ENTITIES may have as a value a space-separated list of unparsed entity names, while attributes of type ENTITY may have as a value a single unparsed entity name.) Retrieving the content referenced by unparsed entities, which by definition is non-XML content, is typically not the purview of generic XML processing software (e.g., an XML parser) but rather a task handed off to tools specialized in the relevant format.

When authoring DTDs, it also is necessary to recognize a distinction between *general entity declarations*, which declare entities that may be parsed or unparsed and are meant to be referenced from within XML document instances conforming to the DTD (as described in the preceding paragraph), and *parameter entity declarations*, which declare entities that are always parsed and meant only to be referenced subsequently within markup declarations included in the DTD itself. A common use for parameter entities is to facilitate adding to attribute-list declarations the names and types of attributes that are associated with multiple elements. Parameter entities facilitate the authoring of DTDs and allow for more modular DTD designs.

Finally, to distinguish parsed from unparsed entity declarations, general entity declarations of unparsed entities must reference a *notation name* (e.g., "image/gif"). Notation names specify the format name associated with an unparsed entity. This format name must be declared elsewhere within the DTD in a notation declaration. Notation declarations may also hint at potential helper applications capable of processing data in a particular format.

The Document Type Declaration

The markup declarations of a DTD are bound together as a DTD and referenced from XML document instances through a *document type declaration* appearing at the top of any XML document instance conforming to the DTD (i.e., after the XML declaration and before the first element of the document instance). The document type declaration, which includes the name of the root (first) element used in all conforming XML document instances, may contain the full set of the DTD's markup declarations, may reference a file elsewhere that contains the full set of markup declarations, or may contain some markup declarations and reference others contained in an external file. Any markup declarations contained along with the document type declaration in the XML document instance are known as the *internal subset* of markup declarations and take precedence over any markup declarations contained in an external file (the *external subset*) in case of disagreement. A DTD can be thought of as the document type declaration plus all of the markup declarations it contains either directly (internal subset) or by reference (external subset).

For reasons of reuse and modularity discussed above, the greatest benefit tends to accrue when at least most of the markup declarations are stored separate from XML document instances as an external subset. This external subset can then be referenced by many documents. Any changes in the external subset are immediately applied to all XML document instances that reference the file. However, it is a feature of XML that nonvalidating parsers (e.g., most Web browsers) are not required to retrieve the external subset of markup declarations. A consequence of this behavior is that general entity declarations should always be included in the internal subset of markup declarations. Otherwise, references to entities in the XML document will not be resolved by nonvalidating parsers, leading to a well-formedness error, even if the general entity declaration referenced in the document instance has been included in the external subset.

Document type declarations that reference an external file containing an external subset of markup declarations do so by including a *system identifier* string that corresponds to the relative or absolute URL at which the external file can be found. By convention, the file extension ".dtd" is normally used for such files, and when disseminated from a Web server, such files are assigned a Multipurpose Internet Mail Extension (MIME) type of *application/xml-dtd*. (MIME types, along with file name extensions, determine how applications such as Web browsers process files.) An optional *public identifier*, the canonical name by which the DTD is known, may also be included (partly as a fallback in case the system identifier fails to resolve). The W3C contains a list of recommended document type declarations with canonical public and system identifiers for certain ubiquitous XML-based grammars maintained by the W3C (i.e., XHTML, MathML, and SVG—the Scalable Vector Graphics markup language).[7]

Examples of Declarations Found in a DTD

Markup and document type declarations are syntactically distinct from all other XML markup. They begin with a two-character sequence "<!" and end with a close angle bracket ">". Unlike XML elements, markup and document type declarations are not intended to contain content (i.e., they do not delineate the content objects of a resource), so they do not have separate start-tags and end-tags.

Figure 7.6 illustrates an XML document instance with a document type declaration that includes all the required markup declarations as an internal subset. Figure 7.7 illustrates an XML document instance that includes a document type declaration that references an external file (Figure 7.8) containing the required external subset of markup declarations. The system identifier given is a relative URL and assumes that the document instance and the markup declaration file

FIGURE 7.6 XML document validated against a DTD; markup declarations included as internal subset.

```
<?xml version="1.0" encoding="UTF-8" ?>
<!DOCTYPE sentence [
<!ELEMENT sentence ( #PCDATA  |  name )*  >
<!ELEMENT name ( #PCDATA )>
]>
<sentence>One author of this book is
    <name>Myung-Ja Han</name>.
</sentence>
```

FIGURE 7.7 XML document validated against a DTD; markup declarations maintained in an external file.

```
<?xml version="1.0" encoding="UTF-8" ?>
<!DOCTYPE sentence SYSTEM "myTest.dtd">
<sentence>One author of this book is
    <name>Myung-Ja Han</name>.
</sentence>
```

FIGURE 7.8 The external markup declarations included by reference in the DTD shown in Figure 7.7.

```
<?xml version="1.0" encoding="UTF-8"?>
<!ELEMENT sentence ( #PCDATA  |  name )*  >
<!ELEMENT name  (  #PCDATA  )>
```

FIGURE 7.9 Three document type declarations.

```
<!DOCTYPE sentence [
      <!ELEMENT sentence  ( #PCDATA | name )* >
      <!ELEMENT name  ( #PCDATA )>
]>

<!DOCTYPE metadata SYSTEM "myTestMeta.dtd">

<!DOCTYPE metadata SYSTEM "myTestMeta.dtd" [
    <!ENTITY myBookCover SYSTEM "http://myuni.....gif" NDATA GIF>
    <!ENTITY myCopyright "&#0169; copyright 2012 by me">
]>
```

are in the same folder. The content of the XML document instances shown in Figures 7.6 and 7.7 is the same as for Figure 1.2 in Chapter 1.

Taking a closer look at the document type and element type declarations above reveals that the declarations shown are in the general form of a declaration open delimiter ("<!"), a key word indicating the kind of declaration, a space, a primary parameter (usually a semantic label), more space-delineated parameters specific to the kind of declaration, and a declaration closing delimiter (">"). This general form is followed by the other types of markup declarations as well. Document type declarations and each kind of markup declaration are described and illustrated below. For more complete documentation, see the XML standard specifications themselves.

The first parameter of a document type declaration is always the name of the root element for the XML metadata grammar. The name of the XML root element for all document instances conforming to the DTD (i.e., sharing the same document type declaration) will be the same and must match the element name of the document type declaration. The rest of the document type declaration may include (in various permutations) a public identifier enclosed in quotes, the word `SYSTEM` followed by the URL in quotes of a file containing a set of markup declarations, and/or a set of markup declarations enclosed within square brackets. The three examples shown in Figure 7.9 illustrate the syntax and semantics of document type declarations. The first declares the root element to be `<sentence>` and includes all necessary markup declarations as part of an internal subset. The second illustration declares the root element to be `<metadata>` and references all markup declarations as part of an external subset. The last illustration also uses `<metadata>` as the root element name and incorporates both an internal subset and reference to an external subset of markup declarations.

The first parameter of an element type declaration is always the name (semantic label) of the element. The remaining parameters of the declaration give the content type and, if applicable, content model for the element. The content type can be expressed in a variety of ways. Certain keywords, such as EMPTY, #PCDATA, and so on, can be used to convey the content type.

FIGURE 7.10 Four examples of element type declarations.

```
<!ELEMENT metadata ( title, coverImage, creator*, copyright ) >
<!ELEMENT title ( #PCDATA ) >
<!ELEMENT coverImage EMPTY >
<!ELEMENT author (#PCDATA | lastName | firstName)* >
```

EMPTY denotes that the element is always empty (i.e., cannot contain child elements or any parsed character data, as discussed in Chapter 3 for this content type). The content type for elements that contain only parsed character data is denoted by the key word #PCDATA in parentheses. Element content models are described by listing allowed child elements in the order they should appear in a comma-separated list enclosed in parentheses. Nesting of lists of allowed child elements is accommodated with nested parentheses. The optional character following a child element name or a list of child element names enclosed in parentheses governs whether the element or the content particles in the list together may occur one or more times ("+"), zero or more times ("*"), or zero or one times ("?"). The absence of such an operator (referred to as an *occurrence indicator*) means that the element or content particle must appear exactly once. To indicate when a choice of elements is allowed in a sequence, child element names in a list are separated with a pipe symbol ("|") rather than a comma. Nested parentheses are used to manage groupings of element lists, choices, and so on. Figure 7.10 illustrates examples of basic element type declarations. A mixed content model can be indicated by the keyword #PCDATA plus the pipe symbol followed by element name(s), but there is no way to use an XML DTD to enforce order between parsed character data and elements in a mixed content model; thus, the last example in Figure 7.10 would allow `<author>` to contain a `<lastName>` element, followed by punctuation and white space (parsed character data), followed by a `<firstName>` element, but it would also allow an order of parsed character data, `<firstName>`, `<lastName>`, and parsed character data.

An attribute-list declaration simultaneously defines one or more attributes and binds this list of attributes to an element. The first parameter of an attribute-list declaration is the name of the element to which the attributes in the list will be bound. Then, for each attribute in the attribute list, an attribute name is provided, followed by the type of attribute or an enumeration of allowed values the attribute can take, followed by the default value of the attribute or a key word indicating whether the attribute is required, optional (#IMPLIED), or fixed (i.e., always a fixed value). A single attribute-list declaration is used to declare and describe all attributes associated with a particular element. Figure 7.11 shows two attributes, `firstAuthor` and `id`, associated with an element named `<creator>`. When many elements can have many of the same attributes, parameter entities are often used for convenience.

FIGURE 7.11 An example of an attribute-list declaration.

```
<!ATTLIST creator firstAuthor (true | false) "false"
                  id ID #REQUIRED>
```

FIGURE 7.12 An example of a parsed general entity declaration.

```
<!ENTITY myCopyright "&#0169; copyright 2012 by me">
```

The first parameter of a general entity declaration is the name of the entity. For internal parsed general entities, the entity name is followed by the replacement string. The replacement string is the snippet of XML that should replace any references to the entity appearing in document instances, as in Figure 7.12. As described in Chapter 3, a parsed general entity is referenced by preceding the entity name with an ampersand and terminating the entity name with a semicolon. Thus, in the example of Figure 7.12, the entity would be referenced as "`&myCopyright;`". Notice that the replacement string in this instance includes a character reference ("`©`") as a placeholder for the copyright symbol ("©").

Alternatively, when declaring an external parsed entity or an unparsed entity (all of the latter are external by virtue of being non-XML), the entity name is followed by the word SYSTEM or a public identifier and then the word SYSTEM. The word SYSTEM is then followed by a system identifier providing the location of the parsed or unparsed content that can be substituted for the entity reference in the XML document instance. Unparsed entity declarations end with the key word NDATA and then the name of the notation for the content referenced. Figure 7.13 is an example of an unparsed general entity declaration, in this case referring to a GIF image.

In parameter entity declarations, the name of the parameter entity is preceded by a percent symbol ("%"), as illustrated in Figure 7.14. This tells processing applications that this is a parameter rather than a general entity declaration. All parameter entities are internal (to the DTD) parsed entities. The replacement text, in this example the names and types of two attributes that are to be allowed on multiple elements, comes after the parameter entity name. Once this parameter entity has been declared, it can be referenced ("`%commonAtts;`") in subsequent declarations in the DTD—in this case in an attribute-list declaration, as illustrated in Figure 7.17.

The first parameter of a notation declaration is the identifier for the notation being declared in the context of the DTD. This is followed optionally by a public identifier, then the word SYSTEM, and finally as a quoted string the name of the format, usually a MIME type, associated with the notation. Figure 7.15 is an example of a notation declaration for GIF-formatted images.

FIGURE 7.13 An example of an unparsed general entity declaration.

```
<!ENTITY myBookCover SYSTEM "http://.../bookCover.gif" NDATA GIF>
```

FIGURE 7.14 An example of a parameter entity declaration.

```
<!ENTITY % commonAtts "id ID #IMPLIED
                       graphic ENTITY #IMPLIED">
```

FIGURE 7.15 An example of a notation declaration.

```
<!NOTATION GIF SYSTEM "image/gif">
```

FIGURE 7.16 XML document referencing an external subset of declarations and simultaneously including an internal subset of declarations.

```
<?xml version="1.0" encoding="UTF-8" ?>
<!DOCTYPE metadata SYSTEM "myTestMeta.dtd" [
    <!ENTITY myBookCover SYSTEM
        "http://myuniversity.edu/myHomepage/graphics/bookCover.gif" NDATA GIF>
    <!ENTITY myCopyright "&#0169; copyright 2012 by me">
]>
<metadata>
    <title id="Book12345">XML is Fun!</title>
    <coverImage graphic="myBookCover"/>
    <creator firstAuthor="true">Han, Myung-Ja</creator>
    <creator>Cole, Timothy</creator>
    <copyright>&myCopyright;</copyright>
</metadata>
```

FIGURE 7.17 An external subset of markup declarations illustrating the use of a parameter entity.

```
<?xml version="1.0" encoding="UTF-8"?>
<!ENTITY % commonAtts "id ID #IMPLIED
                        graphic ENTITY #IMPLIED">
<!ELEMENT metadata ( title, coverImage, creator*, copyright ) >
<!ELEMENT title ( #PCDATA ) >
<!ATTLIST title %commonAtts; >
<!ELEMENT coverImage EMPTY >
<!ATTLIST coverImage %commonAtts; >
<!ELEMENT creator ( #PCDATA ) >
<!ATTLIST creator firstAuthor (true | false) "false"
                   %commonAtts; >
<!ELEMENT copyright ( #PCDATA ) >
<!ATTLIST copyright %commonAtts; >
<!NOTATION GIF SYSTEM "image/gif">
```

Figures 7.16 and 7.17 (repeated from Figure 7.5) consolidate the illustrations above into a complete albeit very simple example. Notice that the internal subset of markup declarations in Figure 7.16 includes the general entity declarations for `&myBookCover;` (an unparsed entity) and `&myCopyright;` (a parsed entity). As mentioned above, this is necessary to avoid a well-formedness error when viewing the XML document instance in a non-validating XML parser, such as a Web browser.

CASE STUDY 7.1
A DTD for Simple Dublin Core

Synopsis: A DTD describes the structure and grammar of a class of XML documents: the names and content models or types of elements, attributes, and entities used; how the data used for each element and attribute should be created and used; and any other information required to validate conforming XML document instances. The XML metadata grammar described in a DTD should be assembled and agreed to within an implementer community before the actual DTD construction. In 1999, as part of a museum metadata test bed project involving multiple institutions, the Consortium for the Computer Interchange of Museum Information (CIMI)[8] developed a DTD for Simple Dublin Core[9] that could be used to facilitate cross-domain, cross-institutional sharing of digitized cultural heritage resources. This case study introduces the CIMI's Simple Dublin Core DTD, illustrating its construction and how it can be used in creating Dublin Core XML metadata records.
Illustrates: DTD for Simple Dublin Core; Dublin Core data model; DTD; XML documents.

The first step in creating a DTD is to design and define the application-specific XML grammar appropriate for use in support of a particular project or recognized domain. This grammar should reflect project or community consensus as to semantic labels, content models, attributes, and so on. Ideally, best-practice and/or usage guidelines should accompany release of the DTD as a way to provide essential context for those who will create metadata records conforming to the DTD.

In existence from 1990 until the end of 2003, the CIMI was an organization dedicated to the goal of bringing museum information to the largest possible audience. In 1999, in support of this goal, the CIMI created and published on the Web a *Guide to Best Practice: Dublin Core*.[10] Included as an appendix to this guide was an XML DTD for Simple Dublin Core created by the authors of the guide. The markup declarations of the CIMI DTD for Simple Dublin Core are depicted in Figure 7.18 as re-created in a current version of the Oxygen XML editor. This XML DTD represented one of the first attempts to formalize an approach for serializing Simple Dublin Core metadata in XML. (The Dublin Core Metadata Initiative (DCMI) did not formally release the first edition of its *Using Dublin Core in XML*, with accompanying DTD, until July 2000.[11]) In the absence of a DCMI XML DTD or other schema, developing its own DTD was the right approach for CIMI to take to establish a baseline standard for the community and for use in its project.

While the authors of the CIMI DTD did not have tools as sophisticated as Oxygen when creating the DTD, Figure 7.19 illustrates the process of re-creating the CIMI Simple Dublin Core DTD today in a tool like Oxygen. As

FIGURE 7.18 CIMI's Simple Dublin Core DTD. Screen shot was made using Oxygen XML Editor (http://www.oxygenxml.com).

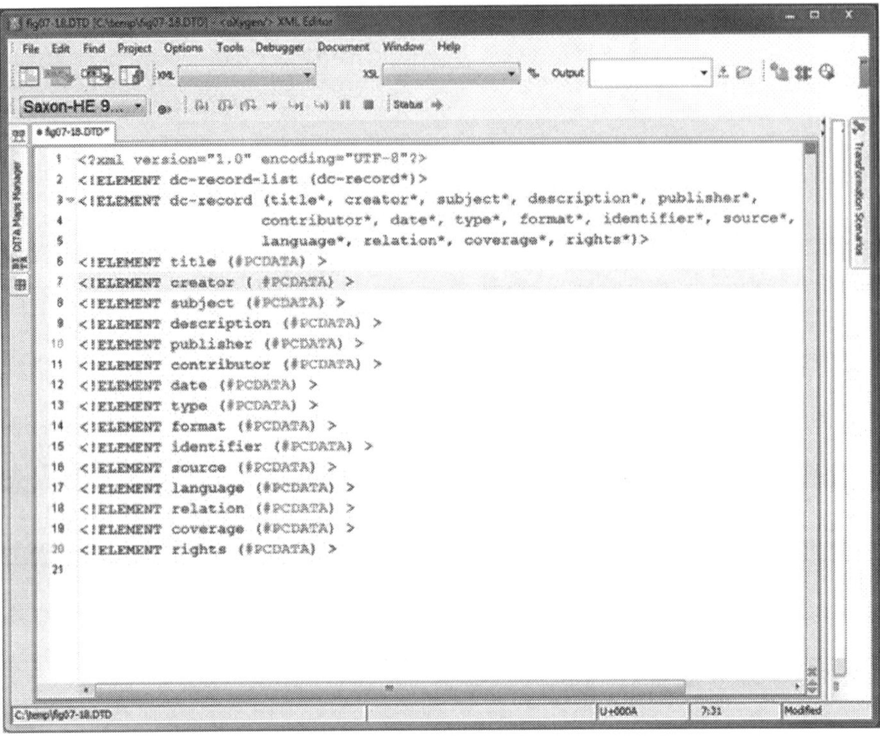

FIGURE 7.19 Authoring markup declarations of a DTD in Oxygen. Screen shot was made using Oxygen XML Editor (http://www.oxygenxml.com).

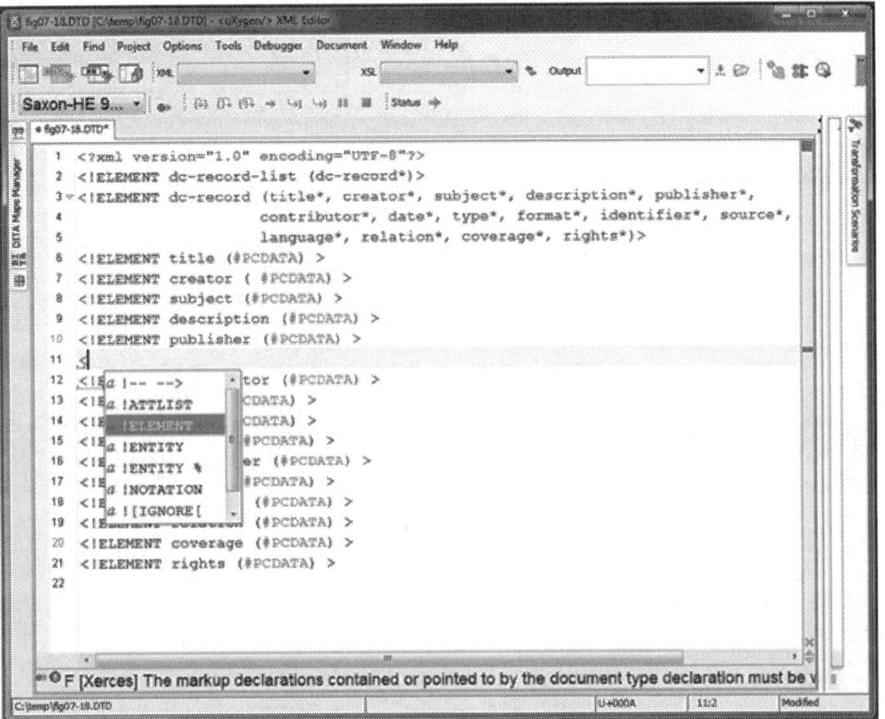

shown in Figure 7.19, when authoring or editing a DTD, Oxygen lists (as helpful hints) the markup declarations of DTD that can be used at the current cursor location in the DTD as it is being authored. As you create the DTD, Oxygen also checks the internal consistency of the DTD being created and warns, for example, if a content model references an undeclared element. This greatly facilitates DTD authoring.

A DTD always includes a document type declaration, `<DOCTYPE>`. For this specific case, the root element as declared in the document type declaration is called "dc-record-list." Markup declarations (in the internal or external subset) list the other elements that can be used in conforming metadata records. The root element `<dc-record-list>` is allowed to contain zero or more (*) `<dc-record>` elements, that is, zero or more Dublin Core XML records. The DTD then lists allowed children of the `<dc-record>` element. In this example, any of the 15 Simple Dublin Core elements are allowed as children of the `<dc-record>` element. All of these elements can be used zero or more times in the `<dc-record>` node (*); that is, the `<dc-record>` element is actually not required by the DTD to have any child elements. (Note that with a relatively minor modification to the declared content model for the `<dc-record>` element—moving the occurrence indicator to the outside the parentheses and changing it to "+"—the DTD could have been constructed to require each `<dc-record>` node to have at least one child element.)

The CIMI DTD for Simple Dublin Core is a relatively simple XML DTD. DTDs can declare and define attributes, entities, and more complex hierarchical structures. However, since Simple Dublin Core content objects do not require elaboration, no attribute declarations are needed in this instance. The external subset of the DTD (i.e., the markup declarations shown in Figure 7.18) consists only of a list of element declarations. Since all Simple Dublin Core content objects are by definition simple strings, the content type of all 15 Simple Dublin Core elements is specified in this DTD as parsed character data, such as `<!ELEMENT title (#PCDATA) >`. Entity declarations are typically not needed for Simple Dublin Core records but can be added when required for specific conforming metadata records. This is done by including entity declarations within the document instance as part of the internal subset, as illustrated in Figure 7.20.

Given the XML DTD, Oxygen can provide hints and otherwise facilitate the creation of conforming metadata records. In order to create a metadata record in Oxygen using CIMI's DTD, a cataloger would start off the record with an XML declaration, `<?xml version="1.0" ?>`. As described in Chapter 3, the XML declaration declares the version of XML specification to which the XML document conforms and may optionally declare encoding used (default is UTF-8). The document type declaration comes after the XML declaration, followed by the root of the XML metadata record, `<dc-record-list>`. The metadata node, `<dc-record>`, follows the root

FIGURE 7.20 When authoring an XML document instance in Oxygen, the tool shows elements that have been declared in DTD. Screen shot was made using Oxygen XML Editor (http://www.oxygenxml.com).

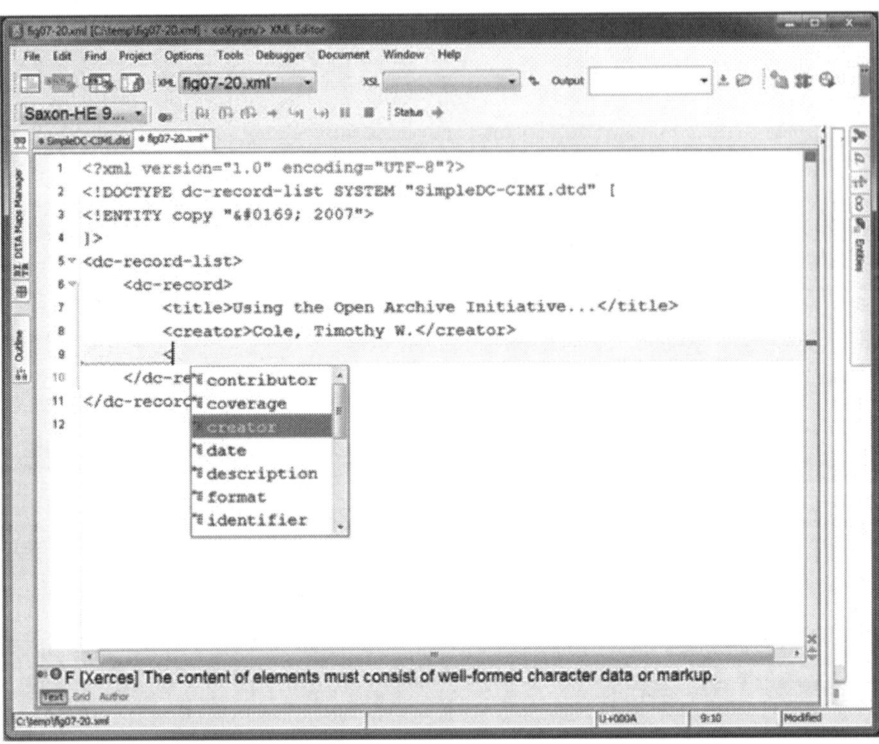

FIGURE 7.21 Dublin Core record created in Oxygen to conform to a DTD. Screen shot was made using Oxygen XML Editor (http://www.oxygenxml.com).

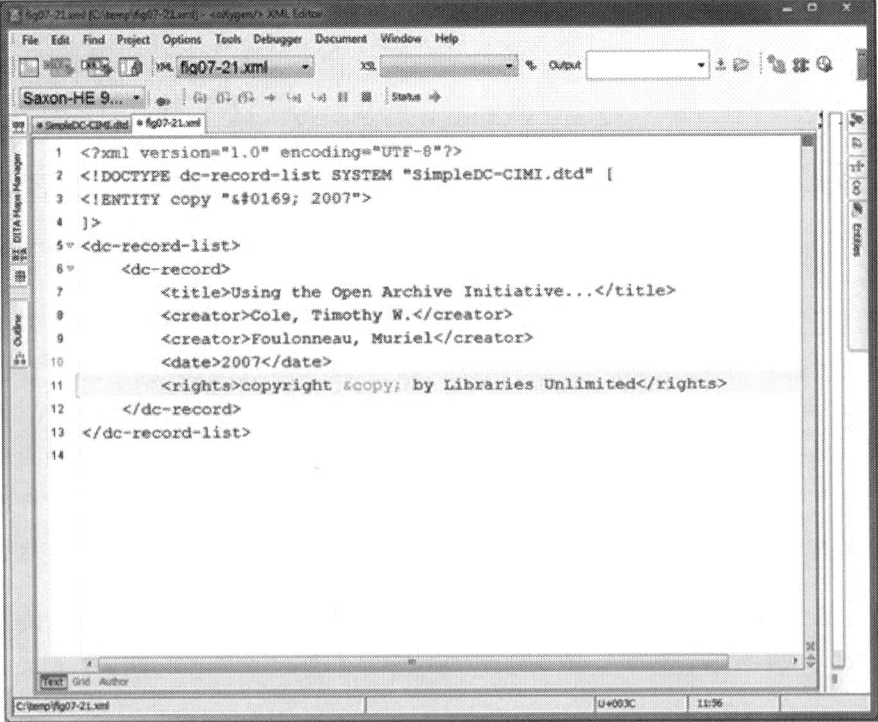

element. Any Simple Dublin Core elements needed for describing the resource are added between the `<dc-record>` and `</dc-record>` tags.

As illustrated in Figure 7.20, when authoring or editing an XML document instance that includes or references markup declarations (e.g., as found in a DTD), Oxygen shows possible elements that can be used at the current cursor location in the XML document as you edit. This facilitates editing and helps to avoid the introduction of errors that would invalidate the XML document instance. A complete (albeit brief) and valid Simple Dublin Core XML metadata record created using Oxygen is shown in Figure 7.21. Note that the external subset of markup declarations, SimpleDC-CIMI.dtd, is included by reference. Note also the entity declaration for "©" (a character reference to Unicode for the copyright symbol) is included in the internal subset of the metadata record illustrated.

QUESTIONS AND TOPICS FOR DISCUSSION

1. What are the potential benefits of using DTDs when authoring or managing metadata records serialized as XML?
2. What are the potential trade-offs and limitations of using DTDs when authoring or managing XML metadata records?
3. When would you use ENTITY declarations in your DTDs? When would you use ATTLIST declarations in your DTDs? How do these help you in creating and processing your XML metadata?

SUGGESTIONS FOR EXERCISES

1. Expand the CIMI's Simple Dublin Core DTD with element refinements from the Qualified Dublin Core standard.
2. Create a new Dublin Core document using CIMI's Simple Dublin Core DTD; that is, create a metadata record in XML that validates against the DTD.
3. Think about what kind of entity declarations you might want to add for documents conforming to the CIMI DTD and how you would do it. Make some conforming metadata records that include entities.

NOTES

1. Latin-1 is more formally a standard of the International Organization for Standardization, *ISO/IEC 8859-1:1998, Information technology—8-bit single-byte coded graphic character sets—Part 1: Latin alphabet No. 1.* (http://www.iso.org/iso/iso_catalogue/catalogue_ics/catalogue_detail_ics.htm?csnumber=28245).
2. http://www.w3.org/TR/xforms.
3. http://www.w3.org/MarkUp/Forms/2003/xforms-faq.html.
4. http://dl.lib.brown.edu:8083/editor.
5. http://www.w3.org/TR/REC-xml.

6. http://www.w3.org/TR/xml11.
7. http://www.w3.org/QA/2002/04/valid-dtd-list.html.
8. http://www.cni.org/pub/CIMI/part1.html.
9. http://www.ukoln.ac.uk/interop-focus/activities/z3950/int_profile/bath/draft/Appendix_D__XML_DTD.htm.
10. http://ddc.aub.edu.lb/projects/museum-catalog/background-info/meta_bestprac_v1_1_210400.pdf.
11. http://dublincore.org/documents/2000/07/14/dcmes-xml.

REFERENCES

Salesky, Winona, and Michael Park. 2008. "XForms for Metadata Creation." Paper presented at the Code4Lib 2008 conference, Portland, OR, February 25–28. Available at: http://code4lib.org/conference/2008/salesky

SoftQuad, Inc. 1991. *The SGML Primer*. 3rd ed. Toronto: SoftQuad, Inc.

CHAPTER 8

Valid XML (Part II): XML Schemas

XML schema documents provide structured views of application-specific grammars built on top of XML's foundational rules and syntax. In the context of this discussion of metadata and XML, a schema can be thought of as a kind of road map to an XML metadata grammar. *XML Document Type Definitions* (DTDs) fit this definition of schema and are in fact a class of XML schema. However, illustrative of one of the major ways in which XML is more suited for use on the Web than generic *Standard Generalized Markup Language* (SGML), DTDs are not the only class of schema supported by XML. XML supports other kinds of schemas as well. Typically, as is done in this book, XML DTDs are treated separately from and given precedence over other classes of XML schema when introducing XML to implementers. Because of the unique syntax of DTD *document type* and *markup declarations* and because the grammar of DTDs is defined in the XML specification itself, XML DTDs require separate attention. There is, however, nothing intrinsically better about XML DTDs as compared to other classes of XML schemas. As a practical matter, a DTD is just one option for describing an XML metadata grammar. In fact, in the development of XML-based metadata applications, DTDs have been largely supplanted in recent years by other forms of XML schema.

Each class of XML schema is defined by its own semantics and rules, its own *schema description grammar* (also known as a *schema language*). Schema description grammars can vary significantly one from another and from the grammar of DTDs, but all non-DTD XML schema grammars must conform to the XML standard's well-formedness requirements (and therefore all non-DTD XML schemas are well-formed XML document instances by definition).When using XML, implementers are able to describe their custom, application-specific metadata grammars using their preferred—or even their own unique custom—XML schema description grammar. This approach to schemas represents another form of XML extensibility. By contrast, generic SGML requires the use of DTDs and does not offer the option of using alternative schema description grammars for validation.

As with XML DTDs, the primary practical use of non-DTD XML schemas is to support document instance validation, that is, metadata record validation in the context of this discussion of XML and metadata. An XML validating parser that understands a particular schema description grammar, given a schema written in this grammar, is able to determine whether an XML metadata record is valid relative to the schema provided. Still, if validation is the main goal, why is there the need for alternatives to DTDs?

At a high level, two rationales are typically offered. First, XML DTDs conform to a different syntax than the rest of XML. This means that authors (and applications) capable of creating and editing well-formed XML document instances will not necessarily be able to create or read XML DTDs. Second, DTDs have significant functional and expressiveness limitations, especially relating to *XML Namespaces* and *data typing*. It is straightforward in an XML DTD to designate that an element called `<zipCode>` should contain parsed character data; it is not practical to specify in an XML DTD that the parsed character data contained by such an element must be exactly five numeric digits. Nor is it possible in a useful way to use DTDs to validate XML document instances incorporating elements and attributes from multiple XML Namespaces.

Given the long history of work with SGML DTDs, the limitations of XML DTDs were well known even before the XML specification became a World Wide Web Consortium (W3C) Recommendation. The potential for alternatives to DTDs was built into the specification, and this resulted almost immediately after the publication of the XML specification in the creation of a plethora of alternative XML schema languages. The online XML Schemas page edited by Robin Cover and hosted by the Organization for the Advancement of Structured Information Standards[1] still lists more than a dozen major XML schema grammars that have been proposed and/or implemented by the XML user community.

This chapter continues the discussion begun in Chapter 7 of valid XML and the authoring of XML metadata by considering alternatives to XML DTDs. First, some of the limitations of XML DTDs that led to the creation of alternative options for validation are examined. Then the basic semantics and structures of schemas conforming to the W3C XML Schema Definition Language,[2] the best-supported and most ubiquitous alternative to XML DTDs, are discussed and illustrated. By convention, a schema document conforming to the W3C XML Schema Definition Language is referenced as an *XML Schema Definition* (XSD); this abbreviation is also used as the file extension for such schema documents. As part of this chapter's introduction to XSDs, the major differences between DTDs and XSDs are examined and illustrated. In XML metadata applications, the use of XSDs has now surpassed the use of XML DTDs. As a case study for XML schemas, the use by the University of Illinois of an XSD created by the Library of Congress to help check the correctness of MAchine-Readable Cataloging (MARC) records contained in the University's library catalog is described. This chapter then closes with brief introductions to two other popular schema languages for XML document instance validation: *RELAX NG*[3] and *Schematron*.[4] Additional advanced features of XSDs and the use of XSDs with XML Namespaces are examined in the next chapter.

THE NEED FOR ALTERNATIVES TO XML DTDs

The W3C began work on a schema alternative to DTDs in 1998, essentially concurrent with the release of the first edition of the XML 1.0 specification. In February 1999, the XML Schema Working Group of the W3C (which, though rechartered from time to time, has been in existence almost continuously since the invention of XML) issued a W3C Note titled *XML Schema Requirements*.[5] This document explains the following:

> For some uses, applications may need definitions of markup constructs more informative, or constraints on document structure tighter than, looser than, or simply different from those which can be expressed using document type definitions as defined in XML 1.0. There is also a widespread desire to allow markup constructs and constraints to be specified in an XML-based syntax, in order to allow tools for XML documents to be used on the specifications.

Syntactical Considerations

The above statement captures the broader markup community's dissatisfaction with XML DTDs at a high level. On the one hand, users see potential benefits in the adoption of valid XML for many emerging Web-based applications; on the other hand, they have concerns in many situations about using DTDs as the mechanism for XML document instance validation. These concerns start with the uniqueness of the syntax used for XML DTD markup declarations. Compare the two expressions in Figure 8.1.

The first expression in Figure 8.1 is a markup declaration for an XML element named "date" as would be found in a DTD. The content type for the element `<date>` is declared to be parsed character data (#PCDATA). The syntax of this first expression is DTD specific and differs significantly from the syntax of non-DTD, well-formed XML document instances. The name of the element being declared and its content type must be inferred from the position of unlabeled parameters in the expression. This approach to markup declarations seems at odds with much of the rest of XML. There should be a more XML-like way to declare element and attribute semantics and structural constraints.

FIGURE 8.1 A DTD element declaration compared to an XSD element declaration.

```
<!ELEMENT date ( #PCDATA ) >

<xsd:element name="date" type="xsd:string"
            minOccurs="0" maxOccurs="unbounded"/>
```

The second expression in Figure 8.1, taken from an XSD file, is immediately recognizable as a snippet of XML. As XML, this expression can be characterized as follows:

- The name of the element is `xsd:element`.
- The element `<xsd:element>` is empty of content.
- `<xsd:element>` has four attributes: `name`, `type`, `minOccurs`, and `maxOccurs`.

In the semantics of the W3C XML Schema Definition Language, this second expression from Figure 8.1 has additional meaning. It serves a roughly equivalent purpose in an XSD as the first expression serves in a DTD. Although it may at first seem counterintuitive that an expression consisting of one XML element (`<xsd:element>`) can be thought of as declaring another XML element (`<date>`), this is exactly what is happening here; that is, `<xsd:element>`, appearing as shown in an XSD, declares an element named "date" and indicates that the element `<date>` may contain `xsd:string` content (i.e., parsed character data). Just as an XML metadata record describes an information resource using elements and attributes, an XSD uses elements and attributes to describe the semantics and grammar of a metadata standard.

As compared to the DTD expression, the `<xsd:element>` declaration does the job in a manner much more consistent with how XML serializes other kinds of information. The name of the element being declared is provided as the value of the attribute "`name`" rather than by position in the declaration as is the case for the DTD expression. Also, instead of "#PCDATA," the attribute "`type`" defines the type of content that this newly declared element is allowed to contain, in this case `xsd:string`. Assuming that the namespace prefix `xsd` has been bound to `<http://www.w3.org/2001/XMLSchema>`, the canonical namespace URI for the W3C XML Schema Definition Language version 1.0, `xsd:string`, is equivalent to parsed character data for most practical purposes. The other two attributes, `minOccurs` and `maxOccurs`, serve the purpose in an XSD element declaration that occurrence indicator symbols "*," "+," and "?" serve in a DTD. These attributes are used to indicate whether the element being declared is optional and/or repeatable. The XSD expression is clearly more verbose than the equivalent DTD expression, but for systems (and human authors) that already understand well-formed XML, it is arguably much easier to parse. As discussed below, this approach also allows schema authors to be more expressive and more precise, for example, in regard to nuances of element content types.

Data Typing

Beyond the syntactical distinctiveness of DTD declarations, another concern that many early implementers had with DTD markup declaration semantics

FIGURE 8.2 An XSD element declaration specifying the <xsd:date> data type.

```
<xsd:element name="date" type="xsd:date"
          minOccurs="0" maxOccurs="unbounded"/>
```

was their limited expressiveness in regard to prescribing the type of data that could be contained in an element. For applications involving strong *data typing*—that is, requirements to constrain the format and scope of information contained within an element—parsed character data are insufficiently prescriptive. For example, in a particular metadata grammar, one element might be designated to always contain a date value, another element to always contain an ISBN, another to always contain a language code, and so on. The monolithic parsed character data content type cannot accommodate such granular nuances. Consider as a simple example the declarations from Figure 8.1. Intuition suggests that having the name "date," the element being declared might be intended to contain date values, such as of the form year-month-day. If so, there is no way in a DTD markup declaration to express such a format constraint on the content type of the element <date>.

By contrast, the W3C Schema Definition Language defines 18 built-in primitive data types (i.e., primitive in that these types are not defined in terms of other data types; they exist ab initio) and another 25 built-in derived data types (i.e., data types built into the XML Schema Definition Language specification that are defined in terms of primitive or other derived data types mentioned in the specification). Further, the specification defines mechanisms by which schema designers can derive as many additional data types as they need. In the example from Figure 8.1, the second expression, the declaration taken from an XSD file, would more likely have been written as shown in Figure 8.2, using the primitive data type for date included in the W3C XML Schema Definition Language specification. This approach would result in validation errors for an XML document instance having a date element that contained a value not conforming to the XSD date data type (any value not of the form year-month-day, such as yyyy-mm-dd). This is just one example of the greater expressiveness and flexibility of XSDs as compared to DTDs. More examples are provided below.

Requirements and Goals for the W3C Schema Definition Language

To identify other concerns with XML DTDs like the two described above, the authors of the *XML Schema Requirements* W3C Note developed several validation use cases. These use cases helped their schema language design process and notably included a metadata interchange use case. The analysis of these cases led to the requirements and key design goals articulated in the W3C Note. Among these goals are that the W3C XML Schema Definition Language should be as follows:

- More expressive than XML DTDs
- Expressed in XML

- Usable by a wide variety of applications that employ XML
- Straightforwardly usable on the Internet
- Optimized for interoperability
- Simple enough to implement with modest design and runtime resources
- Coordinated with relevant W3C specifications (including XML Namespaces; see further discussion in Chapter 9)

The end result is a specification in two parts. *XML Schema Part 1: Structures*[6] defines a grammar for describing the structures and constraining the contents of XML document instances. *XML Schema Part 2: Datatypes*[7] defines a set of built-in primitive and derived data types for use in constructing XML schemas and mechanisms for generating additional derived data types, including implementer-defined derived data types.

Together, the semantics for describing structures and data types defined by these two documents allow schema authors to express everything they can express in a DTD about attributes and elements, plus more about these entities that cannot be expressed in a DTD. The W3C XML Schema Definition Language also implements a kind of inheritance. In addition to supporting data type derivations, XML Schema inheritance allows implementers to create definitions for new elements by extending or restricting already defined element declarations. This facilitates reuse, modularity, and sustainability in XML schema design. Such an approach is not as easily supported by the grammar of DTDs. Also, as described in Chapter 9, XSDs support XML Namespaces intrinsically, something else not supported by DTDs. This allows XML-based applications to make the most of XML Namespaces.

The one area in which XSDs are less expressive than DTDs is in regard to general entity declarations. Since there are alternatives to using named parsed and unparsed entities in XML document instances, one can argue that this is not a significant omission; however, implementers retain the option of using a *document type declaration* with an internal subset of general entity and notation declarations (see Chapter 7) in concert with reference to an XSD. By rule, the general entity declarations of the document type declaration internal subset are processed by a validating parser first, and then the elements and attributes of the XML metadata record are validated against the XSD.

DIFFERENCES BETWEEN DTDs AND XSDs

There are facets of how XSDs declare and define semantics and content models that distinguish them from DTDs. Several of these differences, summarized in Table 8.1, illustrate the markedly different ways that XSDs and DTDs describe application-specific XML grammars. Appreciating these distinctions is one way to understand for which uses one approach or the other might be better. XSD reliance on XML Namespaces, differences in how DTD files

TABLE 8.1 Summary of major differences between DTDs and XSDs.

	DTD	XSD
Associate schema with document instance	Document type declaration; internal and/or external markup declarations	Namespace xsi:shemaLocation Processing instruction schema almost always external
Root element	Specified in document type declaration	Not declared when invoking XSD
Data typing	Parsed character data (#PCDATA)	Built-in primitive & derived data types (~40) Implementer-derived data types (xsd:restriction)
Declaration syntax	DTD-specific	Well-formed XML
Mixed content model	Cannot constrain order of elements mixed with #PCDATA	Can constrain order of elements mixed with #PCDATA
Occurrence indicators	+ ? *	Attributes: minOccurs, maxOccurs
General entity declarations	Supported	Not supported
Inheritance	Not supported	xsd:restriction and xsd: extension
Global and local scope declarations	Not supported	Supported
Validation of elements from multiple namespaces	Not supported	Supported

and XSD files are associated with XML document instances, and related differences in practices for identifying document instance root nodes are especially important and are dealt with in more detail below.

XML Namespaces Are Integral to How XSDs Are Used

It is important to recognize that the W3C XML Schema Definition Language was built from the ground up with XML Namespaces in mind. XSDs, unlike DTDs, are designed to accommodate XML Namespaces. As illustrated below, most XSDs are associated with a namespace. Additionally, references to one or both of the following W3C schema-related namespace URIs will be found not only in XSDs but also in most XML document instances conforming to an XSD. The two primary XML W3C namespaces associated with XSDs are the following:

- *http://www.w3.org/2001/XMLSchema-instance*: The namespace identified by this URI contains attributes helpful for associating XML document instances with the XSD or XSDs to which they conform. Most XML document instances conforming to an XSD reference this namespace URI, typically binding it to a namespace prefix of `xsi` (see Figure 8.3). The namespace prefix `xsi` is used consistently in the illustrations that follow.

- *http://www.w3.org/2001/XMLSchema*: The namespace identified by this URI contains most other elements, primitive data types, built-in derived data types, and attributes described in the W3C XML Schema Definition Language. All XSD schema definition files reference this namespace URI, typically binding it to a namespace prefix of `xsd` or `xs` (see Figure 8.4). The namespace prefix `xsd` is used in the illustrations that follow.

XSDs Do Not Use Document Type Declarations

Figure 8.3 gives the text of an XML document instance that conforms to the XML schema (XSD) given in Figure 8.4. Note the absence of a document type declaration in Figure 8.3. XML metadata records that are meant to be validated against a particular DTD include a document type declaration that associates the internal and/or external markup declaration subsets of the DTD with the metadata record. However, document type declarations are not used to associate an XSD, which is nearly always external to the XML files it validates, with an XML metadata record. Nor do XSDs have internal and external subsets of markup declarations as such. How then is an XSD for validation associated with an XML metadata record?

The XML Schema Parts 1 and 2 specifications do not explicitly prohibit an internal (inline) schema, that is, an XML schema definition embedded within the XML document instance being validated. However, for an in-line XSD scenario, the XSD itself would have to be contained in the document instance as a child node of the document instance root element. This can complicate reference to the XSD, and practice for how to make such references (or whether to make such references explicit) is inconsistent among validating XML parsers that do support in-line XSDs. Also, by default, many validating XML parsers that validate against XSDs, validate starting at the root element of the XML document instance; an internal XSD therefore would have to be self-validating as well as validating for the rest of the document instance. (For some parsers, the behavior to start validating from the root element can be overridden, though there is not currently a standard way across parsers to

FIGURE 8.3 XML document valid against the XSD file shown in Figure 8.4.

```
<?xml version="1.0" encoding="UTF-8"?>
<sentence>
   xmlns:xsi="http://www.w3.org/2001/XMLSchema-instance"
   xsi:noNamespaceSchemaLocation="mySchema.xsd"
   One author of this book is
      <name>Myung-Ja Han</name>.
</sentence>
```

FIGURE 8.4 A simple XSD schema (note the namespace attribute).

```
<?xml version="1.0" encoding="UTF-8"?>
<xsd:schema xmlns:xsd="http://www.w3.org/2001/XMLSchema">
    <xsd:element name="name" type="xsd:string"/>
    <xsd:element name="sentence">
      <xsd:complexType mixed="true">
         <xsd:sequence>
             <xsd:element ref="name" minOccurs="0" maxOccurs="unbounded"/>
         </xsd:sequence>
      </xsd:complexType>
    </xsd:element>
</xsd:schema>
```

invoke this alternate behavior.) Thus, while a few parsers, notably the Microsoft XML Parser (version 6 and subsequent), can support the use of in-line XSDs for piecemeal validation of XML metadata records,[8] in order to avoid the pitfalls and lack of standard practices involved in the use of in-line schemas, in-line XSDs are rarely used in practice for validating XML-serialized metadata records.

Instead, consistent with principles of reuse and modularity (as discussed in Chapter 7 in regard to DTD external subsets), XSD files used for validating XML metadata records are maintained separate from conforming XML metadata records. As XML document instances in their own right, XSD files (i.e., XML-serialized schema definition documents) are served from Web servers with a Multipurpose Internet Mail Extension (MIME) type of application/xml or text/xml in the same way as other XML files. (MIME types,[9] along with file name extensions, determine how applications such as Web browsers process files.) As described in section 4.3.1 of the XML Schema Part 1 specification, XSDs should be "identified by URI and retrieved using the standard mechanisms of the Web" (World Wide Web Consortium 2004). In many instances, it will be most convenient during the early development and testing of a schema to locate the XSD file(s) in the same folder with conforming XML document instance files; this allows the use of relative URI addressing even on one's desktop.

In lieu of document type declarations, section 4.3.2 ("How Schema Definitions Are Located on the Web") of the XML Schema Part 1 specification gives validating XML parsers options for selecting the XSD to use to validate a document instance. This flexibility reflects in part a recognition that for some Web-based use cases (e.g., when XML documents are being retrieved from an untrusted source), it may not be optimal to rely on the document instance itself to identify the schema used for validation. Ultimately, the control over which XSD is used to validate a document should lie with the user or application doing the validation, not with the document being validated.

Because schema definitions often are associated with specific namespaces (e.g., the Library of Congress MARCXML XSD is associated with namespace URI http://www.loc.gov/MARC21/slim), most validating XML parsers first check to see if they have preloaded or otherwise cached a copy of an XSD instance associated with the namespace(s) of the metadata record or specific element being validated. If the answer is yes, they use their cached copy of the XSD for that namespace to perform validation. Normally this works well, but because on the Web multiple XSD files can exist that each assert an association with the same namespace and because an XSD associated with a namespace may be updated from time to time, reliance on namespace for selecting the XSD to use for validation can (rarely) create latency or other related issues.

Thus, if the parser does not find a recently enough cached XSD corresponding to the namespace of the document instance or if the XML document instance or element being validated is not associated with a namespace, most validating parsers will next look in the XML metadata record for either an `xsi:noNamespaceSchemaLocation` attribute or an `xsi:schemaLocation` attribute. For most scenarios (i.e., assuming that the metadata record source is trustworthy), the values of these attributes can be relied on to identify the location of the XSD file(s) to use for validation. However, as defined in the formal W3C XML Schema Definition Language specifications, these attributes are hints only, and validating parsers may ignore the values given by these attributes and rely on other methods to determine the XSD to use for validation (e.g., an XSD location provided by the user or application requesting validation).

Figure 8.3 is a simple test XML document that has been used for illustration in earlier chapters (compare to Figure 1.2 in Chapter 1 and Figure 7.7 in Chapter 7). The elements in this document instance are not associated with any namespace, so to validate this document instance against the XSD shown in Figure 8.4, the `xsi:noNamespaceSchemaLocation` attribute is provided to indicate to the validating parser where to find the XSD file. In this case, the document instance and the XSD file are located in the same folder, so a simple relative address URI can be used.

The use of XSDs with XML Namespaces is discussed in more detail in the next chapter, but for now Figure 8.5 illustrates use of the `xsi:schemaLocation` attribute. Notice that this attribute requires a value consisting of a white space-delineated pair of URIs. The first URI in the pair is the namespace URI, and the second URI is the XSD URI, which gives the location of the XSD file. As will be illustrated in the next chapter, additional URI pairs (separated by white space) can be included when validating a document instance containing elements from multiple namespaces.

FIGURE 8.5 Associating an XML document with an XSD file using `<xsi:schemaLocation>`.

```
<?xml version="1.0" encoding="UTF-8"?>
<oai_dc:dc
   xmlns:oai_dc="http://www.openarchives.org/OAI/2.0/oai_dc/"
   xmlns:dc="http://purl.org/dc/elements/1.1/"
   xmlns:xsi="http://www.w3.org/2001/XMLSchema-instance"
   xsi:schemaLocation="http://www.openarchives.org/OAI/2.0/oai_dc/
                       http://www.openarchives.org/OAI/2.0/oai_dc.xsd">
   <dc:title>Using the Open Archive Initiative Protocol...</dc:title>
   <dc:creator>Cole, Timothy W.</dc:creator>
   <dc:creator>Foulonneau, Muriel</dc:creator>
</oai_dc:dc>
```

While Figures 8.3 and 8.5 illustrate the most common ways to associate an XSD with an XML document instance, this remains an issue under discussion by the W3C. Relatively recently, a W3C Working Group Note titled, *Associating Schemas with XML Documents 1.0* (second edition),[10] was issued, describing a common, schema-agnostic syntax for associating XML schemas with XML document instances. This new approach makes use of a special "xml-model" processing instruction in the prolog of an XML document instance to associate one or more schemas with a document instance. This approach addresses some of the limitations of current approaches, but because as of this writing it remains a work in progress (i.e., not yet a W3C Recommendation), it is not described further here.

XSDs Do Not Declare a Root Element

As described in Chapter 7 and reiterated above, the markup declarations of a DTD are associated with a document instance through a document type declaration. In addition to connecting a set of markup declarations with an XML document instance, a document type declaration declares the root element for the document instance. In practice, though not required, most external subsets of DTD markup declarations are written with a specific document type declaration in mind. This means that most external subsets are written assuming that a particular element will be the root node of all conforming XML document instances. This is not a requirement of DTDs, but the practice of associating an external subset with a single root element is a tendency encouraged by the DTD model of application-specific grammar description. It is a common practice to embed a sample document type declaration in a file containing an external subset of DTD markup declarations (i.e., as an XML Comment near the top of the file).

In contrast, XSDs were built from the ground up with XML Namespaces in mind. XSDs rely on XML namespaces and, as discussed in Chapter 9, can be

FIGURE 8.6 A simple metadata record that includes an element <abstract>.

```
<?xml version="1.0" encoding="UTF-8"?>
<myMeta
   xmlns:xsi="http://www.w3.org/2001/XMLSchema-instance"
   xsi:noNamespaceSchemaLocation="myMetaSchema.xsd">
     <pubInfo>
        <title>Using the Open Archives Initiative Protocol....</title>
        <author>Cole, Timothy W.</author>
        <author>Foulonneau, Muriel</author>
        <date>2007-06-01</date>
     </pubInfo>
     <abstract>This book, published in the <date>summer of 2007</date>,
               describes OAI-PMH and how it is used.</abstract>
</myMeta>
```

used to validate XML document instances that include elements and/or attributes from multiple namespaces. Additionally, XSDs are not associated with XML document instances using DTD-style document type declarations that require the declaration of a root element. As a result, XSDs are being written in anticipation that they may be used to validate document instances having various elements from the XSD's namespace as a root.

Consider as a simple example of this Figures 8.6, 8.7, and 8.8. The XML document instance shown in Figure 8.6 has a root element of <myMeta>. The XML document instance shown in Figure 8.7 has a root element of <abstract>. Both document instances are associated with the same XSD (shown in Figure 8.8), and even though they have different root elements, both document instances are valid against this XSD. In fact, even without resorting to namespaces, the XSD shown in Figure 8.8 could be used to validate documents with any of the following root elements: <abstract>, <author>, <myMeta>, <myMetaList>, <pubInfo>, <title>. (As discussed in Chapter 9, with the use of XML Namespaces, this schema could be used to validate any of these elements even when not the root element of the document instance.) A notable example of a schema developed with multiple root elements in mind is the Library of Congress (2002) MARCXML XSD (Figure 8.10), which was written to support validation of both individual MARCXML

FIGURE 8.7 The <abstract> element from a simple metadata record.

```
<?xml version="1.0" encoding="UTF-8"?>
<abstract
   xmlns:xsi="http://www.w3.org/2001/XMLSchema-instance"
   xsi:noNamespaceSchemaLocation="myMetaSchema.xsd">
     Using OAI-PMH, written in <date>2006</date> and
     published in the <date>summer of 2007</date>,
     describes OAI-PMH and how it is used.
</abstract>
```

FIGURE 8.8 The XSD file for XML document instances in Figures 8.6 and 8.7.

```
<?xml version="1.0" encoding="UTF-8"?>
<xsd:schema xmlns:xsd="http://www.w3.org/2001/XMLSchema">
  <xsd:element name="title" type="xsd:string"/>
  <xsd:element name="author" type="xsd:string"/>
  <xsd:element name="pubInfo">
    <xsd:complexType>
      <xsd:sequence>
        <xsd:element ref="title" minOccurs="1" maxOccurs="1"/>
        <xsd:element ref="author" minOccurs="0" maxOccurs="unbounded"/>
        <xsd:element name="date" type="xsd:date" minOccurs="1" maxOccurs="1"/>
      </xsd:sequence>
    </xsd:complexType>
  </xsd:element>
  <xsd:element name="abstract">
    <xsd:complexType mixed="true">
      <xsd:sequence>
       <xsd:element name="date" type="xsd:string" minOccurs="0"
            maxOccurs="unbounded"/>
      </xsd:sequence>
    </xsd:complexType>
  </xsd:element>
  <xsd:element name="myMeta">
    <xsd:complexType>
      <xsd:sequence>
        <xsd:element ref="pubInfo" minOccurs="1" maxOccurs="1"/>
        <xsd:element ref="abstract" minOccurs="0" maxOccurs="1"/>
      </xsd:sequence>
    </xsd:complexType>
  </xsd:element>
  <xsd:element name="myMetaList">
    <xsd:complexType>
      <xsd:choice minOccurs="1" maxOccurs="unbounded">
        <xsd:element ref="myMeta"/>
      </xsd:choice>
    </xsd:complexType>
  </xsd:element>
</xsd:schema>
```

records (root element <record>) and collections of MARCXML records (root element <collection>).

W3C XML SCHEMA DEFINITION LANGUAGE ILLUSTRATIONS

The fifth edition of the W3C Recommendation defining Extensible Markup Language version 1.0[11] is approximately 40 pages when printed in default font (depending on printer settings). In total, the discussion of DTDs, document type declarations, and markup declarations takes up significantly less than half of the specification (i.e., less than 20 pages). To achieve the additional expressiveness and flexibility desired, the W3C XML Schema Definition Language required a two-part specification totaling over 200 pages when printed (i.e., over 10 times as much as was needed to define DTDs). While it is beyond the scope of this book to provide a comprehensive manual for XSDs, an illustrated outline of some of the most important features of XSDs is provided here—enough to help the reader understand the XSDs most likely to be encountered in the context of XML-based metadata applications. For further details about the W3C XML Schema Definition Language, the reader is referred to the *XML Schema Part 0: Primer*,[12] itself about 70 printed pages in length. The primer is intended to provide an easily readable introduction to and overview of the W3C XML Schema Definition Language. The primer is written to help readers gain a quick understanding of how to create schemas using the W3C XML Schema Definition Language and is a good starting point for those needing a deeper understanding of XSDs before tackling the more technically dense *XML Schema Parts 1 and 2* documents, which were written more for ready reference than for reading start to finish.

The illustrations of the W3C XML Schema Definition Language presented below focus on features most pertinent to XML metadata applications. Examples are drawn from the made-for-illustration XSD depicted in Figure 8.8, from an Oxygen-generated XSD derived from the Simple Dublin Core DTD created by Consortium for the Computer Interchange of Museum Information (CIMI) and used for Case Study 7-1 in Chapter 7 (Figure 8.9), and from the Library of Congress MARCXML XSD as depicted in Figure 8.10 (i.e., with some simplifications and sans annotations and comments present in the canonical copy on the Library of Congress Website).

XSDs can be difficult reading, especially those that are long and complex. Many tools for authoring and editing XSDs can generate visualizations of schema design features as an aid to comprehension. For the longest and most complex of the illustrative schemas presented here, the MARCXML schema, a partial graphical representation of the schema as generated by Oxygen (Figure 8.11), is included both to aid understanding and as a way to better draw attention to schema design facets. Figure 8.11 shows that the MARCXML schema defines a MARC record as having two attributes, `type` and `id`, and a content model of one `<leader>` element, followed by 0 or more `<controlfield>` elements, followed by zero or more `<datafield>` elements. The `<datafield>` element has a content model (expanded in the representation shown in Figure 8.11) allowing as children one or more `<subfield>` elements, which in turn are of content type `xsd:string` (parsed character data). When viewing this graphical representation in Oxygen, additional components can be expanded to show more details of the elements and attributes defined in the schema. Such representations can be very helpful when authoring and reading XSD files.

FIGURE 8.9 An XSD schema for simple Dublin Core auto-generated from the CIMI DTD.

```
<?xml version="1.0" encoding="UTF-8"?>
<xsd:schema xmlns:xs="http://www.w3.org/2001/XMLSchema"
elementFormDefault="qualified">
  <xsd:element name="dc-record-list">
    <xsd:complexType>
      <xsd:sequence>
        <xsd:element minOccurs="0" maxOccurs="unbounded" ref="dc-record"/>
      </xsd:sequence>
    </xsd:complexType>
  </xsd:element>
  <xsd:element name="dc-record">
    <xsd:complexType>
      <xsd:sequence>
      <xsd:element minOccurs="0" maxOccurs="unbounded" ref="title"/>
      <xsd:element minOccurs="0" maxOccurs="unbounded" ref="creator"/>
      <xsd:element minOccurs="0" maxOccurs="unbounded" ref="subject"/>
      <xsd:element minOccurs="0" maxOccurs="unbounded" ref="description"/>
      <xsd:element minOccurs="0" maxOccurs="unbounded" ref="publisher"/>
      <xsd:element minOccurs="0" maxOccurs="unbounded" ref="contributor"/>
      <xsd:element minOccurs="0" maxOccurs="unbounded" ref="date"/>
      <xsd:element minOccurs="0" maxOccurs="unbounded" ref="type"/>
      <xsd:element minOccurs="0" maxOccurs="unbounded" ref="format"/>
      <xsd:element minOccurs="0" maxOccurs="unbounded" ref="identifier"/>
      <xsd:element minOccurs="0" maxOccurs="unbounded" ref="source"/>
      <xsd:element minOccurs="0" maxOccurs="unbounded" ref="language"/>
      <xsd:element minOccurs="0" maxOccurs="unbounded" ref="relation"/>
      <xsd:element minOccurs="0" maxOccurs="unbounded" ref="coverage"/>
      <xsd:element minOccurs="0" maxOccurs="unbounded" ref="rights"/>
      </xsd:sequence>
    </xsd:complexType>
  </xsd:element>
  <xsd:element name="title" type="xsd:string"/>
  <xsd:element name="creator" type="xsd:string"/>
  <xsd:element name="subject" type="xsd:string"/>
  <xsd:element name="description" type="xsd:string"/>
  <xsd:element name="publisher" type="xsd:string"/>
  <xsd:element name="contributor" type="xsd:string"/>
  <xsd:element name="date" type="xsd:string"/>
  <xsd:element name="type" type="xsd:string"/>
  <xsd:element name="format" type="xsd:string"/>
  <xsd:element name="identifier" type="xsd:string"/>
  <xsd:element name="source" type="xsd:string"/>
  <xsd:element name="language" type="xsd:string"/>
  <xsd:element name="relation" type="xsd:string"/>
  <xsd:element name="coverage" type="xsd:string"/>
  <xsd:element name="rights" type="xsd:string"/>
</xsd:schema>
```

FIGURE 8.10 An XSD schema for MARCXML (*Source*: Library of Congress[13]).

```
<?xml version="1.0"?>
<xsd:schema targetNamespace="http://www.loc.gov/MARC21/slim"
  xmlns:xsd="http://www.w3.org/2001/XMLSchema"
  elementFormDefault="qualified" attributeFormDefault="unqualified"
  version="1.1" xml:lang="en">
  <xsd:element name="record" type="recordType" nillable="true"/>
  <xsd:element name="collection" type="collectionType" nillable="true"/>
  <xsd:complexType name="collectionType">
    <xsd:sequence minOccurs="0" maxOccurs="unbounded">
      <xsd:element ref="record"/>
    </xsd:sequence>
    <xsd:attribute name="id" type="idDataType" use="optional"/>
  </xsd:complexType>
  <xsd:complexType name="recordType">
    <xsd:sequence minOccurs="0">
      <xsd:element name="leader" type="leaderFieldType"/>
      <xsd:element name="controlfield" type="controlFieldType"
            minOccurs="0" maxOccurs="unbounded"/>
      <xsd:element name="datafield" type="dataFieldType" minOccurs="0"
            maxOccurs="unbounded"/>
    </xsd:sequence>
    <xsd:attribute name="type" type="recordTypeType" use="optional"/>
    <xsd:attribute name="id" type="idDataType" use="optional"/>
  </xsd:complexType>
  <xsd:simpleType name="recordTypeType">
    <xsd:restriction base="xsd:NMTOKEN">
      <xsd:enumeration value="Bibliographic"/>
      <xsd:enumeration value="Authority"/>
      <xsd:enumeration value="Holdings"/>
      <xsd:enumeration value="Classification"/>
      <xsd:enumeration value="Community"/>
    </xsd:restriction>
  </xsd:simpleType>
  <xsd:complexType name="leaderFieldType">
    <xsd:simpleContent>
      <xsd:extension base="leaderDataType">
        <xsd:attribute name="id" type="idDataType" use="optional"/>
      </xsd:extension>
    </xsd:simpleContent>
  </xsd:complexType>
  <xsd:simpleType name="leaderDataType">
    <xsd:restriction base="xsd:string">
      <xsd:whiteSpace value="preserve"/>
      <xsd:pattern
value="[\d ]{5}[\dA-Za-z ]{1}[\dA-Za-z]{1}[\dA-Za-z ]{3}(2| )(2| )[\d ]{5}[\dA-
Za-z ]{3}(4500|    )"
      />
    </xsd:restriction>
  </xsd:simpleType>
  <xsd:complexType name="controlFieldType">
    <xsd:simpleContent>
      <xsd:extension base="controlDataType">
```

FIGURE 8.10 (Continued)

```
      <xsd:attribute name="id" type="idDataType" use="optional"/>
      <xsd:attribute name="tag" type="controltagDataType"
        use="required"/>
    </xsd:extension>
  </xsd:simpleContent>
</xsd:complexType>
<xsd:simpleType name="controlDataType">
  <xsd:restriction base="xsd:string">
    <xsd:whiteSpace value="preserve"/>
  </xsd:restriction>
</xsd:simpleType>
<xsd:simpleType name="controltagDataType">
  <xsd:restriction base="xsd:string">
    <xsd:whiteSpace value="preserve"/>
    <xsd:pattern value="00[1-9A-Za-z]{1}"/>
  </xsd:restriction>
</xsd:simpleType>
<xsd:complexType name="dataFieldType">
  <xsd:sequence maxOccurs="unbounded">
    <xsd:element name="subfield" type="subfieldatafieldType"/>
  </xsd:sequence>
  <xsd:attribute name="id" type="idDataType" use="optional"/>
  <xsd:attribute name="tag" type="tagDataType" use="required"/>
  <xsd:attribute name="ind1" type="indicatorDataType" use="required"/>
  <xsd:attribute name="ind2" type="indicatorDataType" use="required"/>
</xsd:complexType>
<xsd:simpleType name="tagDataType">
  <xsd:restriction base="xsd:string">
    <xsd:whiteSpace value="preserve"/>
    <xsd:pattern
value="(0([1-9A-Z][0-9A-Z])|0([1-9a-z][0-9a-z]))|(([1-9A-Z][0-9A-Z]{2})|([1-
9a-z][0-9a-z]{2}))"
    />
  </xsd:restriction>
</xsd:simpleType>
<xsd:simpleType name="indicatorDataType">
  <xsd:restriction base="xsd:string">
    <xsd:whiteSpace value="preserve"/>
    <xsd:pattern value="[\da-z ]{1}"/>
  </xsd:restriction>
</xsd:simpleType>
<xsd:complexType name="subfieldatafieldType">
  <xsd:simpleContent>
    <xsd:extension base="subfieldDataType">
      <xsd:attribute name="id" type="idDataType" use="optional"/>
      <xsd:attribute name="code" type="subfieldcodeDataType"
        use="required"/>
    </xsd:extension>
  </xsd:simpleContent>
</xsd:complexType>
<xsd:simpleType name="subfieldDataType">
```

(continued)

FIGURE 8.10 (Continued)

```
    <xsd:restriction base="xsd:string">
      <xsd:whiteSpace value="preserve"/>
    </xsd:restriction>
  </xsd:simpleType>
  <xsd:simpleType name="subfieldcodeDataType">
    <xsd:restriction base="xsd:string">
      <xsd:whiteSpace value="preserve"/>
      <xsd:pattern
value="[\dA-Za-z!&quot;#$%&amp;'()*+,-./:;&lt;=&gt;?{}_^`~\[\]\\]{1}"/>
    </xsd:restriction>
  </xsd:simpleType>
  <xsd:simpleType name="idDataType">
    <xsd:restriction base="xsd:ID"/>
  </xsd:simpleType>
</xsd:schema>
```

Declaring Elements and Attributes in XSDs

In XSDs, element and attribute names and properties are declared and defined using <xsd:element> and <xsd:attribute>, respectively. As illustrated in Figures 8.8, 8.9, and 8.10, these elements of an XSD can be empty or can have child elements. In the case of <xsd:attribute>, the only allowed children are <xs:annotation> (self-explanatory) and <xsd:simpleType>; <xsd:element> can have these as well as other children, including, most important for the current discussion, <xsd:complexType>. The difference between *simple type definitions* and *complex type definitions* is explained below.

FIGURE 8.11 A graphical representation of the MARCXML XSD shown in Figure 8.10. Screen shot was made using Oxygen XML Editor (http://www.oxygenxml.com).

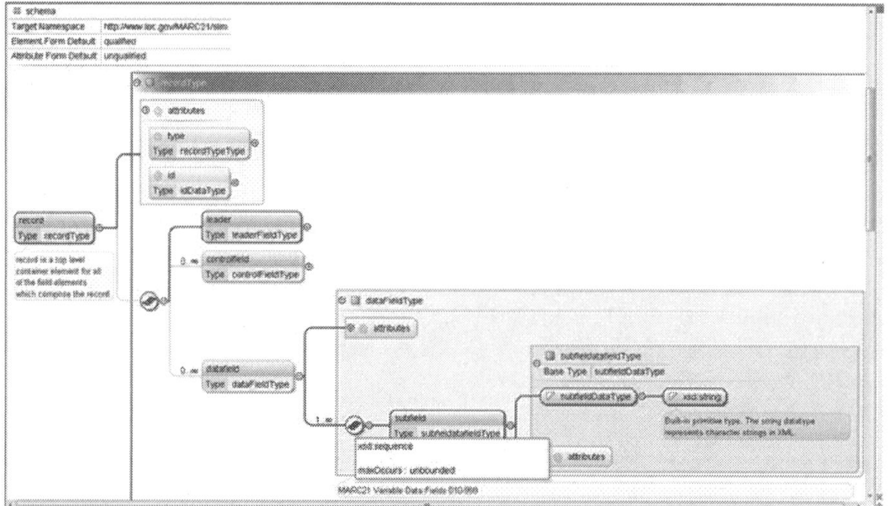

Both `<xsd:attribute>` and `<xsd:element>` can have attributes. The attributes `name`, `ref`, and `type` can appear on both elements. In addition, the attributes `use`, `default`, and `fixed` can appear on `<xsd:attribute>`, and the attributes `minOccurs` and `maxOccurs` can appear on `<xsd:element>`. Either `name` or `ref` is required but never both. If the `name` attribute is used on `<xsd:element>` or `<xsd:attribute>`, then a new element or attribute with that name is being declared. If the `ref` attribute is used, then the `<xsd:element>` or `<xsd:attribute>` occurrence is a placeholder within the XSD structure for the element or attribute referenced, which must be declared elsewhere in the XSD (or in included or imported XSDs). This method, for example, is used when defining an element content model that includes a reference to another element declared somewhere else in the schema, such as depicted in Figure 8.12 (a snippet from the Simple Dublin Core XSD shown in Figure 8.9).

The `type` attribute on `<xsd:element>` and `<xsd:attribute>` associates the declaration with a content type definition for the element or attribute. Content type definitions include descriptions of the element's or attribute's content type or the element's *content model* when applicable (i.e., when the element is allowed child elements). The `type` attribute is not used if a `<xsd:simpleType>` or `<xsd:complexType>` child is present, as is the case for `<dc-record>` in Figure 8.12. (This is called an *anonymous type definition.*) Otherwise, the value of the `type` attribute should be the name of a content type definition (either simple or complex) found elsewhere in the XSD or the name of a built-in primitive or derived data type as defined in *XML Schema Part 2: Datatypes.*

The `minOccurs` attribute on a `<xsd:element>` (element declaration) indicates the minimum number of times that the element being declared should appear; values for this attribute are constrained to 0 (optional) or 1 (required to appear at least once). The `maxOccurs` attribute indicates the

FIGURE 8.12 Snippets from Figure 8.9 illustrating the use of the `ref` attribute.

```
XML to validate:
  <dc-record><publisher>Libraries Unlimited</publisher></dc-record>

From XSD:
  <xsd:element name="dc-record">
    <xsd:complexType>
      <xsd:sequence>
          ...
        <xsd:element minOccurs="0" maxOccurs="unbounded" ref="publisher"/>
          ...
      </xsd:sequence>
    </xsd:complexType>
  </xsd:element>
  ...
  <xsd:element name="publisher" type="xsd:string"/>
```

maximum number of times the element being declared is allowed to appear; values are constrained to 1 or unbounded. Note that an element included in multiple content models by reference may be required to appear in one element's content model (minOccurs=1) while being optional in another element's content model (minOccurs=0). Other aspects of content model definitions are handled using <xsd:choice>, <xsd:sequence>, and <xsd:all>, as detailed below in the discussion of complex type definitions.

The use attribute performs an analogous function to that of <xsd:attribute> (attribute declarations). Thus the value of the use attribute indicates whether the attribute being declared is optional, required, or prohibited (rarely used in metadata applications but can be useful as a way to modify/refine a reference to a previously declared complex type definition). The <xsd:attribute> element is also allowed a default attribute (specifying a value for the attribute that should be assumed when the attribute is not explicitly present in a document instance) and a fixed attribute (specifying the only value the attribute is allowed to have and indicating that the attribute should be assumed with that value even if not explicitly present in a document instance).

Type Definitions

When declaring elements and attributes in an XSD, type definitions are included or referenced as a way to describe the kind of information that the element or attribute being declared is allowed to contain and, in the case of element declarations, any required or optional attributes or child elements allowed. *Simple type definitions* are used when defining attributes and when defining elements that have no child elements and no attributes. Most implementations of Simple Dublin Core today assume that the 15 elements of Simple Dublin Core take plain text strings as values and are not allowed child elements. For XML serializations of such Simple Dublin Core records, the 15 elements of Simple Dublin Core can be declared in an XSD simply by referencing the xsd:string built-in type definition, as illustrated in Figure 8.9.

Complex type definitions must be used when defining elements that are allowed attributes and/or are allowed child elements, have an *empty* content type (i.e., are allowed no content whatsoever), or are of a *mixed* content type (i.e., can contain parsed character data and child elements). (The use of complex type definitions for empty elements is nonintuitive but avoids the need to define an additional type definition model just for empty element definitions.) Notice in Figure 8.9 that a complex type definition is included in the declaration for the <dc-record-list> element (allowed to contain zero or more <dc-record> elements as child nodes) and in the declaration for the <dc-record> element (allowed zero or more of any of the 15 elements of Simple Dublin Core in the order specified). Complex type definitions are required for these two elements because both have element content models (i.e., are allowed child elements).

FIGURE 8.13 Simple type definition for an element allowed to contain `xsd:string` content.

```
XML to validate:
  <title>Using the Open Archives Initiative Protocol....</title>

From XSD:
<xsd:element name="title" type="xsd:string"/>
```

Simple Types

Declarations of attributes and elements that have simple content types either reference one of the built-in primitive or derived data types defined in *XML Schema Part 2: Datatypes* or include or reference a simple content type derived from built-in data types by restricting a data type (including via an enumerated lists) or by specifying a union of built-in or derived data types.

Figures 8.13 and 8.14 illustrate two different declarations involving elements of simple content type. The first example (a snippet from the Simple Dublin Core XSD shown in Figure 8.9) is a declaration for the element `title`. This element declaration defines the content of the title to be the simple data type `xsd:string` (essentially synonymous with parsed character data for most purposes). Because this definition involves a built-in data type, no separate `<xsd:simpleType>` child element is needed. It is sufficient to reference the built-in data type definition as the value of the type attribute of the `<xsd:element>` node.

The second example (Figure 8.14, a snippet from the MARCXML XSD shown in Figure 8.10) uses `<xsd:simpleType>`, `<xsd:restriction>`, and `<xsd:enumeration>` to define a new attribute simple type that is an enumerated list restriction on the `xsd:NMTOKEN` data type (NMTOKEN is

FIGURE 8.14 Simple type definition for attribute restricted to having values from an enumerated list.

```
XML to validate (specifically the attribute "type"):
  <record type="Bibliographic">....</record>

From XSD:
    ...
      <xsd:attribute name="type" type="recordTypeType" use="optional"/>
    ...
<xsd:simpleType name="recordTypeType">
  <xsd:restriction base="xsd:NMTOKEN">
    <xsd:enumeration value="Bibliographic"/>
    <xsd:enumeration value="Authority"/>
    <xsd:enumeration value="Holdings"/>
    <xsd:enumeration value="Classification"/>
    <xsd:enumeration value="Community"/>
  </xsd:restriction>
</xsd:simpleType>
```

a built-in data type carried over from the XML Specification where it is described as a way to support attributes having values from enumerated lists). This enumerated list simple type definition is then given a name and referenced by that name (i.e., as value of the type attribute) when declaring the MARCXML record element.

It is also possible to construct a simple type definition that defines a union data type comprised of multiple other simple type definitions (user-defined derived types) and/or built-in data types. For example, given elsewhere in an XSD declarations for a simple type enumerated list of two-letter state abbreviations and for a ZIP code simple type (i.e., strings of exactly five digits), these types could be combined together as a simple type union to allow a particular element to contain either a state abbreviation or a ZIP code.

Complex Types

If the element being declared is allowed to have attributes and/or child elements (including a mixed #PCDATA and element content model) or is defined as having an empty content model, then the element declaration must reference (through the type attribute) a complex type definition or must include an anonymous complex type definition. Complex type definitions may include one or more attribute declarations and/or references to attributes declared elsewhere in the XSD (i.e., using the <xsd:attribute> element). They may also describe a content model (using one of <xsd:sequence>, <xsd:choice>, or <xsd:all>, as described below). Or they may describe a derived (by restriction or extension) content type/model (i.e., using <xsd:simpleContent> or <xsd:complexContent> elements).

Figure 8.15 shows that a MARC element <datafield> is declared to have a complex type by reference, <xsd:complexType name="dataFieldType">. Through reference to this complex type definition, <datafield> is allowed to contain any number of <subfield> elements. This complex type definition also allows the <datafield> element to have attributes id, tag, ind1, and ind2. Among these attributes, tag, ind1, and ind2 are required.

Most of the complex type definitions shown in the example XSDs (Figures 8.8, 8.9, and 8.10) use <xsd:sequence> to describe element content models. The two other options that can be used in XSDs are <xsd:choice> and <xsd:all>. Each of these elements takes a list of one or more element declarations or element references (except when declaring empty elements) as its content. If the <xsd:sequence> element is used in a complex type definition, then the elements listed (if present in the XML metadata record) must appear in the order listed. Depending on the values of minOccurs and maxOccurs on each child element declaration or reference, each item in the sequence may appear in a conformant metadata record once, more than once, or not at all, but the elements that do appear must appear in the order listed. If not, an error message like

FIGURE 8.15 Complex type definition for MARCXML `<datafield>` element.

```
XML to validate (datafield may contain subfield(s), and have attributes):

<datafield tag="245" ind1="1" ind2="0">
      <subfield code="a">Using the Open Archive Initiative ...</subfield>
      <subfield code="c">by Timothy Cole & Muriel Foulonneau. </subfield>
  </datafield>

  ...
  <xsd:element name="datafield" type="dataFieldType" minOccurs="0"
          maxOccurs="unbounded"/>
  ...
  <xsd:complexType name="dataFieldType">
    <xsd:sequence maxOccurs="unbounded">
      <xsd:element name="subfield" type="subfieldatafieldType"/>
    </xsd:sequence>
    <xsd:attribute name="id" type="idDataType" use="optional"/>
    <xsd:attribute name="tag" type="tagDataType" use="required"/>
    <xsd:attribute name="ind1" type="indicatorDataType" use="required"/>
    <xsd:attribute name="ind2" type="indicatorDataType" use="required"/>
  </xsd:complexType>
```

that depicted in Figure 8.16 can occur. In this example, the <language> element appears out of order in an XML metadata record that purports to conform to the Simple Dublin Core XSD shown in Figure 8.9. The error could be resolved by moving the <language> element in the metadata record below the second <creator> element.

Alternatively, the second complex type definition in the Simple Dublin Core schema shown in Figure 8.9 could be changed to use <xsd:choice> instead of <xsd:sequence> (Figure 8.17); <xsd:choice> allows any one of the elements listed within it to appear in the XML metadata record as a child of the element being declared. Interestingly, an <xsd:choice> with its maxOccurs attribute set to unbounded can be used to define a content model that is similar to a content model defined using <xsd:sequence> and maxOccurs="unbounded" on each of the element declarations or references in the included list. The only difference when using <xsd:choice> this way is that order is no longer constrained. Thus, as Figure 8.18 illustrates, the error from Figure 8.16 can be resolved by changing the XSD rather than the XML metadata record. Graphically, the two variations of the Simple Dublin Core schemas are similarly represented (Figure 8.19).

The last option for describing content models in complex type definitions, <xsd:all>, is more specialized than either <xsd:choice> or <xsd:sequence>, so it is used less often in authoring XSDs. Each element listed in an <xsd:all> element in an XSD may appear zero or one time in that content model in the XML metadata record.

FIGURE 8.16 Invalid Simple Dublin Core metadata record. Record is invalid because schema used <xsd:sequence> in type definition. Screen shot was made using Oxygen XML Editor (http://www.oxygenxml.com).

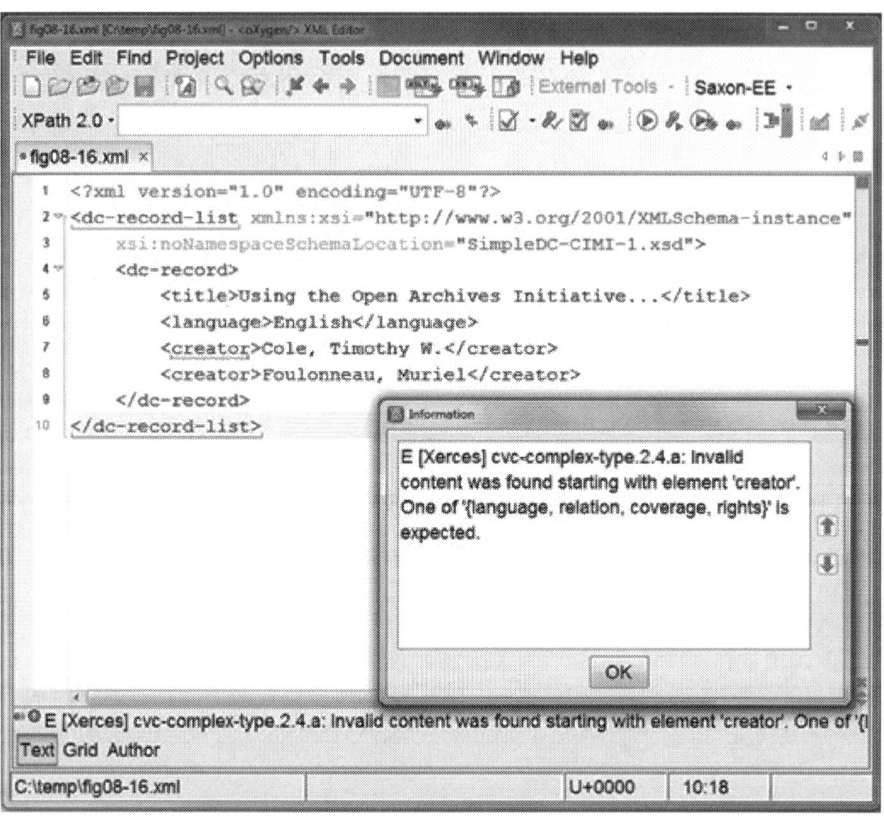

FIGURE 8.17 Complex type definition using <xsd:choice> instead of <xsd:sequence>.

XML to Validate - see Figures 8.18

```
<xsd:element name="dc-record">
    <xsd:complexType>
        <xsd:choice minOccurs="1" maxOccurs="unbounded">
        <xsd:element ref="title"/>
            ...
        <xsd:element ref="rights"/>
        </xsd:sequence>
    </xsd:complexType>
</xsd:element>
```

FIGURE 8.18 Simple Dublin Core record is valid evaluated against schema using <xsd:choice> in type definition. Screen shot was made using Oxygen XML Editor (http://www.oxygenxml.com).

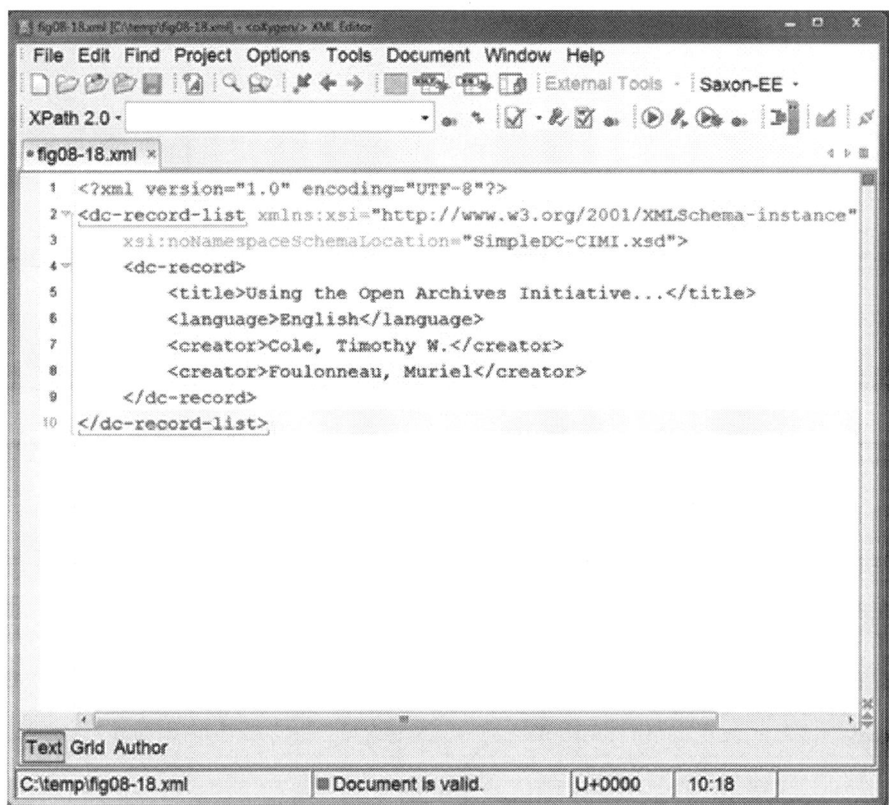

FIGURE 8.19 Comparing schema type definitions using <xsd:sequence> (left) versus <xsd:choice> (right). Screen shot was made using Oxygen XML Editor (http://www.oxygenxml.com).

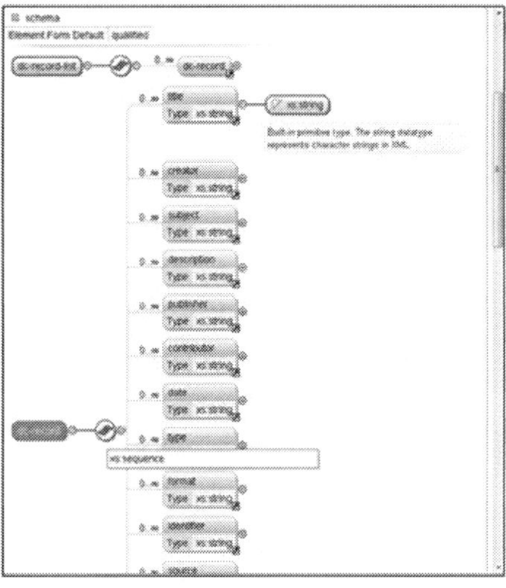

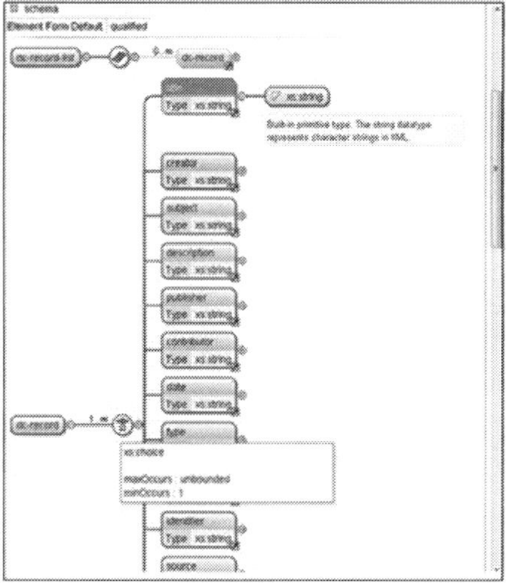

Global versus Local Declarations

There is an important distinction in XSDs between global and local declarations of elements and attributes. As mentioned, it is common within descriptions of content models in an XSD (i.e., within <xsd:sequence>, <xsd:choice> and <xsd:all>) to use references to elements declared elsewhere in the XSD rather than declaring elements within the content model description (type definition) itself. This is possible in an XSD because elements and attributes that are declared using <xsd:element> and <xsd:attribute> nodes that are immediate children of <xsd:schema> are deemed to be declared globally. Globally declared elements and attributes can be referenced elsewhere in the XSD. Globally declared elements can be the root element of a conforming document instance. Elements that are declared (rather than referenced) in a complex type definition are considered locally declared. Definitions of locally declared elements can be used only within the complex type definition in which they are declared.

Figure 8.20 (a snippet of Figure 8.8) illustrates the use of both global and local element declarations. <title> and <author> elements are declared globally elsewhere in the XSD and are included by reference in the content model description for the element <pubInfo>. These elements also can be referenced from elsewhere in the XSD.

The element <date> is declared locally within the <pubInfo> content model description. The element <date> is also declared locally again within

FIGURE 8.20 Globally (title, author) and locally (date) declared elements.

XML to Validate - see Figure 8.21

```
From XSD:
  <xsd:element name="pubInfo">
    <xsd:complexType>
      <xsd:sequence>
        <xsd:element ref="title" minOccurs="1" maxOccurs="1"/>
        <xsd:element ref="author" minOccurs="0" maxOccurs="unbounded"/>
        <xsd:element name="date" type="xsd:date" minOccurs="1" maxOccurs="1"/>
      </xsd:sequence>
    </xsd:complexType>
  </xsd:element>

  <xsd:element name="abstract">
    <xsd:complexType mixed="true">
      <xsd:sequence>
        <xsd:element name="date" type="xsd:string" minOccurs="0"
              maxOccurs="unbounded"/>
      </xsd:sequence>
    </xsd:complexType>
</xsd:element>
```

the content model description for the element <abstract>. For the purposes of validation, an instance of <date> appearing in an XML metadata record in the <pubInfo> element is treated differently than an instance of <date> appearing in the <abstract> element. Each declaration of <date> has scope only within the complex type definition in which it appears, and each instance of <date> in an XML metadata record is valid or not according to the rules of the relevant complex type definition, that is, according to whether the instance of <date> appears in the <pubInfo> element or the <abstract> element.

Although not entirely intuitive, this approach can be useful if an element's data type or content model (in this case the <date> element's data type) needs to be different when appearing in one element (in this case the <pubInfo> element) than when appearing in another element (in this case the <abstract> element). In this example, the objective is to constrain the format of the date value more tightly when it appears in the <pubInfo> element than when it appears in the <abstract> element. Because of this construction in the XSD, the metadata record depicted in Figure 8.21 is invalid, even though the exact same string appears as the value for both occurrences of the <date> element in the record. (The occurrence of <date> in the <pubInfo> element is the invalid value.)

FIGURE 8.21 Local declaration of date within pubInfo is more restrictive. Screen shot was made using Oxygen XML Editor (http://www.oxygenxml.com).

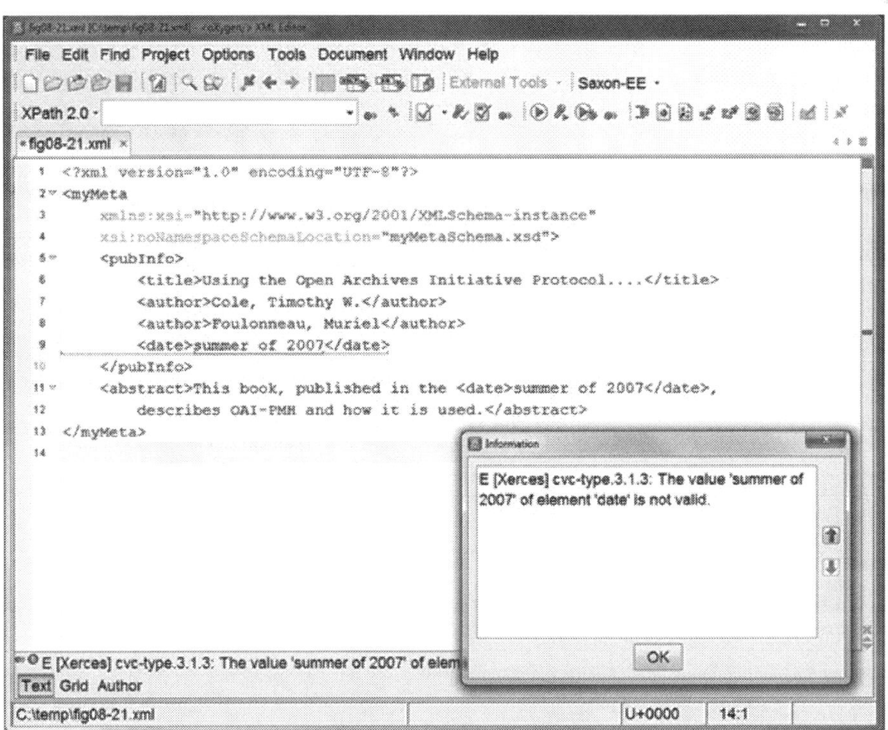

Inheritance Examples

Inheritance is implemented in XSDs using the `<xsd:restriction>` and `<xsd:extension>` elements. These elements allow XSD authors to derive additional content types and content models by restricting and extending simple and complex type definitions. For example, Figure 8.14, discussed above, illustrates the use of `<xsd:restriction>` to derive a new enumerated list simple type with an inheritance from the canonical NMTOKEN type (as a way to constrain values of the type attribute of the MARCXML `<record>` element).

The use of `<xsd:restriction>` in the snippet of the MARCXML XSD shown in Figure 8.22 is a bit more complex. In this example, `<xsd:restriction>` is used to define a new data type named "`indicatorDataType`". The new data type is a restriction on `xsd:string`. A *regular expression*, "`[\da-z]{1}`,", is provided in the `<xsd:pattern>` element to describe the allowed values of attributes conforming to the "`indicatorDataType`." (In computer programming, regular expressions are used as a concise way to express match conditions. In this case, a value matches this particular regular expression if the value is a single digit [1–9], a single lowercase letter [a–z], or a space.) The base `xsd:string` data type is further constrained to preserve white space. (As discussed in Chapter 3, by default, XML parsers normalize white space characters, which in this instance would cause deletion of a single white space character between quotes.) The "`indicatorDataType`" is then referenced when declaring the `ind1` and `ind2` attributes.

Notice that in this instance, the XML validation is less precise than the MARC standard requirement for indicator values. Depending on the format

FIGURE 8.22 Derivation of a new simple content type for `ind1` and `ind2` attributes.

```
XML to Validate (data type of ind1 and ind2):
  <datafield tag="100" ind1="1" ind2=" ">...</datafield>

   <xsd:complexType name="dataFieldType">
       <xsd:sequence maxOccurs="unbounded">
         <xsd:element name="subfield" type="subfieldatafieldType"/>
       </xsd:sequence>
       <xsd:attribute name="id" type="idDataType" use="optional"/>
       <xsd:attribute name="tag" type="tagDataType" use="required"/>
       <xsd:attribute name="ind1" type="indicatorDataType" use="required"/>
       <xsd:attribute name="ind2" type="indicatorDataType" use="required"/>
   </xsd:complexType>
   ...
   <xsd:simpleType name="indicatorDataType">
       <xsd:restriction base="xsd:string">
           <xsd:whiteSpace value="preserve"/>
           <xsd:pattern value="[\da-z ]{1}"/>
       </xsd:restriction>
   </xsd:simpleType>
```

FIGURE 8.23 The use of <xsd:restriction> and <xsd:extension> in tandem.

```
XML to Validate (subfield content and attributes):
  <datafield tag="245" ind1="1" ind2="0">
      <subfield code="a">Using the Open Archive ...</subfield>
      <subfield code="c">by Timothy Cole & Muriel Foulonneau. </subfield>
  </datafield>


  ...
  <xsd:element name="subfield" type="subfieldatafieldType"/>
  ...
  <xsd:complexType name="subfieldatafieldType">
      <xsd:simpleContent>
          <xsd:extension base="subfieldDataType">
              <xsd:attribute name="id" type="idDataType" use="optional"/>
              <xsd:attribute name="code" type="subfieldcodeDataType"
                   use="required"/>
            </xsd:extension>
      </xsd:simpleContent>
    </xsd:complexType>
    ...
    <xsd:simpleType name="subfieldDataType">
        <xsd:restriction base="xsd:string">
            <xsd:whiteSpace value="preserve"/>
        </xsd:restriction>
    </xsd:simpleType>
```

and data field involved, the MARC standard limits valid indicator values to some subset of the digits 0 through 9. Allowed values according to the standard are also context sensitive. It is not currently possible to create in an XSD a truly context-sensitive data type. Validation using XSDs is powerful and will catch many metadata record errors, but for more complete validation, other options may need to be considered (e.g., the use of Schematron, described below).

Finally, Figure 8.23 illustrates the use in the MARCXML XSD of <xsd:restriction> and <xsd:extension> in tandem to derive a new complex type definition, in this case the complex type definition for MARCXML <subfield> elements. First, a new simple type is derived from xsd:string by constraining conforming values to retain white space. In other words, the simple type derivation shown in Figure 8.23 says that XML parsers should not normalize white space appearing in values for any elements or attributes declared as conforming to the subfieldDataType. This simple type definition is then extended to make a new complex type definition named subfielddatafieldType, which requires an attribute. Elements conforming to this new complex type definition, in this instance MARCXML <subfield> elements, must conform to the subfieldDataType as far as content (data type) is concerned but must also include a code attribute (the id attribute is optional).

Although not as full featured as implementations of inheritance models in advanced programming languages, inheritance through the use of `<xsd:restriction>` and `<xsd:extension>` is still quite powerful. It can facilitate the validation of even relatively complex metadata designs, though in a few cases alternative techniques or supplemental approaches (such as adding Schematron statements) may be required.

CASE STUDY 8.1
Checking MARCXML Records Using Oxygen and an XSD

Synopsis: The rigorous validation that XML supports can sometimes reveal latent errors in existing catalog records when these records are converted into MARCXML. The University of Illinois Library found this to be the case when using existing catalog records converted to MARCXML to derive new e-book catalog records describing online resources generated by scanning digitizing volumes from its collections. The University of Illinois Library now uses its work flow of creating new e-book catalog records to identify and correct existing errors in its MARC catalog records.
Illustrates: Validating XML records using Oxygen; working with MARCXML XSD.

When the University of Illinois Library started its large-scale retrospective book digitization work in 2007, the Library decided to create a new, distinct MARC e-book record for each book digitized as it became available online. The Library utilized existing MARC records in its catalog as a starting point for creating new e-book records for the digitized volumes. MARC records were extracted for the books as they were prepared for digitization and then converted to MARCXML to facilitate the derivation of new e-book records. To create the new e-book records, an Extensible Stylesheet Language for Transformations (XSLT) style sheet was written to generate a MARCXML e-book record for each digitized book from the corresponding printed-book MARCXML record. (XSLT style sheets are discussed in Chapter 11.)

When first implemented, the work flow for creating e-book records stopped unexpectedly on a frequent basis. Investigation revealed that stoppages were due to failures when validating the converted print-volume MARCXML records after export from the Library's online catalog. The errors causing the validation problems were traced back to errors in the MARC records in the Library's catalog (i.e., the errors were not being caused by faulty conversion from MARC to MARCXML; there were simply errors in the MARC records).

Most of the books being digitized as part of the University of Illinois digitization project were published before 1923 (i.e., volumes in the public domain). Cataloging practices were not as mature at that time, nor were they as well controlled. Obviously, MARC did not yet exist. Subsequent conversions of catalog records as the Library went through several cataloging system changes introduced additional errors, as did changes over the years in catalog standards supported by the Library. Whenever the Library changed cataloging conventions and subsequently whenever it changed online catalog systems, the mass data conversion that followed introduced some errors. Consequently, it is not altogether surprising (in hindsight) that there are so many latent errors present. What is perhaps slightly more surprising is that the current integrated library system used in the Library has not revealed more of these errors. The Library modified its work flows to identify, review, and deal more quickly with MARC records that fail transformation to XML. The work flow now accommodates these interruptions more routinely. Records that fail XML transformation are reviewed. Once confirmed that a record has a validation problem, the record is corrected both in the work flow for creating new e-book catalog records and by updating the relevant print-volume record as it exists in the Library's production catalog.

Figure 8.24, a screen shot of a MARCXML record in Oxygen, illustrates one common error encountered. In this instance, a `<subfield>` element (a child of the `<datafield tag="245">`) fails validation against the MARCXML schema. Figure 8.25 shows the `xsi:schemaLocation`

FIGURE 8.24 MARCXML record with validation problem. Screen shot was made using Oxygen XML Editor (http://www.oxygenxml.com).

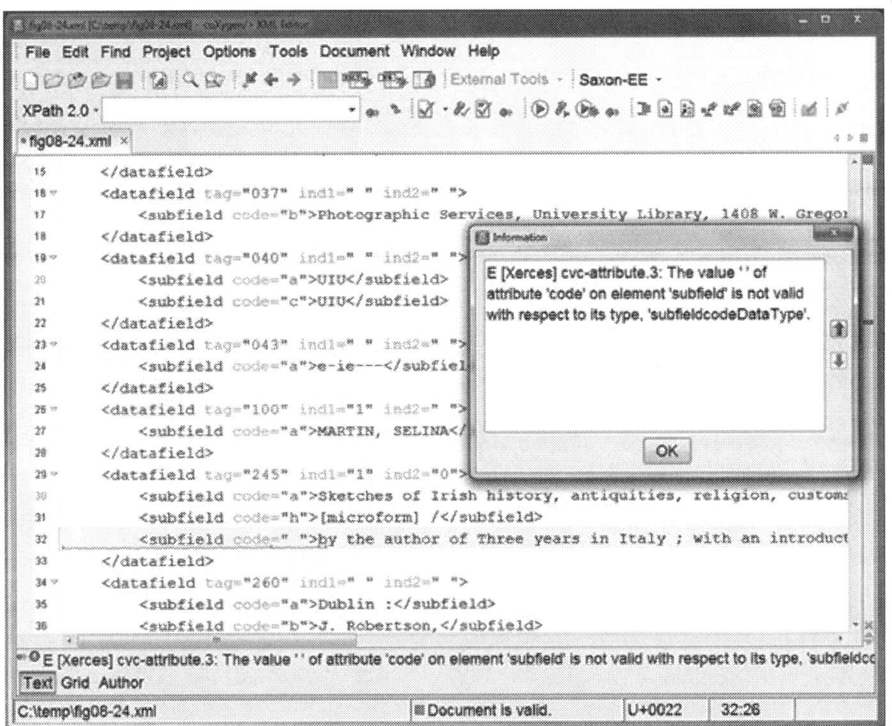

FIGURE 8.25 Header used for the MARCXML record references MARC21 schema.

```
<record
  xsi:schemaLocation="http://www.loc.gov/MARC21/slim
              http://www.loc.gov/standards/marcxml/schema/MARC21slim.xsd"
  xmlns="http://www.loc.gov/MARC21/slim"
  xmlns:xsi="http://www.w3.org/2001/XMLSchema-instance">
```

attribute giving the location of the MARCXML XSD being used for validation. The relevant sections of the schema being used to validate the record are shown in Figure 8.26 (for the complete schema, see Figure 8.10). As shown, the regular expression provided in the MARCXML XSD does require a `code` attribute for all `<subfield>` elements and does not allow the value of that attribute to be empty or a space.

Various other errors were found in other records. For example, the MARCXML schema protected against no indicator or indicators that do not

FIGURE 8.26 MARCXML XSD defines subfield code data type (pattern does not allow for space).

```
<xsd:complexType name="dataFieldType">
  <xsd:sequence maxOccurs="unbounded">
    <xsd:element name="subfield" type="subfieldatafieldType"/>
  </xsd:sequence>
  <xsd:attribute name="id" type="idDataType" use="optional"/>
  <xsd:attribute name="tag" type="tagDataType" use="required"/>
  <xsd:attribute name="ind1" type="indicatorDataType" use="required"/>
  <xsd:attribute name="ind2" type="indicatorDataType" use="required"/>
</xsd:complexType>
...
<xsd:complexType name="subfieldatafieldType">
  <xsd:simpleContent>
    <xsd:extension base="subfieldDataType">
      <xsd:attribute name="id" type="idDataType" use="optional"/>
      <xsd:attribute name="code" type="subfieldcodeDataType"
        use="required"/>
    </xsd:extension>
  </xsd:simpleContent>
</xsd:complexType>
...
<xsd:simpleType name="subfieldcodeDataType">
  <xsd:restriction base="xsd:string">
    <xsd:whiteSpace value="preserve"/>
    <xsd:pattern
value="[\dA-Za-z!&quot;#$%&amp;'()*+,-./:;&lt;=&gt;?{}_^'~\[\]\\]{1}"/>
     <!- "A-Z" added after "\d" May 21, 2009 ->
  </xsd:restriction>
```

FIGURE 8.27 OPAC view of the record with validation problem.

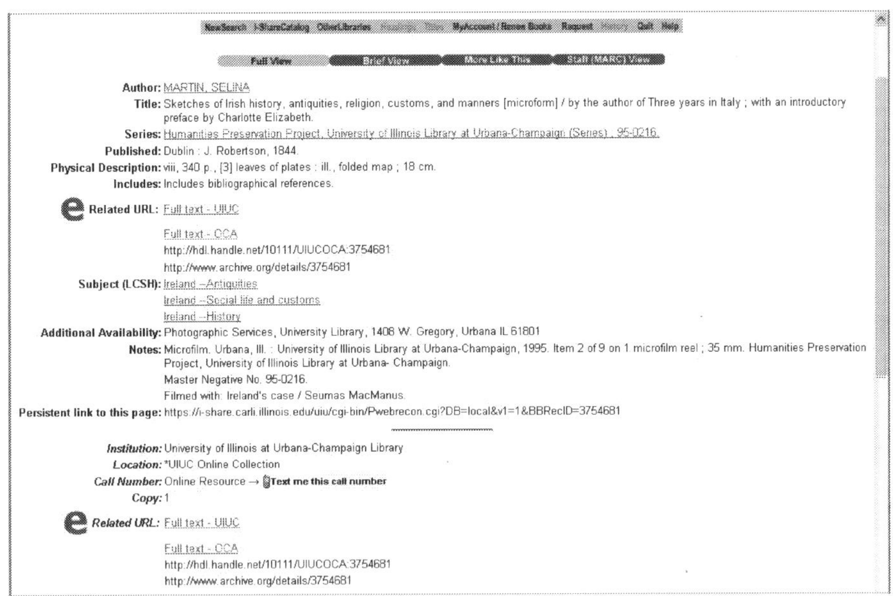

fit the template for indicators generally. However, the schema does not protect against indicator data values that are not allowed based on context. The MARC standard prescribes that when a `datafield` 100 is present in the metadata record, the first indicator of `datafield` 245 must be "0." XSDs generally cannot include constraints of this nature that involve multiple elements (data fields) and attributes (indicators). Validation tests of this sort are more easily expressed using Schematron. (An example at the end of this chapter illustrates how Schematron can work with other, more grammar-based schema languages to facilitate validation of XML documents.)

It is interesting to note that the Library's Online Public Access Catalog (OPAC) displays records with minor errors, such as the examples above, without difficulty (and without reporting the error). Figure 8.27 illustrates the OPAC end-user display of the record with the incorrect code attribute. The error is not apparent. However, the same record in staff view does show the empty value in the subfield code of the 245 field (Figure 8.28). By using XML schema and tools such as Oxygen, the University of Illinois Library can identify and correct catalog records for printed books with validation problems en route to creating catalog records for retrospectively digitized books. Although today the Library uses XML validation only in connection with its retrospective digitization project, there is the potential to use a similar work flow to review and improve other records created during the pre-MARCXML era.

FIGURE 8.28 Staff view of the record with validation problem.

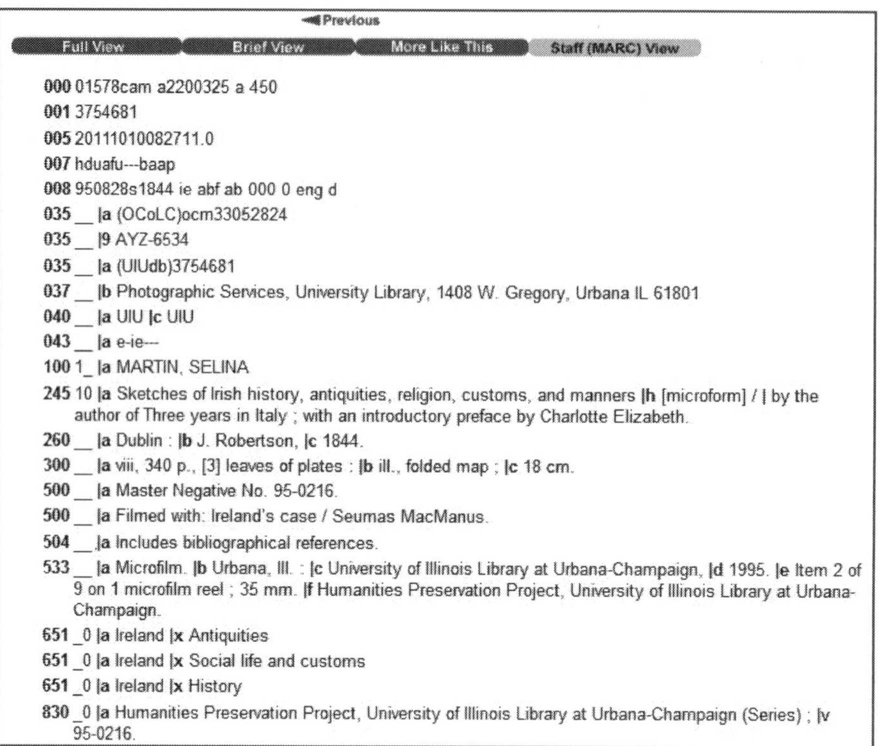

◄Previous

Full View | Brief View | More Like This | Staff (MARC) View

000 01578cam a2200325 a 450
001 3754681
005 20111010082711.0
007 hduafu---baap
008 950828s1844 ie abf ab 000 0 eng d
035 __ |a (OCoLC)ocm33052824
035 __ |9 AYZ-6534
035 __ |a (UIUdb)3754681
037 __ |b Photographic Services, University Library, 1408 W. Gregory, Urbana IL 61801
040 __ |a UIU |c UIU
043 __ |a e-ie---
100 1_ |a MARTIN, SELINA
245 10 |a Sketches of Irish history, antiquities, religion, customs, and manners |h [microform] / | by the author of Three years in Italy ; with an introductory preface by Charlotte Elizabeth.
260 __ |a Dublin : |b J. Robertson, |c 1844.
300 __ |a viii, 340 p., [3] leaves of plates : |b ill., folded map ; |c 18 cm.
500 __ |a Master Negative No. 95-0216.
500 __ |a Filmed with: Ireland's case / Seumas MacManus.
504 __ |a Includes bibliographical references.
533 __ |a Microfilm. |b Urbana, Ill. : |c University of Illinois Library at Urbana-Champaign, |d 1995. |e Item 2 of 9 on 1 microfilm reel ; 35 mm. |f Humanities Preservation Project, University of Illinois Library at Urbana-Champaign.
651 _0 |a Ireland |x Antiquities
651 _0 |a Ireland |x Social life and customs
651 _0 |a Ireland |x History
830 _0 |a Humanities Preservation Project, University of Illinois Library at Urbana-Champaign (Series) ; |v 95-0216.

OTHER SCHEMA LANGUAGES

Beyond DTDs and XSDs, several other XML schema languages have been proposed and/or implemented since the introduction of XML in 1998. One early XML schema language was the *XML Data-Reduced* (XDR) schema language. This schema language was underwritten and developed in large part by Microsoft. Initial release of this schema grammar was in 1998. This language was supported natively by some Microsoft products, in particular some releases of Microsoft SQL Server, and was well suited to applications treating XML as data structures, such as for ingestion into or export from relational databases. Eventually, a mapping between XDR and XSD was established to facilitate interoperability. The use of XDR has faded over time as XSDs have become better established and as XSD has proven an adequate alternative for XDR.

Two other relatively early XML schema grammars of note were *Tree Regular Expressions for XML* (TREX) and *REgular LAnguage Description for XML* (RELAX). In fairly short order, it was recognized that these approaches to schema design were highly complementary. As discussed below, these schema languages, along with elements of other languages, were unified to create one of the languages, REgular LAnguage Descriptions for XML Core New Generation (RELAX NG), described briefly below.

In the context of applications using XML metadata, XSDs and DTDs adequately address most use cases. Both DTDs and XSDs are primarily structure-validation languages, that is, schema languages optimized to express the structural and semantic labeling constraints of a metadata grammar. The data typing available with XSD is generally sufficient for all but the most rigorous metadata validation tasks. For metadata system designers, other XML schema languages will be needed only in unusual circumstances. For those situations, the two most established, most proven alternative schema languages are introduced briefly.

REgular LAnguage Descriptions for XML Core New Generation (RELAX NG)

RELAX NG is a popular alternate schema language for XML. Developed by the RELAX NG Technical Committee of the Organization for the Advancement of Structured Information Standards, version 1.0 of RELAX NG is recognized by the International Organization for Standardization and by the International Electrotechnical Commission (ISO/IEC) (ISO/IEC 10757-2) and as Part 2 of ISO/IEC 19757 DSDL (Document Schema Definition Languages).

As suggested by its acronym, RELAX NG is generally considered a simple and easy-to-learn schema language. As compared to DTDs, RELAX NG has several benefits (some in common with XSDs), including the following:

1. RELAX NG supports XML namespaces.
2. RELAX NG treats attributes uniformly with elements.
3. RELAX NG has unrestricted support for unordered content and mixed content.
4. RELAX NG can be used in conjunction with a separate data typing language, such as W3C XML Schema Definition Language Datatypes.

For these reasons, RELAX NG is put forward as an "evolution and generalization of XML DTDs" (Clark 2001). One of the primary agents behind RELAX NG is James Clark, who also developed TREX.[14] (Not surprisingly therefore, RELAX NG draws heavily on TREX.) In 2002, Clark offered a comparison of RELAX NG and the W3C XML Schema Definition Language in a post to the Internet Engineering Task Force (IETF) and XML ListServ. The main advantage of RELAX NG, Clark suggested, is its support for unordered content and for more attribute use models. When using DTDs or an XSD, the schema author is allowed to define whether attributes are required or optional. However, "RELAX NG integrates attributes into content models, . . . [thereby allowing] more complex constraints between attributes or between attributes and elements" (Clark 2002). This feature has made RELAX NG somewhat more suitable for describing the grammar of the *Resource Description Framework* (RDF) serialized in XML. (RDF is discussed in Chapter 12.)

In addition, RELAX NG has more flexibility with regard to the order of child elements in content models, allowing an "interleave [of] element[s] that gives flexibility in ordering of child elements" (Clark 2002). Another difference between RELAX NG and the W3C XML Schema Definition Language is the way in which an XML document is associated with an XSD file. With XSDs, the `xsi:schemaLocation` attribute is used to give validating parsers a hint as to the location of the schema against which an XML document should be validated. In RELAX NG, an XML document is validated with two independent inputs: a schema and an instance with respect to the schema (Clark 2002). In other words, there is no RELAX NG-specific way in the XML metadata record to prescribe or hint at the location of the schema against which the record should be validated. For developer convenience, some XML tools, such as Oxygen, do recognize tool-specific processing instructions (and the new xml-model processing instruction mentioned above) as ways to fulfill this role during schema development and testing.

RELAX NG is built largely on three earlier and contemporaneous schema languages (comprising a RELAX NG family of schema languages): Regular Language description for XML Core (RELAX or RLX),[15] a specification for describing XML-based grammars; XDuce ("transduce"),[16] a typed programming language specifically designed for processing XML data; and TREX, the type system of XDuce with an XML syntax and additional features that are expressed as easy-to-read plain-text descriptions. In addition, RELAX NG can be used in conjunction with the data types defined as part of the W3C Schema Definition Language.

When creating a RELAX NG schema, the schema follows the structure of the document. RELAX NG does not require markup declarations in the same way as DTDs, such as ELEMENT or ATTLIST. Like XSD, RELAX NG schemas (file extension ".rng") can be created as well-formed XML. Figure 8.29, from the

FIGURE 8.29 Snippets of a DTD and a schema written in RELAX NG (*Source*: RELAX NG Tutorial. Copyright © The Organization for the Advancement of Structured Information Standards [OASIS] 2001. All Rights Reserved).

```
<!DOCTYPE addressBook [
<!ELEMENT addressBook (card*)>
<!ELEMENT card (name, email)>
<!ELEMENT name (#PCDATA)>
<!ELEMENT email (#PCDATA)>
]>
```

```
<element name="addressBook"
        xmlns="http://relaxng.org/ns/
        structure/1.0">
  <zeroOrMore>
      <element name="card">
         <element name="name">
           <text/>
         </element>
         <element name="email">
           <text/>
         </element>
      </element>
   </zeroOrMore>
</element>
```

RELAX NG Tutorial,[17] illustrates the difference between a small DTD and a schema created in RELAX NG. Instead of using markup and document type declarations as present in the DTD (Figure 8.29, left), the schema created in RELAX NG (Figure 8.29, right) nest element definitions much as they would appear in a conforming document, reflecting hierarchy in a more intuitive manner.

RELAX NG has both XML syntax and a compact, non-XML syntax. The XML syntax is based on RELAX Core and TREX. Using XML syntax has multiple benefits; for example, it allows XML tools and technologies to be applied to the schema and makes schema extensible depending on needs. The compact syntax[18] is a non-XML syntax. The compact syntax is supported by tools such as Jing[19] for validation and Trang[20] for translating schemas written in the compact syntax to the standard RELAX NG XML syntax. Figure 8.30 shows a portion of the simple CIMI Dublin Core DTD converted to a RELAX NG schema. Compare to DTD version (Figure 7.19 in Chapter 7) and XSD version (Figure 8.9 in Chapter 8).

Schematron

Known as "a simple and powerful Structural Schema Language" (Jelliffe 2006), *Schematron* is a rule-based schema language for validation. Schematron semantics and syntax allow a metadata grammar developer to define a list of Boolean XPath–based rules; if an XML metadata record passes these rules as expressed in Schematron, the metadata record is considered validated. Otherwise, a validation error message is generated. By contrast DTDs, XSDs and RELAX NG schemas describe the design of an XML metadata grammar. Validation is judged by conformance to that design.

Schematron was published as an ISO/IEC standard in 2006 under the title *Information Technology—Document Schema Definition Languages (DSDL)—Part 3: Rule-Based Validation*. DSDL (ISO 8879:1986) origins predate the advent of XML. DSDL is comprised of a set of languages and validation processes for use with XML or SGML documents. Whereas RELAX NG, as a grammar-based validation approach, fits under DSDL Part 2, Schematron, as a rule-based validation approach, fits under DSDL Part 3. As a rule-based approach, Schematron has flexibility and power not available with the other schema languages discussed in this and the previous chapter. The trade-off is that it can be difficult to create in Schematron a comprehensive schema describing a metadata grammar in full. Often, Schematron is most effective when used in combination with a grammar-based validation schema language, such as RELAX NG.

For example, to validate most constraints associated with a class of XML metadata records, a grammar-based schema language will suffice. Both RELAX NG and the W3C Schema Definition Language can be used for validating value constraints (element data typing) and most structural constraints.

FIGURE 8.30 An RNG for Simple Dublin Core based on the CIMI DTD.

```
<?xml version="1.0" encoding="UTF-8"?>
<grammar xmlns="http://relaxng.org/ns/structure/1.0">
  <start>
    <choice>
      <ref name="dc-record-list"/>
      <ref name="dc-record"/>
    </choice>
  </start>
  <define name="dc-record-list">
    <element name="dc-record-list">
      <ref name="attlist.dc-record-list"/>
      <zeroOrMore>
        <ref name="dc-record"/>
      </zeroOrMore>
    </element>
  </define>
  <define name="attlist.dc-record-list" combine="interleave">
    <empty/>
  </define>
  <define name="dc-record">
    <element name="dc-record">
      <ref name="attlist.dc-record"/>
      <zeroOrMore>
        <ref name="title"/>
      </zeroOrMore>
      <zeroOrMore>
        <ref name="creator"/>
      </zeroOrMore>
  ...
    </element>
  </define>
  <define name="attlist.dc-record" combine="interleave">
    <empty/>
  </define>
  <define name="title">
    <element name="title">
      <ref name="attlist.title"/>
      <text/>
    </element>
  </define>
  <define name="attlist.title" combine="interleave">
    <empty/>
  </define>
  ...
</grammar>
```

Schematron can then be used in a complementary way for validating aspects of usage that are difficult to describe in a grammar-based language, such as a content model that prohibits the presence in one record of two particular child elements having the same content (see example below). Also, as alluded to earlier, Schematron is an option for validating the MARC prohibition against having a first indicator value of 1 on a data field 245 if a data field 100 is also present in the record, something that is not really possible to prohibit using an XSD or a RELAX NG schema.

Figures 8.31 and 8.32 provide a simple, minimal illustration of Schematron used in conjunction with RELAX NG. Assume that a project has defined as metadata best practices for the project's use of Simple Dublin Core the requirement that publisher information (when available) go only in the Simple Dublin Core `<publisher>` element rather than in the `<contributor>` element instead or also. This effectively translates into a prohibition on having any single record containing publisher and contributor elements with identical values.

To achieve this result, a schema author could start with the RELAX NG schema derived from the CIMI Simple Dublin Core DTD (Figure 8.30). Into this schema, he or she could then add a Schematron `<pattern>` element, such as within the node of the RELAX NG schema defining the `<dc-record>` element, as shown in Figure 8.31. This pattern could include a Schematron `<rule>` that checks that when both are present, there are no publisher elements with the same value as any contributor element in the record being validated. The condition to check and the error message to generate when it is violated would appear in the Schematron `<rule>` as an `<assert>` element

FIGURE 8.31 Simple schema example created with Schematron.

```
...
<define name="dc-record">
    <sch:pattern xmlns:sch="http://purl.oclc.org/dsdl/schematron">
      <sch:rule context="dc-record">
        <sch:assert test="(publisher != contributor)
                         or (string-length(publisher[1])=0)
                         or (string-length(contributor[1])=0)">
          Should not have both a publisher element
          and contributor element with same content.</sch:assert>
      </sch:rule>
  </sch:pattern>
  <element name="dc-record">
    <ref name="attlist.dc-record"/>
    <zeroOrMore>
      <ref name="title"/>
    </zeroOrMore>
    ...
</define>
...
```

FIGURE 8.32 A record that generates an error message when evaluated against Schematron schema. Screen shot was made using Oxygen XML Editor (http://www.oxygenxml.com).

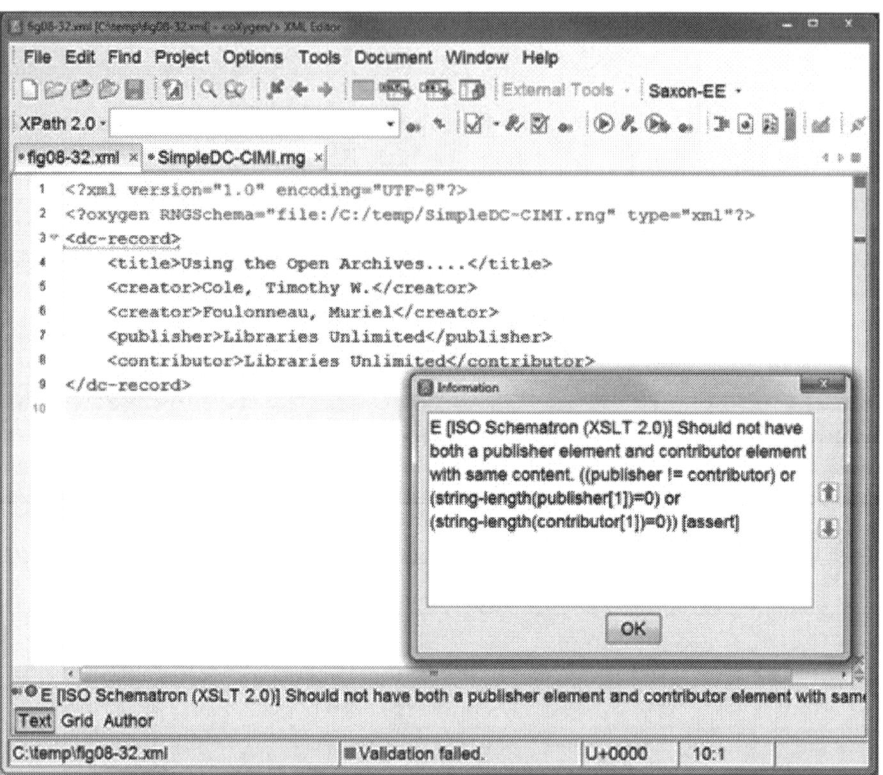

(Figure 8.31). The syntax of the test specified is XPath, which is introduced and illustrated in Chapter 10. Having done this, any attempt to validate a Simple Dublin Core record that violates this rule will result in the validating parser throwing an error message, such as the Oxygen-generated error message shown in Figure 8.32.

QUESTIONS AND TOPICS FOR DISCUSSION

1. Think about the different cases in which you would use DTDs, XSDs, RELAX NG, or Schematron-based schemas.
2. What are the main advantages and disadvantages of using DTDs? What are the main advantages and disadvantages of using XSDs?
3. Chapters 7 and 8 introduced schema languages. Considering also the discussion presented in Chapter 2, discuss how understanding and making greater use of different kinds of XML schemas might impact metadata creation and management and alter current library work flows.

SUGGESTIONS FOR EXERCISES

1. Create a simple XML record describing your class or work schedule. Then create a DTD against which to validate such XML representations of schedules. (Include at least one attribute.)
2. Create an XSD equivalent to the DTD created in exercise 1. Use a `<complexType>` definition that includes either `<sequence>` or `<choice>`.

NOTES

1. http://xml.coverpages.org/schemas.html.
2. http://www.w3.org/TR/xmlschema-0.
3. http://relaxng.org.
4. http://www.schematron.com.
5. http://www.w3.org/TR/NOTE-xml-schema-req.
6. http://www.w3.org/TR/xmlschema-1.
7. http://www.w3.org/TR/xmlschema-2.
8. http://msdn.microsoft.com/en-us/library/windows/desktop/ms759142.
9. http://www.iana.org/assignments/media-types/index.html.
10. http://www.w3.org/TR/xml-model.
11. http://www.w3.org/TR/xml.
12. http://www.w3.org/TR/xmlschema-0.
13. http://www.loc.gov/standards/marcxml/schema/MARC21slim.xsd.
14. http://www.xml.com/pub/a/2001/12/12/schemacompare.html?page=3#b_trex.
15. http://www.xml.gr.jp/relax.
16. http://xduce.sourceforge.net.
17. http://relaxng.org/tutorial-20011203.html.
18. http://relaxng.org/compact-tutorial-20030326.html#id2817637.
19. http://www.thaiopensource.com/relaxng/jing.html.
20. http://www.thaiopensource.com/relaxng/trang.html.

REFERENCES

Clark, James. 2001. "The Design of RELAX NG." Available at: http://www.thaiopensource.com/relaxng/design.html#xml-rec

Clark, James. 2002. "RELAX NG and W3C XML Schema." Available at: http://www.imc.org/ietf-xml-use/mail-archive/msg00217.html

Jelliffe, Rick. 2006. "Schematron: An XML Structure Validation Language using Patterns in Trees." Available at: http://xml.ascc.net/resource/schematron/

Library of Congress. 2002. "MARCXML: The MARC 21 XML Schema." Available at: http://www.loc.gov/standards/marcxml/schema/MARC21slim.xsd

World Wide Web Consortium. 1999. "XML Schema Requirements." Available at: http://www.w3.org/TR/xmlschema-1

World Wide Web Consortium. 2004. "XML Schema Part 1: Structures Second Edition." Available at: http://www.w3.org/TR/xmlschema-1/

CHAPTER 9

Advanced XML Grammars: Schemas and Namespaces, Uniqueness, and Keys

Library applications and services that make use of metadata typically count on a healthy measure of metadata record consistency. Metadata-based search and discovery systems count on the availability of certain fields for creating indexes and for supporting facet-based browsing and search refinement. Systems that display descriptive metadata records to end users, such as library online public access catalogs, rely on the availability of certain fields in order to build record displays and may make assumptions about the data type or format of values contained these fields. Shared cataloging utilities, such as the Online Computer Library Center, enforce consistency with regard to catalog record structure and the format of data entered as a way to ensure interoperability and facilitate record sharing and reuse. *Semantic Web*[1] and *Linked Open Data*[2] tools and services require consistent conformance to the standards and best practices of these communities.

A benefit of using XML to serialize metadata is that desired levels of record-to-record structural and format consistency can be achieved and maintained efficiently and effectively, in large measure at least, through XML validation using Document Type Definitions (DTDs), XML Schema Definition documents (XSDs), and/or other forms of XML schemas. As discussed in Chapters 7 and 8, these approaches support rigorous validation while still allowing for a high degree of application-specific customization. XML schemas can be used to characterize the semantics and structural outlines of a broad range of metadata standards, allowing metadata system developers to express the unique compositional constraints and data type requirements of such standards in a manner that enables automated metadata record validation.

In the basic examples considered so far, metadata record validation has been treated as a *Boolean* proposition; either a metadata record is wholly valid or it is invalid. Validation assessments based on XML DTDs allow no other result. However, for many use cases, piecemeal or even incomplete validation of a metadata record will suffice. For example, to support a particular public access content management service, it may be sufficient to simply ask, Do these metadata records contain the elements, correctly formatted and structured, required for indexing and display? The presence or absence of other elements—or the valid formatting of any other element value—is incidental to the functioning of the content management system. Incomplete record validation suffices.

Other, more advanced use cases may require validating metadata records piecemeal against multiple schema documents. For example, consider a metadata-based service designed to make use of records conforming to a metadata application profile (Chapter 6) that borrows selected (i.e., not all) semantics and rules from both the Library of Congress Metadata Object Description Schema (MODS) standard and the Simple Dublin Core metadata standard. In such a scenario, the relevant question may be, Do the elements borrowed from MODS and Simple Dublin Core that appear in this collection of metadata records conform to the rules of MODS and Simple Dublin Core for these individual elements (i.e., even though none of the records are complete and wholly valid with respect to either MODS or Simple Dublin Core)? For these scenarios and to support many other use cases, there frequently is a need to *partially validate* XML metadata records against one or more XSD files (or alternative schema documents).

Still, other use cases may require more complex forms of validation than illustrated in the basic validation examples provided in Chapters 7 and 8. For example, an application may require that certain elements appear together in a coordinated fashion or not at all. Other applications require that attribute values be unique, such as each value for an attribute designed to indicate order should be unique so as to avoid ambiguity. Often, such requirements can be handled in the World Wide Web Consortium (W3C) XML Schema Definition Language through the use of the `<xsd:unique>`, `<xsd:key>`, and/or `<xsd:keyref>` elements, as described later in the chapter.

This chapter examines the features of XSDs that support more sophisticated grammars and more flexible validation models, including partial validation. The chapter begins by looking at how XSDs can be used with XML Namespaces to support a variety of validation scenarios, including piecemeal validation consistent with a specific metadata application profile. As an example of validation against an application profile, Case Study 9-1 illustrates how an XSD can be designed to integrate (through reference) semantic labels and structural constraints drawn from multiple metadata standards, thereby allowing validation against an application profile designed for describing digitized Renaissance emblem books and their contents. Also discussed in this chapter are advanced features of XSDs that can constrain uniqueness and/or referential integrity within any given XML metadata record, thereby providing a more robust, flexible alternative to the use of XML ID and IDREF attributes (as discussed in Chapter 3). This chapter closes with Case Study 9.2, illustrating the use of these advanced XSD features in the context of the Digital Library Federation Asset Action Experiment (Chavez et al. 2006).

USING XML NAMESPACES AND XML SCHEMAS TOGETHER

As discussed in Chapter 6, XML Namespaces provide a way for metadata application developers to label (i.e., identify) and reference the discrete XML metadata grammars they design and use. For example, the Dublin Core Metadata Initiative uses the *namespace URI* http://purl.org/dc/elements/1.1/, as the collective label (*namespace name*) for the 15 elements of Simple Dublin Core. The Library of Congress uses the namespace URI http://www.loc.gov/mods/v3 as the collective label (namespace name) for its MODS metadata grammar. In XML metadata records, namespace names are bound to *namespace prefixes* through the use of special attributes starting "`xmlns`" that are reserved for this purpose (e.g., `xmlns:mods="http://www.loc.gov/mods/v3"` or `xmlns:dc="http://purl.org/dc/elements/1.1/"`). The purpose of qualifying element, and sometimes attribute, names and values appearing in an XML metadata record with the appropriate namespace prefix, is to enable a user (or a computer application) to recognize, for example, the difference between references in the record to a Simple Dublin Core title element (`<dc:title>`) and a MODS title element (`<mods:title>`).

The `targetNamespace` Attribute in XSD

When creating an XML schema—that is, an XML document that declares the semantic labels (names) of an XML metadata grammar and defines the structural and data type constraints of the grammar—a mechanism is required to associate the names of elements, attributes, and type definitions being declared in the schema with a particular namespace URI. This is managed in XSDs largely through the use of three optional attributes on the `<xsd:schema>` element, the root element of an XSD. (These attributes appear on the root element of an XSD because, though a single XSD file can reference elements, attributes, and type definitions contained in multiple other namespaces, it can declare new elements, attributes, and type definitions for only a single namespace.) The three attributes are `targetNamespace` (discussed here), `elementFormDefault`, and `attributeFormDefault` (discussed later).

To illustrate, consider the XSD for Simple Dublin Core introduced in Chapter 8 (Figure 8.9). This XSD was derived from the Consortium for the Computer Interchange of Museum Information DTD for Simple Dublin Core introduced in Chapter 7 (Figure 7.19). The XSD shown in Figure 8.9 is not tied to a namespace name, and the declarations and definitions of the XSD are not associated with any namespace URI. Accordingly, the sample record (Figure 8.16) illustrating validation against this XSD does not mention the Simple Dublin Core namespace and points to the XSD file using the `xsi:noNamespaceSchemaLocation` attribute from the XML Schema Instance namespace (http://www.w3.org/2001/XMLSchema-instance, typically bound, as here, to the `xsi` namespace prefix).

FIGURE 9.1 XSD associated with the namespace URI for Simple Dublin Core.

```
<?xml version="1.0" encoding="UTF-8"?>
<xsd:schema
   xmlns="http://purl.org/dc/elements/1.1/"
   targetNamespace="http://purl.org/dc/elements/1.1/"
   xmlns:xsd="http://www.w3.org/2001/XMLSchema"
   elementFormDefault="qualified">
   <xsd:element name="dc-record-list">
     <xsd:complexType>
         <xsd:sequence>
             <xsd:element minOccurs="0" maxOccurs="unbounded" ref="dc-record"/>
         </xsd:sequence>
     </xsd:complexType>
   </xsd:element>
   <xsd:element name="dc-record">
       <xsd:complexType>
           <xsd:sequence>
               <xsd:element minOccurs="0" maxOccurs="unbounded" ref="title"/>
               <xsd:element minOccurs="0" maxOccurs="unbounded" ref="creator"/>
               <xsd:element minOccurs="0" maxOccurs="unbounded" ref="subject"/>
               ...
               <xsd:element minOccurs="0" maxOccurs="unbounded" ref="rights"/>
           </xsd:sequence>
       </xsd:complexType>
   </xsd:element>
   <xsd:element name="title" type="xsd:string"/>
   <xsd:element name="creator" type="xsd:string"/>
   <xsd:element name="subject" type="xsd:string"/>
   ...
   <xsd:element name="rights" type="xsd:string"/>
</xsd:schema>
```

An alternative approach would have been to associate global element and attribute declarations in the XSD with a namespace URI, in this case with the namespace URI for Simple Dublin Core, http://purl.org/dc/elements/1.1/, by including a `targetNamespace` attribute in the XSD (see Figure 9.1). The only difference between the XSD shown in Figure 8.9 and the XSD shown in Figure 9.1 is the addition of the `xmlns` and `targetNamespace` attributes (bolded in Figure 9.1 for emphasis). However, simply by adding these two attributes, document instances conforming to the XSD shown in Figure 9.1 must include the appropriate namespace declaration attribute (i.e., `xmlns:dc="http://purl.org/dc/elements/1.1/"`) and should point to the XSD using the `xsi:schemaLocation` attribute, as in Figure 9.2 (compare to Figure 8.16).

Note also in Figure 9.2 that the value of `xsi:schemaLocation` is a pair of strings separated by a space (unlike the value of the attribute `xsi:noNamespaceSchemaLocation`, which is always a single string giving the URL for the XSD). When using `xsi:schemaLocation`, the first string is

FIGURE 9.2 Document instance conforming to XSD shown in Figure 9.1. Screen shot was made using Oxygen XML Editor (http://www.oxygenxml.com).

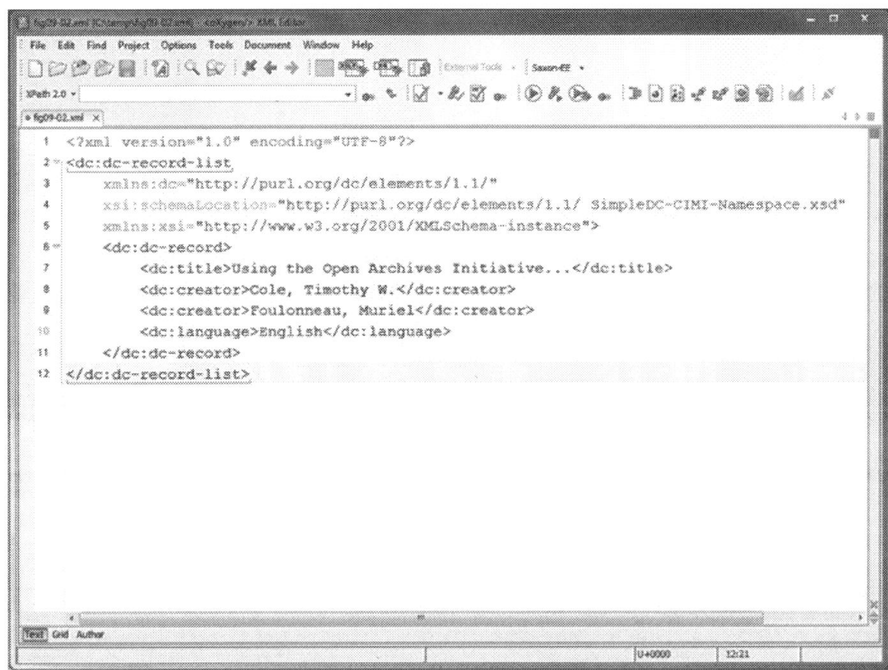

a namespace URI (namespace name). The second string is the location of (URL for) the XSD. This paired approach for pointing to an XSD and associating it with a particular namespace is necessary because a single XML metadata record may contain elements from more than a single namespace. In fact, as illustrated in a subsequent example, `xsi:schemaLocation` can take as a value multiple (white space separated) namespace-URI and XSD-URL pairs.

The `<xsd:import>` Element in XSD

There are two reasons to reference namespace URIs in XSD files and XML metadata records, as illustrated in Figures 9.1 and 9.2. The first is to provide information to librarians and computer applications that make use of an XSD and conforming XML metadata records. While XML provides the means to label the content objects of a metadata record (in this instance, title, creator, language) and while XSD provides a way to validate the occurrence and data types of these content objects, the semantic meaning of metadata record content objects must be described separately. The Dublin Core Metadata Initiative, for instance, maintains reference and best-practice guidelines and an RDF Schema (see Chapter 12) that collectively describe the meaning and semantically appropriate use of the 15 elements of Simple Dublin Core. Although the names of the 15 Simple Dublin Core elements are meant to be intuitive, users of Dublin Core must refer to these guidelines to know for certain how to populate the Simple Dublin Core elements with values, such as how to use the Simple Dublin Core <source> element or to know that in the Simple Dublin Core standard, the names of authors should be expressed using the <creator> element. By associating elements in an XSD and conforming XML metadata records with the Simple Dublin Core namespace URI, the metadata creator is telling consumers of the metadata records that they can use the guidelines posted on the DCMI Web site to interpret the metadata values.

The second reason to reference namespaces in XSD files and XML metadata records, as alluded to above, is to allow mixing of semantics from different standards. For example, in the context of a particular project, a developer might be comfortable using the Simple Dublin Core element <title> to express the title property of a resource being described but might prefer the MODS <name> element (and its content model) for expressing author names. There are multiple ways to describe this preference (as a validation requirement) in an XSD. The most straightforward way is to make use of the <xsd:import> element of the W3C Schema Definition Language, as illustrated in Figures 9.3 and 9.4.

The XSD shown in Figure 9.3 includes a targetNamespace attribute associating the declarations and definitions of the XSD with a fictitious namespace URI created for this illustration, http://myuniversity.edu/myNamespace. The XSD shown in Figure 9.3 also declares namespace prefixes for both Simple Dublin Core and MODS (xmlns:dc and xmlns:mods attributes) and "imports" an XSD for each of these namespaces using the <xsd:import> element. Notice that this element has a required attribute,

FIGURE 9.3 Using <xsd:import> for a content model mixing MODS and Dublin Core.

```
<?xml version="1.0" encoding="UTF-8"?>
<xsd:schema
    targetNamespace="http://myuniversity.edu/myNamespace"
    xmlns="http://myuniversity.edu/myNamespace"
    xmlns:xsd="http://www.w3.org/2001/XMLSchema"
    xmlns:dc="http://purl.org/dc/elements/1.1/"
    xmlns:mods="http://www.loc.gov/mods/v3">
    <xsd:import namespace="http://www.loc.gov/mods/v3"
        schemaLocation="http://www.loc.gov/standards/mods/mods.xsd"/>
    <xsd:import namespace="http://purl.org/dc/elements/1.1/"
    schemaLocation="http://dublincore.org/schemas/xmls/simpledc20021212.xsd"/>
    <xsd:element name="myMetadata" type="baseContentModel"/>
    <xsd:complexType name="baseContentModel">
        <xsd:sequence>
            <xsd:element ref="dc:title" minOccurs="1" maxOccurs="1"/>
            <xsd:element ref="mods:name" minOccurs="0" maxOccurs="unbounded"/>
        </xsd:sequence>
    </xsd:complexType>
</xsd:schema>
```

FIGURE 9.4 Metadata record conforming to XSD of Figure 9.3. Screen shot was made using Oxygen XML Editor (http://www.oxygenxml.com).

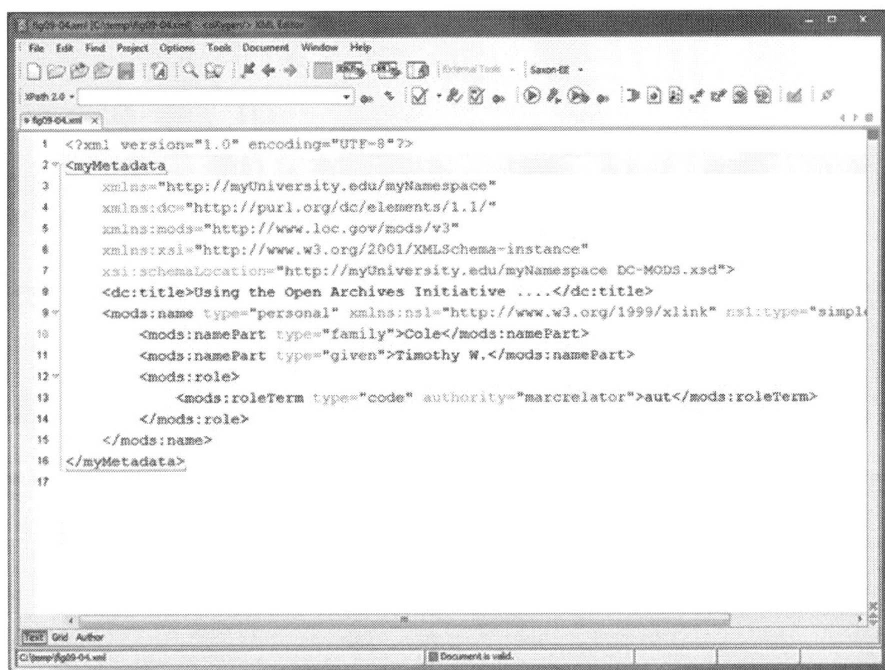

namespace, and an optional (but nearly always included in practice) attribute, schemaLocation (not to be confused with xsi:schemaLocation). The purpose of including an <xsd:import> element at the top of an XSD is to allow references in subsequent XSD declarations and definitions to element names, attribute names, and type definitions from the "imported" XSD. In the example shown in Figure 9.3, the XSD author declares an element, <myMetadata>, in the fictitious "myNamespace" namespace. The XSD author then defines the content model of this element such that an instance of <myMetadata> must contain exactly one occurrence of <dc:title> and may contain an unbounded number of <mods:name> elements. Figure 9.4 shows an XML metadata record that meets these requirements.

The Open Archives Initiative Protocol for Metadata Harvesting (OAI-PMH) provides a simple, real-world example illustrating the use of the <xsd:import> element. To promote interoperability between digital content repositories, OAI-PMH mandates that all metadata items shared using the protocol be made available as XML metadata records conforming to the XSD shown in Figure 9.5. The canonical copy of this XSD is retrievable from a persistent link on the OAI-PMH Web site.[3] (Metadata items held by a repository can be disseminated as XML conforming to other XSDs as well, but at a minimum, all metadata must be shareable as oai_dc records.) The XSD shown in Figure 9.5 describes the OAI-PMH implementation of Simple

FIGURE 9.5 The XSD defining the OAI-PMH implementation of Simple Dublin Core.

```
<schema targetNamespace="http://www.openarchives.org/OAI/2.0/oai_dc/"
        xmlns:oai_dc="http://www.openarchives.org/OAI/2.0/oai_dc/"
        xmlns:dc="http://purl.org/dc/elements/1.1/"
        xmlns="http://www.w3.org/2001/XMLSchema"
        elementFormDefault="qualified" attributeFormDefault="unqualified">

<annotation>
  <documentation>
      XML Schema 2002-03-18 by Pete Johnston.
      Adjusted for usage in the OAI-PMH.
      Schema imports the Dublin Core elements from the DCMI schema for
             unqualified Dublin Core.
      2002-12-19 updated to use simpledc20021212.xsd (instead of
             simpledc20020312.xsd)
  </documentation>
</annotation>

<import namespace="http://purl.org/dc/elements/1.1/"
schemaLocation="http://dublincore.org/schemas/xmls/simpledc20021212.xsd"/>

<element name="dc" type="oai_dc:oai_dcType"/>

<complexType name="oai_dcType">
  <choice minOccurs="0" maxOccurs="unbounded">
    <element ref="dc:title"/>
    <element ref="dc:creator"/>
    <element ref="dc:subject"/>
    <element ref="dc:description"/>
    <element ref="dc:publisher"/>
    <element ref="dc:contributor"/>
    <element ref="dc:date"/>
    <element ref="dc:type"/>
    <element ref="dc:format"/>
    <element ref="dc:identifier"/>
    <element ref="dc:source"/>
    <element ref="dc:language"/>
    <element ref="dc:relation"/>
    <element ref="dc:coverage"/>
    <element ref="dc:rights"/>
  </choice>
</complexType>

</schema>
```

Dublin Core. This XSD is referenced by the more than 3,000 repositories currently supporting OAI-PMH (as of the sping of 2013).[4]

Notice that the XSD includes a `targetNamespace` attribute that associates the declarations of the XSD with the namespace URI `http://`

FIGURE 9.6 XML metadata record that is valid with respect to XSD in Figure 9.5. Screen shot was made using Oxygen XML Editor (http://www.oxygenxml.com).

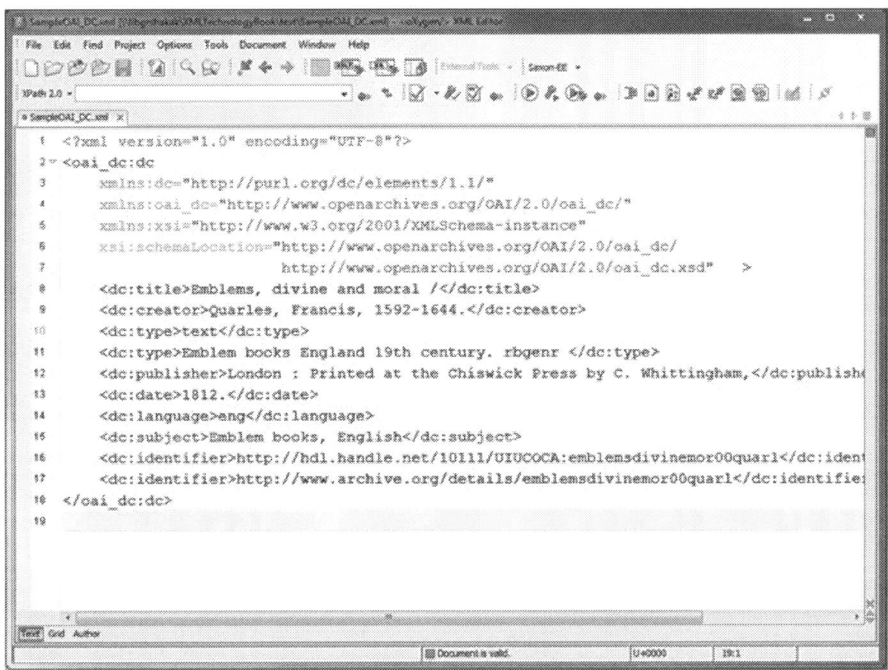

www.openarchives.org/OAI/2.0/oai_dc/, which is owned and maintained by the OAI-PMH initiative. The complex type oai_dcType and the element that conforms to this type definition, <dc>, are contained in this namespace. The XSD also imports a schema from the Dublin Core Metadata Initiative (DCMI) Web site. The namespace URI associated with the "imported" schema (i.e., the value of the <import> element's namespace attribute) is the canonical namespace URI for Simple Dublin Core, http://purl.org/dc/elements/1.1/. The "imported" schema declares and defines the 15 elements of Simple Dublin Core. These 15 definitions are then referenced in the XSD shown in Figure 9.5 to define the content model for its <dc> element such that this element is allowed to contain any Simple Dublin Core element (zero, once, or multiple times) in any order. The XML metadata record shown in Figure 9.6 is valid with respect to the XSD shown in Figure 9.5. The metadata shown in Figure 9.6 was retrieved using OAI-PMH from a University of Illinois Library repository. This record is a transformation of a MARCXML record derived from a University of Illinois Library catalog record for an English-language Renaissance emblem book.

The <xsd:any> and <xsd:anyAttribute> Elements in XSD

An alternative to <xsd:import> as a way to allow elements in metadata records from other namespaces is the W3C XML Schema Definition Language <xsd:any> element. The XSD shown in Figure 9.7 illustrates

FIGURE 9.7 XSD using the <any> element.

```
<?xml version="1.0" encoding="UTF-8"?>
<xsd:schema
    targetNamespace="http://myuniversity.edu/myNamespace"
    xmlns="http://myuniversity.edu/myNamespace"
    xmlns:xsd="http://www.w3.org/2001/XMLSchema">
    <xsd:element name="myMetadata" type="baseContentModel2"/>
    <xsd:complexType name="baseContentModel2">
        <xsd:choice minOccurs="0" maxOccurs="unbounded">
            <xsd:any namespace="http://purl.org/dc/elements/1.1/"/>
            <xsd:any namespace="http://www.loc.gov/mods/v3"/>
        </xsd:choice>
        <xsd:anyAttribute namespace="##any"/>
    </xsd:complexType>
</xsd:schema>
```

the use of this element. Similar to the XSD shown in Figure 9.3, this schema declares the <myMetadata> element and assigns it to the fictitious namespace with the namespace URI http://myuniversity.edu/myNamespace. The XSD in Figure 9.3 requires that <myMetadata> contain exactly one <dc:title> element and an unbounded number of <mods:name> elements. In contrast, the XSD in Figure 9.7, while supporting this content model, is more permissive, allowing <myMetadata> to contain an unbounded number of any of the elements from the Simple Dublin Core namespace, intermingled in any order with any number of any of the elements from the MODS namespace.

The XSD shown in Figure 9.7 also makes use of the <xsd:anyAttribute> element, which in this instance allows attributes from any namespace (the meaning of ##any) to appear on the <myMetadata> element, such as the xml:lang attribute as in Figure 9.8. Other special values of namespace allowed on the <xsd:any> and <xsd:anyAttribute> elements are ##other, ##local, and ##targetNamespace, allowing, respectively, elements or attributes from namespaces other than the target namespace of the XSD, from no namespace (unqualified), or from the target namespace of the XSD only.

Because the XSD in Figure 9.7 is not explicit about which elements from the Simple Dublin Core and MODS namespaces are to be allowed in the content model for <myMetadata>—the schema simply says that any elements from the two namespaces are allowed as children of <myMetadata>—the schema does not have to make explicit reference to any of the semantic labels from these namespaces. This in turn means that the XSD shown in Figure 9.7 does not need to use the <xsd:import> element. (Use of the <xsd:import> element in this XSD is allowed but not required.) However, while this simplifies construction of the XSD, the absence of explicit <xsd:import> elements in the XSD means that any XML metadata records conforming to the

FIGURE 9.8 XML metadata record valid with respect to the XSD shown in Figure 9.7. Screen shot was made using Oxygen XML Editor (http://www.oxygenxml.com).

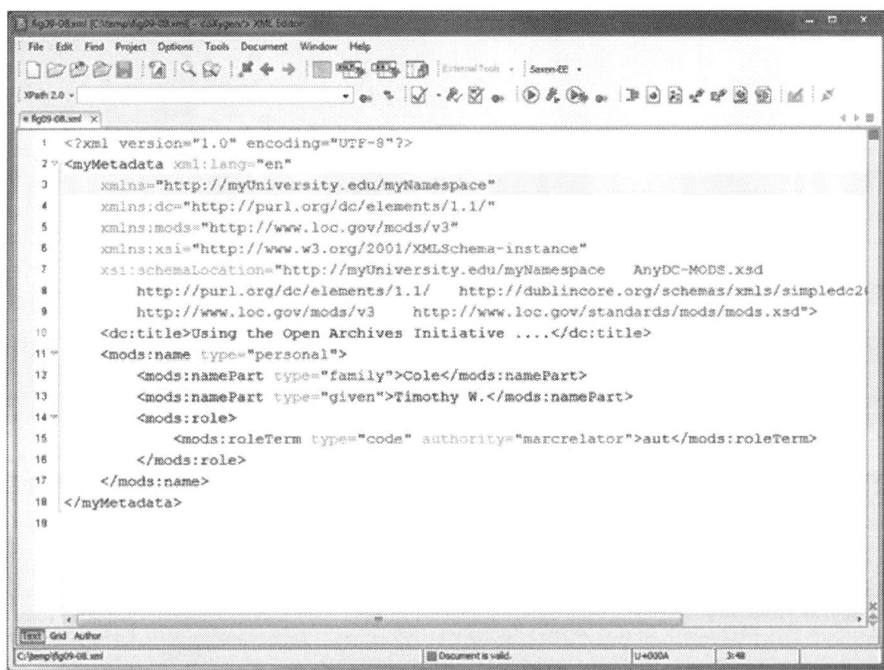

```
<?xml version="1.0" encoding="UTF-8"?>
<myMetadata xml:lang="en"
    xmlns="http://myUniversity.edu/myNamespace"
    xmlns:dc="http://purl.org/dc/elements/1.1/"
    xmlns:mods="http://www.loc.gov/mods/v3"
    xmlns:xsi="http://www.w3.org/2001/XMLSchema-instance"
    xsi:schemaLocation="http://myUniversity.edu/myNamespace   AnyDC-MODS.xsd
        http://purl.org/dc/elements/1.1/   http://dublincore.org/schemas/xmls/simpledc2
        http://www.loc.gov/mods/v3    http://www.loc.gov/standards/mods/mods.xsd">
    <dc:title>Using the Open Archives Initiative ....</dc:title>
    <mods:name type="personal">
        <mods:namePart type="family">Cole</mods:namePart>
        <mods:namePart type="given">Timothy W.</mods:namePart>
        <mods:role>
            <mods:roleTerm type="code" authority="marcrelator">aut</mods:roleTerm>
        </mods:role>
    </mods:name>
</myMetadata>
```

XSD shown in Figure 9.7 should reference the XSD for Simple Dublin Core and the XSD for MODS. This reference is accomplished by including additional namespace-URI and XSD-location-URL pairs in the `xsi:schema Location` attribute value, as shown in Figure 9.8 (compare to Figure 9.4). Alternatively, if `<xsd:import>` is used in the XSD, a reference to other XSD URLs in the XML metadata record is not needed (and likely would be ignored).

The `processContents` Attribute in XSD

In his aptly titled paper "How Schema-Validity Is Different from Being Married," Sperberg-McQueen (2005) notes that it is often "unhelpful to reduce validity to a single bit of information," that is, to a simple True/False Boolean assessment of an XML document instance considered as an indivisible whole. In the context of the Web, some applications consuming XML metadata records, in most cases Web browsers, do not need to check validity. As long as the XML metadata record is well-formed (with no unresolved general entities), a Web browser is able to parse and present the XML record as received. Other applications, such as content management systems, Web syndication tools, and shared cataloging utilities, require XML metadata records that conform, at least in part, to a particular metadata standard or application profile. These applications do not function properly if the metadata records provided do not include the elements, properly formatted, on which the application relies. However, many of these applications need to parse and use only selected portions of a metadata record; therefore, they need confirmation of conformance over only selected elements and attributes of a record. Providing these applications with only a True/False assessment of an XML metadata record's validity in its entirety can result in such applications skipping some partially valid metadata records that they could process. A rigid, whole record binary approach to validity assessment can make it harder to use a single XML metadata record for multiple purposes (some requiring validation and some not) and can have a chilling effect on experimentation with extensibility.

Web syndication applications, Web-based services that facilitate current awareness tracking of updates to Web sites (e.g., allowing readers to keep up with breaking news via regularly updated "feeds" viewable in their Web browsers), are a good example of the class of applications that are satisfied with partial validation. (See Chapter 6 for an example of how Web syndication tools and protocols are used in libraries to support current awareness services for library users.) The two most popular protocols for Web Syndication services, RSS 2.0[5] and Atom 1.0,[6] rely on XML metadata records. (Initially, the acronym RSS stood for "RDF Site Summary," later for "Rich Site Summary," and most commonly today for "Really Simple Syndication.") Both formats allow for the inclusion in syndication metadata records of well-formed XML fragments that may or may not be valid against any schema. For purposes of extensibility, the RSS 2.0 format explicitly supports the inclusion in syndication records of elements and attributes not mentioned in the RSS 2.0 specification, as long as these elements and attributes are associated with a non-RSS 2.0 namespace. Similarly, the Atom 1.0 specification explicitly allows markup from other vocabularies in Atom records, that is, as "foreign markup," in the terminology of the Atom specification (section 6, "Extending Atom").

So how is partial validation implemented in practice? Most common scenarios relying on XSDs still involve starting validation at the root element of the XML metadata record. Although some validating parsers allow this behavior to be overridden, in practice partial validation of XML-serialized metadata typically is accomplished by instructing or allowing validating parsers to selectively skip or bypass the validation of child nodes below the root level. Protocol standards and documents like the Atom Syndication Format Proposed Standard (Internet Engineering Task Force Request for Comment 4287) levy specific requirements on validating parsers in this regard:

> Atom Processors that encounter foreign markup in a location that is legal according to this specification MUST NOT stop processing or signal an error. It might be the case that the Atom Processor is able to process the foreign markup correctly and does so. Otherwise, such markup is termed "unknown foreign markup." When unknown foreign markup is encountered as a child of `atom:entry`, `atom:feed`, or a `Person Construct`, Atom Processors MAY bypass the markup and any textual

> content and MUST NOT change their behavior as a result of the markup's presence. When unknown foreign markup is encountered in a `Text Construct` or `atom:content` element, software SHOULD ignore the markup and process any text content of foreign elements as though the surrounding markup were not present. (Nottingham and Sayre 2005)

In order to support partial validation of XML document instances, the W3C XML Schema Definition Language Part I specification[7] defines an approach to validation assessment that is more nuanced than that allowed by XML DTDs. The specification allows for more granular validation, for example, at the level of individual XML elements and attributes as well as at the level of an entire XML document instance. The specification requires validating parsers to report validation actions and results at the level of each element and attribute and allows parsers to report skipping validation of particular elements or attributes, for example, because no XSD is available for the namespace containing these elements or attributes. When skipping the validation of an element and its children entirely or in part, validating parsers are allowed to report a "not known" validation result in lieu of a valid or invalid result. Accommodation for partial validation is signaled in an XSD through the use of the `processContent` attribute, which can appear on both the `<xsd:any>` element and the `<xsd:anyAttribute>` element. Allowed values for `processContent` attribute are the following:

- "`strict`" (Default. The elements or attributes allowed by the `<xsd:any>` or `<xsd:anyAttribute>` element must be validated.)
- "`lax`" (The elements or attributes allowed by the `<xsd:any>` or `<xsd:anyAttribute>` element should be validated if mentioned in an XSD available to the parser; otherwise, validation of these elements or attributes may be skipped.)
- "`skip`" (The elements or attributes allowed by the `<xsd:any>` or `<xsd:anyAttribute>` element should be skipped, that is, should not be validated.)

The availability of the `processContent` attribute allows XSD authors to control where and when partial validation is allowed; however, care must be taken to ensure that the desired validation does take place. The XSD shown in Figure 9.9 is identical to that shown in Figure 9.7 except for the addition of the `processContent` attribute on the second `<xsd:any>` element. The value of "`lax`" for this attribute allows validating parsers to skip any MODS elements when validating an XML metadata record if no XSD for MODS is available. In practical terms, for most validating XML parsers that rely on the `xsi:schemaLocation` hint to locate XSDs for validation, this value means that if the MODS XSD reference is left out of the `xsi:schemaLocation` attribute value, then erroneous MODS elements and attribute values will not be reported, as illustrated in Figure 9.10. In this instance, the reference to the MODS XSD URL was neglected and is not present in the metadata record. The values of the `type` attributes on the `<mods:namePart>` elements in Figure 9.10 are invalid according to the MODS standard.

FIGURE 9.9 XSD allowing partial validation.

```
<?xml version="1.0" encoding="UTF-8"?>
<xsd:schema
    targetNamespace="http://myuniversity.edu/myNamespace"
    xmlns="http://myuniversity.edu/myNamespace"
    xmlns:xsd="http://www.w3.org/2001/XMLSchema">
    <xsd:element name="myMetadata" type="baseContentModel3"/>
    <xsd:complexType name="baseContentModel3">
         <xsd:choice minOccurs="0" maxOccurs="unbounded">
             <xsd:any namespace="http://purl.org/dc/elements/1.1/"/>
             <xsd:any namespace="http://www.loc.gov/mods/v3"
                       processContents="lax"/>
         </xsd:choice>
         <xsd:anyAttribute namespace="##any"/>
    </xsd:complexType>
</xsd:schema>
```

In spite of this fact, validation in Oxygen appears to succeed because, in the absence of an XSD for MODS, validation of the elements from the MODS namespace is skipped.

The approach for allowing partial validation of XML metadata records is frequently used in real-world metadata-based applications. Often, the goal is to allow metadata standard extensibility, facilitate the implementation of

FIGURE 9.10 XML metadata record reported as valid in spite of errors. Screen shot was made using Oxygen XML Editor (http://www.oxygenxml.com).

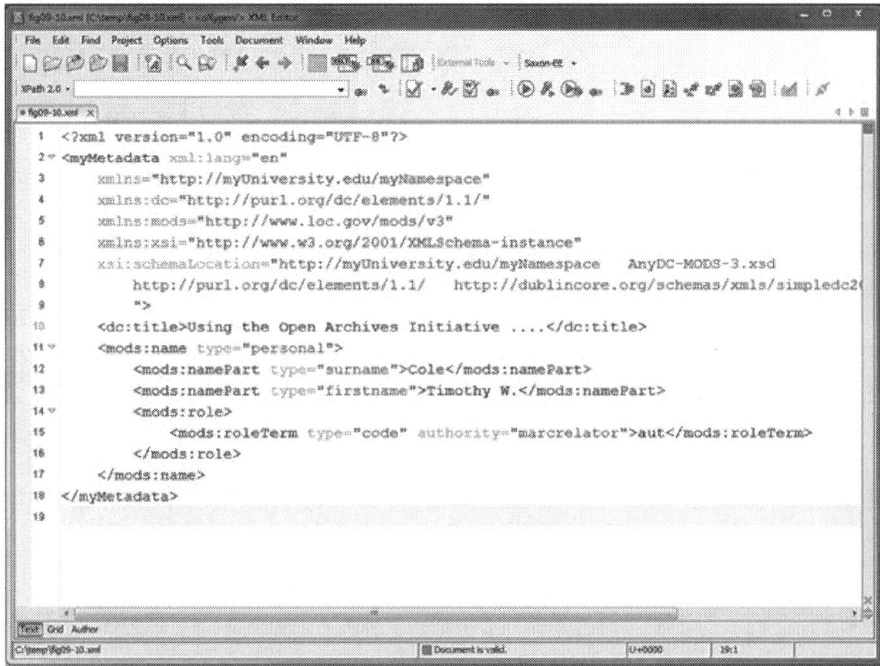

```
<?xml version="1.0" encoding="UTF-8"?>
<myMetadata xml:lang="en"
    xmlns="http://myUniversity.edu/myNamespace"
    xmlns:dc="http://purl.org/dc/elements/1.1/"
    xmlns:mods="http://www.loc.gov/mods/v3"
    xmlns:xsi="http://www.w3.org/2001/XMLSchema-instance"
    xsi:schemaLocation="http://myUniversity.edu/myNamespace   AnyDC-MODS-3.xsd
        http://purl.org/dc/elements/1.1/   http://dublincore.org/schemas/xmls/simpledc2
        ">
    <dc:title>Using the Open Archives Initiative ....</dc:title>
    <mods:name type="personal">
        <mods:namePart type="surname">Cole</mods:namePart>
        <mods:namePart type="firstname">Timothy W.</mods:namePart>
        <mods:role>
            <mods:roleTerm type="code" authority="marcrelator">aut</mods:roleTerm>
        </mods:role>
    </mods:name>
</myMetadata>
```

FIGURE 9.11 Snippet from the MODS XSD (*Source*: Library of Congress).

```
...
<xsd:element name="extension" type="extensionDefinition"/>
...
<xsd:complexType name="extensionDefinition" mixed="true">
   <xsd:sequence>
      <xsd:any processContents="lax" minOccurs="0" maxOccurs="unbounded"/>
   </xsd:sequence>
   <xsd:attribute name="displayLabel" type="xsd:string"/>
   <!-- displayLabel added to <extension> in 3.4. -->
</xsd:complexType>
...
```

metadata application profiles (Chapter 6), and/or support broader interoperability. As described below, the MODS XSD provides a real-world illustration of partial validation through the use of `<xsd:any>` and the `processContents` attribute. Other notable real-world examples include Jorgen Thelin's XSD for RSS 2.0[8] and the XSD for docBook.[9]

The authors of the MODS standard anticipated that on some occasions and for some use cases, there would be properties or attributes of a digital resource or of an agent or entity associated with a digital resource not expressible using solely the elements of the MODS standard. For such circumstances, they created a special element, `<extension>`, to contain properties or attributes related to a resource description expressed using non-MODS semantics and content models. Figure 9.11 are the snippets from the MODS XSD declaring the `<mods:extension>` element and defining its content model. Note the use of the `<xsd:any>` element and the `processContent` attribute with the "`lax`" value. The absence of a namespace attribute on the `<xsd:any>` element and the presence of the `mixed="true"` attribute allows the `<mods:extension>` element to contain any mix of parsed character text and child elements, whether associated with a namespace or not.

Figure 9.12, from the Library of Congress *MODS User Guidelines*,[10] is a snippet of a MODS XML metadata record illustrating the use of the `<mods:extension>` element. In this instance, the element is being used to provide information about an agent associated with an electronic thesis or dissertation that cannot be provided satisfactorily using elements from the MODS namespace alone. A namespace customized for use in connection with electronic theses and dissertations is used instead of MODS, but because no `<xsi:schemaLocation>` attribute is provided and given the value ("`lax`") of the `processContents` attribute in the MODS XSD definition of the `<mods:extension>` element, the elements from the electronic theses and dissertations namespace (i.e., as indicated by the `etd:` namespace prefix) likely will be skipped during any validation of this metadata record.

FIGURE 9.12 Part of a MODS XML metadata record illustrating <mods:extension>.

```
...
<extension
      xmlns:etd="http://www.ntltd.org/standards/metadata/etdms/1.0/etdms.xsd">
   <etd:degree>
      <etd:name>Doctor of Philosophy</etd:name>
      <etd:level>Doctoral</etd:level>
      <etd:discipline>Educational Administration</etd:discipline>
   </etd:degree>
</extension>
...
```

The elementFormDefault and attributeFormDefault Attributes in XSD

As described in Chapter 8, XSDs may contain both global and local element and attribute declarations. Declarations that appear as immediate children of the <xsd:schema> element are global in scope. These can be referenced by name elsewhere in the XSD. All other element and attribute declarations are local in scope (as are anonymous type definitions).

When XSDs are used in conjunction with XML Namespaces, the global/local distinction has additional ramifications. Elements and attributes declared globally are considered *qualified* and are contained in the namespace of the XSD as set by the targetNamespace attribute of the XSD root <xsd:schema> element. By default, elements and attributes declared locally are deemed unqualified and are not contained in the namespace of the XSD. Such locally declared elements and attributes have no target namespace and can be used only to validate unqualified elements and attributes in an XML metadata record, that is, elements and attributes not bound to a default namespace and having no namespace prefix.

This latter behavior can be overridden using the elementFormDefault and attributeFormDefault attributes on the XSD root <xsd:schema> element or by the form attribute on individual element or attribute declaration nodes in the XSD. These attributes take as values either "qualified" or "unqualified" (the default). Common practice in XSDs for metadata applications is to set the <xsd:schema> element's elementFormDefault to "qualified" and its attributeFormDefault to "unqualified" (the default). Since attributes tend to be declared in named or anonymous types (i.e., rather than globally), this results in XML metadata records in which all element names are qualified with a namespace prefix and most attribute names are left unqualified. This is why, for example, all the attributes in the illustrations involving elements declared in the MODS XSD (e.g., Figures 9.8, 9.10, and so on) are unqualified. An illustration involving the use of a qualified attribute name is provided in Figures 9.15 through 9.17 later in this chapter.

The <xsd:include> and <xsd:redefine> Elements in XSD

The root `<xsd:schema>` element of an XSD file is allowed only a single `targetNamespace` attribute, and that attribute can take only a single namespace URI as its value. Therefore, though an XSD author can make references to elements, attributes, and type definitions from other namespaces declared in other XSDs, all the type definitions, qualified elements, and qualified attributes declared in any single XSD must be in the same namespace (or in no namespace at all). If a metadata application requires declaring some elements in one namespace and other elements in a different namespace, at least two XSD files are required, one for each namespace.

How is the inverse situation handled? Given the benefits of reuse and modular design, what if a metadata creator wants to locate the element declarations, attribute declarations, and type definitions of a single namespace in multiple XSD files rather than all in a single XSD file? How are type definitions changed and updated and element and attribute declarations augmented over time while still protecting currently working applications, that is, while not changing XSD files already in use? These needs can be addressed using the `<xsd:include>` and `<xsd:redefine>` elements.

The first of these two elements, the `<xsd:include>` element, is similar to the `<xsd:import>` element in that the type definitions and element and attribute declarations of the "included" XSD become available for reference and use within an XSD (and to parsers validating records against that XSD). The primary difference is that the `<xsd:include>` element has no `namespace` attribute. Instead, the "included" declarations and definitions are deemed to be in the same namespace as the target namespace of the "including" XSD. This translates to a requirement that the "included" XSD either have no `targetNamespace` attribute of its own or have a `targetNamespace` attribute that exactly matches the `targetNamespace` of the XSD into which it is being "included." This approach allows XSD authors to put frequently used sets of type definitions into individual XSD files having no target namespaces. Then, as needed, these type definition XSD files can be "included" into newly created XSDs that need to reference these type definitions when declaring elements and attributes. These "including" XSDs may or may not have a target namespace. If they do, then in the scope of that XSD, the type definitions from the "included" XSD share this target namespace.

The `<xsd:redefine>` element integrates an existing XSD in a somewhat analogous fashion to how `<xsd:include>` does with the added benefit that, in the new XSD, an XSD author can redefine the complex and simple type definitions from the XSD "integrated" through the use of the <xsd:redefine> element. All elements and attributes referencing any redefined type definitions are automatically redefined as well, whether newly declared in the new XSD or previously declared in the "integrated" XSD. In practical terms, this means that XSD authors can evolve and update content models, attribute value lists, and so on without revising existing XSD files directly. The trade-off is that since the old XSD (i.e., the "integrated" XSD) is left unchanged, the new XSD will have a different location (i.e., different URL). This means that XSD URL references in records and document instances will need to be updated to take advantage of the updated definitions.

Use of the <xsd:redefine> element is illustrated in Figures 9.13 through 9.17. The XSD shown in Figure 9.13 redefines the simple XSD shown in Figure 9.3, which declared the element <myMetadata> in the fictitious namespace http://myuniversity.edu/myNamespace and defined a content model for this element (the complex type definition named "baseContentModel") consisting of one <dc:title> element and zero or more <mods:name> elements. The XSD shown in Figure 9.13 redefines the "baseContentModel" content model to require the addition of a <dc:publisher> element. Note that it is not necessary in the XSD shown in Figure 9.13 to mention the <myMetadata> element explicitly; redefining the definition of "baseContentModel," on which the declaration of <myMetadata> depends, is sufficient. Figure 9.14 shows an XML metadata record that validates against the XSD shown in Figure 9.13. Compare this to

FIGURE 9.13 XSD schema redefining the content model of the XSD depicted in Figure 9.3.

```
<?xml version="1.0" encoding="UTF-8"?>
<xsd:schema
    targetNamespace="http://myuniversity.edu/myNamespace"
    xmlns="http://myuniversity.edu/myNamespace"
    xmlns:xsd="http://www.w3.org/2001/XMLSchema"
    xmlns:dc="http://purl.org/dc/elements/1.1/">
    <xsd:import namespace="http://purl.org/dc/elements/1.1/"
     schemaLocation="http://dublincore.org/schemas/xmls/simpledc20021212.xsd"/>
    <xsd:redefine schemaLocation="DC-MODS.xsd">
     <xsd:complexType name="baseContentModel">
       <xsd:complexContent>
         <xsd:extension base="baseContentModel">
           <xsd:sequence>
             <xsd:element ref="dc:publisher" minOccurs="1" maxOccurs="1"/>
           </xsd:sequence>
       </xsd:extension>
     </xsd:complexContent>
    </xsd:complexType>
  </xsd:redefine>
</xsd:schema>
```

FIGURE 9.14 XML metadata record conforming to redefined content model. Screen shot was made using Oxygen XML Editor (http://www.oxygenxml.com).

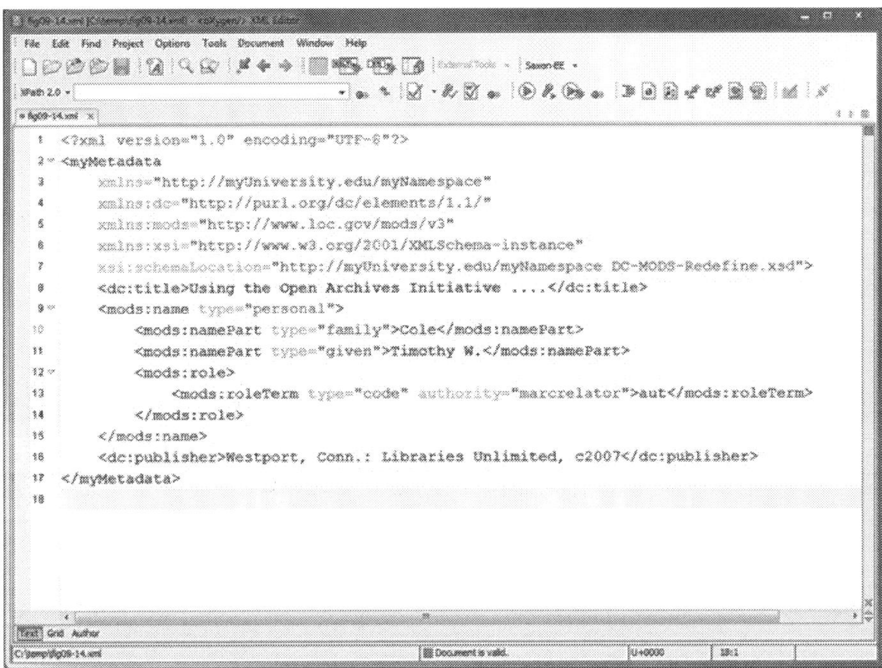

the XML metadata record shown in Figure 9.4. The only difference is the addition of the `<dc:publisher>` node.

Refinement in XSD is a powerful tool and potentially open to abuse. Care should be taken when using it. For example, because information on the Web is so distributed and decentralized, it is possible to locally redefine type definitions from canonical XSDs created and maintained by other entities. While this can be useful for local applications and for experimentation, doing so may result in the creation of XML metadata records that no longer conform to the canonical, authoritative XSD. This in turn may jeopardize interoperability.

Figure 9.15 shows an XSD that extends the definition of the content model used in the Library of Congress MODS XSD for its `<mods:name>` element to allow an optional attribute `mods:gender`. A simple type is defined to restrict values for this attribute to "`male`" or "`female`." The schema shown in Figure 9.16 is a version of the XSD in Figure 9.3, modified to point to the XSD of Figure 9.15 rather than to the canonical MODS XSD on the Library of Congress Web site. The XML metadata record shown in Figure 9.17 is the same as that shown in Figure 9.4, with the addition of this new attribute for author gender, and is valid according to XSD shown in Figure 9.16. However, the record shown in Figure 9.17 would no longer validate with respect to the canonical MODS XSD maintained by the Library of Congress.

FIGURE 9.15 XSD schema redefining the MODS <name> element.

```
<?xml version="1.0" encoding="UTF-8"?>
<xsd:schema
    targetNamespace="http://www.loc.gov/mods/v3"
    xmlns="http://www.loc.gov/mods/v3"
    xmlns:xsd="http://www.w3.org/2001/XMLSchema">
    <xsd:redefine schemaLocation="http://www.loc.gov/standards/mods/mods.xsd">
      <xsd:complexType name="nameDefinition">
        <xsd:complexContent>
          <xsd:extension base="nameDefinition">
            <xsd:attribute name="gender" type="genderList" use="optional"/>
          </xsd:extension>
        </xsd:complexContent>
      </xsd:complexType>
    </xsd:redefine>
    <xsd:simpleType name="genderList">
      <xsd:restriction base="xsd:string">
        <xsd:enumeration value="male"/>
        <xsd:enumeration value="female"/>
      </xsd:restriction>
    </xsd:simpleType>
</xsd:schema>
```

FIGURE 9.16 XSD schema referencing the XSD redefining MODS <name> element (Figure 9.15).

```
<?xml version="1.0" encoding="UTF-8"?>
<xsd:schema
    targetNamespace="http://myuniversity.edu/myNamespace"
    xmlns="http://myuniversity.edu/myNamespace"
    xmlns:xsd="http://www.w3.org/2001/XMLSchema"
    xmlns:dc="http://purl.org/dc/elements/1.1/"
    xmlns:mods="http://www.loc.gov/mods/v3">
    <xsd:import namespace="http://www.loc.gov/mods/v3"
      schemaLocation="MODS-Name-Redefine.xsd"/>
    <xsd:import namespace="http://purl.org/dc/elements/1.1/"
      schemaLocation="http://dublincore.org/schemas/xmls/simpledc20021212.xsd"/>
    <xsd:element name="myMetadata" type="baseContentModel"/>
    <xsd:complexType name="baseContentModel">
        <xsd:sequence>
            <xsd:element ref="dc:title" minOccurs="1" maxOccurs="1"/>
            <xsd:element ref="mods:name" minOccurs="0" maxOccurs="unbounded"/>
        </xsd:sequence>
    </xsd:complexType>
</xsd:schema>
```

FIGURE 9.17 Metadata record with `<gender>` attribute allowed by use of `<xsd:redefine>` in XSD schema (Figure 9.15). Screen shot was made using Oxygen XML Editor (http://www.oxygenxml.com).

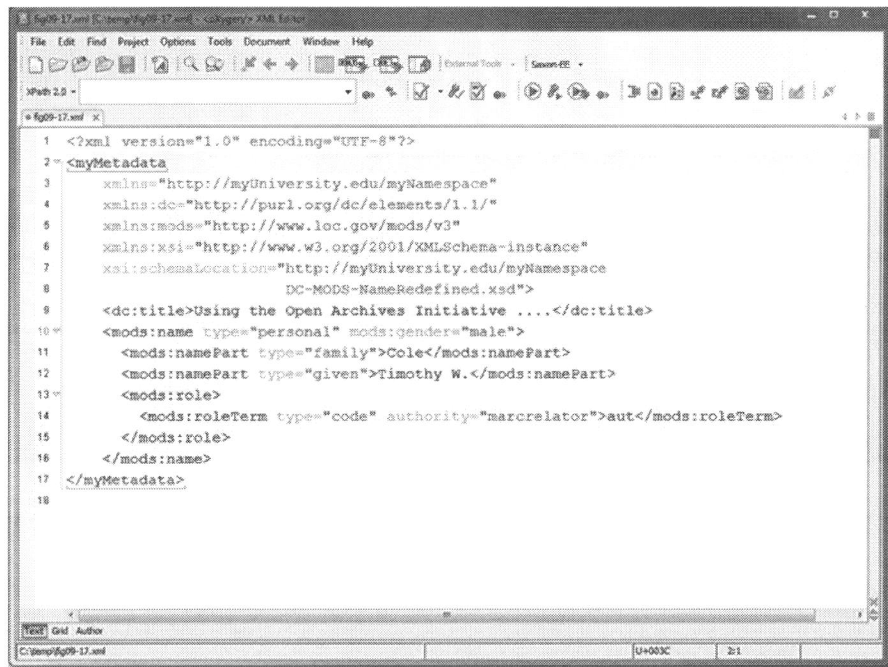

```
<?xml version="1.0" encoding="UTF-8"?>
<myMetadata
    xmlns="http://myUniversity.edu/myNamespace"
    xmlns:dc="http://purl.org/dc/elements/1.1/"
    xmlns:mods="http://www.loc.gov/mods/v3"
    xmlns:xsi="http://www.w3.org/2001/XMLSchema-instance"
    xsi:schemaLocation="http://myUniversity.edu/myNamespace
                        DC-MODS-NameRedefined.xsd">
    <dc:title>Using the Open Archives Initiative ....</dc:title>
    <mods:name type="personal" mods:gender="male">
      <mods:namePart type="family">Cole</mods:namePart>
      <mods:namePart type="given">Timothy W.</mods:namePart>
      <mods:role>
        <mods:roleTerm type="code" authority="marcrelator">aut</mods:roleTerm>
      </mods:role>
    </mods:name>
</myMetadata>
```

CASE STUDY 9.1
A "Spine" of Metadata for Digitized Emblem Books

Synopsis: Emblem books are illustrated books published in Europe during the sixteenth and seventeenth centuries. The "emblems" in these books consist of an emblematic image (the *pictura*) accompanied by a motto and a *subscriptio*, an explanatory text. After several institutions in America and Europe, including the University of Illinois, started digitizing their emblem books to provide better access to these resources, the need for a new metadata schema to properly describe these resources emerged. Both books and emblems contained in books are of interest to Renaissance emblem scholars, so the new metadata schema needed to accommodate emblem-level descriptions in addition to book-level bibliographic descriptions. A *SPINE* XML schema[11] was developed to meet emblem scholars' needs, that is, to provide metadata necessary to describe a book and its emblems in a single record supporting multiple points of access. Since there are already well-established schemas for bibliographic description, the SPINE XML schema borrows elements and attributes from existing XSDs to describe the book. To describe emblems, elements are borrowed from the Simple Knowledge Organization System (SKOS)[12] and the Resource Description Framework (RDF).[13] The SPINE namespace also contains its own elements and attributes for describing emblem components, the physical book digitized, and the resulting digital manifestations.

Illustrates: Namespaces and XSDs; application profiles; multigranular descriptions.

The foundation for the SPINE schema was introduced by Stephen Rawles (2004) in his chapter titled "A SPINE of Information Headings for Emblem-Related Electronic Resources." Rawles identified a set of core properties describing emblem books and the emblems they contain. The SPINE XSD consists of three main segments: one for bibliographic description, one for describing relationships between printed source and digital manifestations and for providing appropriate liminary text, and one for descriptions of emblem motto, pictura, and subscriptio.

FIGURE 9.18 SPINE XML schema uses semantics from other namespaces.

```
<xs:schema
      xmlns="http://diglib.hab.de/rules/schema/emblem"
      xmlns:xlink="http://www.w3.org/1999/xlink"
      xmlns:tei="http://www.tei-c.org/ns/1.0"
      xmlns:mods="http://www.loc.gov/mods/v3"
      xmlns:rdf="http://www.w3.org/1999/02/22-rdf-syntax-ns#"
      xmlns:skos="http://www.w3.org/2004/02/skos/core#"
      xmlns:xs="http://www.w3.org/2001/XMLSchema"
      targetNamespace="http://diglib.hab.de/rules/schema/emblem"
      elementFormDefault="qualified"
      attributeFormDefault="unqualified">
      <xs:import namespace="http://www.w3.org/XML/1998/namespace"
         schemaLocation="xml.xsd"/>
      <xs:import namespace="http://www.tei-c.org/ns/1.0"
         schemaLocation="http://diglib.hab.de/rules/schema/teiP5/teiP5.xsd"/>
      <xs:import namespace="http://www.loc.gov/mods/v3"
         schemaLocation="mods-3-4.xsd"/>
      <xs:import namespace="http://www.w3.org/1999/02/22-rdf-syntax-ns#"
         schemaLocation="rdf-dummy.xsd"/>
      <xs:import namespace="http://www.w3.org/2004/02/skos/core#"
         schemaLocation="skos-dummy.xsd"/>
```

FIGURE 9.19 Root element of SPINE and its content model.

```
<xs:element name="biblioDesc">
      <xs:complexType>
        <xs:sequence>
          <xs:choice>
              <xs:element ref="tei:teiHeader" minOccurs="0"/>
              <xs:element ref="mods:mods" minOccurs="0"/>
          </xs:choice>
          <xs:element ref="copyDesc" maxOccurs="unbounded"/>
          <xs:element ref="liminaryText" minOccurs="0"/>
          <xs:choice>
              <xs:element ref="sectionTitle" minOccurs="0"/>
              <xs:element ref="emblem" maxOccurs="unbounded"/>
          </xs:choice>
        </xs:sequence>
      <xs:attribute name="workID" type="xs:string" use="optional"/>
      <xs:attribute name="globalBookID" type="xs:anyURI" use="optional"/>
   </xs:complexType>
 </xs:element>
```

The namespaces (including the `targetNamespace` for the XSD) and the imported XSDs (`<xsd:import>` elements) referenced by the SPINE XSD are shown in Figure 9.18. Figure 9.19 shows the XSD declaration for the `<biblioDesc>` element (the typical root element for SPINE metadata records) and its content model. For bibliographic information, the SPINE XML schema gives implementers a choice (Figure 9.19) between using MODS or the `<teiHeader>` element of the Text Encoding Initiative (TEI) XSD.[14] Figure 9.20 is a segment of a SPINE record showing emblem book bibliographic metadata serialized as MODS XML.

FIGURE 9.20 Segment of the SPINE metadata record describing an emblem book digitized by the University of Glasgow.

```
<mods:mods version="3.4" xmlns:xlink="http://www.w3.org/1999/xlink"
  xmlns:xsi="http://www.w3.org/2001/XMLSchema-instance"
  xmlns:mods="http://www.loc.gov/mods/v3"
  xsi:schemaLocation="http://www.loc.gov/mods/v3
                        http://www.loc.gov/standards/mods/mods.xsd">
  <mods:titleInfo>
    <mods:nonSort>Le</mods:nonSort>
    <mods:title>premier livre des emblemes. Composé par Guillaume...</mods:title>
  </mods:titleInfo>
  <mods:name type="personal">
    <mods:namePart>Guéroult, Guillaume</mods:namePart>
    <mods:role>
      <mods:roleTerm authority="marcrelator" type="text">creator</mods:roleTerm>
    </mods:role>
  </mods:name>
  <mods:typeOfResource>text</mods:typeOfResource>
  <mods:genre authority="rbgenr">Emblem books-France</mods:genre>
  <mods:genre authority="marcgt">bibliography</mods:genre>
  <mods:originInfo>
    <mods:place>
      <mods:placeTerm authority="marccountry" type="code">fr</mods:placeTerm>
    </mods:place>
    <mods:place>
      <mods:placeTerm type="text">Lyon</mods:placeTerm>
    </mods:place>
    <mods:publisher>Balthazar Arnoullet</mods:publisher>
    <mods:dateIssued>1550</mods:dateIssued>
    <mods:issuance>monographic</mods:issuance>
  </mods:originInfo>
  <mods:language>
    <mods:languageTerm authority="iso639-2b" type="code">fre</mods:languageTerm>
  </mods:language>
  <mods:physicalDescription>
    <mods:form authority="marcform">print</mods:form>
    <mods:extent>36 leaves : ill ; 8vo.</mods:extent>
  </mods:physicalDescription>
  <mods:note>Arnoullet, Balthasar</mods:note>
```

(continued)

FIGURE 9.20 (Continued)

```
  <mods:note>Item 1 of 2 bound together</mods:note>
  <mods:note>Stirling Maxwell</mods:note>
  <mods:subject authority="lcsh">
    <mods:topic>Emblem books, French.</mods:topic>
    <mods:geographic>France</mods:geographic>
    <mods:temporal>16th century</mods:temporal>
  </mods:subject>
  <mods:location>
    <mods:physicalLocation>University of Glasgow Library</mods:physicalLocation>
    <mods:physicalLocation>Level 12 Spec Coll</mods:physicalLocation>
    <mods:shelfLocator>Sp Coll S.M. 535</mods:shelfLocator>
    <mods:url displayLabel="Full text - University of Glasgow" usage="primary
display">http://www.emblems.arts.gla.ac.uk/french/books.php?id=FGUa&amp;o=</mods:
url>
  </mods:location>
  <mods:recordInfo>
    <mods:recordCreationDate encoding="marc">970701</mods:recordCreationDate>
    <mods:recordIdentifier>b1652570</mods:recordIdentifier>
    <mods:descriptionStandard>aacr2</mods:descriptionStandard>
  </mods:recordInfo>
</mods:mods>
```

The next part of a SPINE XML record describes the printed book that was the source digitized, identifies the resulting digital manifestations, and describes the relationships between them. A work can have many different digital manifestations sourced from one or more print manifestations. Digital manifestations derived from the same print original may be available via different portals and may have multiple disparate derivatives. In a SPINE metadata record, each print source is described in a <copyDesc> element. As shown in Figure 9.21, <copyDesc> can contain several subelements, including <copyID> and <owner>, as well as one or more <digDesc> elements, one for each digital manifestation from the same print source. A sample of the <copyDesc> part of a SPINE metadata record is shown in Figure 9.22.

The last part of the SPINE metadata record describes emblems included in the book. Since describing an emblem requires specific semantics, most of the elements and attributes used for this section of a SPINE record are contained in the SPINE namespace, although some attributes for linking are borrowed from the XLink namespace, and some elements used for pictura descriptors are borrowed from the RDF and SKOS namespaces. The SPINE element <emblem> is used for describing an emblem in a book. This element contains descriptions of all three parts of the emblem—<motto>, <pictura>, and <subscriptio>—as shown in Figure 9.23. Figure 9.24 shows the description of an emblem in a SPINE metadata record; for example, the <pictura>

FIGURE 9.21 SPINE XSD schema defining elements <copyDesc> and <digDesc>.

```
...
<xs:element name="copyDesc">
    <xs:complexType>
        <xs:sequence>
            <xs:element ref="copyID"/>
            <xs:element ref="owner"/>
            <xs:element ref="digDesc" minOccurs="0" maxOccurs="unbounded"/>
        </xs:sequence>
        <xs:attribute name="globalID" type="xs:anyURI" use="optional"/>
        <xs:attribute ref="xlink:href"/>
    </xs:complexType>
</xs:element>
<xs:element name="digDesc">
    <xs:complexType mixed="true">
        <xs:complexContent mixed="true">
            <xs:extension base="stringWithAttrib">
                <xs:sequence>
                    <xs:element ref="copyID" minOccurs="0"/>
                    <xs:element ref="owner" minOccurs="0"/>
                </xs:sequence>
                <xs:attribute name="scope" type="digCodeBook"/>
                <xs:attribute name="comp" type="digCodeDigit"/>
                <xs:attribute name="globalID" type="xs:anyURI" use="optional"/>
                <xs:attribute name="pageImages" type="xs:anyURI" use="optional"/>
            </xs:extension>
        </xs:complexContent>
    </xs:complexType>
</xs:element>
```

FIGURE 9.22 A <copyDesc> element from a SPINE metadata record.

```
<copyDesc>
  <copyID>ugb1652570</copyID>
  <owner countryCode="GB">University of Glasgow</owner>
  <digDesc comp="complete" scope="all" xml:id="FGUa"
    globalID="http://www.emblems.arts.gla.ac.uk/french/books.php?id=FGUa&amp;o=">
      <copyID>ugb1652570:FGUa</copyID>
      <owner countryCode="GB">University of Glasgow</owner>
  </digDesc>
</copyDesc>
```

element can include in its <iconclass> child element semantics borrowed from the RDF and SKOS namespaces. These semantics are used in associating controlled vocabulary terms from the Iconclass thesaurus in a manner consistent with linked data principles.

Instead of creating new schemas from scratch, the SPINE XML schema uses the elements and attributes from already well-established XML schemas

FIGURE 9.23 SPINE XSD schema defining the <emblem> element and its content model.

```
<xs:element name="emblem">
  <xs:complexType>
    <xs:sequence>
      <xs:element name="motto" maxOccurs="unbounded">
        <xs:complexType>
          <xs:complexContent>
            <xs:extension base="emblemParts">
              <xs:attribute name="globalID" type="xs:anyURI" use="optional"/>
              <xs:attribute name="src" type="xs:anyURI"/>
              <xs:attribute name="page" type="xs:token"/>
              <xs:attribute name="citeNo" type="xs:token"/>
              <xs:attribute name="standNo" type="xs:token"/>
              <xs:attribute ref="xml:id" use="optional"/>
            </xs:extension>
          </xs:complexContent>
        </xs:complexType>
      </xs:element>
      <xs:element ref="pictura" minOccurs="0" maxOccurs="unbounded"/>
      <xs:element name="subscriptio" minOccurs="0" maxOccurs="unbounded">
        <xs:complexType>
          <xs:complexContent>
            <xs:extension base="emblemParts">
              <xs:sequence>
                <xs:element name="metreOrig" type="xs:token" minOccurs="0"/>
                <xs:element name="metreEdit" type="xs:token" minOccurs="0"/>
              </xs:sequence>
              <xs:attribute ref="xml:id" use="optional"/>
              <xs:attribute ref="xml:lang" use="optional"/>
              <xs:attribute ref="xlink:href" use="optional"/>
              <xs:attribute name="globalID" type="xs:anyURI" use="optional"/>
              <xs:attribute name="src" type="xs:anyURI"/>
              <xs:attribute name="page" type="xs:token"/>
              <xs:attribute name="citeNo" type="xs:token"/>
              <xs:attribute name="standNo" type="xs:token"/>
            </xs:extension>
          </xs:complexContent>
        </xs:complexType>
      </xs:element>
    </xs:sequence>
  </xs:complexType>
</xs:element>
```

to describe two levels of resources. This combination of schemas resulted in a standard that can be used to describe digitized emblem resources. The SPINE XML schema facilitates the sharing of emblem resources between institutions and aids Renaissance emblem scholars by providing different levels of access (e.g., book, emblem, and Iconclass heading) using SPINE metadata records.

FIGURE 9.24 An <emblem> element from a SPINE metadata record.

```
<emblem
  xmlns:xlink="http://www.w3.org/1999/xlink"
  xmlns:rdf="http://www.w3.org/1999/02/22-rdf-syntax-ns#"
  xmlns:skos="http://www.w3.org/2004/02/skos/core#"
  xlink:href="http://www.emblems.arts.gla.ac.uk/french/images/pic_1/
FGUa001.jpg"
  globalID="http://www.emblems.arts.gla.ac.uk/french/emblem.php?id=FGUa001"
  xml:id="FGUa001">
    <motto>
       <transcription xml:lang="fr">
                          Amour oste sens &amp; raison.</transcription>
    </motto>
    <pictura
  xlink:href="http://www.emblems.arts.gla.ac.uk/french/images/pic_1/
FGUa001.jpg"
  xml:id="FGUa001_P1">
       <figDesc>woman stands pointing at a man ....</figDesc>
       <iconclass rdf:about="http://www.iconclass.org/rkd/25G3/">
           <skos:notation>25G3</skos:notation>
           <skos:prefLabel xml:lang="en">trees</skos:prefLabel>
           <skos:prefLabel xml:lang="fr">arbres</skos:prefLabel>
           <keyword xml:lang="en">earth</keyword>
           <keyword xml:lang="en">nature</keyword>
           <keyword xml:lang="en">plant</keyword>
           <keyword xml:lang="en">tree</keyword>
           <keyword xml:lang="en">world</keyword>
       </iconclass>
    </pictura>
</emblem>
```

KEYS, KEY REFERENCES, AND UNIQUENESS CONSTRAINTS

As described in Chapter 3, the W3C XML Specification[15] defines special tokenized attribute types (ID, IDREF, and IDREFS) to support needs for uniqueness and internal linking within a document instance. The value of an ID attribute must be unique within a given XML document instance. This uniqueness constraint means that other elements in the document instance with attributes of type IDREF or IDREFS can unambiguously link to an element via the value of its ID attribute. This mechanism for uniqueness and cross-reference, inherited from Standard Generalized Markup Language, is useful but limited and a bit cumbersome. While basic uniqueness and referential constraints can be implemented through these special kinds of attributes, what if an XSD author wants to articulate more complex uniqueness and/or referential constraints?

The W3C XML Schema Definition Language, while it supports ID, IDREF, and IDREFS attribute types, also provides alternative, more flexible mechanisms for achieving similar purposes using the <xsd:unique>, <xsd:key>, and <xsd:keyref> elements. When declaring an element,

FIGURE 9.25 XSD schema illustrating the use of <xsd:unique>.

```
<xsd:schema xmlns:xsd="http://www.w3.org/2001/XMLSchema"
      xmlns:my="http://myuniversity.edu/myNamespace"
      targetNamespace="http://myuniversity.edu/myNamespace"
      elementFormDefault="qualified" attributeFormDefault="unqualified">
  <xsd:element name="myMetadata">
    <xsd:complexType>
      <xsd:sequence>
        <xsd:element minOccurs="0" maxOccurs="unbounded" ref="my:title"/>
        <xsd:element minOccurs="0" maxOccurs="unbounded" ref="my:author"/>
      </xsd:sequence>
    </xsd:complexType>
    <xsd:unique name="creatorOrder">
      <xsd:selector xpath="./my:author"/>
      <xsd:field xpath="@order"/>
    </xsd:unique>
  </xsd:element>
  <xsd:element name="title" type="xsd:string"/>
  <xsd:element name="author" type="my:elementType"/>
  <xsd:complexType name="elementType">
    <xsd:simpleContent>
      <xsd:extension base="xsd:string">
        <xsd:attribute name="order" type="xsd:integer" use="required"/>
      </xsd:extension>
    </xsd:simpleContent>
  </xsd:complexType>
</xsd:schema>
```

<xsd:unique> allows an XSD author to define a test within the scope of the element being declared on the uniqueness of a child element or attribute value, singly or in combination with the value(s) of other elements or attributes.

As illustration, the XSD shown in Figure 9.25 declares an element, <author>, for expressing the name of a resource author. This element is repeated for each author name when describing a resource having multiple authors. An attribute "order" is required for each <author> element in the metadata record, giving the order in which that author should be listed. To be sure that no instance of <author> appears in the metadata record with a duplicative value for the order attribute, the XSD includes an <xsd:unique> declaration in its definition of the root element <my:myMetadata>. If more than one instance of the author order attribute appears with the same value in the metadata record, a validation error occurs (see Figure 9.26).

As illustrated in Figure 9.25, the children of <xsd:unique> are the <xsd:selector> element (cannot be repeated) and the <xsd:field> element (repeatable). The <xsd:selector> element describes in its "xpath" attribute the scope of the uniqueness constraint, in this case <my:author>, a child element of the root element <my:myMetadata>.

FIGURE 9.26 An error message indicating attribute `order="1"` was used with more than one `<author>` in a metadata record. Screen shot was made using Oxygen XML Editor (http://www.oxygenxml.com).

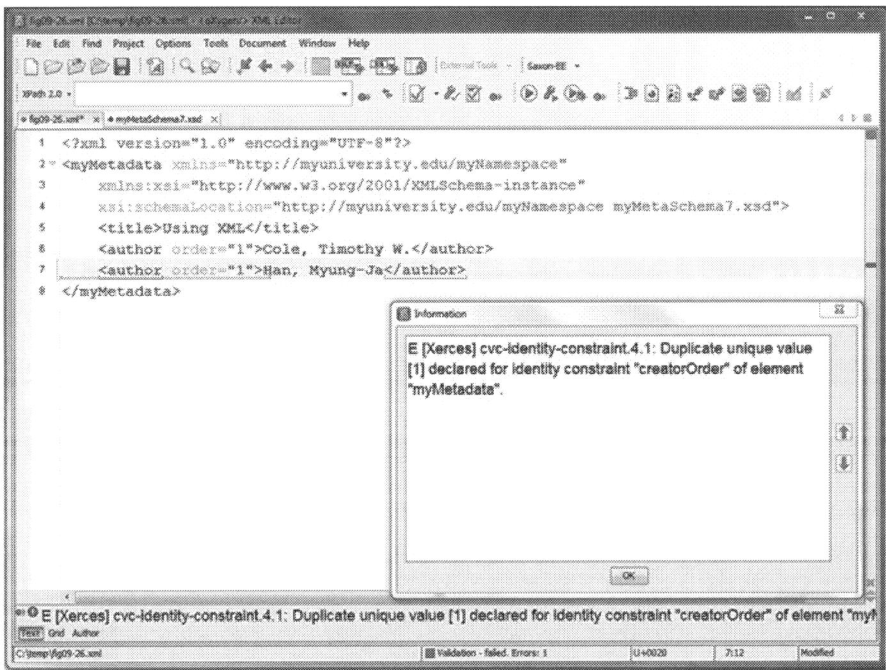

The `<xsd:field>` element specifies in its `xpath` attribute, the attribute or element value to be tested for uniqueness, in this case the `order` attribute. If multiple `<xsd:field>` elements are included, it is the combination of all the values specified by the `<xsd:field>` elements that must be unique. (XPath syntax and semantics are described in Chapter 10.)

The `<xsd:key>` and `<xsd:keyref>` have similar content models to the `<xsd:unique>` element, each is required to have one `<xsd:selector>` and at least one `<xsd:field>` element as children. Like the `<xsd:unique>` element, the `<xsd:key>` element has a required "`name`" attribute. The `<xsd:keyref>` element has two required attributes, its own `name` attribute, and a "`refer`" attribute. The `refer` attribute value must match with the value of a `<xsd:key>` element `name` attribute. This match is what ties an `<xsd:key>` to an `<xsd:keyref>`.

Like `<xsd:unique>`, `<xsd:key>` ensures uniqueness, that is, for each concatenated value composed from the specified `<field>`(s) within the specified `<selector>`. The value of the `name` attribute of `<xsd:key>` makes certain that the key can be referenced from a corresponding `<xsd:keyref>` elsewhere in the metadata record. This `<xsd:keyref>` then additionally requires that for each concatenated value composed from the specified

<field>s and <selector> within <xsd:keyref>, there is a matching value composed from the <field>s and <selector> of the corresponding <xsd:key> element. These elements and attributes are further described in Case Study 9.2.

CASE STUDY 9.2
Creating the DLF Aquifer Asset Action XML Schema

Synopsis: Many metadata records harvested using OAI-PMH do not include clearly typed URLs; it can be unclear what representations of the resource described are available. For example, the resource described may be an image, but it is often unclear whether the URL provided points to a medium-resolution view of the image, to the highest-resolution view of the image available, or to a low-resolution view of the image surrounded by XHTML metadata about the image (e.g., to a splash screen for the resource). Complicating matters even more, multiple undifferentiated URLs may be provided in each metadata record. This makes it difficult for metadata-based aggregation service providers to give their users a proper sense of where the link(s) in a displayed metadata record might take them. In 2006, the Digital Library Federation (DLF) Aquifer Technology/Architecture Working Group demonstrated the utility of harvestable XML metadata records that include multiple typed actionable URLs or "asset actions" (Chavez et al. 2006). The experiment dealt specifically with digital image resources. By having a consistent set of well-labeled URLs for all images (e.g., pointing to thumbnails, in-context presentations of images on a data provider's Web site, or medium- and high-resolution views), the service provider in this experiment was able to ensure consistent results with metadata harvested from multiple institutions. One of the XSDs developed as part of this experiment is described in this case study.
Illustrates: Practical use of uniqueness and referential constraints on XML metadata.

Figure 9.27 shows a sample asset action XML metadata record from the experiment. The structure of the record is relatively simple. The only children allowed for the <assetActions> root element are <actionGroup> elements. These elements enumerate (as <action> elements) a list of URLs providing access to representations of a resource. The name attribute of the <actionGroup> element describes which set of representations (by group) is being enumerated. All resources are assumed to have representations that collectively can fulfill certain basic functions: for example, provide a preview of the resource, provide a Simple Dublin Core record describing the resource, provide a view of the resource optimized for Web delivery, and so on. These constitute the "defaultActionGroup." Different types of resources will have additional action groups describing representations appropriate to that particular resource type, such as representations that all Web-accessible static images should have. The example shown in Figure 9.27 is for a still

FIGURE 9.27 A sample asset action metadata record.

```
<?xml version="1.0" encoding="UTF-8"?>
<assetActions objid="12345" type="image" xmlns="http://dca.tufts.edu/ad"
    xmlns:xsi="http://www.w3.org/2001/XMLSchema-instance"
    xsi:schemaLocation="http://dca.tufts.edu/ad assetActions-Test.xsd">

  <actionGroup name="defaultActionGroup" label="default Action Group">
    <action name="getAssetDefinition" format="text/xml" label="..." uri="..."/>
    <action name="getPreview" format="image/jpeg" label="..." uri="..."/>
    <action name="getLabel" format="text/plain" label="..." uri="..."/>
    <action name="getDCRecord" format="text/xml" label="..." uri="..."/>
    <action name="getWebView" format="text/html" label="..." uri="..."/>
    <action name="getDefaultContent" format="image/jpeg" label="..." uri="..."/>
  </actionGroup>

  <actionGroup name="basicImageActionGroup" label="basic Image Action Group">
    <action name="getThumbnail" format="image/jpeg" label="..." uri="..."/>
    <action name="getScreenSize" format="image/jpeg" label="..." uri="..."/>
    <action name="getMaxSize" format="image/jpeg" label="..." uri="..."/>
    <action name="getDynamicView" format="text/html" label="..." uri="..."/>
  </actionGroup>

</assetActions>
```

image resource; accordingly, the second group described is the "basic ImageActionGroup."

In constructing the XSD for this metadata model, the experiment designers wanted to ensure that all asset action metadata records included exactly one set of default actions (i.e., one defaultActionGroup), that no asset action metadata records included more than one action group of a particular type (i.e., no action groups with the same name), and that actions of an included action group were represented in each asset action metadata record with no duplication. This was achieved through an XSD uniqueness constraint, a fixed attribute, and a `key-keyref` pair constraint in the XSD.

Figure 9.28 shows the XSD for an Asset Actions metadata record, illustrating the use of `<xsd:unique>`, `<xsd:key>`, and `<xsd:keyref>`. Note the `<xsd:unique>` declaration included as part of the anonymous complex type definition for the `<actionGroup>` element. This instance of `<xsd:unique>` ensures that no two children of any `<actionGroup>` (i.e., no two `<action>` elements within an `<actionGroup>`) can have `name` attributes with duplicative values.

The XSD shown in Figure 9.28 also defines a fixed attribute, `requiredAG`, for the `<assetActions>` element. This attribute has a fixed value of "defaultActionGroup" and is assumed for all instances of `<assetActions>` even if not explicitly included in the XML (as it is not in Figure 9.27). The

FIGURE 9.28 XSD schema for validating Asset Action metadata record shown in Figure 9.27.

```
<xsd:schema
  targetNamespace="http://dca.tufts.edu/ad"
  xmlns:xsd="http://www.w3.org/2001/XMLSchema"
  xmlns="http://dca.tufts.edu/ad" elementFormDefault="qualified">
    <xsd:element name="assetActions">
    <xsd:complexType>
      <xsd:sequence>
        <xsd:element name="actionGroup" type="actionGroupType" minOccurs="1"
                maxOccurs="unbounded" >

          <xsd:unique name="uniqueAction">
            <xsd:selector xpath="./*"/>
            <xsd:field xpath="@name"/>
          </xsd:unique>

        </xsd:element>
      </xsd:sequence>
      <xsd:attribute name="objid" type="xsd:string" use="required" />
      <xsd:attribute name="type" type="xsd:string" use="required" />
      <xsd:attribute name="requiredAG" type="xsd:string"
                fixed="defaultActionGroup" />
    </xsd:complexType>

    <xsd:key name="reqActionGroupKey">bg:linebreak/>
      <xsd:selector xpath="./*" />
      <xsd:field xpath="@name"/>
    </xsd:key>
    <xsd:keyref name="reqActionGroupRef" refer="reqActionGroupKey">
      <xsd:selector xpath="." />
      <xsd:field xpath="@requiredAG"/>
    </xsd:keyref>

  </xsd:element>
  <xsd:complexType name="actionGroupType">
    <xsd:sequence>
      <xsd:element name="action" type="actionType" minOccurs="1"
                maxOccurs="unbounded" />
    </xsd:sequence>
    <xsd:attribute name="name" use="required" type="xsd:string"/>
    <xsd:attribute name="label" use="required" type="xsd:string"/>
  </xsd:complexType>
  <xsd:complexType name="actionType">
    <xsd:attribute name="name" use="required">
      <xsd:simpleType>
        <xsd:restriction base="xsd:string">
          <xsd:enumeration value="getAssetDefinition" />
          <xsd:enumeration value="getDCRecord" />
```

FIGURE 9.28 (Continued)

```
        <xsd:enumeration value="getWebView" />
        <xsd:enumeration value="getDefaultContent" />
        <xsd:enumeration value="getThumbnail" />
        <xsd:enumeration value="getScreenSize" />
        ...
      </xsd:restriction>
    </xsd:simpleType>
  </xsd:attribute>
  <xsd:attribute name="format" use="required" type="xsd:string"/>
  <xsd:attribute name="label" use="required" type="xsd:string"/>
  <xsd:attribute name="uri" type="xsd:anyURI" use="required"/>
 </xsd:complexType>
</xsd:schema>
```

instance of <xsd:key> in the definition of the <assetActions> element ensures the uniqueness of <actionGroup> name attributes within any asset action metadata record. The instance of <xsd:keyref> in the definition of the <assetActions> element, tied by its refer attribute to the <xsd:key> mentioned above, ensures that exactly one of the <actionGroup> elements will have a name attribute with the value "defaultActionGroup", that is, the value of the requiredAG attribute referenced by the <selector> and <field> elements associated with <xsd:keyref>.

QUESTIONS AND TOPICS FOR DISCUSSION

1. Describe how the elements and attributes introduced in this chapter can be used to enforce additional constraints and rules for XML schemas.
2. Discuss some instances where the following constraints may be useful: xsd:any, xsd:redefine, and xsd:unique.
3. After learning about additional features of XSDs, in what instances would an XSD be advantageous over a DTD and why?

SUGGESTIONS FOR EXERCISES

1. Choose a nontraditional object/item and devise an application profile for this item's metadata. What schemas would be useful to describe this object? What elements would you use or reject?
2. What constraints (or lack thereof) are necessary for a collection of metadata records for objects like the one you chose? What XSD elements or attributes can be used to enforce these rules?
3. Create an XSD schema representing this application profile and its rules.

NOTES

1. http://www.w3.org/2001/sw.
2. http://www.w3.org/standards/semanticweb/data.
3. http://www.openarchives.org/OAI/2.0/oai_dc.xsd.
4. Repository count from the University of Illinois OAI-PMH Data Provider Registry, http://oai.grainger.uiuc.edu/registry.
5. http://www.rssboard.org/rss-specification.
6. http://tools.ietf.org/html/rfc4287.
7. http://www.w3.org/TR/2011/CR-xmlschema11-1-20110721/
8. http://rss2schema.codeplex.com.
9. http://www.docbook.org/xml/5.0b3/xsd/docbook.xsd.
10. http://www.loc.gov/standards/mods/v3/mods-userguide.html.
11. http://diglib.hab.de/rules/schema/emblem/emblem-1-2.xsd.
12. http://www.w3.org/2004/02/skos/core#.
13. http://www.w3.org/1999/02/22-rdf-syntax-ns#.
14. http://diglib.hab.de/rules/schema/teiP5/teiP5.xsd.
15. http://www.w3.org/TR/REC-xml.

REFERENCES

Chavez, Robert, Timothy W. Cole, Jon Dunn, Muriel Foulonneau, Thomas G. Habing, William Parod, and Thorton Staples. 2006. "DLF-Aquifer Asset Actions Experiment: Demonstrating Value of Actionable URLs." *D-Lib Magazine* 12, no. 10. Available at: http://www.dlib.org/dlib/october06/cole/10cole.html

Nottingham, M., and R. Sayre, eds. 2005. *The Atom Syndication Format. Internet Engineering Task Force Request for Comments 4287* (Proposed Standard). The Internet Society. Available at: http://www.apps.ietf.org/rfc/rfc4287.html

Rawles, Stephen. 2004. "A SPINE of Information Headings for Emblem-Related Electronic Resources." In *Digital Collections and the Management of Knowledge: Renaissance Emblem Literature as a Case Study for the Digitization of Rare Texts and Images*, 19–28, edited by Mara Wade. Salzburg: DigiCULT.

Sperberg-McQueen, C. M. 2005. "How Schema-Validity Is Different from Being Married." Paper presented at the XML 2005 conference, Atlanta, November 14–18. Available at: http://www.pdfpower.com/XML2005Proceedings/abstracts/paper166.HTML

PART IV

METADATA CROSSWALKS, XML TRANSFORMATIONS, AND RDF XML

CHAPTER 10

Transforming XML (Part I): Metadata Crosswalking and XPath

Increasingly in their cataloging and metadata work flows, libraries must deal with multiple descriptive standards and must integrate metadata from diverse sources. This in turn assumes interoperability at the syntactic level (accomplished through the use of XML) and mandates the development of semantic mappings that can bridge metadata standards and application profiles. Documents describing semantic mappings from one metadata grammar to another, often representing these mappings in tables or as graphs, are referred to as crosswalk specifications. Mapping is "the intellectual activity of comparing and analyzing two or more metadata schemas," and crosswalks are "the visual and textual product of the mapping process" (Woodley 2008). Thus, a crosswalk specification for transforming MARCXML records to Simple Dublin Core XML records might specify that MAchine-Readable Cataloging (MARC) data field 245, subfield a (e.g., `<datafield tag="245" ind1="1" ind2="0"> <subfield code="a">`), maps to the Simple Dublin Core `<title>` element. This is a fairly simple example of a crosswalk specification mapping. More complex mappings are often required. Additionally, when developing crosswalks involving metadata grammars that rely on differing data value and/or data content standards, the crosswalk specification may also need to include rules that describe how to convert values from one data standard to another.

As discussed in earlier chapters, XML is well suited for serializing structured metadata in part because it is designed to facilitate the maintenance, organization, sharing, and reuse of these metadata, including the integration of metadata gathered from multiple sources and the transformation of records (i.e., in accord with a crosswalk specification) from one metadata grammar to another or from a metadata standard to XHTML (e.g., for presentation of metadata to end users via the Web). Conformance to the XML specification ensures syntactic metadata interoperability; however, to support semantic interoperability and scalable algorithmic transformation (i.e., automated batch-mode crosswalk implementation), ancillary specifications and processing rules are provided by the World Wide Web Consortium (W3C) for use with XML.

The XML Path Language (XPath) and the Extensible Stylesheet Language for Transformations (XSLT) are two of the tools in the XML arsenal that facilitate metadata record reuse and sharing and make batch-mode, algorithmic transformation of metadata feasible on a large scale. XPath provides the semantics, including special operators and functions, for selecting specific segments of the record hierarchy, specific content objects, individual element values, and individual element attribute values from XML metadata records. Style sheets conforming to the XSLT standard (which is discussed and illustrated in Chapter 11) incorporate XPath expressions and are used to transform an XML metadata record from one XML metadata grammar to another XML metadata grammar, to XHTML, or to plain text. Although separately described, the XSLT and XPath standards are meant to work together. The W3C Recommendations defining XPath (version 1.0[1] and version 2.0[2]) and XSLT (version 1.0[3] and version 2.0[4]) were initially drafted by the W3C XSL Working Group as components of an Extensible Stylesheet Language family of specifications.[5]

When transforming XML metadata records, the expressions, operators, and functions of XPath are used to select the structures and values from the source XML document(s) that need to be analyzed, manipulated, and potentially included in the transformation result. The XSLT standard defines the complementary semantics required to manage the end-to-end transformation process and construct a transformation result based on the structures and values selected using XPath. For example, an implementer can retrieve and concatenate subfields a and b of the 245 data field (title statement) of a MARCXML record by using XPath; then this concatenated value can be saved as the content of a `<title>` element in a Simple Dublin Core XML metadata record created as the outcome of a transformation implemented using XSLT. In combination, XPath and XSLT are well suited for implementing metadata crosswalks.

This chapter briefly introduces metadata crosswalking and a few of the most common issues associated with defining crosswalks in the context of XML-based metadata applications. For more extensive discussions of metadata crosswalking and attendant issues, the reader is referred to Woodley (2008); Godby Smith, and Childress (2008); Lightle and Ridgway (2003); and St. Pierre and LaPlant (1998). The general and high-level introduction to metadata crosswalking provided here is intended as a motivation and a source of metadata mapping illustrations for the discussion that follows about the XPath W3C Recommendations. This discussion of XPath focuses on examples illustrating how XPath can be used to isolate and extract specific information from a source XML metadata record and help crosswalk this information to a destination record conforming to a different XML metadata grammar. The next chapter describes the XSLT standards and examines how XPath is used within XSLT style sheets that implement complete metadata crosswalks.

METADATA CROSSWALKS

Metadata crosswalking is the process of implementing a crosswalk specification to translate records from one metadata format to another, such as from one XML metadata grammar to another: MARC to Simple Dublin Core, MARC to Metadata Object Description Schema (MODS), MODS to Qualified Dublin Core, and so on. Crosswalking allows a metadata search and discovery application designed around Simple Dublin Core XML to also ingest for indexing MARCXML and MODS XML metadata records. Non-XML serialized metadata can be crosswalked, but the following discussion will focus on crosswalking metadata serialized as XML.

In any metadata crosswalking process, there are source items conforming to a specific metadata grammar—call it metadata grammar A. The crosswalking process creates from each of these source items corresponding new metadata records conforming to a different metadata grammar—call it metadata grammar B. The crosswalking process, i.e., the translation from metadata grammar A to metadata grammar B, is often imperfect. The transformation may be lossy. The created (destination) metadata records conforming to grammar B may not contain all the information that was present in the source items conforming to grammar A. Lossiness may be due to limitations of the transformation process itself or to limitations of grammar B as compared to grammar A. As described below, other kinds of crosswalking/translation issues can occur. Such errors are acceptable as long as they do not compromise the goals of the crosswalk, for example, as long as the errors and data loss do not compromise the ability to usefully index MARCXML and MODS XML records in a unified search and discovery application initially designed around Simple Dublin Core XML. Practically speaking, crosswalking imperfections are inevitable; nonetheless, crosswalking remains a useful metadata interoperability approach, as articulated by Coyle (2004):

> The more metadata experience we have, the more it becomes clear that metadata perfection is not attainable, and anyone who attempts it will be sorely disappointed. When metadata is crosswalked between two or more unrelated sources, there will be data elements that cannot be reconciled in an ideal manner. The key to a successful metadata crosswalk is intelligent flexibility. It is essential to focus on the important goals and be willing to compromise in order to reach a practical conclusion to projects. (91)

Mapping Metadata Semantics and Hierarchies

By definition, a metadata crosswalk specification describes a mapping between distinct metadata standards or metadata application profiles. The process of creating a crosswalk specification spanning different XML metadata grammars begins by identifying which elements and attributes contained in the source metadata items being crosswalked (i.e., items conforming to metadata grammar A) map to which elements and attributes in the destination metadata records being created (i.e., records conforming to metadata grammar B). To develop such intellectual mappings, one must discover and understand the differences in the semantics, content standards, and hierarchical organization of the XML metadata grammars involved. This requires carefully analyzing the relevant XML schemas, metadata standards, application profiles, and data content guidelines associated with each of the XML grammars being crosswalked.

Understanding the Semantics of a Metadata Grammar

Although a good starting point, looking at the XML schemas alone is typically not enough. To create an accurate crosswalking result, it is important to look beyond the XML schemas themselves—that is, beyond the XML Schema Definition (XSD) files on their own—to the standards, data models, and usage guidelines for the grammars being described by the XSD files. For instance, as discussed in previous chapters, similarity in semantic labels declared in an XSD does not necessarily mean semantic equivalence. The MODS concept of *subject*, which encompasses both geographic and temporal subjects, as well as topical subjects, overlaps in semantic meaning with both *subject* and *coverage* in Simple Dublin Core but is synonymous with neither. In order to appreciate the nuanced differences between MODS subject and Simple Dublin Core subject, it is necessary to look beyond the XSD files on their own; for example, it is necessary to look at the *MODS User Guide*[6] and the *Dublin Core User Guide*[7] for in-depth rules and limitations for each grammar.

Development of a crosswalk specification is greatly facilitated if the properties of the elements and attributes that make up each metadata grammar are themselves well described. As a minimum, St. Pierre and LaPlant (1998) suggest that to simplify crosswalk development, the following six properties should be available for describing each element of a metadata grammar:

1. A unique identifier or name for the element (e.g., tag, label, or field name)
2. Whether the element is mandatory or optional
3. Whether the element can appear multiple times in a single record
4. The hierarchical parent–child relationships involving the element
5. An enumeration of any constraints on the value (content) of the element
6. A semantic definition of the element

When available, an XSD declaring the elements of a particular metadata grammar is a good source for the first five of the properties listed above; usage guides, the associated metadata standard itself, and/or other ancillary documentation are likely sources for the semantic definition of an element.

More extensive properties about the elements and attributes that make up a distinct metadata grammar may be available, and, when available, these can be useful for developing mappings. Just as there are many metadata standards for describing digital information resources, there are multiple meta-metadata schemes for describing the elements of a metadata standard. Increasingly, authors of metadata standards are choosing to define the elements of their metadata grammar using terminology borrowed from the data model of the Resource Description Framework (RDF; see further discussion in Chapter 12). Thus, the Simple Dublin Core element `<creator>` is defined by the Dublin Core Metadata Initiative (DCMI) Usage Board as having a range of "Agent." Agent is defined elsewhere[8] by the DCMI as "a resource that acts or has the power to act. . . . Examples of Agent include person, organization, and software agent." So in this instance, range (a term borrowed from RDF and first-order predicate logic), as part of the definition of the Simple Dublin Core `<creator>` element, conveys the scope of what exactly can be a creator, such as a person, an organization, a software agent, or anything else that "acts or has the power to act" (DCMI Usage Board 2010). This information is helpful in understanding the semantic meaning of `<creator>` as used in Simple Dublin Core.

Altogether, Simple and Qualified Dublin Core elements are defined by as many as 17 properties (DCMI Usage Board 2010). The characteristics of elements that make up other metadata standards may be defined according to other schemes in accord with various parts of ISO/IEC 11179, *Information Standards—Metadata Registries*.[9] Among other things, this standard, in six parts (Framework, Classification, Registry Metamodel and Basic Attributes, Formulation of Data Definition, Naming and Identification Principles, and Registration), defines properties and best practices useful for formulating descriptions of elements used in a metadata grammar.

Semantic and Value Mappings

Once the semantics of each grammar involved in a crosswalk have been fully explored and assimilated, the next challenge in creating a crosswalk specification is to identify where and how the grammars overlap. Are there elements in the source item's grammar that match the semantic meaning of elements in the destination record's grammar on a one-to-one basis? Or are there multiple elements in the source item's grammar that map to a single element in the destination record's grammar? The latter is a many-to-one mapping. Are there one-to-many mappings?

One-to-one mappings are the easiest to address when creating a crosswalk specification and one-to-one crosswalk specifications are the easiest to implement in practice. The Library of Congress (LC) maintains several crosswalk specifications involving metadata standards used in the library domain. Table 10.1 shows the one-to-one mappings from LC's recommended Simple Dublin Core to MARC crosswalk.[10] Note that `<title>` and `<identifier>` are not

TABLE 10.1 Summary of one-to-one mappings of Simple Dublin Core to MARC crosswalk (*Source*: Library of Congress).

Simple Dublin Core Elements	MARC Data Fields
contributor	720 $a — added entry, uncontrolled name
coverage	500 $a — general note
creator	720 $a — added entry, uncontrolled name
date	260 $c — date of publication
description	520 $a — note: summary, etc.
format	856 $q — electronic format type
language	546 $a — note: language
publisher	260 $b — publication, distribution, . . .
relation	787 $n — non-specific relationship entry. . .
rights	540 $a — note: terms governing use . . .
source	786 $n — data source entry / note
subject	653 $a — index term – uncontrolled
type	655 $a ($2=local) — genre/form index term

one-to-one mappings and hence are not included in Table 10.1 (see further discussion below).

Notice the compromises inherent even in some of the relatively simple one-to-one mappings from Simple Dublin Core to MARC shown in Table 10.1. For example, because the Simple Dublin Core metadata standard provides no way to differentiate between corporate and personal authors (creators) and no way to express order among creators, the LC crosswalk recommends mapping all Simple Dublin Core `<creator>` elements to the uncontrolled name added-entry field in MARC. The crosswalk provides no way to populate MARC 1XX main-entry fields by crosswalking from a Simple Dublin Core metadata record. While this can impact how crosswalked records are displayed, overall the approach is deemed acceptable because most search and discovery applications that consume MARC records provide a merged (10X, 11X, 70X, 71X, 72X) name index for end-user searching.

Similarly, many values found in the Simple Dublin Core subject element would most properly belong in MARC data field 600 (subject added entry personal name), 610 (subject added entry corporate name), or 650 (subject added entry topical term). However, because Simple Dublin Core provides no semantics for identifying the kind of subject heading in a `<subject>` element of a record, there is no easy way to accomplish this mapping reliably. So the Simple Dublin Core `<subject>` element is mapped to the MARC data field 653 (index term-uncontrolled). This has relatively little impact on indexing but may impact the range of faceted browsing that can be supported.

Although they tend to make crosswalking work flows simple and easy, one-to-one mappings of the sort illustrated in Table 10.1 are not the only kind included in crosswalk specifications or even the most common. Crosswalk specifications may also describe many-to-one and one-to-many mappings.

There are at least three kinds of many-to-one mappings to consider. The first stems from the situation where the source record's metadata grammar allows repeatable elements but the destination record's metadata grammar or application profile does not. For example, when mapping from a metadata grammar that allows the <subject> element to be repeated (i.e., once for every subject heading assigned) to a metadata grammar that does not, it is necessary to concatenate together all of the subject heading values from the source record (the many), usually integrating a delimiter (e.g., semicolon) as a separator between headings, in order to create a sensible and complete value for the single <subject> element of the destination record (the one).

Another kind of many-to-one mapping covers the situation where the source item's metadata grammar is more granular. In this situation, it may be necessary to concatenate together values (sometimes reordered with added punctuation) from discrete elements of a source item to create a single, less granular value that maps to a single element conforming to the destination record's metadata grammar. Consider the subfields of the MARC data field 662 (subject added entry-hierarchical place name) as illustrated in the snippet shown in Figure 10.1 from a hypothetical MARCXML record. The MARCXML grammar allows a location or political jurisdiction to be broken down into segments, such as country, county, city name, city subsection, and so on. The Simple Dublin Core data model does not provide that level of granularity for specifying location values. The mapping shown in Figure 10.1 is the result.

A related third kind of many-to-one mapping covers the situation where the source item's grammar is more expressive than the destination record's grammar. For example, as alluded to above, the MARC metadata standard differentiates between personal and corporate agents involved in the creation of the resource being described. MARC also differentiates between main entry named entities and added entry named entities. The Simple Dublin Core

FIGURE 10.1 Example of many-to-one mapping necessary due to granularity differences between schemas.

```
Snippet from a MARCXML record:
        <datafield tag="662" ind1=" " ind2=" ">
                <subfield code="b">Maryland</subfield>
                <subfield code="c">Montgomery</subfield>
                <subfield code="d">Silver Spring.</subfield>
        </datafield>

Maps to this snippet in destination Simple Dublin Core XML record:
        <coverage>Maryland, Silver Spring (Montgomery).</coverage>
```

TABLE 10.2 An incomplete summary of the Library of Congress MAchine-Readable Cataloging (LC MARC) to Simple DC crosswalk illustrating many-to-one mappings.[11]

MARC Data Fields	Simple Dublin Core Elements
100, 110, 111, 700, 710, 711, 720	contributor (some LC XSLTs map to creator)
500-599 (except 506, 530, 540, 546)	description
600, 610, 611, 630, 650, 653	subject
020 $a, 02 2$a, 024 $a, 856 $u	identifier
260 $a and $b	publisher
008 (characters 07–10), 260 $c and $g	date

standard does not. As shown in Table 10.2, this results in six different data fields in MARC (100, 110, 111, 700, 711, and 720), all mapping individually to the Simple Dublin Core `<contributor>` element. Since `<contributor>` is a repeatable field according to the Simple Dublin Core standard, notice that concatenation is not required; each MARC name entry maps individually to its own `<contributor>` field in the destination record. However, also notice that information differentiating between personal and corporate names and information defining the order of names is lost since Simple Dublin Core offers no way to record this information.

Together, Tables 10.1 and 10.2 (the latter showing some of the many-to-one mappings inherent in the LC MARC to Simple Dublin Core crosswalk) illustrate that crosswalks are directional. Mappings from MARC to Simple Dublin Core (Table 10.2) are not the exact inverse of mappings from Simple Dublin Core to MARC (Table 10.1). This difference has the practical consequence that some metadata crosswalks are inherently lossy; that is, metadata and/or semantic meaning are lost during the transformation. To illustrate, consider the round-trip transformation sequence depicted in Figure 10.2, which extends the one-way transformation shown in Figure 10.1. The XML

FIGURE 10.2 A round-trip crosswalk.

Snippet from a MARCXML record:

```
<datafield tag="662" ind1=" " ind2=" ">
    <subfield code="b">Maryland</subfield>
    <subfield code="c">Montgomery</subfield>
    <subfield code="d">Silver Spring.</subfield>
</datafield>
```

Maps to this snippet in destination Simple Dublin Core XML record:

```
<coverage>Maryland, Silver Spring (Montgomery).</coverage>
```

Mapped back to MARCXML:

```
<datafield tag="500" ind1=" " ind2=" ">
    <subfield code="a">Maryland, Silver Spring (Montgomery).</subfield>
</datafield>
```

resulting from crosswalking a snippet of metadata from MARC to Simple Dublin Core and then back to MARC does not match the original. In this example, the original source item contained values in the subfields of MARC data field 662 (subject added entry-hierarchical place name). Crosswalked to Simple Dublin Core, these values were concatenated and put into the Simple Dublin Core `<coverage>` element in the destination record (as specified in the LC MARC to Simple Dublin Core crosswalk). If this metadata record is then crosswalked back to MARC per the mappings shown in Table 10.1, the value ends up as subfield a of MARC data field 500 (general note), which is not at all where this information was serialized originally.

In addition to one-to-one and many-to-one mappings, crosswalks may also specify one-to-many mappings. Generally, these mappings are the hardest to implement. Often, one-to-many mappings require parsing values into component parts. For instance, as an alternative to the Simple Dublin Core to MARC mapping depicted in Figure 10.2, a crosswalk could specify that the contents of the Simple Dublin Core element `<coverage>` should be parsed and mapped into the appropriate subfields of MARC data field 662. Assuming that the values found in the `<coverage>` element for the collection of Simple Dublin Core items being crosswalked to MARC are consistently punctuated and similar in form (e.g., always consist of a state name, a city name, and county), it is feasible to implement such a crosswalk specification. In practice, though, the realities of limited data quality and inconsistent data often get in the way.

Slightly easier are one-to-many mappings that require the mapping of source item elements based on their position in the node list of the record. The LC Simple Dublin Core to MARC crosswalk specifies such a one-to-many mapping. This mapping requires that the first occurrence of the `<title>` element in a Simple Dublin Core source item be mapped to MARC data field 245, subfield a, in the destination record. All subsequent occurrences of `<title>` in the source item should be mapped to data field 246, subfield a, in the destination record. This mapping is illustrated in Figure 10.3.

Beyond mapping semantic labels, crosswalks may also include rules for converting values. For example, date values found in data field 260, subfield c, of MARC records (publication date) can vary in format according to how such dates were recorded in the item cataloged. At times, it has been common for the publication date of a book to be recorded in the item in Roman numerals. This can lead to date values in MARC records, such as "MDLXXIIII [1574]." Many application profiles of Simple Dublin Core, on the other hand, require that date values conform to the W3C Date-Time Format (W3CDTF).[12] Roman numeral dates are not supported by the W3CDTF specification and therefore must be removed or converted as part of the process of migrating values from MARC date fields to Simple Dublin Core date fields. Any comprehensive crosswalk specification for mapping from generic MARC to a profile of Simple Dublin Core requiring W3CDTF dates must specify rules for

FIGURE 10.3 Example of one-to-many mapping based on order of element in source record.

```
Snippet from a Simple Dublin Core XML record:
    <title>Meditationes emblematicae de restaurata pace Germaniae</title>
    <title>Sinnebilder von dem widergebrachten Teutschen Frieden</title>
    <title>Meditationes de restaurata pace</title>

Maps to this snippet in destination MARCXML record:
    <datafield tag="245" ind1="0" ind2="0">
        <subfield code="a">Meditationes emblematicae de restaurata pace
            Germaniae</subfield>
    </datafield>
    <datafield tag="246" ind1="3" ind2="3">
        <subfield code="a"> Sinnebilder von dem widergebrachten Teutschen
            Frieden </subfield>
    </datafield>
    <datafield tag="246" ind1="3" ind2="3">
        <subfield code="a">Meditationes de restaurata pace</subfield>
    </datafield>
```

converting date values found in MARC records into a format consistent with the W3CDTF specification. Conversion rules for handling Julian calendar dates, approximate dates, and date ranges may also be required in order to deal with the different data content guidelines used in conjunction with various metadata standards. Analogous conversions may be required for other metadata values.

Crosswalk Issues

Although the implementation of metadata crosswalks has been facilitated by the emergence of XML, library experience with crosswalks predates XML. Karen Coyle describes one early experience with metadata crosswalks. In the late 1980s, the University of California's Division of Digital Library Automation (one of the precursors of today's California Digital Library) wanted to better integrate searches of the University of California library online catalog with searches of select journal article abstract and indexing databases for which the University of California had license to load and maintain copies locally (e.g., the National Library of Medicine's *Medline* database and the Institute of Scientific Information's *Current Contents* database). This integration was accomplished by crosswalking metadata from local copies of *Medline*, *Current Contents*, and similar databases to MARC for ingestion into the library's online catalog system, MELVYL (Coyle 2004). As a result of this metadata integration, library users were able to search and discover books and journal articles through the same interface, exploiting merged comprehensive indexes of article and book metadata.

As would be expected, a number of challenges and issues arose during the development of the crosswalks to support the California project

(Coyle 2004). Many of these issues, as well as additional issues that have surfaced in other library projects involving metadata crosswalks, have come to be recognized as endemic to the metadata crosswalk process (St. Pierre and LaPlant 1998; Woodley 2008). Highlighted here as examples are a few of these issues:

1. Differences in unit of description: Both Simple and Qualified Dublin Core adhere to the "one-to-one" principle (Powell et al. 2007, sec. 3). This principle mandates that a metadata record describe a single discrete resource, such as a single digital photograph of a painting or a digitized facsimile of a single letter. By contrast, a single metadata record conforming to Visual Resources Association (VRA) Core or Categories for the Description of Works of Art (CDWA)-Lite (see Chapter 5) typically describes a work (e.g., a painting) as well as multiple digital representations of that work. Or a metadata record conforming to the Encoded Archival Description (EAD) standard (see Chapter 5) might describe a digitized surrogate of a letter in the context of the complete set of correspondence included in an archive of an individual's papers. For this reason, it is uncommon to try to crosswalk Simple Dublin Core XML to VRA Core XML, CDWA-Lite XML, or EAD XML, though sometimes it is possible to crosswalk a single metadata record conforming to one of these non-Dublin Core standards to multiple Dublin Core XML records.
2. Fuzzy or imprecise mappings: Often an element in the source item's schema will have no exact analog in the destination record's schema. A common example is an element that has a narrower meaning (e.g., personal author) in the source record's schema than the meaning of the closest match element (e.g., creator) in the destination record's schema. In these instances, it is often acceptable to "dumb down" the metadata in order to have somewhere to put the metadata in the destination record; however, this is clearly an example of a lossy transform. In other cases, it may be a matter of poor alignment. For example, should the contents of the VRA Core *stylePeriod* map to Simple Dublin Core *subject*, *coverage*, both, or neither (i.e., not be mapped)? This question usually is answered not generically but rather in light of local context for the contemplated crosswalk. Zeng and Qin (2008, 120) suggest the terms "absolute crosswalk" and "relative crosswalk" to capture the two extremes of the options available in these situations. In their model, absolute crosswalks map only exactly aligned elements, leaving out unmapped fuzzy or imprecise mappings. Relative crosswalks strive to map every element in the source item to a closest match in the destination record.
3. Missing required elements: A particularly vexing issue can arise when the destination record's schema or application profile requires metadata not present in the source item. For example, many application profiles based on the MODS metadata standard require all records to contain a `<titleInfo>` element in order to build short-record search result displays. However, digital surrogates for natural history museum specimens, untitled works of art, and other classes of nonbibliographic content often have no title (in the strictest sense of the term). "Books and articles have titles in a way that bones and viruses do not" (Yale University 2008, 2). This absence can result in metadata records that do not include any values that can be mapped (strictly speaking) to the MODS `<titleInfo>` element. One way to deal with this is to generate a fixed value for absent destination elements, such as "no title," "untitled," "not applicable."

Another option is to generate a fuzzy, approximate mapping sufficient to ensure that `<titleInfo>` is always populated.

4. Changes in standards over time: Metadata crosswalk specifications can be challenging to maintain over time as schemas and standards change. Crosswalks may also break if the processes change by which source items (i.e., the metadata items to be crosswalked) are generated. Metadata crosswalks often have latent dependencies and assumptions about both the metadata standards involved and the elements that can be encountered in source items. These can make it difficult to anticipate what changes might break a previously working crosswalk.

This list of crosswalk issues is incomplete and cursory, but it illustrates the scope of the challenges faced in constructing crosswalk specifications as well as the scope of crosswalk mappings that must be accommodated in any implementation. Fortunately, catalogers and metadata librarians today have access to a number of well-established, community-vetted crosswalk specifications on which to build local implementations. In particular, the LC Network Development and MARC Standards Office,[13] which maintains canonical schemas and documentation for MARCXML, MODS, EAD, VRA Core, and a number of other metadata standards, maintains a number of crosswalk specifications and XSLT-based implementations of these crosswalks. Many of the examples and illustrations included in this chapter draw on these crosswalks.

USING XPATH TO ANALYZE AND NAVIGATE XML METADATA RECORDS

The XPath W3C Recommendation defines a syntax and set of semantics for analyzing and navigating XML documents, such as XML metadata records. Using XPath to navigate XML metadata records is one step in automating metadata crosswalks. The XPath version 1.0 W3C Recommendation was initially published in 1999 and is widely supported. XPath version 2.0 became a W3C Recommendation in 2007. While version 2.0 does introduce some new features (a few of which are not yet widely supported), in terms of practical functionality in the context of XML-based metadata applications, it is largely an incremental update and backward compatible with version 1.0 in most respects. The 2.0 specification itself, however, is richer and more detailed regarding data models and description of XPath semantics. The 2.0 specification is more than three times as long when printed and references three new W3C Recommendations, each of which is longer than the original 1.0 XPath specification:

The XQuery 1.0 and XPath 2.0 Data Model (XDM) Second Edition[14]

XQuery 1.0 and XPath 2.0 Formal Semantics[15]

XQuery 1.0 and XPath 2.0 Functions and Operators Second Edition[16]

The introduction to XPath presented here relies primarily on the data models and terminology of the XPath version 2.0 W3C Recommendation and related documentation; however, unless otherwise noted, the illustrations are equally valid in XPath 1.0 and XPath 2.0.

Basic Concepts

XPath models XML documents as hierarchical trees of *nodes* and *atomic values*. XML elements and attributes are examples of entities that XPath models as nodes (there are several other kinds of nodes, enumerated below). Nodes may have accessible properties, such as *node-names* and *typed-values*. Nodes are arranged relative to one another along *axes*, such as *parent* axis, *child* axis, *ancestor* axis, *descendant* axis, *preceding-sibling* axis, and *following-sibling* axis, and so on. Specific axes may be empty for specific nodes. An atomic value always has a data type matching one of the primitive data types defined in the W3C Recommendation *XML Schema Part 2: Datatypes*[17] (e.g., string, Boolean, decimal, date, and so on) or a data type derived by restriction from one of those primitive data types (e.g., integer, NMTOKEN, IDREF, and so on). See Chapters 8 and 9 for more discussion about the XML Schema W3C Recommendations. The typed-value of a node is an atomic value or comprised of a sequence of atomic values. Thus, for most practical purposes, XPath models XML documents as trees of nodes and node-values, the latter broken down into primitive data types as required. XPath version 2.0 also defines *sequences* of *items* (i.e., sequences of nodes and/or atomic values) as a way to deal with units of an XML document larger than a single node or a single atomic value. Sequences in XPath version 2.0 supplant the concept of *node-sets* in XPath version 1.0. For purposes of the XPath data model, sequences may be empty or contain only a singleton item (i.e., a single node or atomic value). Sequences are flat (i.e., not hierarchical) and do not nest but can be combined.

XPath is an *expression*-based language that includes a set of built-in core operators and functions to give the language additional intrinsic programming power. The simplest kind of XPath expression is a string or numeric *literal*, such as "hello" or 7.5. For the most part, pairs of single or double quotes can be used interchangeably to delineate a string literal in an XPath expression. For example, the string literals 'hello' and "hello" are equivalent in XPath. This flexibility makes it easier to embed string literals inside XPath expressions that appear as part of an XML attribute value, which itself is contained between quote marks or apostrophes (e.g., when using XPath within an XSLT style sheet). Also, this flexibility is helpful when expressing string literals that include embedded quotes or apostrophes, such as the string literal "O'Brien". Alternatively, if necessary, to avoid confusion or ambiguity, character entities may be used to represent quotes or apostrophes that are embedded in string literals, such as "O'Brien". This is a form of what is commonly called *character escaping*. XPath 2.0 allows other forms of character escaping, such as two consecutive quotes or two consecutive apostrophes, to represent a quote or apostrophe embedded in a string literal.

In addition to string and numeric literals, XPath supports other kinds of expressions, including the following (incomplete list):

Path expressions (used to locate specific nodes within a tree structure)

Arithmetic expressions (return the result of an arithmetic operation)

Comparison expressions (return true or false according to result of comparison)

Logical expressions (used to perform Boolean operations)

For expressions (used to iterate; version 2.0 only)

Conditional expressions (supports branching in processing flow; version 2.0)

Sequence expressions (1.0 supports combining; 2.0 adds support for manipulation)

XPath is a composable language, meaning that an XPath expression may be composed of multiple other XPath expressions (i.e., subexpressions), which in turn may be composed of XPath expressions and so on. XPath expressions can embed calls to intrinsic XPath functions. XPath provides functions for operating on atomic values, such as numeric values, strings, Boolean values, date and time values, nodes, and sequences, as well as various other, more specialized functions. In addition to taking atomic values as arguments, many XPath functions may take an XPath expression as an argument. XPath also supports references to variables; in XPath, variable names are prefixed with a "$." Parentheses can be used to enforce order of precedence during expression evaluation.

In XPath, *context* and *scope* are also fundamental concepts. As path expressions are used to navigate the structure of an XML metadata record, the context can change according to what portion of the record hierarchy was navigated by the last path expression; subsequent XPath expressions referencing nodes of the XML metadata record are evaluated according to the current context, that is, according to where in the XML metadata record hierarchy the last path expression left off. Similarly, variables and other references used in XPath expressions are scoped according to context, such as where in the sequence of the XSLT the variable was declared. Context and scope will be illustrated in XSLT examples given in the next chapter.

Path Expressions and Predicates

As mentioned, XPath models XML metadata records as hierarchical trees of nodes. There are seven kinds of nodes in the XPath data model of XML: element, attribute, text, namespace, processing-instruction, comment, and document nodes. The document node represents the root of the tree and encapsulates the complete XML of the metadata record. The document node "contains" (i.e., has as child node) the root element node of the XML metadata record and may also have immediate children processing instruction, comment, and/or text nodes. The distinction between the document node and the root element node in XPath is a bit nuanced. In practical terms, the distinction means that the URI of an XML metadata record (i.e., the string used to identify and typically retrieve an XML metadata record on the Web) is a property of the document node, while the name of the top-level element in the XML metadata record hierarchy of content objects is a property of the root element node. In XPath version 1.0, the document node was called the root node. The name was changed in XPath 2.0 to avoid confusion.

XPath (and XSLT as well) are best understood by example. These specifications are difficult to assimilate in the abstract. To facilitate this introduction, XPath illustrations used through the remainder of this chapter assume one or the other of the XML metadata records shown in Figure 10.4 (a Simple Dublin Core XML record) and Figure 10.5 (a MARCXML record). These records, introduced in Chapter 5 (Figure 5.1) and Chapter 1 (Figures 1.11 through 1.15), respectively, have been used throughout this book as a source of illustrations. Additionally, keep in mind that XPath is meant to be embedded within a host language such as XSLT. For this reason, it can be difficult to debug and test XPath syntax and semantics independently. Some XML editors, such as SyncRO Soft Ltd's Oxygen XML Editor, do provide an integrated tool for constructing and debugging XPath expressions (as illustrated in Figure 10.9). Often in practice, testing and debugging of XPath goes hand in hand with XSLT testing and debugging.

XPath gets its name from its support for path expressions, which are used to locate nodes and values within an XML document or fragment. Path expressions are built-up stepwise, with steps separated by instances of "/" or

FIGURE 10.4 Example of a Simple Dublin Core record (used for XPath and XSLT illustrations).

```
<?xml version="1.0" encoding="UTF-8"?>
<?xml-stylesheet type="text/xsl" href="DC2XHTML.xsl"?>
<oai_dc:dc xmlns:oai_dc="http://www.openarchives.org/OAI/2.0/oai_dc/"
    xmlns="http://purl.org/dc/elements/1.1/"
    xmlns:dc="http://purl.org/dc/elements/1.1/"
    xmlns:xsi="http://www.w3.org/2001/XMLSchema-instance"
    xsi:schemaLocation="http://www.openarchives.org/OAI/2.0/oai_dc/
                        http://www.openarchives.org/OAI/2.0/oai_dc.xsd">
    <creator>Cole, Timothy W</creator>
    <creator>Foulonneau, Muriel</creator>
    <title>Using the Open Archives Initiative protocol ...</title>
    <publisher>Westport, Conn. : Libraries Unlimited</publisher>
    <date>2007</date>
    <format>xv, 208 p. : ill. ; 26 cm. </format>
    <language>eng</language>
    <description>Includes bibliographical ....</description>
    <description>Definition and origins ....</description>
    <subject>Open Archives Initiative</subject>
    <subject>Metadata harvesting</subject>
    <identifier>http://www.loc.gov/catdir/toc/....html</identifier>
</oai_dc:dc>
```

FIGURE 10.5 Example of a MARCXML record (used for XPath and XSLT illustrations).

```
<?xml version="1.0" encoding="UTF-8"?>
<record xmlns="http://www.loc.gov/MARC21/slim"
        xmlns:marc="http://www.loc.gov/MARC21/slim"
        xmlns:xsi="http://www.w3.org/2001/XMLSchema-instance">
  <leader>01698cam 22003614a 4500</leader>
  <controlfield tag="001">5439928</controlfield>
  <controlfield tag="005">20080104135038.0</controlfield>
  <controlfield tag="008">070313s2007    ctua    b    001 0 eng    </controlfield>
  <datafield tag="010" ind1=" " ind2=" ">
    <subfield code="a"> 2007009006</subfield></datafield>
  <datafield tag="035" ind1=" " ind2=" ">
    <subfield code="a">(OCoLC)ocn105428765</subfield></datafield>
  <datafield tag="040" ind1=" " ind2=" ">
    <subfield code="a">DLC</subfield>
    <subfield code="c">DLC</subfield>...</datafield>
  <datafield tag="020" ind1=" " ind2=" ">
    <subfield code="a">9781591582809 (alk. paper)</subfield></datafield>
  <datafield tag="020" ind1=" " ind2=" ">
    <subfield code="a">1591582806 (alk. paper)</subfield></datafield>
  <datafield tag="029" ind1="1" ind2=" ">
    <subfield code="a">NLGGC</subfield>
    <subfield code="b">302541152</subfield></datafield>
  <datafield tag="042" ind1=" " ind2=" ">
    <subfield code="a">pcc</subfield></datafield>
  <datafield tag="050" ind1="0" ind2="0">
    <subfield code="a">Z666.7</subfield>
    <subfield code="b">.C65 2007</subfield></datafield>
  <datafield tag="082" ind1="0" ind2="0">
    <subfield code="a">025.3</subfield>
    <subfield code="2">22</subfield></datafield>
  <datafield tag="049" ind1=" " ind2=" ">
    <subfield code="a">UIUU</subfield></datafield>
  <datafield tag="100" ind1="1" ind2=" ">
    <subfield code="a">Cole, Timothy W.</subfield></datafield>
  <datafield tag="245" ind1="1" ind2="0">
    <subfield code="a">Using the Open Archives Initiative... /</subfield>
    <subfield code="c">Timothy... and Muriel Foulonneau</subfield></datafield>
  <datafield tag="260" ind1=" " ind2=" ">
    <subfield code="a">Westport, Conn. :</subfield>
    <subfield code="b">Libraries Unlimited,</subfield>
    <subfield code="c">c2007.</subfield></datafield>
  <datafield tag="300" ind1=" " ind2=" ">
    <subfield code="a">xv, 208 p. :</subfield>
    <subfield code="b">ill. ;</subfield>
    <subfield code="c">26 cm.</subfield></datafield>
  <datafield tag="440" ind1=" " ind2="0">
    <subfield code="a">Third millennium cataloging</subfield></datafield>
  <datafield tag="504" ind1=" " ind2=" ">
    <subfield code="a">Includes bibliographical ....</subfield></datafield>
  <datafield tag="505" ind1="0" ind2=" ">
    <subfield code="a">Definition and origins of OAI...</subfield></datafield>
```

FIGURE 10.5 (Continued)

```
  <datafield tag="650" ind1=" " ind2="0">
    <subfield code="a">Metadata harvesting.</subfield></datafield>
  <datafield tag="610" ind1="2" ind2="0">
    <subfield code="a">Open Archives Initiative.</subfield></datafield>
  <datafield tag="700" ind1="1" ind2=" ">
    <subfield code="a">Foulonneau, Muriel.</subfield></datafield>
  <datafield tag="856" ind1="4" ind2="1">
    <subfield code="3">Table of contents only</subfield>
    <subfield code="u">http://www.loc.gov/catdir/toc...</subfield></datafield>
</record>
```

"//." Each step generates a sequence of items that is refined by subsequent steps or filtered through the use of a predicate (XPath expressions enclosed in square brackets). The first step is evaluated against the current context node, unless proceeded by "/," in which case the first step is evaluated against the ultimate parent node (i.e., document node) of the current context.

XPath supports both *unabbreviated* and *abbreviated* path expression syntax. The abbreviated syntax is used for most of the illustrations that follow. Namespace prefixes and bindings are inherited from context, except that in XPath 1.0 the default namespace binding is not recognized. (For this reason, `dc` and `marc` are bound as namespace prefixes in Figures 10.4 and 10.5, respectively, even though default namespace bindings are also provided.)

Figure 10.6 shows two examples of path expressions and an example of a function expression taking the singleton node sequence result of a path

FIGURE 10.6 Examples of XPath expressions and results when evaluated against the Simple Dublin Core record shown in Figure 10.4.

```
Expression (unabbreviated): /child::oai_dc:dc/child::dc:creator
           (abbreviated): /oai_dc:dc/dc:creator
Results in a sequence of 2 nodes:
           <creator> Cole, Timothy W</creator>
           <creator>Foulonneau, Muriel</creator>

Expression (unabbreviated): /child::oai_dc:dc/child::dc:title/child::text()
           (abbreviated): /oai_dc:dc/dc:title/text()
Results in the singleton text node child of <title>:
           Using the Open Archives Initiative protocol ...

Expression (unabbreviated): string(/child::oai_dc:dc/child::dc:creator[2])
  (2.0 alternative version): /child::oai_dc:dc/child::dc:creator[2]/fn:string(.)
           (abbreviated): string(/oai_dc:dc/dc:creator[2])
           (2.0 abbreviated): /oai_dc:dc/dc:creator[2]/string(.)
Results a value of data type string:
  "Foulonneau, Muriel"
```

expression (with predicate) as an argument. Also shown are the results of evaluating these expressions using the Simple Dublin Core XML record shown in Figure 10.4 as the context. Both unabbreviated and abbreviated syntax is shown. An XPath version 2.0 alternative way of invoking functions is also illustrated. The first step in all three path expressions shown is "oai_dc:dc," the root element (i.e., child of the document node) of the record shown in Figure 10.4. The second step of all three expressions references one or more children of this root element. As illustrated, if an axis is not included explicitly as part of a step, the abbreviated syntax generally assumes "/" on its own is a stand-in for the child:: axis.

Path expressions typically resolve (as in these examples) to a sequence containing zero, one, or more than one node. The first path expression in Figure 10.6 results in a sequence of two nodes, that is, the two <creator> nodes found in the metadata record. The second retrieves a singleton sequence consisting of the text node child of the <title> element. Document and element nodes may have text nodes as children. Text nodes encapsulate the character content of an XML element. Technically, text nodes are nodes, not atomic values. The third example in Figure 10.6 illustrates a path expression containing a predicate. In this case, the predicate is a simple numeric literal: 2. As used here, this predicate specifies the selection of the second <creator> node from the metadata record shown in Figure 10.4, so this third path expression returns a singleton sequence containing the second creator node.

Note that the function expression as a whole (which takes this third path expression as an argument) returns a string value (i.e., an atomic value), not a node. If evaluated against a metadata record that did not contain at least two creator nodes, the function would have returned an empty result (because its argument would have been an empty sequence). Because the invoked function accepts as an argument only sequences containing zero or one item (e.g., zero or one node), this expression would have returned an error if the predicate were not included in the path expression used as the function argument (i.e., because the path expression without the predicate would have returned a sequence of two nodes). The XPath 2.0 alternative version of the third example uses "." to represent the context node. In this case, because the "." appears immediately at the end of a path expression, the context node is the result of the path expression to that point.

Beyond allowing implementers to omit explicit mention of the child:: axis, XPath abbreviated syntax allows other shortcuts as well. For example, a "//" before the first step or any subsequent step is shorthand for the descendant-or-self axis. This highlights the difference between the child:: axis and the descendant:: axis. The former axis contains just the immediate children of the context node (i.e., only a single level in the hierarchy), while the latter is the transitive closure of the child axis. As such, the descendant::axis encompasses all children, children's children, children's

FIGURE 10.7 Examples of XPath expressions and results when evaluated against the MARCXML record shown in Figure 10.5.

```
Expression: //marc:subfield[3]
Results in a sequence of 2 nodes:
        <subfield code="c">c2007.</subfield>
        <subfield code="c">26 cm.</subfield>

Expression: //marc:datafield[@tag="260"]/marc:subfield[3]
Results in a sequence of 1 node:
        <subfield code="c">c2007.</subfield>

Expression: string(//marc:datafield[@tag="260"])
Results in a value of data type string:
       "Westport, Conn : Libraries Unlimited, c2007"

Expression: string(//marc:datafield[@tag="260"]/*[@code="b"])
Results in a value of data type string:
        "Libraries Unlimited,"
```

children's children, and so on. This means that the "//" can be used to essentially ignore intermediate levels of hierarchy. Thus, the first path expression example in Figure 10.6 could have been written as `//dc:creator`. There are, however, some nuances when combined with predicates, as illustrated in the first example of Figure 10.7. Evaluating this expression resulted in a node sequence containing all of the third subfield elements from all data field elements containing at least three subfield elements.

The other path expression examples in Figure 10.7 illustrate the use of predicates that filter results based on attribute values. The "`@`" symbol is the abbreviated syntax for the `attribute::` axis. Thus, "`@tag`" and "`@code`" are expressions for the `tag` and `code` attributes. The expression `@tag="260"` is a comparison expression that is true only for elements with a value of `260` for the tag attribute. As used here (i.e., contained in square brackets), it acts as a filter for the path expression step `//marc:datafield`. Notice in the examples given in Figure 10.7 that each step in a path expression can have its own filter. The last example in Figure 10.7 also illustrates the use of "*" as a wild card character; in this instance used in a step specifying any child element (regardless of element name) having a `code` attribute with value "`b`."

XPATH OPERATORS AND FUNCTIONS

XPath includes additional operators and functions beyond those illustrated above. In addition to basic operators for addition, subtraction, multiplication, and division involving numeric values, XPath also supports an operator for finding the modulus (division remainder) of two numbers (e.g., `10.2 mod 4` results in the numeric value 2.2) as well as mathematical functions for rounding

FIGURE 10.8 Examples of using XPath string functions evaluated against the MARCXML record shown in Figure 10.5.

```
Expression:
   //marc:datafield[starts-with(@tag, '6')]/marc:subfield[@code='a']
Returns subfield a of all the 6XX fields in the MARCXML record:
   <subfield code="a">Metadata harvesting.</subfield>
   <subfield code="a">Open Archives Initiative.</subfield>

Expression:
   //marc:datafield[starts-with(@tag,'1') or
                   @tag='245'][1]/marc:subfield[@code='a']
Returns subfield a of first 1XX or 245 datafield in the XML hierarchy:
   <subfield code="a">Cole, Timothy W.</subfield>

Expression:
   concat(
     substring-after(substring-before
        (//marc:datafield[@tag='700'][1]/marc:subfield[@code='a'],'.'),
        ','),
     ' ',
     substring-before
        (//marc:datafield[@tag='700'][1]/marc:subfield[@code='a'], ',')
   )
Results in a value of data type string:
   Muriel Foulonneau
```

and calculating the floor/ceiling of numeric values (largest integer not greater than number/smallest integer greater than or equal to number). XPath also supports several node and string manipulation operators and functions, which can be especially useful when manipulating XML metadata records. A few string manipulation functions are illustrated in the examples shown in Figure 10.8. For full definitions and a comprehensive listing of intrinsic XPath operators and functions, see the W3C Recommendation *XQuery 1.0 and XPath 2.0 Functions and Operators.*

XPath string manipulation functions are powerful and cover most use cases required for manipulating metadata value strings. Figure 10.8 illustrates the `concat`, `substring-before`, `substring-after`, and `starts-with` XPath functions. The `starts-with` function returns Boolean True or False; the other functions return strings. As shown in the first expression in Figure 10.8, `starts-with` is used to help return a node sequence of all subfield as from MARC data fields in a record having `tag` attributes that start with the numeral "6." Because `starts-with` returns a Boolean type value, it can be used in compound XPath predicates involving Boolean operators such as "`and`" and "`or`" as illustrated in the second expression in Figure 10.8.

Most other XPath string functions return string data type results. For example, `concat`, `string-before`, and `string-after` are XPath functions

FIGURE 10.9 Constructing an XPath expression (third expression from Figure 10.8) using Oxygen XPath Builder graphical user interface. Screen shot was made using Oxygen XML Editor (http://www.oxygenxml.com).

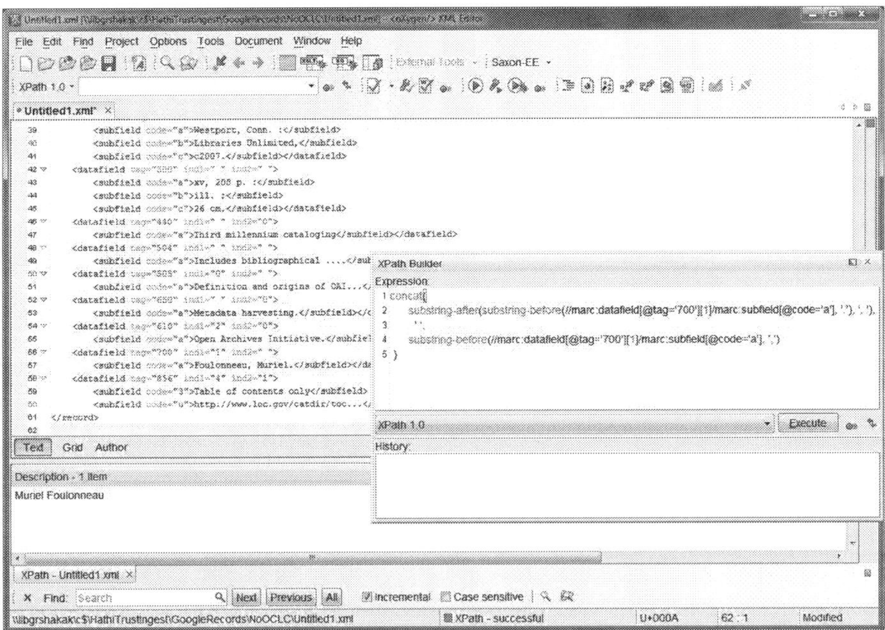

that result in values of data type string. Often, these functions are nested to achieve desired results. The third expression in Figure 10.8 (repeated in Figure 10.9 to illustrate visually the use of a typical tool for building and debugging XPath expressions) is an expression for converting a name in inverted name order (i.e., of the form surname comma given-name) into a direct order name (i.e., given-name surname). This expression uses the `substring-before` function to extract the surname ('Foulonneau'), which appears before the comma, from the string value of subfield a of the first MARC data field 700 in the record. The expression also uses the `substring-before` and `substring-after` in combination (i.e., nested) to extract the given name (Muriel, which appears between the comma and the period in the same MARC element value. The expression then uses the `concat` function to concatenate the extracted given-name and extracted surname together, with an intervening space character added for readability.

XPath provides a few operators and functions for manipulating sequences (nodelists). For example, the "|" symbol is an operator for combining (computing the union of) two sequences. The first expression in Figure 10.10 computes the union of all `<creator>` and `<title>` elements in a Dublin Core record and then returns the first one in the combined sequence (where first is based on order of elements in the record, i.e., document order). A commonly used aggregate function for sequences is "`count`." Given a sequence as an argument (e.g., a path expression resolving to a sequence), the `count`

FIGURE 10.10 Illustrations of XPath node and sequence operators and functions evaluated against the Simple Dublin Core record shown in Figure 10.4.

```
Expression:
        (//dc:creator | //dc:title)[1]
Returns:
        <creator>Cole, Timothy W</creator>

Expression:
        count(//dc:creator)
Returns integer value:
        2

Expression:
        //dc:creator[count(//dc:creator)]
Alternative expression:
        //dc:creator[last()]
Returns:
        <creator>Foulonneau, Muriel</creator>

Expression:
        name((/oai_dc:dc/*)[position() = 5])
Alternative expression:
        name((/oai_dc:dc/*)[5])
Returns string value:
        "date"

Expresion (Version 2.0 only):
        if (exists(//dc:creator)) then //dc:creator[1] else //dc:title[1]
Returns:
        <creator>Cole, Timothy W</creator>
```

function returns the number of items in that sequence, as illustrated by the second expression in Figure 10.10. If the path expression resolves to an empty sequence, `count` returns zero. The third expression in Figure 10.10 illustrates how the result of a `count` expression can be used as a predicate to select the final expression in a sequence. An alternative is to use the context function "`last`" as the predicate instead. Context functions `last` and "`position`" take no arguments; rather, the context node is implicitly the argument. When used as a predicate, the context node for `last` and `position` are the path expressions to that point.

The use of `position` is illustrated in the fourth expression in Figure 10.10. Note that the number returned by `position` is relative to the sequence, not necessarily relative to the number of elements with the same name. This expression also illustrates the use of the XPath "`name`" function, one of several functions that take as argument a single node (or a path expression resolving to a sequence with a node as the only item). The function name returns the node name (as a string value) essentially the way it appears in the XML record, including the namespace prefix when present. To reliably return the name of the element without namespace prefix, use the function `local-name`. The final expression illustrates the `exists` function and the use of an XPath inline Boolean logic expression, two enhancements added in XPath version 2.

SUMMARY

A core goal of XPath is to facilitate the manipulation of information serialized as XML. The authors of the XPath W3C Recommendations wanted to develop a language that could support the reuse and interoperability of information serialized as XML by supporting use cases centered on the transformation of XML documents conformant to one XML schema into XML documents conformant to a different XML schema. They also wanted a language robust and flexible enough to support use cases requiring precise and powerful query functionality. They achieved their objectives by creating a language founded on predicate-based path expressions, semantics for manipulating structured nodes and sequences of nodes, extensive logical and comparison operators and functions, and expressive semantics for manipulating strings as well as numeric values.

Metadata crosswalking involves the mapping of specific metadata record elements and values expressed in one metadata scheme to corresponding and analogous structures in another metadata scheme. XPath is well suited for implementing the first part of this mapping process. The preceding illustrations demonstrate how XPath provides semantics for navigating XML-serialized metadata, analyzing the structure and content of XML metadata records, and selecting values and nodes from such records for further manipulation and/or reuse. Using XPath, catalogers and metadata librarians can isolate, test, and manipulate the structures and values of a source metadata record and prepare these structures and values for crosswalking to destination records corresponding to a different metadata standard or application profile.

The XPath language on its own is not a complete solution for metadata crosswalking. Additional semantics are required to complete the mapping process and create destination metadata records. The path expressions, operators, and functions of XPath are meant to be embedded within a host language, such as XSLT. The next chapter introduces XSLT and illustrates how XPath is used in concert with XSLT to implement complete metadata crosswalking solutions.

QUESTIONS AND TOPICS FOR DISCUSSION

1. Why have crosswalks become an increasingly important part of cataloging and metadata work flows in recent years?
2. Crosswalks can map one-to-one, many-to-one, one-to-many, and many-to-many relationships. Come up with concrete scenarios for crosswalks involving

each type of relationship and discuss the potential impacts of implementing these types of crosswalks on metadata quality.

3. Discuss how and why XPath can help facilitate metadata crosswalking. Consider crosswalks involving a many-to-one mapping.

SUGGESTIONS FOR EXERCISES

1. Currently, there are many reliable MARC to Simple or Qualified Dublin Core crosswalks available but few Dublin Core to MARC crosswalks, none of which are completely satisfactory. Think about the reasons why and create a crosswalk from Simple Dublin Core to MARC.
2. Crosswalks from MARC to Simple Dublin Core typically require that the values of some MARC data fields and subfields be manipulated in various ways. Create expressions using XPath string functions to create values suitable for `<dc:date>` from MARC data field 008 and MARC data field 260 subfield c.
3. Elements in Simple and Qualified Dublin Core can be repeated. For example, a Dublin Core record can have more than one `<dc:creator>` element. Assume that a Dublin Core record has three `<dc:creator>` elements. Create expressions using XPath string functions that would allow the first `<dc:creator>` to be mapped to the MARC 100 data field, while the other two creator values could be mapped to the MARC 700 field.

NOTES

1. http://www.w3.org/TR/xpath.
2. http://www.w3.org/TR/xpath20.; work is underway on XPath 3.0, but as of this writing XPath 3.0 is not yet an approved W3C Recommendation.
3. http://www.w3.org/TR/xslt.
4. http://www.w3.org/TR/xslt20. ; work is underway on XSLT 3.0, but as of this writing XSLT 3.0 is not yet an approved W3C Recommendation.
5. http://www.w3.org/Style/XSL.
6. http://www.loc.gov/standards/mods/userguide.
7. http://wiki.dublincore.org/index.php/User_Guide.
8. http://purl.org/dc/terms/Agent.
9. http://www.iso.org/iso/iso_catalogue/catalogue_tc/catalogue_detail.htm?csnumber=35343.
10. http://www.loc.gov/marc/dccross.html.
11. http://www.loc.gov/marc/marc2dc.html.
12. http://www.w3.org/TR/NOTE-datetime.
13. http://www.loc.gov/marc/ndmso.html.
14. http://www.w3.org/TR/xpath-datamodel.
15. http://www.w3.org/TR/2007/REC-xquery-semantics-20070123.
16. http://www.w3.org/TR/xpath-functions.
17. http://www.w3.org/TR/xmlschema-2.

REFERENCES

Coyle, Karen. 2004. "Crosswalking Citation Metadata: The University of California's Experience." In *Metadata in Practice*, ed. Diane I. Hillmann and Elaine L. Westbrooks (Chicago: American Library Association), 89–103.

DCMI Usage Board. 2010. *DCMI Metadata Terms*. Singapore: Dublin Core Metadata Initiative. Available at: http://dublincore.org/documents/2010/10/11/dcmi-terms (latest version: http://dublincore.org/documents/dcmi-terms)

Godby, Carol Jean, Devon Smith, and Eric Childress. 2008. "Encoding Application Profiles in a Computational Model of the Crosswalk." In *Proceedings of International Conference on Dublin Core and Metadata Applications*. Singapore: Dublin Core Metadata Initiative. Available at: http://dcpapers.dublincore.org/ojs/pubs/article/view/914

Lightle, Kimberly S., and Judith S. Ridgway. 2003. "Generation of XML Records across Multiple Metadata Standards." *D-Lib Magazine*. Available at: http://www.dlib.org/dlib/september03/lightle/09lightle.html

Powell, Andy, Mikael Nilsson, Ambjörn Naeve, Pete Johnston, and Thomas Baker. 2007. *DCMI Abstract Model*. Singapore: Dublin Core Metadata Initiative. Available at: http://dublincore.org/documents/2007/06/04/abstract-model

St. Pierre, Margaret, and William P. LaPlant Jr. 1998. *Issues in Crosswalking Metadata Standards: A NISO Whitepaper*. Washington, DC: National Information Standards Organization. Available at: http://www.niso.org/publications/white_papers/crosswalk

Woodley, Mary S. 2008. "Crosswalks, Metadata Harvesting, Federated Searching, Metasearching: Using Metadata to Connect Users and Information." In *Introduction to Metadata*, by Tony Gill, Anne J. Gilliland, Maureen Whalen, and Mary S. Woodley, online ed., ver. 3.0., ed. Murtha Baca (Los Angeles: Getty Publications). Available at: http://www.getty.edu/research/publications/electronic_publications/intrometadata

Yale University. 2008. *Best Practices for Descriptive Metadata May 2008 Version 0.5*. New Haven, CT: Digital Production and Integration Program, Yale University Library. Available at: http://www.library.yale.edu/dpip/bestpractices/BestPracticesForDescriptiveMetadata.doc

Zeng, Marcia Lei, and Jian Qin. 2008. *Metadata*. New York: Neal-Schuman Publishers.

CHAPTER 11

Transforming XML (Part II): Extensible Stylesheet Language for Transformations

Recognition of the need to define a language for transforming, presenting, and interacting with structured information (e.g., XML metadata records) predates the release of XML version 1.0 in 1998. Formal work within the World Wide Web Consortium (W3C) on what became the Extensible Stylesheet Language (XSL) family of W3C Recommendations dates from a technical note titled "A Proposal for XSL," which was submitted to the W3C in August 1997.[1] This technical note proposed that the W3C develop a new style sheet language optimized to work with the then still-under-development XML approach to serialization that went beyond the functionality possible using the Cascading Style Sheet (CSS) language,[2] a preexisting standard maintained by the W3C and still used today for formatting HTML and occasionally XML documents. As an example of the limitations of CSS, the 1997 proposal to the W3C noted a need to reorder elements of a markup language document, a function not supported by CSS. The proposal also recommended that XSL be based largely on the Document Style Semantics and Specification Language (DSSSL),[3] another preexisting style sheet language designed for use with Standard Generalized Markup Language (SGML), a precursor to XML. While more powerful and in many ways well suited to the then nascent versions of what became XML, DSSSL was not well optimized for the Web. The result of the 1997 proposal to the W3C was a rudimentary and, as it turned out, rather incomplete working draft version of XSL.[4]

Interest in XSL for more than just presentation (e.g., for general purpose transformation and for searching XML document instances) quickly expanded the initial scope of the XSL activity. In trying to develop the 1.0 XSL working draft into a full-fledged W3C Recommendation, it quickly became apparent that a single specification document for XSL would not suffice. As mentioned in the previous chapter, the W3C Recommendations defining XPath (version 1.0[5] and version 2.0[6]) and Extensible Stylesheet Language for Transformations (XSLT) (version 1.0[7] and version 2.0[8]) were initially drafted by the W3C XSL Working Group as part of an XSL family of specifications,[9] which also includes an XML vocabulary for specifying formatting object semantics (XSL-FO). Ongoing work on XSL-FO, which can be used, for instance, to convert XML to a PDF document, is now the responsibility of a separate

W3C working group. Ongoing work on XPath has been integrated with work on the XML Query Language (XQuery), which was initially developed by the W3C XQuery Working Group. Other ancillary XML specifications maintained by the W3C that are related to XPath and/or XSLT include the following:

The XML Linking Language (XLink),[10] which allows linking to resources from XML documents

The XML Pointer Language (XPointer)[11] (multiple W3C Recommendations), which supports direct citing of individual components of an XML document

XML Inclusions (XInclude),[12] which provides syntax and a processing model for merging together segments of separate XML documents

It was originally envisioned that style sheets created in accord with XSL specifications would be analogous to style sheets conforming to the CSS standards; that is, they would be used primarily to describe how to display or format XML document instances of a certain class. Style sheets conforming to the CSS specifications are used on many Web sites today to describe how to render static and dynamic HTML pages in Web browser windows and for printing. Although XSL is XML based and in many ways more powerful than CSS, the XSL-to-CSS analogy holds true in large part with regard to XSL-FO. Both XSL-FO and CSS are primarily about formatting.

However, as implemented today, the analogy does not hold up well for XSLT style sheets that do not include XSL-FO semantics. XSLT is currently used in combination with XPath for general purpose XML processing and to transform between classes of XML documents conforming to different XML schemas. While XSLT can be used without XSL-FO to transform XML documents into XHTML, a presentation-oriented XML grammar, it is typical to invoke a CSS-conformant style sheet to handle the final styling of the XHTML created. XSLT is really not about style; rather, XSLT as used today is better thought of as a declarative, functional programming language for manipulating XML. When used in conjunction with XPath and without XSL-FO, XSLT is much better suited for implementing metadata crosswalks than it is for formatting XML metadata records.

This chapter briefly introduces and illustrates the use of the current XSLT W3C Recommendations, building on the discussion of metadata crosswalking and the XPath W3C Recommendations presented in the previous chapter. Many of the illustrations in this chapter draw on the crosswalk specifications and XPath examples described in Chapter 10. This chapter closes with an examination of two case studies, the first describing how XSLT is used to transform MARCXML records into XHTML and the second describing how XSLT is used to generate e-book MARCXML metadata records from existing printed-book records.

INTRODUCTION TO XSLT

In most programming language taxonomies, XSLT is classified as a declarative, functional programming language as opposed to an imperative, procedural programming language. Procedural language code constitutes a written sequence of instructions to a computer defining a procedure to be followed with iterative loops as needed and branches defined at appropriate decision points during the instruction work flow. Functional programming emphasizes rules, pattern-matching, recursion, and, of course, functions. Functional programming is often more concise, but it is also often less intuitive and harder to learn. Some things are harder to do in a procedural language, and some things harder to do in a functional language. In general, XSLT and its functional language approach is well suited as a language for implementing XML metadata record crosswalks and transformations.

An XSLT processor is required to test, debug, and implement XSLT style sheets. (Common usage is that *XML parsers* can read and optionally may be able to validate XML; *XSLT processors* can parse XML but also can process requests to output transformed XML. Terminology is imprecise, however, so readers also may encounter references to XML transforming parsers.) As shown in Table 11.1, there are a number of good stand-alone transforming processors available both commercially and as open source (i.e., for free). All of those listed in Table 11.1 can be used with SyncRO Soft's Oxygen XML Editor, and with the command-line version of Xsltproc which is typically installed as part of the standard Oxygen XML Editor installation. The examples in this chapter were authored and debugged using Oxygen XML Editor and the SAXON XSLT processor, taking advantage of the advanced user interface of Oxygen XML Editor for creating and testing XSLT style sheets.

Most modern XSLT processors include command-line and/or other kinds of application programming interfaces to facilitate integration of the processor into locally created batch processing work flows. Additionally, most current Web browsers support XSLT version 1.0 and have their own embedded XSLT

TABLE 11.1 Ubiquitous XSLT processor software.

XSLT Processor	Description
SAXON	Developed by Michael Kay of Saxonica Limited in the United Kingdom.[13] Available in both an open source basic version (now called Home Edition)[14] and commercial versions.
Apache Xalan	Developed as part of the Apache Software Foundation XML Project,[15] this parser is available open source in both Java[16] and C++[17] programming languages.
Xsltproc	Based on libxml,[18] the C language parser and XML tool kit developed for the open source Gnome project.[19]
MSXML	Developed by Microsoft[20] for use with its Windows operating system.

FIGURE 11.1 Using processing instructions to specify which XSLT style sheet to apply.

```
<?xml-stylesheet type="text/xsl" href="DC2XHTML.xsl"?>

<?xml-stylesheet type="text/xsl" href="/spineToHTML.xsl"?>

<?xml-stylesheet type="text/xsl" href="http://myserver.edu/MODS2DC.xsl"?>
```

processor. This allows implementers to test simple stand-alone XSLT 1.0 style sheets using a Web browser. To do this, a processing instruction must be included in the source XML file telling the Web browser's XSLT processor to retrieve and apply a specific style sheet. Three such processing instructions are illustrated in Figure 11.1. All three processing instructions give the type of style sheet to apply (in this case "`text/xsl`," that is, an XSLT style sheet) and the location of the style sheet. The first illustration specifies XSLT style sheet location relative to the location of the XML file being transformed. The second specifies style sheet location relative to the the Web server's root folder. The third gives an absolute URL for the location of the style sheet. The style sheet type value "`text/xsl`" was never registered as an official Multipurpose Internet Mail Extensions media type; instead, the W3C registered the value `application/xslt+xml` as the official media type for XSLT style sheets. However, by that time, "`text/xsl`" was well established and widely supported. In practice, it remains the de facto standard media type for XSLT style sheets.

The second processing instruction shown in Figure 11.1, specifying XSLT style sheet location relative to the Web server's root folder, can give implementers added flexibility. Reverse proxy Web servers are used in some environments to better manage and control access to content served to the general public. For instance, library staff may retrieve and edit XML files using a Web server that allows read-write access to staff working on the library's internal network. External users are given read-only access to these files via a reverse proxy server. Behind the scenes (but unbeknownst to the external users), the proxy server fetches the requested XML files from the original Web server via the library's internal network. By providing a value for the style sheet's `href` attribute that is relative to the server's root directory, XML files can be transformed by one style sheet when retrieved by staff Web browsers connecting via the library's internal network and by a different style sheet (i.e., one residing on the proxy server) when retrieved by the general public over the Internet. Both style sheets have the same file name, but one resides on the library's inward-facing, staff Web server, while the other style sheet resides on the library's public-facing proxy Web server. This *conditional transformation by proxy* allows implementers to vary the transformation applied based on whether a user is retrieving content directly from the host Web server or via proxy. As discussed in Case Study 13.1, this approach is used by the University of Illinois Library in its *Emblematica Online* Project, which provides enhanced access to digitized emblem book content.

THE STRUCTURE OF AN XSLT STYLE SHEET

An XSLT style sheet is a valid XML document conforming to an XML Schema Definition document.[21] The root element of an XSLT style sheet is `<stylesheet>` in the XSL Transform namespace (as illustrated in Figures 11.2 and 11.3). Notice that attributes are provided on the root element to express the version of XSLT (and implicitly XPath) implemented by the style sheet as well as to exclude namespace prefix bindings that are referenced in the style sheet but not needed in the output (transformed) XML.

An XSLT style sheet consists of one or more rule sets for transformation that are called *templates*. Each template tells the XSLT processor how to handle specific elements and attributes in the XML document being transformed. Templates may be invoked by name from within other templates or may be used to process specific fragments of an XML metadata record based on matching a pattern, such as, an XPath path expression, that is the value of the template's *match* attribute. Typically, the top-level template of a stand-alone XSLT style sheet will match on the XML document root, that is, will have a `match="/"` attribute. The output of a complete transform is a *result-tree*, which is then serialized in accord with the attributes of the style sheet's `<output>` element. XSLT is a host language for XPath and depends on XPath for much of its processing power, as illustrated in the sample XSLT style sheets shown in Figures 11.2 and 11.3. Figure 11.2 transforms MARCXML into Simple Dublin Core. This style sheet implements the crosswalk outlined in Table 10.1 and is based on the MARCXML to RDF-Simple Dublin Core XML crosswalk maintained by the Library of Congress,[22] which is used in Case Study 11.1. The style sheet shown in Figure 11.3 transforms Simple Dublin Core to XHTML. These examples illustrate many XSLT basics as described below.

The Elements of XSLT

The starting point for most XSLT style sheets is a *source-tree* representation of an XML document. (XSLT style sheets can be defined that have no input, only output, but this is a rare use case ignored for purposes of this discussion.) An XSLT style sheet contains the rules used to go from a source-tree (or source-trees if multiple XML input files are required for the transform; see Case Study 13.1) to a final result-tree, which is then serialized for use, typically as another XML document. A style sheet may generate intermediate result-tree fragments for use along the way. Elements in the XSL Transform namespace are categorized as either *instruction* elements or *declaration* elements. Elements from other namespaces included in an XSLT style sheet are incorporated directly into result-trees. XSLT declaration elements set the properties of the final result-tree

FIGURE 11.2 A portion of an XSLT style sheet that transforms MARCXML to Simple Dublin Core.

```
<?xml version="1.0" encoding="UTF-8"?>
<xsl:stylesheet version="1.0" exclude-result-prefixes="marc"
  xmlns:xsl="http://www.w3.org/1999/XSL/Transform" xmlns:xsi="http://www.w3.org/2001/XMLSchema-instance"
  xmlns:oai_dc="http://www.openarchives.org/OAI/2.0/oai_dc/" xmlns:marc="http://www.loc.gov/MARC21/slim"
  xmlns:dc="http://purl.org/dc/elements/1.1/" xmlns="http://purl.org/dc/elements/1.1/">
<xsl:output method="xml" indent="yes" encoding="UTF-8"/>
<xsl:template match="/">
   <oai_dc:dc xmlns:oai_dc="http://www.openarchives.org/OAI/2.0/oai_dc/" xmlns="http://purl.org/dc/elements/1.1/">
    <xsl:attribute name="schemaLocation" namespace="http://www.w3.org/2001/XMLSchema-instance"
      >http://www.openarchives.org/OAI/2.0/oai_dc/ http://www.openarchives.org/OAI/2.0/oai_dc.xsd</xsl:attribute>
    <xsl:if test="/marc:record/marc:datafield[@tag=245]">
      <xsl:element name="title" namespace="http://purl.org/dc/elements/1.1/">
        <xsl:value-of select="/marc:record/marc:datafield[@tag=245][1]/marc:subfield[@code='a']"/>
      </xsl:element>
    </xsl:if>
    <xsl:for-each select="//marc:datafield[@tag=100] | //marc:datafield[@tag=110] | //marc:datafield[@tag=111] |
    //marc:datafield[@tag=700] | //marc:datafield[@tag=710] | //marc:datafield[@tag=711] | //marc:datafield[@tag=720]">
      <xsl:element name="creator" namespace="http://purl.org/dc/elements/1.1/">
        <xsl:value-of select="marc:subfield[@code='a']"/></xsl:element>
    </xsl:for-each>
    <xsl:for-each select="marc:record/marc:datafield[500 &lt;= @tag and @tag &lt;= 599][not(@tag=506
    or @tag=530 or @tag=540 or @tag=546)]">
      <xsl:element name="description" namespace="http://purl.org/dc/elements/1.1/">
        <xsl:value-of select="marc:subfield[@code='a']"/></xsl:element>
    </xsl:for-each>
    <xsl:for-each select="//marc:datafield[@tag=600] | //marc:datafield[@tag=610] | //marc:datafield[@tag=611] |
    //marc:datafield[@tag=630] | //marc:datafield[@tag=650] | //marc:datafield[@tag=653] ">
      <xsl:element name="subject" namespace="http://purl.org/dc/elements/1.1/">
```

```
    <xsl:value-of select="marc:subfield[@code='a']"/></xsl:element>
</xsl:for-each>
<xsl:for-each select="//marc:datafield[@tag=020] | //marc:datafield[@tag=022] | //marc:datafield[@tag=024]">
  <xsl:element name="identifier" namespace="http://purl.org/dc/elements/1.1/">
    <xsl:value-of select="marc:subfield[@code='a']"/></xsl:element>
</xsl:for-each>
<xsl:for-each select="marc:record/marc:datafield[@tag=856]/marc:subfield[@code='u']">
  <xsl:element name="identifier" namespace="http://purl.org/dc/elements/1.1/">
    <xsl:value-of select="."/></xsl:element>
</xsl:for-each>
<xsl:for-each select="marc:record/marc:datafield[@tag=260]">
  <xsl:element name="publisher" namespace="http://purl.org/dc/elements/1.1/">
    <xsl:value-of select="concat(marc:subfield[@code='a'], ' ', marc:subfield[@code='b'])"/>
  </xsl:element>
</xsl:for-each>
<xsl:if test="string-length(marc:record/marc:controlfield[@tag=008]/text()) &gt; 37">
  <xsl:element name="language" namespace="http://purl.org/dc/elements/1.1/">
    <xsl:value-of select="substring(marc:record/marc:controlfield[@tag=008],36,3)"/>
  </xsl:element>
</xsl:if>
<xsl:element name="date" namespace="http://purl.org/dc/elements/1.1/">
  <xsl:choose>
    <xsl:when test="marc:record/marc:datafield[@tag='260']/marc:subfield[@code='c']">
      <xsl:value-of select="marc:record/marc:datafield[@tag='260']/marc:subfield[@code='c']"/>
    </xsl:when>
    <xsl:otherwise>
      <xsl:value-of select="substring(marc:record/marc:controlfield[@tag=008],8,4)"/>
    </xsl:otherwise>
  </xsl:choose>
```

(continued)

FIGURE 11.2 (Continued)

```
    </xsl:element>
    <xsl:apply-templates select="/marc:record/marc:leader"/>
  </oai_dc:dc>
</xsl:template>
<xsl:template match="/marc:record/marc:leader">
  <xsl:element name="type" namespace="http://purl.org/dc/elements/1.1/">
    <xsl:choose>
      <xsl:when test="substring(.,7,1)='a' or substring(.,7,1)='t'">text</xsl:when>
      <xsl:when test="substring(.,7,1)='e' or substring(.,7,1)='f'">cartographic</xsl:when>
      <xsl:when test="substring(.,7,1)='c' or substring(.,7,1)='d'">notated music</xsl:when>
      <xsl:when test="substring(.,7,1)='i' or substring(.,7,1)='j'">sound recording</xsl:when>
      <xsl:when test="substring(.,7,1)='k'">still image</xsl:when>
      <xsl:when test="substring(.,7,1)='g'">moving image</xsl:when>
      <xsl:when test="substring(.,7,1)='r'">three dimensional object</xsl:when>
      <xsl:when test="substring(.,7,1)='m'">software, multimedia</xsl:when>
      <xsl:when test="substring(.,7,1)='p'">mixed material</xsl:when>
    </xsl:choose>
  </xsl:element>
</xsl:template>
</xsl:stylesheet>
```

FIGURE 11.3 XSLT style sheet that transforms Simple Dublin Core to XHTML.

```
<?xml version="1.0" encoding="UTF-8"?>
<xsl:stylesheet version="1.0" exclude-result-prefixes="oai_dc dc"
  xmlns:xsl="http://www.w3.org/1999/XSL/Transform"
  xmlns:oai_dc="http://www.openarchives.org/OAI/2.0/oai_dc/"
  xmlns:dc="http://purl.org/dc/elements/1.1/"
  xmlns="http://www.w3.org/1999/xhtml">
  <xsl:output indent="yes" method="xml" encoding="UTF-8"/>
  <xsl:template match="/">
    <xsl:element name="html" namespace="http://www.w3.org/1999/xhtml">
      <xsl:element name="head" namespace="http://www.w3.org/1999/xhtml">
        <xsl:element name="title" namespace="http://www.w3.org/1999/xhtml">
          XHTML version of Simple Dublin Core Record</xsl:element>
      </xsl:element>
      <xsl:element name="body" namespace="http://www.w3.org/1999/xhtml">
        <xsl:for-each select="oai_dc:dc/*">
          <xsl:element name="p" namespace="http://www.w3.org/1999/xhtml">
            <xsl:attribute name="class">
              <xsl:value-of select="local-name(.)"/></xsl:attribute>
            <i><xsl:value-of select="local-name(.)"/></i>: <b><xsl:value-of
select="."/></b>
          </xsl:element>
        </xsl:for-each>
      </xsl:element>
    </xsl:element>
  </xsl:template>
</xsl:stylesheet>
```

(`<xsl:output>`), declare and define the rules of the transform (`<xsl:template>`), define variables and parameters used in the style sheet (`<xsl:variable>`, `<xsl:param>`), and so on. Instruction elements make up the sequence constructors of the transform. Sequence constructors are used to construct fragments of intermediate or final result-trees. The `<xsl:value-of>` element is an example of an instruction element used in sequence constructors. This element retrieves from the source-tree the value of the node identified by the XPath expression given in the `select` attribute of the `<xsl:value-of>` element.

Table 11.2 lists some of the XSLT elements used frequently in XML metadata record crosswalking applications. The use of these elements is illustrated below and in Cases Studies 11.1 and 11.2.

Navigating a Metadata Record Source-Tree

In the context of metadata crosswalking, XSLT style sheets are most often used to take fragments of the input source-tree (i.e., XML from the source metadata record being crosswalked) and use these fragments as the basis for constructing corresponding fragments in the result-tree (i.e., the destination XML metadata record that is the result of the crosswalk). The elements

TABLE 11.2 Frequently used XSLT elements.

Element	Use
<xsl:output>	Immediate child of <xsl:stylesheet>; sets attributes for result-tree serialization, such as encoding, whether to include XML declaration in final result serialization, and so on.
<xsl:template>	Declares rule(s), that is, sequence constructor(s), for creating result-tree nodes and/or atomic values.
<xsl:variable> <xsl:param>	Declares a variable (binding between name and a value) that can be referenced during a subsequent step of the transform. Parameter values are set when style sheet or template is invoked.
<xsl:apply-templates>	An instruction that allows the invocation of templates matching context node or node pattern specified by `select` attribute.
<xsl:call-template> <xsl:with-param>	Used to invoke templates by name rather than by match. The <xsl:with-param> is optional child of <xsl:call-template>, used to set value of parameter in called template.
<xsl:element> <xsl:attribute>	Instructions used to add a new node or attribute to the result-tree.
<xsl:text>	An instruction used to add atomic string values to result-tree.
<xsl:value-of>	Used to construct a new text node in the result tree. Value is value of node specified in `select` attribute or result of evaluating contained sequence constructor.
<xsl:for-each>	Used to transform a sequence node by node by evaluating the contained sequence constructor for each node.
<xsl:if>	Contained sequence constructor is evaluated if value of `test` attribute is True; otherwise skipped.
<xsl:choose> <xsl:when> <xsl:otherwise>	<xsl:choose> is used to express an ordered series of conditional tests. <xsl:when> and <xsl:otherwise> are children of <xsl:choose> that each contain a sequence constructor. The sequence constructor of the first <xsl:when> Which evaluates True is implemented. If no <xsl:when> conditional evaluates True and an <xsl:otherwise> is present, then the sequence constructor of the <xsl:otherwise> is implemented. Each <xsl:choose> must contain at least one <xsl:when> and no more than one <xsl:otherwise>.
<xsl:document>	Used as root of an XML source-tree referenced by the transform (i.e., in addition to the primary source-tree being transformed).

<xsl:apply-templates> and <xsl:for-each> are commonly used to navigate the source-tree in order to select fragments to transform one by one. Both elements have an attribute named select. The values of these attributes are sequences (node-lists) that specify the fragments in the source-tree that are to be transformed. The actual sequence constructors that generate the result-tree fragments from corresponding source-tree fragments are contained within the <xsl:for-each> element or within the <xsl:template> element having a match attribute with a value that corresponds to the value of the <xsl:apply-templates> select attribute.

If the value of the select attribute of a <xsl:for-each> evaluates to an empty sequence, the sequence constructor contained in the <xsl:for-each> (i.e., the instruction elements that are children of the <xsl:for-each>) are skipped. If the attribute value evaluates to a sequence of one item, the contained sequence constructor is processed once to transform that single item. If the attribute evaluates to a multi-item sequence, the sequence constructor is processed multiple times, once for each item in the sequence.

Similarly the value of the select attribute of a <xsl:apply-templates> is evaluated, and each node in the resulting sequence is compared to the patterns of the match attributes for each <xsl:template> element in the style sheet. Matching nodes are then transformed in accordance with the rules contained in the matching <xsl:template> element in document order (unless an alternate sort order is specified). Dissimilarly from how <xsl:for-each> is handled, however, if no matching template is found for a node included in the select sequence of a <xsl:apply-templates> element, the node is processed against the appropriate built-in template rule. For example, the built-in or default template rule for text and attribute nodes is to return a text node with the string value of the original. Figures 11.4 and 11.5 illustrate examples of <xsl:for-each> and <xsl:apply-templates> as used in the style sheets shown in Figures 11.2 and 11.3.

FIGURE 11.4 Illustrations of <xsl:for-each> from Figures 11.2 and 11.3.

```
<xsl:for-each select="oai_dc:dc/*">

<xsl:for-each select="marc:record/marc:datafield[@tag=260]">

<xsl:for-each select="marc:record/marc:datafield[@tag=856]/marc:subfield
[@code='u']">

<xsl:for-each select="marc:record/marc:datafield[500 &lt;= @tag and @tag &lt;= 599]
[not(@tag=506 or @tag=530 or @tag=540 or @tag=546)]">

<xsl:for-each select="//marc:datafield[@tag=600] | //marc:datafield[@tag=610] | //
marc:datafield[@tag=611] | //marc:datafield[@tag=630] | //marc:datafield[@tag=650] |
//marc:datafield[@tag=653]">
```

FIGURE 11.5 Illustration of <xsl:apply-templates> from Figure 11.2.

```
<xsl:template match="/">
      ...
      <xsl:apply-templates select="/marc:record/marc:leader"/>
      ...
</xsl:template>
...
<xsl:template match="/marc:record/marc:leader">
      ...
</xsl:template>
```

Building Result-Trees

There are two common ways to insert nodes into a result-tree created by an XSLT style sheet. These are illustrated in Figures 11.6 and 11.7. The first option is to include <xsl:element>, <xsl:attribute>, or <xsl:text> at the appropriate point in the sequence constructor. These are used to construct element, attribute, and text nodes in the result-tree. The attribute values present on each element determine properties of the nodes constructed, such as the name and namespace of an inserted element node. Sometimes an easier way is to simply include the node directly in the sequence constructor. Figure 11.6 shows both ways of inserting nodes into the result-tree. The XHTML <p> element and its class attribute are constructed using <xsl:element> and <xsl:attribute>. The XHTML <b> and <i> elements

FIGURE 11.6 Transforming Simple Dublin Core to XHTML.

```
Source-tree snippet:
    <creator>Cole, Timothy W</creator>
    <creator>Foulonneau, Muriel</creator>
     ...
    <subject>Open Archives Initiative</subject>
    <subject>Metadata harvesting</subject>

XSLT snippet:
    <xsl:for-each select="oai_dc:dc/*">
      <xsl:element name="p" namespace="http://www.w3.org/1999/xhtml">
         <xsl:attribute name="class">
           <xsl:value-of select="local-name(.)"/>
         </xsl:attribute>
         <i><xsl:value-of select="local-name(.)"/></i>:
         <b><xsl:value-of select="."/></b>
      </xsl:element>
    </xsl:for-each>

Result-tree (XHTML) snippet:
    <p class="creator"><i>creator</i>: <b>Cole, Timothy W.</b></p>
    <p class="creator"><i>creator</i>: <b>Foulonneau, Muriel</b></p>
    ...
    <p class="subject"><i>subject</i>: <b>Open Archives Initiative</b></p>
    <p class="subject"><i>subject</i>: <b>Metadata Harvesting</b></p>
```

FIGURE 11.7 Transforming MARCXML to Simple Dublin Core XML.

```
Source-tree snippet:
    <datafield tag="260" ind1=" " ind2=" ">
        <subfield code="a">Westport, Conn. :</subfield>
        <subfield code="b">Libraries Unlimited,</subfield>
        <subfield code="c">c2007.</subfield>
    </datafield>

XSLT stylesheet snippet:
  <xsl:for-each select="marc:record/marc:datafield[@tag=260]">
    <xsl:element name="publisher" namespace="http://purl.org/dc/elements/1.1/">
<xsl:value-of select="concat(marc:subfield[@code='a'],' ',marc:subfield[@code='b'])"/>
    </xsl:element>
  </xsl:for-each>

Result-tree (Dublin Core XML) snippet:
      <publisher>Westport, Conn. : Libraries Unlimited,</publisher>
```

are simply embedded in the sequence constructor contained in the `<xsl:for-each>`.

In general, use of `<xsl:element>`, `<xsl:attribute>`, or `<xsl:text>` is to be preferred if attributes are involved or if properties (e.g., node name) or values of the nodes being constructed depend on the source-tree. Direct embedding of non-XSL Transform namespace elements in sequence constructors may be appropriate when these conditions do not apply. Two other XSLT elements (not illustrated), `<xsl:copy>` and `<xsl:copy-of>`, are frequently used to insert nodes into the result-tree. The former element copies the context item only (no attributes, no children) from the source-tree directly to the result-tree (*shallow copy*). The latter element, which has a required `select` attribute, copies complete sequences, including attributes and descendant when applicable, from the source-tree to the result-tree (*deep copy*).

Context and Conditional Expressions in XSLT

As with XPath, context is important in XSLT. Many implementers initially find the rules of context in XSLT to be nonintuitive. For example, the XSLT style sheet shown in Figure 11.2 uses both `<xsl:if>` and `<xsl:for-each>`. When the source-tree can contain at most one instance of an element to be transformed, `<xsl:if>` can be used in lieu of `<xsl:for-each>`. If the element is present, it is transformed. If not, the sequence constructor contained in the `<xsl:if>` element is ignored. However, when using `<xsl:for-each>` for the same purpose, the context within the scope of the `<xsl:for-each>` becomes the source-tree node being processed. This is not the case within the `<xsl:if>`, which has no `select` attribute. Figure 11.8, two snippets drawn from Figure 11.2, illustrates this distinction. Within the scope of the `<xsl:for-each>` shown in Figure 11.8, the context

FIGURE 11.8 Illustrations of <xsl:if> and <xsl:for-each> from Figure 11.2.

```
<xsl:if test="marc:record/marc:datafield[@tag=245]">
   <xsl:element name="title" namespace="http://purl.org/dc/elements/1.1/">
      <xsl:value-of
select="marc:record/marc:datafield[@tag=245][1]/marc:subfield[@code='a']"/>
   </xsl:element>
</xsl:if>

<xsl:for-each select="marc:record/marc:datafield[@tag=856]/marc:subfield[@code='u']">
   <xsl:element name="identifier" namespace="http://purl.org/dc/elements/1.1/">
      <xsl:value-of select="."/>
   </xsl:element>
</xsl:for-each>
```

is subfield $u of MARC data field 856. Within <xsl:if>, the context remains "/," as can be seen from the <xsl:value-of>. Figure 11.9 illustrates how context is affected within <xsl:template> (analogous to <xsl:for-each>) and within <xsl:when> (analogous to <xsl:if>).

The predicate of the <xsl:if> element, the value of the test attribute, can be used to test for conditions beyond the presence or absence of a particular element in the source-tree. For example, <xsl:if> can be used to apply a conditional transformation segment based on the value of a particular element in a source-tree or based on a comparison of multiple values found in a source-tree. (This is not something that is easily done using the <xsl:for-each> element.) While the <xsl:if> element in XSLT supports simple *if-then* conditionality, there is no <xsl:else> element in XSLT. In order to support conditional processing when there is more than one possibility to be considered, XSLT provides the <xsl:choose> element. Figure 11.9 illustrates <xsl:choose> as used in the style sheet shown in Figure 11.2.

FIGURE 11.9 Illustration of <xsl:choose> from Figure 11.2.

```
Source item XML snippet:
      <leader>01698cam 22003614a 4500</leader>

XSLT stylesheet snippet:
  <xsl:template match="/marc:record/marc:leader">
    <xsl:element name="type" namespace="http://purl.org/dc/elements/1.1/">
      <xsl:choose>
        <xsl:when test="substring(.,7,1)='a' or substring(.,7,1)='t'">text</xsl:when>
              ....
        <xsl:when test="substring(.,7,1)='m'">software, multimedia</xsl:when>
        <xsl:when test="substring(.,7,1)='p'">mixed material</xsl:when>
      </xsl:choose>
    </xsl:element>
  </xsl:template>

Snippet from transformed record:
      <type>text</type>
```

The allowed children of `<xsl:choose>` are `<xsl:when>` (mandatory, repeatable) and `<xsl:otherwise>` (optional, not repeatable). These elements contain sequence constructors, that is, rule sets for adding nodes to the result-tree. Each `<xsl:when>` has a test attribute. The value of the test attribute for each `<xsl:when>` element is evaluated in order until a Boolean True result is encountered. When this happens, the result of the sequence constructor of the associated `<xsl:when>` is returned as the result of the `<xsl:choose>` instruction. All other sequence constructors within the `<xsl:choose>` are ignored. If none of the `<xsl:when>` elements have a test attribute value evaluating to True, then the sequence constructor of the `<xsl:otherwise>`, if present, is evaluated and returned as the result of the `<xsl:choose>` instruction. If no `<xsl:otherwise>` is present and none of the `<xsl:when>` test attributes evaluate to True, nothing is returned by the `<xsl:choose>` instruction. As illustrated in Figure 11.9, `<xsl:choose>` is a good way to extract and transform a granular property, in this case the type of record, embedded within a less granular value, the MARC leader.

Transform Results

Figures 11.10 and 11.11 show the end result of applying the XSLT transforms shown in Figures 11.3 and 11.2 to the XML metadata records shown in Figures 10.4 and 10.5. XSLT can also be used to transform XML metadata records into XHTML or plain text. Examples introduced above illustrate how XSLT can be used to transform a source-tree into a new result-tree

FIGURE 11.10 Complete result of transforming Simple Dublin Core from Figure 10.4 to XHTML using the XSLT style sheet shown in Figure 11.3.

```
<?xml version="1.0" encoding="UTF-8"?>
<html xmlns="http://www.w3.org/1999/xhtml">
  <head><title>XHTML version of Simple Dublin Core Record</title></head>
  <body>
    <p class="creator"><i>creator</i>: <b> Cole, Timothy W</b></p>
    <p class="creator"><i>creator</i>: <b>Foulonneau, Muriel</b></p>
    <p class="title"><i>title</i>: <b>Using the Open Archives Initiative ...</b></p>
    <p class="publisher">
      <i>publisher</i>: <b>Westport, Conn. : Libraries Unlimited</b></p>
    <p class="date"><i>date</i>: <b>2007</b></p>
    <p class="format"><i>format</i>: <b>xv, 208 p. : ill. ; 26 cm. </b></p>
    <p class="language"><i>language</i>: <b>eng</b></p>
    <p class="description">
      <i>description</i>: <b>Includes bibliographical ....</b></p>
    <p class="description"><i>description</i>: <b>Definition and origins ....</b></p>
    <p class="subject"><i>subject</i>: <b>Open Archives Initiative</b></p>
    <p class="subject"><i>subject</i>: <b>Metadata harvesting</b></p>
    <p class="identifier"><i>identifier</i>:
      <b>http://www.loc.gov/catdir/toc/...html</b></p>
  </body>
</html>
```

FIGURE 11.11 Complete result of transforming MARCXML from Figure 10.5 to Simple Dublin Core using the XSLT style sheet shown in Figure 11.2.

```
<?xml version="1.0" encoding="UTF-8"?>
<oai_dc:dc
    xmlns:oai_dc="http://www.openarchives.org/OAI/2.0/oai_dc/"
    xmlns="http://purl.org/dc/elements/1.1/"
    xmlns:xsi="http://www.w3.org/2001/XMLSchema-instance"
    xsi:schemaLocation="http://www.openarchives.org/OAI/2.0/oai_dc/
    http://www.openarchives.org/OAI/2.0/oai_dc.xsd">
    <title>Using the Open Archives Initiative... /</title>
    <creator>Cole, Timothy W.</creator>
    <creator>Foulonneau, Muriel.</creator>
    <description>Includes bibliographical ....</description>
    <description>Definition and origins of OAI...</description>
    <subject>Metadata harvesting.</subject>
    <subject>Open Archives Initiative.</subject>
    <identifier>9781591582809 (alk. paper)</identifier>
    <identifier>1591582806 (alk. paper)</identifier>
    <identifier>http://www.loc.gov/catdir/toc...</identifier>
    <publisher>Westport, Conn. : Libraries Unlimited,</publisher>
    <language>eng</language>
    <date>c2007.</date>
    <type>text</type>
</oai_dc:dc>
```

conforming to a different XML metadata grammar or application profile. However, not all results of XSLT need to be XML result-trees. One project at the University of Illinois uses XSLT to transform metadata records into plain-text relational database insert statements (i.e., for ingesting XML metadata records into a database application). This use case is described in Case Study 13.1 in Chapter 13. The next two sections describe some advanced features of XSLT that can be useful for transforming XML metadata records.

VARIABLES AND PARAMETERS IN XSLT

XSLT variables allow style sheet authors to set a value in one location in the style sheet and then reference it subsequently in the style sheet or a sequence constructor. The `<xsl:variable>` element is used to bind such a value to a name or identifier (given by the mandatory name attribute of `<xsl:variable>` element). The value of an XSLT variable is set either by the sequence constructor contained in the `<xsl:variable>` node or by evaluating the node's optional `select` attribute (which is an XPath expression). XSLT parameters are created in a similar way using the `<xsl:param>` element, except that the value of a parameter can be set by the agent invoking the style sheet or template in which they are used (i.e., rather than the value being set within the style sheet or template as is the case with variables). XSLT variables are a convenience for style sheet authors, allowing them to avoid reentering complicated XPath expressions every time used or providing a way

FIGURE 11.12 Using <xsl:call-template> and <xsl:with-param>.

```
<xsl:for-each select="marc:datafield[@tag=260]">
   <dc:publisher>
      <xsl:call-template name="subfieldSelect">
         <xsl:with-param name="codes">ab</xsl:with-param>
      </xsl:call-template>
   </dc:publisher>
</xsl:for-each>

<xsl:template name="subfieldSelect">
    <xsl:param name="codes">abcdefghijklmnopqrstuvwxyz</xsl:param>
    <xsl:for-each select="marc:subfield">
       <xsl:if test="contains($codes, @code)">
            <xsl:value-of select="text()"/><xsl:text> </xsl:text>
       </xsl:if>
    </xsl:for-each>
</xsl:template>
```

to globally change a value used throughout the style sheet in one place. Parameters can be essential when invoking general purpose style sheets, templates, or functions, especially when using recursion.

The use of XSLT parameters is illustrated in Figure 11.12, taken from the Library of Congress MARCXML to RDF-Dublin Core XSLT style sheet. In this illustration, a general purpose template (named subfieldSelect) has been created to return, for a given MARC data field, the text values of all the subfields with code attributes having values mentioned in the parameter. In this instance, the template is being invoked to return concatenation of subfields $a and $b from the MARC date field 260 (imprint). The use of XSLT variables is illustrated in Case Study 11.1 and in Figure 11.14. Notice in Figure 11.12 that the default value of the parameter, "abcdefghijklmnopqrstuvwxyz," is overridden when the template is called by the value of the <xsl:with-param> element.

To programmers used to imperative, procedural programming languages, XSLT variables and parameters will seem a lot like scoped constants rather than variables as used in procedural programming languages. The <xsl:variable> and <xsl:param> elements bind a name to a value globally for a style sheet or over the scope of particular sequence constructor (depending on where in the hierarchy of the style sheet these elements are placed). Once this binding happens, there is no statement in XSLT for altering the value of a variable or parameter; there is no assignment operator as is common in many programming languages. If the element declaring the variable or parameter is an immediate child of <xsl:stylesheet>, then the variable or parameter is said to have global scope. Globally scoped variables and parameters can be referenced from anywhere in a style sheet. The value of a globally declared variable or parameter is determined at the start of a transform (or for a parameter, set when the style sheet is invoked) before template processing and cannot be changed once determined. If the element declaring the variable or parameter is embedded within a sequence constructor or template, the variable or parameter has local scope. The variable or parameter can be referenced only within that sequence constructor or template. The value is set each time the template or sequence constructor is invoked.

RECURSION AND ADVANCED USES OF AXES IN XSLT

Recursion is a feature of XSLT that can be quite useful for metadata processing. Figure 11.13 illustrates a simple use of recursion. This illustration assumes that multiple subject headings have been concatenated together and included in the `<dc:subject>` element of the metadata record to be crosswalked (presumably because the application profile used to create this record did not allow repeated `<dc:subject>` nodes). The destination application profile has a `<subject>` element that is repeatable. Assuming that a semicolon character (";") was used as a delineator between the concatenated subject headings, the template `separateHeadings` as shown in Figure 11.13 will separate the subject headings as serialized in the original record, returning a result-tree

FIGURE 11.13 Using recursion in XSLT style sheet to separate subject heading values.

Snippet of Simple Dublin Core XML metadata record:

```
<subject>Open Archives Initiative; Metadata harvesting; Metadata crosswalks</subject>
```

Snippet of XSLT stylesheet:

```
  <xsl:call-template name="separateHeadings">
    <xsl:with-param name="hdgString" select="//dc:subject"/>
  </xsl:call-template>
...
<xsl:template name="separateHeadings">
  <xsl:param name="hdgString"/>
  <xsl:choose>
    <xsl:when test="contains($hdgString, '; ')">
      <subject><xsl:value-of select="substring-before($hdgString, '; ')"/></subject>
      <xsl:call-template name="separateHeadings">
        <xsl:with-param name="hdgString" select="substring-after($hdgString, '; ')"/>
      </xsl:call-template>
    </xsl:when>
    <xsl:otherwise>
      <subject><xsl:value-of select="$hdgString"/></subject>
    </xsl:otherwise>
  </xsl:choose>
</xsl:template>
```

Result:

```
        <subject>Open Archives Initiative</subject>
        <subject>Metadata harvesting</subject>
        <subject>Metadata crosswalks</subject>
```

FIGURE 11.14 Grouping Simple Dublin Core properties together in XHTML table rows.

```
Snippet of Simple Dublin Core XML metadata record:
    <creator>Cole, Timothy W</creator>
    <title>Using the Open Archives Initiative protocol ...</title>
    <subject>Open Archives Initiative</subject>
    <creator>Foulonneau, Muriel</creator>
    <subject>Metadata harvesting</subject>

Snippet of a version 2.0 XSLT stylesheet:
<xsl:for-each select="oai_dc:dc/*">
  <xsl:variable name="currentLocalName" select="local-name(.)"/>
  <xsl:if test="not(preceding-sibling::*/local-name()[contains(.,$currentLocalName)])">
  <tr><td><i><xsl:value-of select="$currentLocalName"/></i>:</td>
    <td><b>
      <xsl:for-each select="self::* | following-sibling::*">
        <xsl:if test="local-name(.)=$currentLocalName">
          <xsl:value-of select="."/>
          <br/>
        </xsl:if>
      </xsl:for-each>
    </b></td>
  </tr>
</xsl:if>
</xsl:for-each>

Result in XHTML table rows:
  <tr><td><i>creator</i>:</td>
      <td><b>Cole, Timothy W<br/>
              Foulonneau, Muriel<br/></b></td>
  </tr>
   <tr><td><i>title</i>:</td>
       <td><b>Using the Open Archives Initiative protocol ...<br/></b></td>
   </tr>
   <tr><td><i>subject</i>: </td>
       <td><b>Open Archives Initiative<br/>
               Metadata harvesting<br/></b></td>
  </tr>
```

fragment with each heading in its own `<subject>` element. The first time invoked, the template is passed the complete value from the original record containing three subject headings concatenated. The XPath `substring-before` function is used to extract the first subject heading and add it to the result-tree in its own `<subject>` element. The template then invokes itself (i.e., recursively), passing the remainder of the original, concatenated subject heading (i.e., without the first subject heading, which has already been processed). The sequence constructor of the template is repeated for the second subject heading, and the template invokes itself again, passing this time the third and final subject heading. Because there are no more semicolon characters in the parameter value, recursive calls end. The concatenated subject heading has been parsed and added to the result-tree as three separate `<subject>` elements.

Figure 11.14 suggests an alternative version of the full Simple Dublin Core to XHTML XSLT transform shown in Figure 11.3. The key difference is that the sequence constructor shown in the `<xsl:for-each>` in Figure 11.14 will group all values for a particular Dublin Core metadata property together in a single row rather than having multiple paragraphs for repeated subject and creator metadata properties as in the XHTML shown in Figure 11.10 (the final result-tree of the XSLT style sheet shown in Figure 11.3 applied to the Simple Dublin Core XML metadata record shown in Figure 10.4). This is accomplished by making use of the `self`, `preceding-sibling`, and `following-sibling` XPath axes. For each node in the Simple Dublin Core XML metadata record, a test is performed to see if the element has occurred earlier in the record (`preceding-sibling` axis). If yes, the element is ignored (because it has already been transformed). If no, then a new table row is created and labeled with the local-name of the Simple Dublin Core element. The value of the current node (`self` axis) and all subsequent nodes (`following-sibling` axis) in the Simple Dublin Core XML metadata record that match on local-name are added to the table row in the result-tree, each value separated with an XHTML `<br/>` element.

As libraries collect more and more resources in digital format and develop digital collections to provide their users a better access service, catalogers and metadata librarians need to create, transform, and manage cataloging records for an increasing number of resources. In order to work with resources in bulk and in a timely manner, cataloging and metadata librarians must develop sustainable and scalable work flows. XSLT is a powerful tool that can be implemented in cataloging and metadata work flows to make editing, reusing, and sharing of XML metadata easier and quicker. Although learning XPath and XSLT requires an investment of time, the efficiencies possible with these technologies make it well worth it in the long run.

CASE STUDY 11.1
Generating XHTML Splash Page from MARCXML

***Synopsis*:** After the University of Illinois Library started its retrospective mass book digitization project, the library decided to create an Extensible HyperText Markup Language (XHTML) [23] splash page for each digitized book. These splash pages serve as a landing point on the Web from which users interested in a digitized book can link to different online views of it and see bibliographic metadata about the book. Available views vary according to digitization and postprocessing, but typical derivatives offered in addition to page images are PDF, DjVu, Flip Book (the Internet Archive's page-turner tool), and plain-text transcripts generated from optical character recognition (OCR) processing. As part of the digitization process, the Library's MARC catalog record for the print resource being digitized is converted to MARCXML and updated to include links to digital derivatives created. This allows the Library to create XHTML splash pages directly from MARCXML

(*continued*)

records using an XSLT style sheet. This case study describes the XSLT features and XPath expressions used to create the XHTML splash pages.
Illustrates: XHTML; XSLT; MARCXML; splash page.

XHTML is an enhanced version of HTML (currently the most ubiquitous Web page markup language). Although HTML, like XML, is based on SGML, it is not as strict as XML with regard to case sensitivity of names, closing tags, attribute form, and so on. XHTML, which does conform to the syntactical requirements of XML, is generally regarded as a stricter and cleaner version of HTML (W3Schools 2004). Additionally, generic XML tools, including validating parsers and transforming processors, can be used with XHTML.

As part of the digitization work flow, each print volume's MARC record in the university's online catalog is retrieved and converted to MARCXML. Records are retrieved using the Z39.50 protocol.[24] Conversion from tape-based MARC format to MARCXML is accomplished using locally developed utilities that are based on an open source MARC to MARCXML converter.[25] Metadata records are provided to the Internet Archive at the time of digitization and subsequently augmented, with links to digitization outcomes. Figure 11.15 is an example of such an augmented record.

FIGURE 11.15 MARCXML record describing print copy of a retrospectively digitized book, augmented with links to digital surrogates.

```
<record xmlns="http://www.loc.gov/MARC21/slim">
  <leader>00853cam a22001811 4500</leader>
  <controlfield tag="001">2895515</controlfield>
  <controlfield tag="005">20080826231130.0</controlfield>
  <controlfield tag="008">900530s1622  sz         ger u</controlfield>
  <datafield tag="035" ind1=" " ind2=" ">
    <subfield code="a">(OCoLC)ocm77326353</subfield>
  </datafield>
  <datafield tag="035" ind1=" " ind2=" "><subfield code="9">ASZ-9709</subfield>
    </datafield>
  <datafield tag="035" ind1=" " ind2=" "><subfield code="9">UC 11051371</subfield>
    </datafield>
  <datafield tag="035" ind1=" " ind2=" "><subfield code="a">urb00135250</subfield>
    </datafield>
  <datafield tag="040" ind1=" " ind2=" ">
    <subfield code="d">UtOrBLW</subfield>
    <subfield code="d">UIU</subfield>
  </datafield>
  <datafield tag="100" ind1="1" ind2=" ">
    <subfield code="a">Murer, Christoph,</subfield>
    <subfield code="d">1558-1614.</subfield>
  </datafield>
  <datafield tag="245" ind1="1" ind2="0">
    <subfield code="a">XL [i.e. Quadraginta] emblemata miscella nova :</subfield>
```

(*continued*)

FIGURE 11.15 (Continued)

```
    <subfield code="b">Das ist : XL. underschiedliche Auszerlesene.../</subfield>
    <subfield code="c">durch Christoff Murern inventiret, unnd mit....</subfield>
  </datafield>
  <datafield tag="260" ind1=" " ind2=" ">
    <subfield code="a">Zürych :</subfield>
    <subfield code="b">Gedruckt bey J. Rüdolff Wolffen,</subfield>
    <subfield code="c">1622.</subfield>
  </datafield>
  <datafield tag="300" ind1=" " ind2=" ">
    <subfield code="a">[8], xxxx p. :</subfield>
    <subfield code="b">41 ill. ;</subfield>
    <subfield code="c">20 cm.</subfield>
  </datafield>
  <datafield tag="700" ind1="1" ind2=" ">
    <subfield code="a">Rordorff, Johann Heinrich.</subfield>
  </datafield>
  <datafield tag="776" ind1="1" ind2=" ">
    <subfield code="c">Original</subfield>
    <subfield code="w">(IU)</subfield>
  </datafield>
  <datafield tag="852" ind1=" " ind2=" ">
    <subfield code="a">University of Illinois at Urbana-Champaign</subfield>
    <subfield code="b">stos</subfield>
    <subfield code="u">http://hdl.handle.net/10111/UIUCOCA...</subfield>
  </datafield>
  <datafield tag="856" ind1="4" ind2="0">
    <subfield code="3">Full text - UIUC</subfield>
    <subfield code="u">http://hdl.handle.net/10111/UIUCOCA...</subfield>
  </datafield>
  <datafield tag="856" ind1="4" ind2="0">
    <subfield code="3">Full text - OCA</subfield>
    <subfield code="u">http://www.archive.org/details/...</subfield>
  </datafield>
</record>
```

For the splash page, the Library decided to display important bibliographic information, such as book title(s), creator(s)/contributor(s), publication information, physical description, date(s), description, subject(s), and rights information, in a pane labeled "About this book." The active links in this pane allow users to view the MARCXML record from which the splash page is derived and link to the online public access catalog record for the print volume that was digitized. Links to digital derivatives that users can retrieve, such as PDF, DjVu, Flip Book, OCR text, and/or page-by-page views, are shown in a separate pane below a thumbnail of a page image from the book. A persistent link for the splash page (i.e., a handle-based URL)[26] is provided at the bottom of the page along with the usual links to institution and project-related information. Figure 11.16 illustrates a generated splash page as viewed in a Web browser. The raw XHTML behind this view is shown in Figure 11.21.

FIGURE 11.16 Splash page for a digitized book.

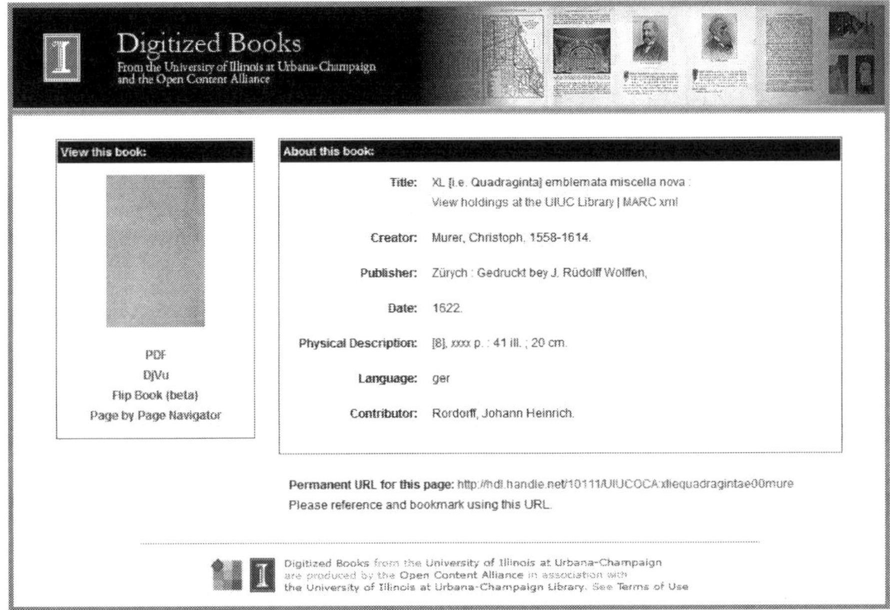

Because XHTML is a display-oriented XML grammar, intellectual mappings (crosswalks) from other XML grammars, such as MARCXML, must be developed on two levels. On one level, it is necessary to decide how the various content objects of the source-tree should be labeled, ordered, and displayed when viewed in a Web browser. Table 11.3 illustrates this level of mapping as developed by Illinois metadata librarians for this particular use case.

The second level is the XML itself. In order to generate the desired display, it is typically necessary to create in the XHTML output of the transform a structure containing several XML elements with attributes (e.g., a table row) in order to handle even a single XML content object of interest in the MARCXML source (i.e., a one-to-many mapping). Sometimes, it is necessary to define at the XML level many-to-many mappings as well, as in this case for Creator, Contributor, Physical Description, and Subject. Table 11.4 illustrates an example of what, at the XML level, is a one-to-many mapping. In this illustration, the publication date information in the MARCXML (data field 260, subfield $c) is mapped to an XHTML table row (`<tr>`) containing two cells. The first cell contains a label ("Date:"), and the second cell contains the actual date value from the MARCXML record. Additional elements and attributes are included in the generated XHTML to more precisely specified formatting.

Figure 11.17 shows the root element (`<xsl:stylesheet>`), the `<xsl:output>` element, and the elements used to define three global style sheet variables as these elements appear in the XSLT that generates the XHTML

TABLE 11.3 Mapping from MARC to display labels used in splash page.

MARC Source	Splash Page <strong>
245 $a	Title
246 $a	Alternative title
245 $n	Volume
100 $a and $d	Creator
260 $b	Publisher
260 $a	Place of publication
260 $c	Date
300 $a, $b, and $c	Physical description
Control field 008 value string location 4 to 7	Language
500 and 546	Notes
510	References
700	Contributor
650 $a, $x, $y, and $z	Subject
540 $a	Copyright status

splash page. The attributes of the root element indicate that the XSLT conforms to version 1.0 of the XSLT W3C Recommendation and provides a namespace binding (`m:`) for the namespace of the source MARCXML. The `<xsl:output>` element specifies that the XML created should be UTF-8 encoded, be indented (to facilitate human readability), and be in XML format (but the XML declaration should be omitted). For convenience and to save repetition of XPath path location expressions elsewhere in the style sheet, three global variables, `$bibID`, `$controlField008`, and `$medium`, are defined. Note that the XPath expression resolved to set the value of `$medium` uses `string-length` and `substring` functions. This is because the value string of subfield $h of data field 245 is enclosed in square brackets; the metadata librarians who created this XSLT wanted to display the value of medium (when present) without square brackets. Only five other XSLT elements are

TABLE 11.4 Illustration of mapping from MARCXML to XHTML.

MARCXML (Source)	XHTML (Splash Page)
<datafield tag="260" ind1=" " ind2=" "> ... <subfield code="c">1622.</subfield> </datafield>	<tr> <td align="right" valign="top"> <strong>Date:</strong> </td> <td>1622.</td> </tr>

FIGURE 11.17 Root and global elements appearing in XSLT style sheet for creating XHTML.

```
<?xml version="1.0" encoding="UTF-8"?>
<xsl:stylesheet version="1.0" xmlns:xsl="http://www.w3.org/1999/XSL/Transform"
   xmlns:m="http://www.loc.gov/MARC21/slim">
  <xsl:output encoding="UTF-8" indent="yes" method="xml" omit-xml-declaration=
"yes"/>
  <xsl:variable name="bibID" select="/m:record/m:controlfield[@tag=001]"/>
  <xsl:variable name="controlField008" select="/m:record/m:controlfield
[@tag=008]"/>
<xsl:variable name="medium"
   select="substring(/m:record/m:datafield[@tag='245']/m:subfield[@code='h'],
         1, string-length(.)-2)"/>
```

FIGURE 11.18 Using XSLT `<xsl:value-of>` to extract text node value of data field 245, subfield $a from the source tree.

```
<xsl:if test="m:datafield[@tag='245']">
  <tr>
    <td align="right" valign="top" width="25%">
      <strong>Title:</strong>
    </td>
    <td>
      <xsl:value-of select=" m:datafield[@tag='245']/m:subfield[@code='a']/text()"/>
      <br/>
    </td>
  </tr>
</xsl:if>
```

used elsewhere in the style sheet: `<xsl:template>`, `<xsl:if>`, `<xsl:for-each>`, `<xsl:text>`, and `<xsl:value-of>`.

Figure 11.18 illustrates how the mapping of data field 245, subfield $a (title proper), is crosswalked to XHTML. Since not all MARCXML records will contain all of the elements identified for crosswalking, `<xsl:if>` is used to decide whether a table row needs to be written out for each class of bibliographic information (e.g., title, creator, subject, and so on). The `<xsl:value-of>` element extracts a text node value, in this case the value of the title proper, from the MARCXML record. In the absence of child nodes, it is not necessary to specify explicitly the text node (i.e., it is not necessary to specify `/text()` if there are no child nodes).

Figure 11.19 illustrates the use of a variable (`$controlField008`). The value for this variable is assigned as shown in Figure 11.17. As illustrated in Figure 11.19 for crosswalking language, XPath string functions can be used in conjunction with `<xsl:value-of>` to extract only part of a variable or element value.

As discussed above, mappings of MARCXML subjects are typically many-to-one crosswalks because MARC defines multiple data fields for subject

FIGURE 11.19 Using XSLT <xsl:value-of> to select a substring of a MARC control field.

```
<xsl:if test="$controlField008">
  <tr>
    <td align="right" valign="top">
      <strong>Language:</strong>
    </td>
    <td>
      <xsl:value-of select="substring($controlField008,36, 3)"/><br/>
    </td>
  </tr>
</xsl:if>
```

information and also further subdivides many of these data fields into multiple subfields, such as subfield $x for general subdivision, $y for chronological subdivision, and $z for geographic subdivision. As illustrated in Figure 11.20 for crosswalking the MARC 650 data field (subject added entry-topical term),

FIGURE 11.20 Nesting <xsl:value-of> and <xsl:text> within <xsl:if> and <xsl:for-each>.

```
<xsl:if test="m:datafield[@tag='650'] | m:datafield[@tag='610']">
  <tr>
    <td align="right" valign="top">
      <strong>Subject:</strong>
    </td>
    <td>
      <xsl:for-each select="m:datafield[@tag='650']">
        <xsl:if test="m:subfield[@code='a']">
          <xsl:value-of select=" m:subfield[@code='a']"/>
          <xsl:for-each select="m:subfield[@code='v']">
            <xsl:text> -- </xsl:text>
            <xsl:value-of select="."/>
          </xsl:for-each>
          <xsl:for-each select="m:subfield[@code='x']">
            <xsl:text> -- </xsl:text>
            <xsl:value-of select="."/>
          </xsl:for-each>
          <xsl:for-each select="m:subfield[@code='y']">
            <xsl:text> -- </xsl:text>
            <xsl:value-of select="."/>
          </xsl:for-each>
          <xsl:for-each select="m:subfield[@code='z']">
            <xsl:text> -- </xsl:text>
            <xsl:value-of select="."/>
          </xsl:for-each>
          <br/>
        </xsl:if>
      </xsl:for-each>
    </td>
  </tr>
</xsl:if>
```

the XSLT style sheet for the splash page uses nested `<xsl:if>` and `<xsl:for-each>` to deal with optional subfields and makes use of `<xsl:text>` to add "– –" between subfield components of a compound subject heading.

Nesting `<xsl:for-each>` within `<xsl:if>` is useful when processing bibliographic properties that are both optional and repeatable, that is, as a way to collocate (one per line) repeated properties in a single table cell of the result-tree, such as for subjects, notes, and so on. Figure 11.21 shows the complete XHTML record created by transforming the MARCXML record shown in Figure 11.15 using mappings and XSLT methods such as those described above.

FIGURE 11.21 XHTML document created by XSLT style sheet.

```
<?xml version="1.0" encoding="UTF-8"?>
<!DOCTYPE html PUBLIC "-//W3C// XHTML 1.1//EN"
                    "http://www.w3.org/TR/xhtml11/DTD/xhtml11.dtd">
<html xmlns="http://www.w3.org/1999/xhtml" xml:lang="en" lang="en">
<table xmlns:m="http://www.loc.gov/MARC21/slim" border="0" cellspacing="5"
        cellpadding="5"
        align="center"
        width="100%">
    <tr>
        <td align="right" valign="top" width="25%">
            <strong>Title:</strong>
        </td>
        <td>XL [i.e. Quadraginta] emblemata miscella nova :<br/>
            <a href="https://i-share.carli.illinois.edu/uiu/cgi-bin/
Pwebrecon.cgi?BBID=2895515">View holdings at the UIUC Library</a><br/>
        </td>
    </tr>
    <tr>
        <td align="right" valign="top">
            <strong>Creator:</strong>
        </td>
        <td>Murer, Christoph,1558-1614.<br/>
        </td>
    </tr>
    <tr>
        <td align="right" valign="top">
            <strong>Publisher:</strong>
        </td>
        <td>Zürych :Gedruckt bey J. Rüdolff Wolffen,<br/>
        </td>
    </tr>
    <tr>
        <td align="right" valign="top">
            <strong>Date:</strong>
        </td>
        <td>1622.<br/>
        </td>
```

(continued)

FIGURE 11.21 (Continued)

```
    </tr>
    <tr>
        <td align="right" valign="top">
            <strong>Physical Description:</strong>
        </td>
        <td>[8], xxxx p. :41 ill. ;20 cm.<br/>
        </td>
    </tr>
    <tr>
        <td align="right" valign="top">
            <strong>Language:</strong>
        </td>
        <td>ger<br/>
        </td>
    </tr>
    <tr>
        <td align="right" valign="top" width="15%">
            <strong>Contributor:</strong>
        </td>
        <td>Rordorff, Johann Heinrich.<br/>
        </td>
    </tr>
</table></html>
```

CASE STUDY 11.2
Creating E-Book Records for Retrospectively Digitized Books

Synopsis: The University of Illinois Library began digitizing books from its collections in the late 1990s. Today, the Library routinely creates separate e-book MARC records for each book digitized in order to provide access to these digital resources via the Library's online public access catalog (OPAC) and in order to share e-book records describing these resources through the Online Computer Library Center (OCLC). Since 2007 (when the scale of book digitization projects at Illinois increased dramatically), the Library has exploited XML technologies when creating e-book records. This facilitates the use of automated batch processes in record creation work flows and allows for the creation of e-book records en masse and in a more timely fashion. The use of XML schemas also facilitates quality control during the record creation process. This case study illustrates how Illinois creates e-book records for digitized books using XSLT style sheets and existing printed book MARC records retrieved from the Library's OPAC.
Illustrates: Creating new MARCXML metadata records for digitized books; various XSLT elements used in metadata transformation.

Digitization involves processes in addition to scanning. Many postdigitization processes involve making retrospectively digitized resources discoverable and available to users. Metadata help to make digitized resources discoverable by users. In the library domain, since the OPAC is still regarded as a main gateway to the library resources, the University of Illinois Library chooses to provide access to its digitized books via its OPAC as well as via project-specific portals, such as the Internet Archive for books scanned for the Library by the Open Content Alliance (OCA).

There are two ways to provide access to retrospectively digitized resources through an OPAC. One option is to add electronic links to existing OPAC records for the associated print volumes. Another option is to create a new, separate (albeit linked) e-book record for each digitized book. While the University of Illinois Library does update OPAC records describing print volumes that have been digitized, it also creates a separate e-book record for each digitized book, in keeping with the interpretation that a digitized copy of a book is a reproduction of that printed book as defined in the Library of Congress Rule of Interpretation (LCRI) 1.11A. However, creating records for a large volume of digitized books requires significant time and effort. As Christina Powell (2008) points out in her article discussing lessons learned by the University of Michigan from their collaboration with Google, in order to provide OPAC access to digitized books produced by mass digitization projects, libraries must develop new automated work flows more appropriate for a "large scale production model" (24–25).

The work flow that the University of Illinois Library developed for creating e-book records takes advantage of the fact that volumes being digitized have existing MARC records in the Library's OPAC. These are retrieved and converted to XML as part of the digitization work flow. Although exact procedures vary according to project, when books are sent to vendors for digitization, typically MARCXML and Simple Dublin Core XML metadata records are generated from existing printed-book MARC records. These XML records are used to manage the digitization processing and during postdigitization processing. For example, when a book is scanned by OCA, the corresponding MARC record from the Library's OPAC is fetched and converted to MARCXML and Simple Dublin Core XML. These records are then ingested by the Internet Archive and made available with the digital copy of the book and its derivatives.

Postdigitization, the University of Illinois Library uses an XSLT style sheet to augment the MARCXML derived from the OPAC MARC record, adding links to the digital instance(s). In the case of OCA-digitized volumes, the Library links to the digital instances at the Internet Archive and on the Library's server; a third link to an archival copy of the digital files also is added. Figure 11.15 (as used also in previous case study) shows a typical MARCXML record after these links have been added. To facilitate internal work flows and allow external harvesting, these augmented MARCXML records are then made available via the Open Archives Initiative Protocol for Metadata Harvesting.

The e-book records that will be uploaded to OCLC are created from these augmented MARCXML records. Although the MARCXML record

FIGURE 11.22 Root and global elements in XSLT style sheet.

```
<?xml version="1.0" encoding="UTF-8" ?>
<xsl:stylesheet version="2.0" xmlns="http://www.loc.gov/MARC21/slim"
     xmlns:marc="http://www.loc.gov/MARC21/slim"
xmlns:xsl="http://www.w3.org/1999/XSL/Transform"
     exclude-result-prefixes="marc">
     <xsl:import href="MARC21slimUtils.xsl"/>
     <xsl:output method="xml" encoding="UTF-8" indent="yes"/>
     <xsl:param name="sourcefile"/>
     <xsl:strip-space elements="*"/>
```

technically describes the print copy, not the digital copy, the record still contains nearly all the bibliographic and descriptive information required to create an e-book record conforming to the requirements of the LCRI 1.11A and the *Cataloging Electronic Resources: OCLC-MARC Coding Guidelines* (2006). According to LCRI 1.11A, the catalog record for the reproduction of the print copy has the same descriptive information as print copy's catalog record, such as publication and physical description information. Additionally, it recommends adding to the e-book record the reproduction information in 533 notes.

For electronic format specific information, the Library follows the *Cataloging Electronic Resources: OCLC-MARC Coding Guidelines* (2006), such as with regard to encoding fixed field 006 and 007. The XSLT style sheet for creating the e-book MARCXML does three things:

1. It copies elements and values from the print MARCXML to the e-book record.
2. It adds information into the new e-book MARCXML record.
3. It corrects punctuation as required when copying values into the e-book record.

Global elements and the root open tag of the XSLT are shown in Figure 11.22. Since the XSLT style sheet is meant to be applied as part of a batch process, a parameter, `<xsl:param name="sourcefile"/>`, is provided to specify the name of the source MARCXML to process.

Copying Elements and Element Values to the New E-Book Record

An e-book MARCXML metadata record will have the same descriptive information as the corresponding printed-book record (in accordance with LCRI 1.11a). When a `<datafield>` can be copied intact, including child nodes and attributes, XSLT `<xsl:copy-of>` is used. Thus, if the new record will have same MARC 050 field, `<xsl:copy-of>` is used, as shown in the first line of Figure 11.23. For digitized book records, most descriptive fields (e.g., 1XX, 2XX, 3XX, 4XX, 5XX, 6XX, 7XX, and 8XX fields) of the print record are copied without change, except that punctuation in the 100, 260, and 300 data fields needs to be corrected as recommended by International Standard Bibliographic Description. This adjustment is done in an `<xsl:template>`,

FIGURE 11.23 Using XSLT <xsl:copy-of> element.

```
<xsl:copy-of select="marc:datafield[@tag='050']"/>
<xsl:copy-of select="marc:datafield[@tag='310']"/>
<xsl:copy-of select="marc:datafield[@tag='321']"/>
<xsl:copy-of select="marc:datafield[@tag='362']"/>
<xsl:copy-of select="marc:datafield[@tag='440']"/>
<xsl:copy-of select="marc:datafield[@tag='490']"/>
<xsl:copy-of select="marc:datafield[@tag='500']"/>
<xsl:copy-of select="marc:datafield[@tag='501']"/>
<xsl:copy-of select="marc:datafield[@tag='502']"/>
<xsl:copy-of select="marc:datafield[@tag='504']"/>
<xsl:copy-of select="marc:datafield[@tag='505']"/>
<xsl:copy-of select="marc:datafield[@tag='508']"/>
<xsl:copy-of select="marc:datafield[@tag='510']"/>
<xsl:copy-of select="marc:datafield[@tag='511']"/>
<xsl:copy-of select="marc:datafield[@tag='515']"/>
<xsl:copy-of select="marc:datafield[@tag='518']"/>
<xsl:copy-of select="marc:datafield[@tag='520']"/>
<xsl:copy-of select="marc:datafield[@tag='521']"/>
<xsl:copy-of select="marc:datafield[@tag='522']"/>
<xsl:copy-of select="marc:datafield[@tag='524']"/>
<xsl:copy-of select="marc:datafield[@tag='525']"/>
<xsl:apply-templates select="marc:datafield[@tag='100']"/>
<xsl:apply-templates select="marc:datafield[@tag='260']"/>
<xsl:apply-templates select="marc:datafield[@tag='300']"/>
<xsl:apply-templates select="marc:datafield[@tag='245']"/>
```

so <xsl:apply-templates> is used instead of <xsl:copy-of> (Figure 11.23). A template is also used when copying data field 245 in order to insert a subfield $h (electronic resource).

The content of some data fields in the print record must be copied to different data fields in the e-book record. For example, to keep the relationship between printed book and e-book, the printed-book local bibliographic number (control field 001) and OCLC number (data field 035) are each copied to a 776 data field (Additional Physical Form Entry) in the e-book record. As described in OCLC Bibliographic Format, subfield $c of the 776 data field can be used for *Qualifying Information*. For the printed-book local bibliographic number and OCLC record number, the library uses "Original" as the value of subfield $c. This value is added in the XSLT style sheet, as illustrated in Figure 11.24.

FIGURE 11.24 Using XSLT <xsl:if> element.

```
<datafield tag="776" ind1="1" ind2=" ">
      <subfield code="c">Original</subfield>
      <subfield code="w">
         <xsl:text>(IU)</xsl:text>
         <xsl:value-of select="marc:controlfield[@tag='001']"/>
      </subfield>
</datafield>
```

FIGURE 11.25 Adding control field 006 and 007 values using <xsl:text> element.

```
<controlfield tag="006">
        <xsl:text>m     d     </xsl:text>
</controlfield>

<controlfield tag="007">
        <xsl:text>cr unu</xsl:text>
</controlfield>

<datafield tag="040" ind1=" " ind2=" ">
        <subfield code="a">UIU</subfield>
        <subfield code="c">UIU</subfield>
</datafield>
```

The value of the 001 control field is copied to subfield $w of the 776. The text value (IU) is added as a prefix in subfield $w using <xsl:text>.

Adding New Data Fields

The e-book record must also include format-specific information in the 006 and 007 fields as defined in the *Cataloging Electronic Resources: OCLC-MARC Coding Guidelines* (2006). Since all the digitized books have the same format, the information can be added as a default value in the XSLT style sheet. In order to add the new fields and data, simply start with the element, in this case control fields 006 and 007. Then add the default data using the <xsl:text> element, as shown in Figure 11.25.

Other than format-specific information, the e-book record also includes a 533 data field for the reproduction information, a 690 data field for the local digitization project name, and 049 and 852 data fields for the holdings record. Values for these elements are institution specific.

SUMMARY

It is important to differentiate between XSLT and other style sheet languages, such as CSS and XSL-FO. These other style sheet languages are concerned largely with formatting and readability of HTML and XML by human agents. XSLT, especially when used in conjunction with XPath and without XSL-FO, is more about manipulation and reuse of content objects and values within XML documents. XSLT is optimized to transform and restructure the contents of one or more source XML documents into output document(s) conforming to different schemas and designs. XSLT exploits XML reusability and the intrinsic ordered hierarchy of content objects data model of XML, design features that make the language so well suited as a serialization approach for library metadata records.

As illustrated in the examples and case studies discussed in this chapter, style sheets conforming to XSLT can be used to create batch work flows in the library to support the conversion of MARCXML catalog records to Dublin Core records, XHTML records, and new, derivative MARCXML records. Today, XSLT-based work flows are routinely used in libraries to transform between a broad range of XML metadata grammars, including to and from Metadata Object Description Schema, Encoded Archival Description, and Visual Resources Association Core. XSLT style sheets also are routinely used to process and manipulate large collections of XML metadata records. For example, at the University of Illinois Library at Urbana–Champaign, XSLT style sheets are used to help assemble batches of MARCXML records provided to Google Books, the HathiTrust, and the OCA as part of large-scale digitization efforts. Other XSLT style sheets are used on large aggregations of MARCXML records to filter out those having or lacking certain characteristics, such as having or not having an OCLC number or being assigned a base call number within a certain range.

These examples illustrate the power of XSLT and demonstrate why it is considered a programming language in its own right. Although many real-world applications of XSLT result in relatively simple and straightforward style sheets, XSLT support for advanced features, such as parameters, the use and creation of multiple source and result-trees (version 2.0), template processing, conditional processing (`<xsl:case>` and `<xsl:if>` elements), and recursion (`<xsl:call-template>` and `<xsl:apply-templates>` elements), also allows XSLT to support the development of complex XML processing and manipulation work flows. This support makes XSLT a useful technology in the library and enhances the utility of XML as a serialization approach for library metadata.

QUESTIONS AND TOPICS FOR DISCUSSION

1. XSLT is a powerful tool for transforming metadata records from one metadata standard into another or into Web pages. However, in order to facilitate this tool, metadata should be in XML format. Discuss the current bibliographic environments, such as integrated library systems, Web-scale discovery, next-generation cataloging, and digital asset management tools, with regard to how these systems work with metadata in XML format.
2. In what ways can XSLT impact, or has already impacted, your library's or project's XML work flows? What are the advantages and disadvantages? What technologies are necessary?

SUGGESTIONS FOR EXERCISES

1. Qualified Dublin Core elements are refined elements of Simple Dublin Core elements. Taking this into account, create an XSLT for transforming Qualified Dublin Core to Simple Dublin Core. A list of Qualified Dublin Core and Simple Dublin Core elements can be found at http://dublincore.org/documents/2000/07/11/dcmes-qualifiers.

2. Several figures depicting fragments of XSLTs introduced in Case Study 11-1 are based on the Table 11.3 crosswalk. Try to complete the XSLT from MARCXML to XHTML.
3. Try to create an XHTML page from Simple Dublin Core metadata using an XSLT style sheet.
4. Compare the XSLT elements used in exercises 2 and 3 and think about what affected the use of XSLT elements in each XSLT.

NOTES

1. http://www.w3.org/TR/NOTE-XSL.
2. http://www.w3.org/Style/CSS.
3. http://www.iso.org/iso/catalogue_detail.htm?csnumber=18196.
4. http://www.w3.org/TR/1998/WD-xsl-19980818.
5. http://www.w3.org/TR/xpath.
6. http://www.w3.org/TR/xpath20.; work is underway on XPath 3.0, but as of this writing XPath 3.0 is not yet an approved W3C Recommendation.
7. http://www.w3.org/TR/xslt.
8. http://www.w3.org/TR/xslt20. ; work is underway on XSLT 3.0, but as of this writing XSLT 3.0 is not yet an approved W3C Recommendation.
9. http://www.w3.org/Style/XSL.
10. http://www.w3.org/TR/xlink11.
11. http://www.w3.org/TR/WD-xptr.
12. http://www.w3.org/TR/xinclude.
13. http://www.saxonica.com.
14. http://saxon.sourceforge.net.
15. http://xml.apache.org.
16. http://xml.apache.org/xalan-j.
17. http://xml.apache.org/xalan-c.
18. http://www.xmlsoft.org.
19. http://www.gnome.org.
20. http://msdn.microsoft.com/xml.
21. http://www.w3.org/2007/schema-for-xslt20.xsd.
22. http://www.loc.gov/standards/marcxml/xslt/MARC21slim2RDFDC.xsl.
23. http://www.w3.org/TR/xhtml1.
24. http://www.niso.org/standards/resources/Z39.50_Resources.
25. http://marcpm.sourceforge.net.
26. http://www.handle.net.

REFERENCES

Cataloging Electronic Resources: OCLC-MARC Coding Guidelines. 2006. Available at: http://www.oclc.org/support/documentation/worldcat/cataloging/electronicresources.

Powell, Christina Kelleher. 2008. "OPAC Integration in the Era of Mass Digitization: The MBooks Experience." *Library Hi Tech* 26, no. 1: 24–32.

W3Schools. 2004. "HTML vs XHTML." Available at: http://www.w3schools.com/html/html_xhtml.asp

CHAPTER 12

RDF and XML: Serializing Triples (Statements) in XML

XML allows catalogers and metadata librarians to serialize structured metadata about information resources in a manner that facilitates validation and transformation. As a meta-markup language, XML has the flexibility to accommodate a broad range of standardized metadata grammars. To facilitate authoring and enable more rigorous validation of grammar-specific rules, metadata grammars can be described using XML Document Type Definitions (DTDs) or other forms of XML schema. However, the utility of the unadorned XML data model for tasks like advanced inferencing and reasoning over an aggregation of metadata is limited.

As described in Chapter 1, XML is based on the idea that documents, including metadata records, can be modeled as an ordered hierarchy of content objects. Using XML, one can represent this hierarchy and give the content objects within it names and additional attributes. XML is a good and useful way to exchange, validate, and use structured information such as metadata. What XML on its own does not allow its users to do (or, more to the point, does not allow a computer application to do) is extract meaning from this hierarchy. Consider the snippet of well-formed XML shown in Figure 12.1.

The information in Figure 12.1 is nicely structured, but not much real meaning can be inferred from this XML, not even after taking into consideration the XSD or DTD that might be provided for validation. The meaning of "tag1," "tag2," and "attrib1" is opaque. Other resources describing the meaning behind the semantic labels and grammar being used are required to draw useful inferences. Of course, for consumption by humans, it might help to have more intuitive element and attribute names, such as in Figure 12.2.

A human reader of the XML in Figure 12.2 might now be able to intuit that this snippet of XML metadata conveys the title of the book identified by ISBN 9781591582809, but the more human-intuitive tag names do not help a computer application make such inferences. Computer applications have to be highly sophisticated to begin making such inferences from unadorned XML without human assistance (for some interesting research in this realm, see Dubin et al. 2003). The point is that while XML exposes the intellectual structure of a metadata record, it cannot convey the meaning of this structure

FIGURE 12.1 A snippet of well-formed XML.

```
<tag1 attrib1="URN:ISBN:9781591582809">
   <tag2>Using the Open Archives Initiative Protocol for Metadata Harvesting</tag2>
</tag1>
```

FIGURE 12.2 Figure 12.1 with more intuitive element and attribute names.

```
<Description about="URN:ISBN:9781591582809">
   <title>Using the Open Archives Initiative Protocol for Metadata Harvesting</title>
</Description>
```

on its own. For that, one needs ancillary information and/or an additional framework with an intrinsically more semantic data model.

The Resource Description Framework (RDF)[1] is one such framework. RDF was designed for conveying descriptions of Web resources. The RDF data model is designed to support simple three-part propositions called triples consisting of a *Subject*, a *Predicate*, and an *Object*. Each triple asserts a relationship between the Subject and the Object. For example, an RDF triple could be used to say that a book (Subject) has a title (Predicate) that is a particular string (Object), such as along the lines of the illustration shown in Figure 12.2. This articulates in a machine-actionable way the relationship between the book and the string of characters that is its title.

RDF is dependent on identifiers for accurately and unambiguously identifying subjects and objects that are resources. RDF is also dependent on well-defined vocabularies and ontologies that enumerate unambiguous, meaningful predicates. Given these prerequisites, RDF supports robust descriptions of Web resources using triples. When serialized as XML according to specification, XML metadata records conforming to the RDF data model facilitate inferencing and make metadata more machine actionable. World Wide Web Consortium (W3C) Working Drafts describing RDF date from early 1998, essentially concurrent with the release of the XML 1.0 Specification as a formal W3C Recommendation. The first serialization used for RDF was XML, though it is important to keep in mind that RDF can be serialized in other ways besides XML. RDF remains a foundational component of the W3C Semantic Web Activity[2] and the related library-linked open data initiative.[3]

This chapter introduces the data model of RDF and discusses its relationship to XML. The chapter also describes RDF Schema, a vocabulary description language for RDF, and a few of the key differences between XML Schemas and RDF Schemas. In addition, the chapter includes a brief introduction to RDF-in-Attributes (RDFa), an alternate way to serialize RDF assertions in XHTML, and a case study illustrating select RDF and RDFa Web services and the derivation from MARCXML of an XHTML Web page with embedded RDFa metadata.

AN INTRODUCTION TO RDF IN XML

"The Resource Description Framework (RDF) is a language for representing information about resources in the World Wide Web. It is particularly intended for representing metadata about Web resources such as the title, author, and modification date of a Web page, copyright and licensing information about a Web document, or the availability schedule for some shared resource" (Marola and Miller 2004). The underlying motivation for developing RDF was to create a simple data model to support machine processing of Web resource metadata. To achieve this, RDF provides a framework for expressing information about resources that facilitates exchange between applications without loss of meaning. The goal, given enough metadata about a set of resources and about the vocabularies and ontologies referenced by these metadata, is to enable computer applications to draw additional inferences about resource properties and relationships.

Subjects, Predicates, and Objects

The RDF data model is straightforward but must be applied rigorously. RDF is an assertional language designed to support the expression of simple propositions and reliant on properly constructed identifiers and formal vocabularies. Creating an RDF statement (called a proposition) involves identifying the Subject, Predicate, and Object of the statement. Sets of RDF statements, known as triples, are often represented as a graph, such as the one shown in Figure 12.3. An RDF triple makes a statement about a relationship between two resources or between a resource and a value (i.e., a literal string). The resource being described is the Subject of the statement. The Predicate identifies the relationship, that is, the attribute or characteristic of the Subject, being specified. The Object is the value of that attribute or characteristic and may be either a simple string or a pointer to another resource. The kinds of propositions that metadata authors need to express with RDF are along the lines of "The book titled *Using* the *Open Archive Initiative Protocol for Metadata Harvesting* (Subject) has a creator (Predicate) Timothy W. Cole (Object)." Another statement would be "This book (Subject) is titled (Predicate) '*Using Open Archive Initiative Protocol for Metadata Harvesting*' (Object)." However, even these seemingly simple statements conflate too much and are too imprecise to be expressed directly in RDF.

Because RDF is about Web resources, the distinction between different kinds of resources is important. In an RDF statement, both the Subject and the Predicate must be identifiable by Uniform Resource Identifiers (URIs). The Subject, the resource being described, must have a URI because it is by definition a resource on the Web. In order for

FIGURE 12.3 An RDF triple represented as a graph.

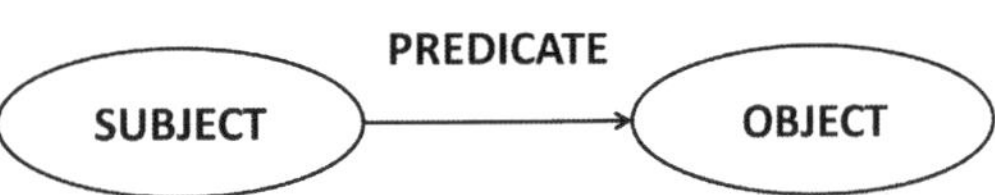

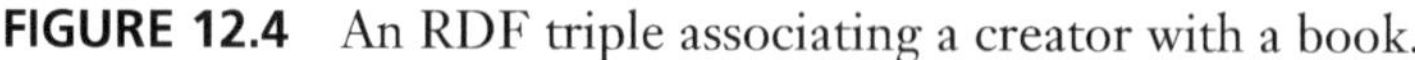

FIGURE 12.4 An RDF triple associating a creator with a book.

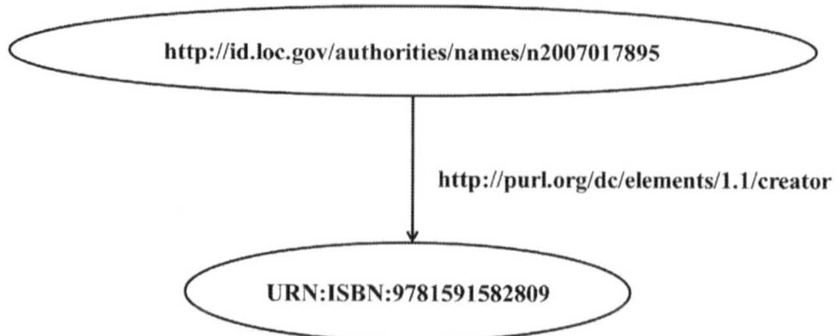

computer applications to reason over collections of RDF statements, the attribute or characteristic of the resource being described must be unambiguous and recognizable to a computer, hence the requirement that the Predicate also be identifiable by URI. More latitude is allowed for the Object. In RDF, the Object can either have a URI reference or be a literal value represented by a character string.

Constraints like those of RDF require that the examples given above be stated more rigorously. The granularity of the Object should be atomic. RDF also requires agreements on how conceptual properties (e.g., creator) and tangible entities (e.g., human authors) should be identified on the Web. The Library of Congress Authorities and Vocabularies Web service for Names[4] provides a URI for the author known as Timothy W. Cole. In this service, Cole has been assigned the URI http://id.loc.gov/authorities/names/n2007017895. The book mentioned above can be identified unambiguously (for this example) by creating a Uniform Resource Name (URN) based on its ISBN (i.e., URN:ISBN:9781591582809). For the Predicates required, a statement can use the URIs declared by the Dublin Core Metadata Initiative,[5] that is, http://purl.org/dc/elements/1.1/creator and http://purl.org/dc/elements/1.1/title. This leads to the RDF triples depicted graphically in Figures 12.4 and 12.5. Note that by common convention, ovals are used for resources identified by a URI, rectangles are used for Objects that are literal string values, and directed, labeled lines or arcs are used to depict predicates.

As discussed above, RDF is limited to simple triple-based propositions (statements). In order to express more complex descriptions, such descriptions need to be broken down into sets of triple statements. The same resource can appear as the Subject for many RDF statements. Objects from

FIGURE 12.5 An RDF triple describing the title of a book.

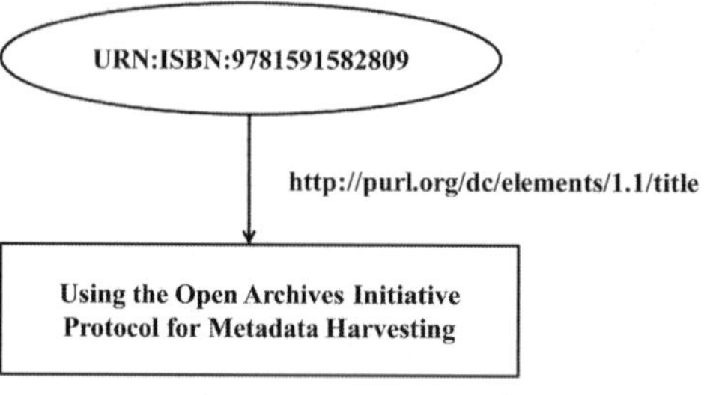

FIGURE 12.6 Multiple RDF statements in a graph (*Source:* Marola and Miller 2004).

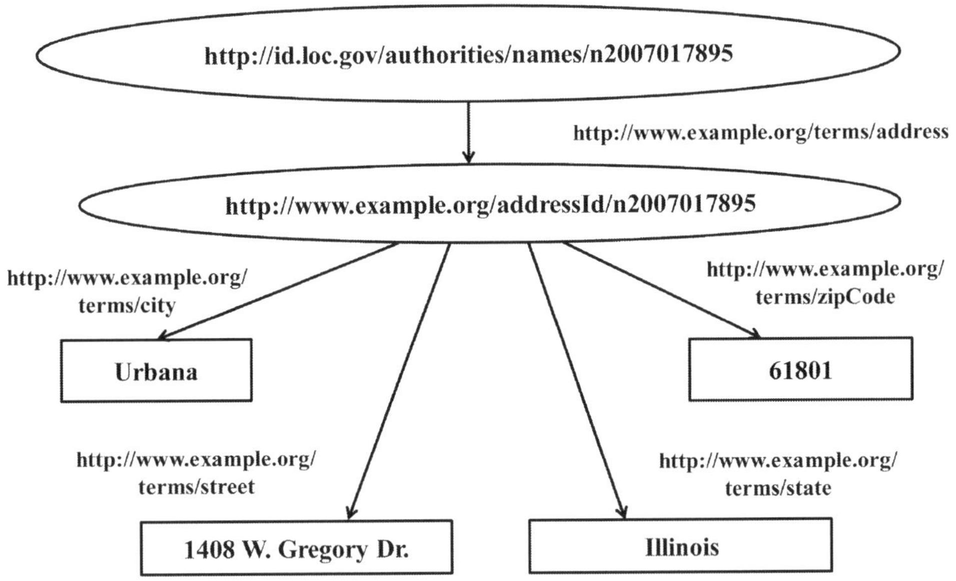

one statement that are resources identified by a URI can be the Subject of other statements. For example, when describing an address for a person, the whole address can be described as one object, a literal string. Alternatively, if the address as a whole has an identifier and is divisible into components or parts, such as state, city, street address, and ZIP code, the RDF *graph* (the graphical representation of a set of RDF triples, that is, Subject-Predicate-Object propositions) might look as depicted in Figure 12.6. This can be helpful because some of the more granular components of the address (e.g., the 5-digit numeric ZIP code) may be more amenable to machine processing than the address as a whole. In this figure, the address as a resource is both a Subject and an Object node.

However, as discussed above the Subject of an RDF triple is expected to be identified by a URI. What if the address as a whole does not have its own URI? How can the address then be broken down into finer granularity sub-components of information? To allow for this, RDF defines the concept of *blank nodes* that can be used when the granularity of an Object needs to be further broken down but a URI for the Object resource is not available. A blank node functions effectively as a resource of local scope within a particular RDF graph or a specific set of RDF triples. It may serve as the Object or Subject (but never the Predicate) of RDF statements within that context, as depicted in Figure 12.7. Within the scope of the graph or triple set only, a blank node may be given a *blank node identifier*. This blank node identifier allows the blank node to be used as Subject of a RDF triple and referenced from within its graph or set of triples, but one should keep in mind that a blank node identifier is not useful for external referencing.

FIGURE 12.7 Blank node used in RDF graph (*Source:* Marola and Miller 2004).

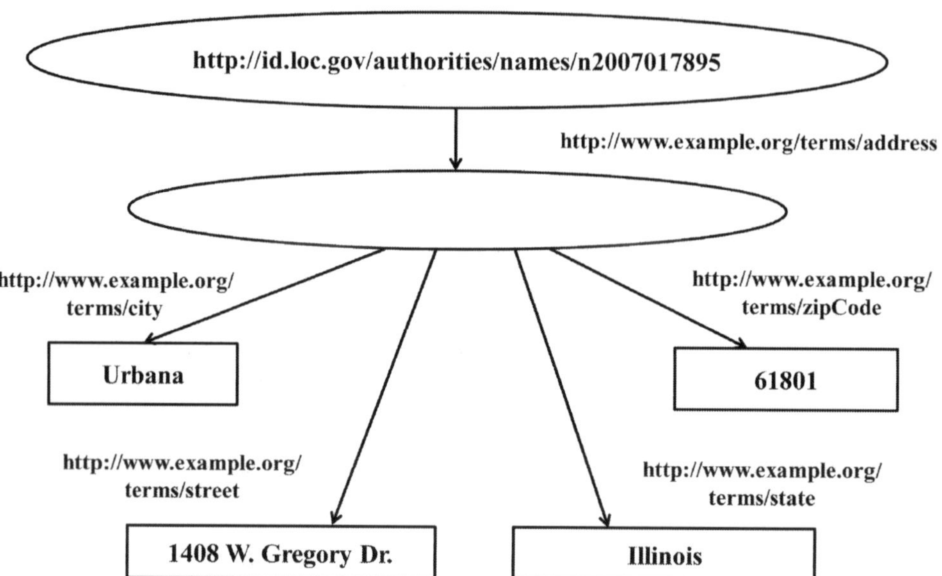

RDF Serialized as XML

XML serialization was the first approach used for serializing RDF. XML remains a good option for serializing RDF (the W3C maintains guidelines for serializing RDF in XML[6]) but is by no means the only option. By design RDF can be serialized more than one way. Figure 12.8 illustrates one way to serialize a simple RDF triple as XML.

When serializing RDF in XML, it is important to keep in mind the additional, implicit constraints levied by RDF semantics. As discussed above, RDF provides extra semantics that are not intrinsic to XML. An RDF statement asserts a relationship between a Subject and an Object using a Predicate to define that relationship. The structure of an RDF statement contains

FIGURE 12.8 The RDF of Figure 12.5 serialized as XML.

```
<?xml version="1.0"?>
<rdf:RDF xmlns:dc="http://purl.org/dc/elements/1.1/"
    xmlns:rdf="http://www.w3.org/1999/02/22-rdf-syntax-ns#"
    xmlns:rdfs="http://www.w3.org/2000/01/rdf-schema#">
    <rdf:Description rdf:about="URN:ISBN:9781591582809">
      <dc:title>Using Open Archive Initiative Protocol for Metadata
              Harvesting</dc:title>
    </rdf:Description>
</rdf:RDF>
```

implicit "knowledge" beyond the base hierarchy of content objects captured by XML. This gives flexibility "in expressing facts about a wide range of things, drawing on information from a wide range of sources" (Tauberer 2008). As early as 1998, Tim Berners-Lee noted that there is "a clear difference of view between those who want to query documents and those who want to extract the 'meaning' in some form and query that" (Berners-Lee 1998). He went on in a subsequent paper to comment that although the data model of XML supports the querying of documents and is "a good basis" for communicating documents between machines as well as humans, on its own it is not an effective means by which to extract meaning and allow that to be queried. XML is designed for the *document* and its structure, not for the data and the semantic meaning it delivers (Berners-Lee 2009).

The W3C guidelines for RDF in XML allow some flexibility in how to serialize RDF XML. An RDF graph typically can be expressed in a single XML hierarchy encompassing one or more `<rdf:Description>` elements (or equivalent) tied together by attribute values. Certain shortcuts are allowed as illustrated below. Both Figure 12.9 and Figure 12.10 are equally valid XML serializations of the RDF graph depicted in Figure 12.6.

As illustrated in both Figure 12.9 and Figure 12.10, the typical root element for an RDF record serialized as XML is `<rdf:RDF>`. This element takes triple statements as its children. The RDF namespace provides the `<rdf:Description>` element for serializing a triple. The URI of the Subject of

FIGURE 12.9 One XML serialization for the RDF graph shown in Figure 12.6.

```
<?xml version="1.0" encoding="UTF-8"?>
<?oxygen RNGSchema="http://www.w3.org/TR/REC-rdf-syntax/rdfxml.rng" type="xml"?>
<rdf:RDF
    xmlns:ex="http://www.example.org/terms/"
    xmlns:rdf="http://www.w3.org/1999/02/22-rdf-syntax-ns#"
    xmlns:rdfs="http://www.w3.org/2000/01/rdf-schema#">
    <rdf:Description rdf:about="http://id.loc.gov/authorities/names/n2007017895">
        <ex:address rdf:resource="http://www.example.org/addressId/n2007017895"/>
    </rdf:Description>
    <rdf:Description rdf:about="http://www.example.org/addressId/n2007017895">
        <ex:city>Urbana</ex:city>
    </rdf:Description>
    <rdf:Description rdf:about="http://www.example.org/addressId/n2007017895">
        <ex:street>1408 W. Gregory Dr.</ex:street>
    </rdf:Description>
    <rdf:Description rdf:about="http://www.example.org/addressId/n2007017895">
        <ex:state>Illinois</ex:state>
    </rdf:Description>
    <rdf:Description rdf:about="http://www.example.org/addressId/n2007017895">
        <ex:zipCode>61801</ex:zipCode>
    </rdf:Description>
</rdf:RDF>
```

FIGURE 12.10 An alternate way of serializing the RDF graph from Figure 12.6.

```
<?xml version="1.0" encoding="UTF-8"?>
<?oxygen RNGSchema="http://www.w3.org/TR/REC-rdf-syntax/rdfxml.rng" type="xml"?>
<rdf:RDF xmlns:ex="http://www.example.org/terms/"
    xmlns:rdf="http://www.w3.org/1999/02/22-rdf-syntax-ns#"
    xmlns:rdfs="http://www.w3.org/2000/01/rdf-schema#">
    <rdf:Description rdf:about="http://id.loc.gov/authorities/names/n2007017895">
        <ex:address>
            <rdf:Description rdf:about="http://www.example.org/addressId/n2007017895">
                <ex:city>Urbana</ex:city>
                <ex:street>1408 W. Gregory Dr.</ex:street>
                <ex:state>Illinois</ex:state>
                <ex:zipCode>61801</ex:zipCode>
            </rdf:Description>
        </ex:address>
    </rdf:Description>
</rdf:RDF>
```

the triple is typically expressed as the value of the `rdf:about` attribute of this element. Elements from other namespaces may be used in lieu of `<rdf:Description>` as long as they accommodate a way to express the URI of the Subject resource. In RDF XML, the Predicate of the triple is subordinate to `<rdf:Description>`, typically as a child element; however, note that a shortcut allowed in RDF XML when the same resource is the subject of multiple triples is to include more than one predicate in the same `<rdf:Description>` (illustrated in Figure 12.10).

Most Predicates are from non-RDF namespaces, but RDF does define a few Properties (i.e., Predicates), such as `<rdf:type>`, that can be useful in a metadata application context. Literal text (i.e., as the Object of a triple) may appear in an RDF XML triple serialization as the content of the Predicate element. Alternatively, the URI of an Object that is a resource can be provided through the `rdf:resource` attribute. Another shortcut allowed in RDF XML when the object of a RDF triple is also a Subject of one or more RDF triples is to nest `<rdf:Description>` elements, as shown in Figure 12.10. RDF XML also allows the `rdf:parseType` attribute with value of "`Resource`" as a serialization shortcut for expressing blank nodes without specifying a blank node identifier, illustrated in the RDF XML metadata record shown in Figure 12.11, which is a serialization of the graph shown in Figure 12.7. Additional serialization techniques and shortcuts are detailed in the W3C guidelines for serializing RDF in XML mentioned above.

In the context of metadata applications, the use of RDF XML is on the increase. Recently, the Library of Congress made its Name Authority File (NAF) records available as RDF descriptions via a Web service.[7] With over 8 million descriptions of names created over many decades, the NAF has long

FIGURE 12.11 RDF XML for graph shown in Figure 12.7, including blank node.

```
<?xml version="1.0" encoding="UTF-8"?>
<?oxygen RNGSchema="http://www.w3.org/TR/REC-rdf-syntax/rdfxml.rng" type="xml"?>
<rdf:RDF xmlns:ex="http://www.example.org/terms/"
  xmlns:rdf="http://www.w3.org/1999/02/22-rdf-syntax-ns#"
  xmlns:rdfs="http://www.w3.org/2000/01/rdf-schema#">
  <rdf:Description rdf:about="http://id.loc.gov/authorities/names/n2007017895">
          <ex:address rdf:parseType="Resource">
             <ex:city>Urbana</ex:city>
             <ex:street>1408 W. Gregory Dr.</ex:street>
             <ex:state>Illinois</ex:state>
             <ex:zipCode>61801</ex:zipCode>
          </ex:address>
  </rdf:Description>
</rdf:RDF>
```

been an authoritative source for names of persons and organizations (especially of those involved in the authoring and publication of books) and includes significant numbers of names of events and places as well. By expressing the NAF records (and records from other Library of Congress vocabularies) as RDF, giving each record its own persistent identifier (URI), and making these RDF records publicly available, the Library of Congress has enabled programmatic access to its authority data from many more computer-based tools and services, helping to expose and interconnect data on the Web. Through this service, the records of the NAF become dereferenceable Web resources, meaning that the identifier assigned to each NAF record can be used to retrieve information about that NAF entry. This makes the NAF more useful in creating machine-actionable metadata. Figure 12.12 shows a typical NAF

FIGURE 12.12 Library of Congress Name Authority File record in RDF XML.

```
<rdf:RDF xmlns:rdf="http://www.w3.org/1999/02/22-rdf-syntax-ns#"
   xmlns:skos="http://www.w3.org/2004/02/skos/core#"
   xmlns:cs="http://purl.org/vocab/changeset/schema#">
  <rdf:Description rdf:about="http://id.loc.gov/authorities/names/n2007017895">
   <rdf:type rdf:resource="http://www.w3.org/2004/02/skos/core#Concept"/>
   <skos:prefLabel xml:lang="en">Cole, Timothy W.</skos:prefLabel>
   <skos:exactMatch rdf:resource="http://viaf.org/viaf/sourceID/LC%7Cn+2007017895#skos:Concept"/>
   <skos:inScheme rdf:resource="http://id.loc.gov/authorities/names"/>
   <skos:changeNote xmlns:skos="http://www.w3.org/2004/02/skos/core#">
    <cs:ChangeSet>
     <cs:subjectOfChange rdf:resource="http://id.loc.gov/authorities/names/n2007017895"/>
     <cs:creatorName>Library of Congress, Network Development and MARC...</cs:creatorName>
     <cs:createdDate rdf:datatype="http://www.w3.org/2001/XMLSchema#dateTime">2007-
03-13T00:00:00</cs:createdDate>
     <cs:changeReason rdf:datatype="http://www.w3.org/2001/XMLSchema#string">new</cs:changeReason>
    </cs:ChangeSet>
   </skos:changeNote>
  </rdf:Description>
</rdf:RDF>
```

record disseminated as RDF XML. Notice the use of the Simple Knowledge Organization System (`skos:`)[8] and Changeset (`cs:`)[9] vocabularies for some Predicates shown in Figure 12.12. These vocabularies provide useful, RDF-compatible semantics for expressing descriptions of concepts and changes in records over time.

RDF SCHEMA

There is currently no XSD for RDF. XSD cannot properly capture all of the constraints of the RDF data model. As an alternative, the grammar of RDF XML is described using a RELAX NG Compact Schema,[10] although even this schema cannot fully validate all constraints of RDF in XML. RDF also provides its own specialized schema language for describing relationships between *Classes* (types of resources that can be Subjects and Objects) and *Properties* (Predicates) used in RDF statements. RDF Schema is a vocabulary description language for RDF[11] rather than a language primarily for validation. RDF schemas define Predicates in terms of their domains and ranges where:

1. A Predicate's *domain* references the Classes of resources that can be the Subject of the Predicate
2. A Predicate's *range* references the Classes of resources that can be the Object of the Predicate

In RDF, a Class is referred to as a "kind of thing" and represents types or categories. The members of a Class are called instances. For example, if you want to reference people you know collectively, then you could (for the purposes of authoring metadata) treat "People-You-Know" as an RDF Class (McBride 2004).

Figure 12.13 is a portion of the RDF Schema for Simple Dublin Core showing the declarations for a few of the Classes defined by Simple Dublin Core: *Agent*, *AgentClass*, and *BibliographicResource*. Notice the use of the `<rdfs:subClassOf>` element to express hierarchical relationships between Classes. Table 12.1 summarizes some of the Classes defined and contained in the RDF and RDF Schema namespaces. One of the main functions of RDF Schemas is to express relationships among Classes and between Classes and Properties in ways that can facilitate reasoning and inference.

Property is used in RDF for describing specific attributes that characterize Classes of things. For example, "mother" might be a Property used with a Class called "Family." As alluded to above, Properties are used as Predicates in RDF statements. There are some Properties built into RDF, but most Properties (and therefore most Predicates) are from other namespaces.

FIGURE 12.13 Fragment of the RDF Schema describing Simple Dublin Core classes.

```
<?xml version="1.0" encoding="UTF-8"?>
<rdf:RDF xmlns:owl="http://www.w3.org/2002/07/owl#"
  xmlns:skos="http://www.w3.org/2004/02/skos/core#"
     xmlns:dcam="http://purl.org/dc/dcam/"
     xmlns:dcterms="http://purl.org/dc/terms/"
     xmlns:rdf="http://www.w3.org/1999/02/22-rdf-syntax-ns#"
     xmlns:rdfs="http://www.w3.org/2000/01/rdf-schema#">
  <rdf:Description rdf:about="http://purl.org/dc/terms/">
     <dcterms:title xml:lang="en-US">DCMI Metadata Terms ...</dcterms:title>
     <dcterms:publisher rdf:resource="http://purl.org/dc/aboutdcmi#DCMI"/>
     <dcterms:modified>2010-10-11</dcterms:modified>
  </rdf:Description>
  <rdf:Description rdf:about="http://purl.org/dc/terms/Agent">
    <rdfs:label xml:lang="en-US">Agent</rdfs:label>
    <rdfs:comment xml:lang="en-US">A resource that acts or has the power to
                              act.</rdfs:comment>
    <dcterms:description xml:lang="en-US">Examples of Agent include person,
                              organization, and software agent.</dcterms:description>
    <rdfs:isDefinedBy rdf:resource="http://purl.org/dc/terms/"/>
    <dcterms:issued>2008-01-14</dcterms:issued>
    <rdf:type rdf:resource="http://www.w3.org/2000/01/rdf-schema#Class"/>
    <rdf:type rdf:resource="http://purl.org/dc/terms/AgentClass"/>
    <dcterms:hasVersion
         rdf:resource="http://dublincore.org/usage/terms/history/#Agent-001"/>
  </rdf:Description>
  <rdf:Description rdf:about="http://purl.org/dc/terms/AgentClass">
    <rdfs:label xml:lang="en-US">Agent Class</rdfs:label>
    <rdfs:comment xml:lang="en-US">A group of agents.</rdfs:comment>
    <dcterms:description xml:lang="en-US">Examples of Agent Class include groups seen
      as classes, such as students, women, charities, lecturers.</dcterms:description>
    <rdfs:isDefinedBy rdf:resource="http://purl.org/dc/terms/"/>
    <dcterms:issued>2008-01-14</dcterms:issued>
    <rdf:type rdf:resource="http://www.w3.org/2000/01/rdf-schema#Class"/>
    <dcterms:hasVersion
      rdf:resource="http://dublincore.org/usage/terms/history/#AgentClass-001"/>
    <rdfs:subClassOf rdf:resource="http://purl.org/dc/terms/AgentClass"/>
  </rdf:Description>
  <rdf:Description rdf:about="http://purl.org/dc/terms/BibliographicResource">
    <rdfs:label xml:lang="en-US">Bibliographic Resource</rdfs:label>
    <rdfs:comment xml:lang="en-US">A book, article, or other documentary
         resource.</rdfs:comment>
    <rdfs:isDefinedBy rdf:resource="http://purl.org/dc/terms/"/>
   <dcterms:issued>2008-01-14</dcterms:issued>
   <rdf:type rdf:resource="http://www.w3.org/2000/01/rdf-schema#Class"/>
   <dcterms:hasVersion
  rdf:resource="http://dublincore.org/usage/terms/history/#BibliographicResource-001"/>
  </rdf:Description>
  <!-- Additional Descriptions Skipped for Brevity  -->
</rdf:RDF>
```

TABLE 12.1 Classes in the RDF and RDF Schema namespaces (*Source:* Brickley and Guha 2004).

RDF Vocabulary	Definition
rdf:Resource	The class of resource, everything
rdfs:Literal	The class of literal values, such as strings and integers
rdf:XMLLiteral	The class of XML literal values
rdfs:Class	The class of classes
rdf:Property	The class of properties
rdfs:Datatype	The class of RDF data types
rdf:Statement	The class of RDF statements
rdf:Alt, rdf:Bag, rdf:Seq	Containers of alternatives, unordered containers, and ordered containers (rdfs:Container is a superclass of the three) rdfs:Container—the class of RDF containers
rdfs:ContainerMembershipProperty	The class of container membership properties, rdf:_1, rdf:_2, . . ., all of which are subproperties of rdfs:member
rdf:List	The class of RDF Lists
rdf:nil	An instance of rdf:List representing the empty list

Figure 12.14 is a portion of the RDF Schema for Simple Dublin Core showing the declarations for the Properties Title and Creator. Notice the difference in ranges allowed by these two definitions. As defined, the range (allowed Object Classes) for the Simple Dublin Core Title Property must be literal strings, while those of the Creator Property are declared as a subclass of the Dublin Core "Agents" Class and thus are more likely to be resources identified by URIs. Table 12.2 summarizes some of the Properties defined and contained in the RDF and RDF Schema namespaces. These Properties can be used as Predicates in RDF and RDF Schema statements.

RDFa

RDF was developed to help applications use metadata to reason about relationships between Web resources and infer additional metadata regarding Web resources. However, the same metadata statements (title, author, subject, and so on) captured as RDF are also of interest to human users. RDFa defines a set of attributes that can be embedded in Extensible HyperText Markup Language (XHTML) Web pages as an alternative way to serialize RDF

FIGURE 12.14 Fragment of the RDF Schema describing Simple Dublin Core properties.

```
<?xml version="1.0" encoding="UTF-8"?>
<rdf:RDF xmlns:owl="http://www.w3.org/2002/07/owl#"
    xmlns:skos="http://www.w3.org/2004/02/skos/core#"
    xmlns:dcam="http://purl.org/dc/dcam/"
    xmlns:dcterms="http://purl.org/dc/terms/"
    xmlns:rdf="http://www.w3.org/1999/02/22-rdf-syntax-ns#"
    xmlns:rdfs="http://www.w3.org/2000/01/rdf-schema#">
  <rdf:Description rdf:about="http://purl.org/dc/terms/">
    <dcterms:title xml:lang="en-US">DCMI Metadata Terms ...</dcterms:title>
    <dcterms:publisher rdf:resource="http://purl.org/dc/aboutdcmi#DCMI"/>
    <dcterms:modified>2010-10-11</dcterms:modified>
  </rdf:Description>
  <rdf:Description rdf:about="http://purl.org/dc/terms/title">
    <rdfs:label xml:lang="en-US">Title</rdfs:label>
    <rdfs:comment xml:lang="en-US">A name given to the resource.</rdfs:comment>
    <rdfs:isDefinedBy rdf:resource="http://purl.org/dc/terms/"/>
    <dcterms:issued>2008-01-14</dcterms:issued>
    <dcterms:modified>2010-10-11</dcterms:modified>
    <rdf:type rdf:resource="http://www.w3.org/1999/02/22-rdf-syntax-ns#Property"/>
    <dcterms:hasVersion
       rdf:resource="http://dublincore.org/usage/terms/history/#titleT-002"/>
    <rdfs:range rdf:resource="http://www.w3.org/2000/01/rdf-schema#Literal"/>
    <rdfs:subPropertyOf rdf:resource="http://purl.org/dc/elements/1.1/title"/>
  </rdf:Description>
  <rdf:Description rdf:about="http://purl.org/dc/terms/creator">
    <rdfs:label xml:lang="en-US">Creator</rdfs:label>
    <rdfs:comment xml:lang="en-US">An entity primarily responsible for making the
          resource.</rdfs:comment>
    <dcterms:description xml:lang="en-US">Examples of a Creator include a person, an
          organization, or a service.</dcterms:description>
    <rdfs:isDefinedBy rdf:resource="http://purl.org/dc/terms/"/>
    <dcterms:issued>2008-01-14</dcterms:issued>
    <dcterms:modified>2010-10-11</dcterms:modified>
    <owl:equivalentProperty rdf:resource="http://xmlns.com/foaf/0.1/maker"/>
    <rdf:type rdf:resource="http://www.w3.org/1999/02/22-rdf-syntax-ns#Property"/>
    <dcterms:hasVersion
       rdf:resource="http://dublincore.org/usage/terms/history/#creatorT-002"/>
    <rdfs:range rdf:resource="http://purl.org/dc/terms/Agent"/>
    <rdfs:subPropertyOf rdf:resource="http://purl.org/dc/elements/1.1/creator"/>
    <rdfs:subPropertyOf rdf:resource="http://purl.org/dc/terms/contributor"/>
  </rdf:Description>
  <!-- Additional Descriptions Skipped for Brevity  -->
</rdf:RDF>
```

metadata records. XHTML + RDFa is defined by and can be validated using an XSD. As described in the following case study, the W3C maintains a special Web-based service that can distill RDF statements from XHTML documents with embedded RDFa content. Using RDFa, "XHTML authors can markup

TABLE 12.2 Properties in the RDF and RDF Schema namespaces (*Source*: Brickley and Guha 2004).

RDF Vocabulary	Definition	Domain	Range
rdf:type	An instance of rdf:Property used to state that a resource is an instance of a class	rdfs:Resource	rdfs:Class
rdfs:subClassOf	The subject is a subclass of a class	rdfs:Class	rdfs:Class
rdfs:subPropertyOf	The subject is a subproperty of a property	rdf:Property	rdf:Property
rdfs:domain	A domain of the subject property	rdf:Property	rdfs:Class
rdfs:range	A range of the subject property	rdf:Property	rdfs:Class
rdfs:label	A human-readable name for the subject	rdfs:Resource	rdfs:Literal
rdfs:comment	A description of the subject resource	rdfs:Resource	rdfs:Literal
rdfs:member	A member of the subject resource	rdfs:Resource	rdfs:Resource
rdf:first	The first item in the subject RDF list	rdf:List	rdfs:Resource
rdf:rest	The rest of the subject RDF list after the first item	rdf:List	rdf:List
rdfs:seeAlso	Further information about the subject resource	rdfs:Resource	rdfs:Resource
rdfs:isDefinedBy	The definition of the subject resource	dfs:Resource	rdfs:Resource
rdf:value	Idiomatic property used for structured values	rdfs:Resource	rdfs:Resource
rdf:subject	The subject of the subject RDF statement	rdf:Statement	rdfs:Resource
rdf:predicate	The predicate of the subject RDF statement	rdf:Statement	rdfs:Resource
rdf:object	The object of the subject RDF statement	rdf:Statement	rdfs:Resource

human-readable [i.e., Web-browser mediated] data with machine-readable indicators for browsers and other programs to interpret" (Adida and Birbeck 2008). Although the current version of RDFa has been specified for XHTML 1.1,[12] the RDFa markup can be embedded inside of HTML4 as well to have the same result. Case Study 12.1 illustrates an RDFa work flow for University of Illinois Library metadata records derived from the online catalog.

CASE STUDY 12.1
RDFa from MARCXML and Dublin Core

Synopsis: RDF using Simple Dublin Core Predicates can be created from a MARCXML document using the Extensible Stylesheet Language for Transformations (XSLT). Using RDFa, such descriptions can be disseminated in an XHTML file. This case study showcases this process and the use of the RDF Validator[13] and RDFa Distiller Web services.[14]
Illustrates: Simple Dublin Core expressed as RDF and RDFa; catalog record conversions.

MarcEdit[15] can be used to create MARCXML from library catalog MAchine-Readable Cataloging (MARC) records as discussed in Chapter 4. Figure 12.15 shows the MARCXML record created from a University

FIGURE 12.15 A MARCXML record (from Case Study 10.1).

```
<record xmlns="http://www.loc.gov/MARC21/slim"
   xmlns:xsi="http://www.w3.org/2001/XMLSchema-instance"
   xsi:schemaLocation="http://www.loc.gov/MARC21/slim
                    http://www.loc.gov/standards/marcxml/schema/MARC21slim.xsd" >
   <leader>01698cam 22003614a 4500</leader>
   <controlfield tag="001">5439928</controlfield>
   <controlfield tag="005">20080104135038.0</controlfield>
   <controlfield tag="008">070313s2007    ctua    b    001 0 eng    </controlfield>
   <datafield tag="010" ind1=" " ind2=" ">
      <subfield code="a"> 2007009006</subfield>
   </datafield>
   ...
   <datafield tag="100" ind1="1" ind2=" ">
      <subfield code="a">Cole, Timothy W.</subfield>
   </datafield>
   <datafield tag="245" ind1="1" ind2="0">
      <subfield code="a">Using the Open Archives Initiative ....</subfield>
      <subfield code="c">Timothy W. Cole and Muriel Foulonneau.</subfield>
   </datafield>
   <datafield tag="260" ind1=" " ind2=" ">
      <subfield code="a">Westport, Conn. :</subfield>
      <subfield code="b">Libraries Unlimited,</subfield>
      <subfield code="c">c2007.</subfield>
   </datafield>
   <datafield tag="300" ind1=" " ind2=" ">
      <subfield code="a">xv, 208 p. :</subfield>
      <subfield code="b">ill. ;</subfield>
      <subfield code="c">26 cm.</subfield>
   </datafield>
   <datafield tag="440" ind1=" " ind2="0">
      <subfield code="a">Third millennium cataloging</subfield>
```

(continued)

FIGURE 12.15 (Continued)

```
    </datafield>
    <datafield tag="504" ind1=" " ind2=" ">
        <subfield code="a">Includes bibliographical references and index.</subfield>
    </datafield>
    <datafield tag="505" ind1="0" ind2=" ">
        <subfield code="a">Definition and origins of OAI-PMH ....</subfield>
    </datafield>
<datafield tag="650" ind1=" " ind2="0">
      <subfield code="a">Metadata harvesting.</subfield>
    </datafield>
    <datafield tag="610" ind1="2" ind2="0">
        <subfield code="a">Open Archives Initiative.</subfield>
    </datafield>
    <datafield tag="700" ind1="1" ind2=" ">
        <subfield code="a">Foulonneau, Muriel.</subfield>
    </datafield>
</record>
```

FIGURE 12.16 RDF Simple Dublin Core record from the MARCXML record depicted in Figure 12.15.

```
<?xml version="1.0" encoding="UTF-8"?>
<?oxygen RNGSchema="http://www.w3.org/TR/REC-rdf-syntax/rdfxml.rng" type="xml"?>
<rdf:RDF
    xmlns:rdf="http://www.w3.org/1999/02/22-rdf-syntax-ns#"
    xmlns:dc="http://purl.org/dc/elements/1.1/">
  <rdf:Description rdf:about="URN:ISBN:9781591582809">
    <dc:title>Using the Open Archives Initiative protocol for metadata
harvesting/</dc:title>
    <dc:creator>Cole, Timothy W.</dc:creator>
    <dc:creator>Foulonneau, Muriel.</dc:creator>
    <dc:type>text</dc:type>
    <dc:publisher>Westport, Conn. : Libraries Unlimited,</dc:publisher>
    <dc:date>c2007.</dc:date>
    <dc:language>eng</dc:language>
    <dc:description>Includes bibliographical references and index.</dc:description>
    <dc:description>Definition and origins of OAI-PMH -- Underlying technologies and the
technical development of OAI-PMH -- Context for OAI-PMH : eprints, institutional reposi-
tories, and open access -- Technical details of the protocol -- Implementing an OAI data
provider -- Creating metadata to share -- Post-harvest metadata normalization & augmenta-
tion -- Using aggregated metadata to build digital library services -- Concluding
thoughts.</dc:description>
    <dc:subject>Metadata harvesting.</dc:subject>
    <dc:identifier>URN:ISBN:9781591582809</dc:identifier>
    <dc:identifier>URN:ISBN:1591582806</dc:identifier>
  </rdf:Description>
</rdf:RDF>
```

FIGURE 12.17 XHTML with RDFa displayed in the Firefox Web browser.

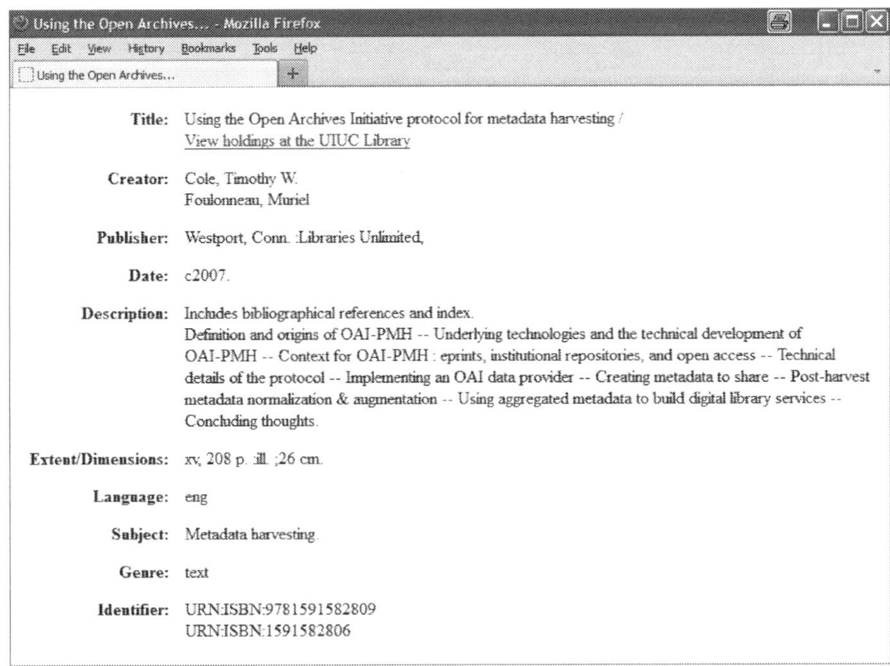

of Illinois Library catalog. The Library of Congress provides a style sheet conforming to the XSLT standard[16] (described in Chapter 11) that can generate RDF using Dublin Core Predicates from a MARCXML record. The outcome of the transformation of MARCXML into RDF-Dublin Core (slightly edited) is shown in Figure 12.16. (Note that this serialization of RDF-Dublin Core does not reflect the most recent updates of the Dublin Core Abstract Model.[17]) Separately, using an XSLT style sheet developed by the University of Illinois Library, the MARCXML can be transformed into XHTML for display. RDFa can simultaneously be generated and embedded within the XHTML. Figure 12.17 shows XHTML + RDFa generated from MARCXML as viewed in a Web browser. The RDFa has no effect on the rendering of the XHTML.

The actual XHTML encoding with RDFa is shown in Figure 12.18. Extra `<div>` and `<span>` elements are included in the XHTML to support the inclusion of RDFa-specific attributes (`about`, `property`, `rel`, and `resource`). These attributes are added as needed to record the URIs and references required to express RDF Subjects, Predicates, and some Objects. For Objects that are literal text, existing XHTML element content is used. The RDFa shown in Figure 12.18 is enriched slightly as compared to the RDF in Figure 12.16. Multiple triples are used to express creator and subject metadata, that is, to express both the preferred label for a property and the URI of the property value as a concept on the Web. Thus, in the XHTML table cell containing subject information, both the concept preferred label (string)

FIGURE 12.18 XHTML document depicted in Figure 12.17, showing embedded RDFa.

```
<html xmlns="http://www.w3.org/1999/xhtml"
  xsi:schemaLocation="http://www.w3.org/1999/xhtml
                      http://www.w3.org/MarkUp/SCHEMA/xhtml-rdfa-1.xsd"
  xmlns:xsi="http://www.w3.org/2001/XMLSchema-instance"
  xmlns:rdf="http://www.w3.org/1999/02/22-rdf-syntax-ns#"
  xmlns:dc="http://purl.org/dc/elements/1.1/"
  xmlns:skos="http://www.w3.org/2004/02/skos/core#">
  <head><title>Using the Open Archives...</title></head>
  <body><div about="URN:ISBN:9781591582809">
    <table border="0" cellspacing="5" cellpadding="5">
     <tr>
      <td align="right" valign="top"><strong>Title:</strong></td>
      <td><span property="dc:title">Using the Open Archives ....</span><br />
          <a href="https://i-share.carli.illinois.edu/...">View holdings...</a>
      </td>
     </tr>
     <tr>
      <td align="right" valign="top"><strong>Creator:</strong></td>
      <td><div rel="dc:creator" xml:lang="en"
                resource="http://id.loc.gov/authorities/names/n2007017895" >
          <span property="skos:prefLabel">Cole, Timothy W.</span>
          <span rel="skos:inScheme"
                resource="http://id.loc.gov/authorities/names"/></div>
         <div rel="dc:creator" xml:lang="en"
              resource="http://id.loc.gov/authorities/names/n2007017897" >
          <span property="skos:prefLabel">Foulonneau, Muriel</span>
          <span rel="skos:inScheme"
                resource="http://id.loc.gov/authorities/names"/></div>
      </td>
     </tr>
     <tr>
      <td align="right" valign="top"><strong>Publisher:</strong></td>
      <td property="dc:publisher">Westport, Conn. :Libraries Unlimited,</td>
     </tr>
     <tr>
      <td align="right" valign="top"><strong>Description:</strong></td>
      <td><span property="dc:description">Includes bibliographical....</span><br/>
          <span property="dc:description">Definition and origins of OAI-...</span>
      </td>
     </tr>
     <td align="right" valign="top"><strong>Subject:</strong></td>
     <td rel="dc:subject" xml:lang="en"
         resource="http://id.loc.gov/authorities/subjects/sh2007001751">
        <span rel="rdf:type"
              resource="http://www.w3.org/2004/02/skos/core#Concept"/>
        <span property="skos:prefLabel">Metadata harvesting.</span>
        <span rel="skos:inScheme"
              resource="http://id.loc.gov/authorities/subjects"/>
     </td>
    </tr>
     <td align="right" valign="top"><strong>Identifier:</strong></td>
```

FIGURE 12.18 (Continued)

```
    <td><span property="dc:identifier">URN:ISBN:9781591582809</span><br/>
        <span property="dc:identifier">URN:ISBN:1591582806</span>
    </td>
   </tr> ...Additional Rows & Some Text Content Omitted for Brevity...
  </table>
 </div></body>
</html>
```

FIGURE 12.19 RDF XML document distilled from XHTML RDFa document.

```
<?xml version="1.0" encoding="utf-8"?>
<rdf:RDF xmlns:dc="http://purl.org/dc/elements/1.1/"
  xmlns:rdf="http://www.w3.org/1999/02/22-rdf-syntax-ns#"
  xmlns:rdfs="http://www.w3.org/2000/01/rdf-schema#"
  xmlns:skos="http://www.w3.org/2004/02/skos/core#"
  xmlns:xhv="http://www.w3.org/1999/xhtml/vocab#"
  xmlns:xml="http://www.w3.org/XML/1998/namespace"
  xmlns:xsi="http://www.w3.org/2001/XMLSchema-instance">
  <rdf:Description rdf:about="URN:ISBN:9781591582809">
    <dc:description>Definition and origins of OAI-PMH ....</dc:description>
    <dc:description>Includes bibliographical references and index.</dc:description>
    <dc:title>Using the Open Archives Initiative...</dc:title>
    <dc:subject>
      <skos:Concept rdf:about="http://id.loc.gov/authorities/subjects/sh2007001751">
        <skos:prefLabel xml:lang="en">Metadata harvesting.</skos:prefLabel>
        <skos:inScheme rdf:resource="http://id.loc.gov/authorities/subjects"/>
      </skos:Concept>
    </dc:subject>
    <dc:language>eng</dc:language>
    <dc:creator>
      <rdf:Description rdf:about="http://id.loc.gov/authorities/names/n2007017897">
        <skos:prefLabel xml:lang="en">Foulonneau, Muriel</skos:prefLabel>
        <skos:inScheme rdf:resource="http://id.loc.gov/authorities/names"/>
      </rdf:Description>
    </dc:creator>
    <dc:creator>
      <rdf:Description rdf:about="http://id.loc.gov/authorities/names/n2007017895">
        <skos:prefLabel xml:lang="en">Cole, Timothy W.</skos:prefLabel>
        <skos:inScheme rdf:resource="http://id.loc.gov/authorities/names"/>
      </rdf:Description>
    </dc:creator>
    <dc:date>c2007. </dc:date>
    <dc:publisher>Westport, Conn. :Libraries Unlimited,</dc:publisher>
    <dc:format>xv, 208 p. :ill. ;26 cm.</dc:format>
    <dc:type>text</dc:type>
    <dc:identifier>URN:ISBN:1591582806</dc:identifier>
    <dc:identifier>URN:ISBN:9781591582809</dc:identifier>
  </rdf:Description>
</rdf:RDF>
```

FIGURE 12.20 Validation result of the distilled RDF XML displayed in triples.

W3C RDF Powered Validation Service

Home Documentation Feedback

Validation Results

Your RDF document validated successfully.

Jump To: Source Triples Messages Graph Feedback Back to Validator Input

Triples of the Data Model

Number	Subject	Predicate	Object
1	URN:ISBN:9781591582809	http://purl.org/dc/elements/1.1/description	"Definition and origins of OAI-PMH ...."
2	URN:ISBN:9781591582809	http://purl.org/dc/elements/1.1/description	"Includes bibliographical references and index."
3	URN:ISBN:9781591582809	http://purl.org/dc/elements/1.1/title	"Using the Open Archives Initiative ..."
4	http://id.loc.gov/authorities/subjects/sh2007001751	http://www.w3.org/1999/02/22-rdf-syntax-ns#type	http://www.w3.org/2004/02/skos/core#Concept
5	URN:ISBN:9781591582809	http://purl.org/dc/elements/1.1/subject	http://id.loc.gov/authorities/subjects/sh2007001751
6	http://id.loc.gov/authorities/subjects/sh2007001751	http://www.w3.org/2004/02/skos/core#prefLabel	"Metadata harvesting."@en
7	http://id.loc.gov/authorities/subjects/sh2007001751	http://www.w3.org/2004/02/skos/core#inScheme	http://id.loc.gov/authorities/subjects
8	URN:ISBN:9781591582809	http://purl.org/dc/elements/1.1/language	"eng"
9	URN:ISBN:9781591582809	http://purl.org/dc/elements/1.1/creator	http://id.loc.gov/authorities/names/n2007017897
10	http://id.loc.gov/authorities/names/n2007017897	http://www.w3.org/2004/02/skos/core#prefLabel	"Foulonneau, Muriel"@en
11	http://id.loc.gov/authorities/names/n2007017897	http://www.w3.org/2004/02/skos/core#inScheme	http://id.loc.gov/authorities/names
12	URN:ISBN:9781591582809	http://purl.org/dc/elements/1.1/creator	http://id.loc.gov/authorities/names/n2007017895
13	http://id.loc.gov/authorities/names/n2007017895	http://www.w3.org/2004/02/skos/core#prefLabel	"Cole, Timothy W."@en
14	http://id.loc.gov/authorities/names/n2007017895	http://www.w3.org/2004/02/skos/core#inScheme	http://id.loc.gov/authorities/names
15	URN:ISBN:9781591582809	http://purl.org/dc/elements/1.1/date	"c2007."
16	URN:ISBN:9781591582809	http://purl.org/dc/elements/1.1/publisher	"Westport, Conn. :Libraries Unlimited,"
17	URN:ISBN:9781591582809	http://purl.org/dc/elements/1.1/format	"xv, 208 p. :ill. ;26 cm."
18	URN:ISBN:9781591582809	http://purl.org/dc/elements/1.1/type	"text"
19	URN:ISBN:9781591582809	http://purl.org/dc/elements/1.1/identifier	"URN:ISBN:1591582806"
20	URN:ISBN:9781591582809	http://purl.org/dc/elements/1.1/identifier	"URN:ISBN:9781591582809"

"Metadata Harvesting" and the concept URI "http://id.loc.gov/authorities/subjects/sh2007001751" in the Library of Congress Authorities and Vocabularies Service are provided.

The W3C maintains two Web services to facilitate the creation and use of RDF and RDFa. The RDFa Distiller Web services will read XHTML containing RDFa and "distill" out the embedded RDF triples. These can then be

FIGURE 12.21 Validation result of the distilled RDF XML displayed in graph.

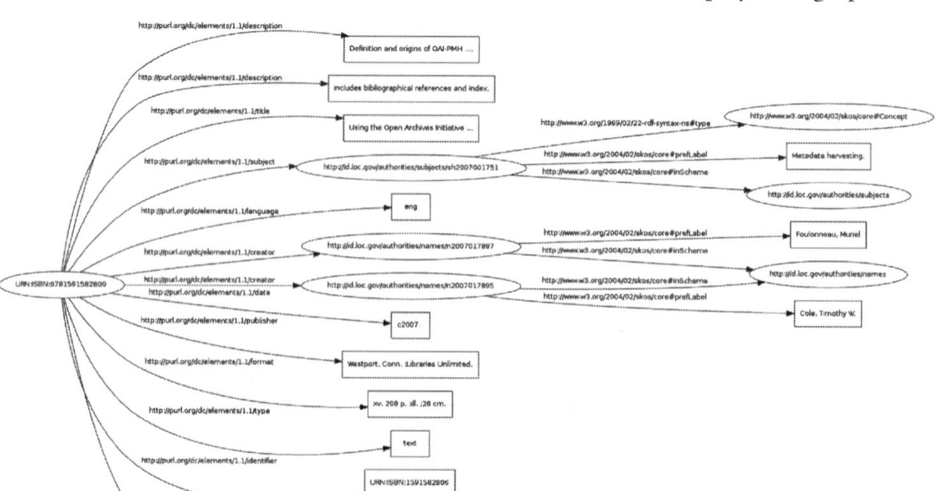

viewed as RDF serialized in XML (Figure 12.19). Compare to the RDF XML created directly from the MARCXML (Figure 12.16).

The W3C RDF Validation Service can both validate RDF serialized as XML and summarize the triples of the submitted RDF. Triples can be either listed (Figure 12.20) or displayed as a graph (Figure 12.21).

QUESTIONS AND TOPICS FOR DISCUSSION

1. Describe the meaning of `<domain>` and `<range>` as defined in the context of RDF Schema. How do `<domain>` and `<range>` values define or limit the values used as Subjects and Objects in an RDF XML statement?
2. In practical terms, what are the differences between XML Schema and RDF Schema?
3. What are the challenges of representing bibliographic records in RDF? Are metadata records conforming to standards like Simple Dublin Core easier to represent in RDF than metadata records conforming to MARCXML? Why?

SUGGESTIONS FOR EXERCISES

1. Create at least three simple RDF statements describing one of your favorite books, including a title, author, and other attributes facilitating discovery.
   a. Think about the domains and ranges that define the Predicates used in each statement.
   b. Serialize your descriptive statements about the book in XML format.
   c. Validate your RDF XML document using W3C RDF Validator. Select the option to view both triples and the RDF graph.
2. Enrich your book description with the use of an empty node in a graph in order to express an attribute of the book that can be broken down into a more granular set of statements.
3. Convert the RDF XML statement into XHTML + RDFa to display in a Web browser.

NOTES

1. http://www.w3.org/RDF.
2. http://www.w3.org/2001/sw.
3. http://www.w3.org/2005/Incubator/lld/XGR-lld-20111025.
4. http://id.loc.gov/authorities/names.html.
5. http://dublincore.org/documents/dces.
6. http://www.w3.org/TR/rdf-syntax-grammar.
7. http://id.loc.gov/authorities/names.html.
8. http://www.w3.org/TR/skos-primer.
9. http://vocab.org/changeset/schema.html.
10. http://www.w3.org/TR/REC-rdf-syntax/rdfxml.rnc.
11. http://www.w3.org/TR/rdf-schema.

12. http://www.w3.org/TR/xhtml11.
13. http://www.w3.org/RDF/Validator.
14. http://www.w3.org/2007/08/pyRdfa.
15. http://people.oregonstate.edu/~reeset/marcedit/html/index.php.
16. http://www.loc.gov/standards/marcxml/xslt/MARC21slim2RDFDC.xsl.
17. http://dublincore.org/documents/abstract-model.

REFERENCES

Adida, Ben, and Mark Birbeck, eds. 2008. *RDFa Primer: Bridging the Human and Data Webs* (W3C Working Group Note). Boston: World Wide Web Consortium. Available at: http://www.w3.org/TR/xhtml-rdfa-primer

Berners-Lee, Tim. 2009. *Axioms of Web Architecture*. Online. Available at: http://www.w3.org/DesignIssues/XML-Semantics.html

Berners-Lee, Tim. 1998. *Semantic Web: Why RDF Is More Than XML*. Available at: http://www.w3.org/DesignIssues/RDF-XML.html

Brickley, Dan, and R. V. Guha, eds. 2004. *RDF Vocabulary Description Language 1.0: RDF Schema* (W3C Recommendation). Boston: World Wide Web Consortium. Available at: http://www.w3.org/TR/rdf-schema

Dubin, David, Allen Renear, C. M. Sperberg-McQueen, and Claus Huitfeldt. 2003. "A Logic Programming Environment for Document Semantics and Inference." *Literary and Linguistic Computing: Journal of the Association for Literary and Linguistic Computing* 18, no. 2: 225–33.

Marola, Frank, and Eric Miller, eds. 2004. *RDF Primer* (W3C Recommendation). Boston: World Wide Web Consortium. Available at: http://www.w3.org/TR/rdf-primer

Tauberer, Joshua. 2008. *What Is RDF and What Is It Good For?* Available at http://www.rdfabout.com/intro/#Comparing%20RDF%20with%20XML

CHAPTER 13

XML and the Future of Descriptive Cataloging

Metadata records are key to opening up access to resources. Metadata make resources discoverable and accessible to patrons, now and in the future. Metadata can facilitate the use of information resources. Information-rich, well-structured, and properly granular metadata allow libraries to organize and manage their collections efficiently. As discussed in earlier chapters of this book, library technical service units have a long tradition of creating and providing high-quality metadata records (e.g., catalog records) for resources held in libraries. Although the roles and responsibilities of catalogers and metadata librarians remain firmly rooted in this tradition, the methods and technologies used to create and manage metadata have changed significantly in recent years. Catalogers and metadata librarians no longer work with only one type of metadata standard, create records exclusively by hand, deal only with a single system for library resource metadata, or work only within a technical service division. The scope of metadata has changed. Provenance and resource-linking metadata have become increasingly important with the advent of the Semantic Web[1] and Library Linked Open Data[2] initiatives. Dollar resources for creating and managing metadata are shrinking even as the volume of information requiring metadata is increasing. The evolution of cataloging methodology and metadata work flows in recent years is driven by changes in environment, the availability of emerging technologies, and new challenges faced by catalogers and metadata librarians.

XML has many features that make it a suitable technology for serializing, manipulating, repurposing, and exchanging library metadata. XML is an open standard that facilitates computer-assisted maintenance, organization, and use of structured information. Powerful in practice, XML is a conceptually straightforward, text-based format for representing structured information such as metadata. XML makes explicit the intellectual and hierarchical structure of metadata records in ways that computer applications can easily recognize. By using XML to serialize metadata records, catalogers and metadata librarians can preserve metadata record structure and expose the granularity of metadata records, thereby facilitating metadata processing and reuse.

Today, generic XML applications are used to author and serialize metadata as XML. Multiple standards exist to facilitate metadata interoperability and

XML metadata record interchange. XML Document Type Definitions (DTDs) and schemas have been created to describe many consensus-based community metadata grammars. As discussed and illustrated in previous chapters, XML DTDs or schemas currently exist for serializing bibliographic and bibliographic-like information in MAchine-Readable Cataloging (MARC), Metadata Object Description Schema (MODS), Dublin Core (both Simple and Qualified), Visual Resources Association (VRA) Core, Encoded Archival Description (EAD), and numerous other metadata grammars. XML validating parsers can be used to verify the conformance of metadata records to a specific XML DTD or schema or, through the use of XML Namespaces, to an application profile that borrows from multiple XML schemas. The integration of XML DTDs and schemas into library work flows helps to ensure the quality and consistency of metadata, even as metadata records today are increasingly created collaboratively by multiple units within a library and by librarians collaborating with domain experts and users. Style sheets conforming to the Extensible Stylesheet Language for Transformations (XSLT) standard can be used by XML processor applications to crosswalk metadata records from one schema to another or from XML to Extensible Hyper Text Markup Language (XHTML), such as to present metadata to an end user. XHTML with resource descriptions embedded in accord with community standard syntax and processing rules for embedding RDF through attributes (RDFa Version 1.1)[3] can be used to create views of metadata that are at once human-readable in a Web browser and machine actionable.

This concluding chapter revisits and summarizes many of the most important observations and conclusions that surfaced in earlier chapters of this introduction to and discussion of XML in the library. This summation begins with a review of some of the workplace changes and challenges faced by catalogers and metadata librarians today and their implications for the use of technologies such as XML. Next, a few of the ways that XML is being incorporated into library work flows are revisited. An end-to-end case study follows to illustrate the multiple ways XML is employed in the implementation of a specialized portal for discovering and using digitized Renaissance and Baroque emblem literature. This case study description is followed by a few concluding observations.

CHANGES AND CHALLENGES

Changing Environment

Libraries function today in a rapidly evolving environment, requiring librarians to reexamine their current work flows for collecting, curating, providing access to, and preserving the resources that they hold. Changes in user expectations and work flow parameters impact the ways catalogers and metadata librarians fulfill their roles and carry out their responsibilities.

Diverse formats of resources and metadata: Libraries have always collected and provided access to resources other than printed books. In many libraries, the volume of nonprint materials requiring cataloging has been increasing steadily since the 1960s, when microform was introduced on a large scale as a new carrier for information. More recently, libraries have been purchasing an increasing number of resources in digital format, including books, journals, games, videos, and sound recordings. In addition, libraries actively produce digital resources by retrospectively digitizing library print holdings in order to make these resources available to patrons regardless of where they are and when the resources are needed. Digitization of nonbook and special collection holdings, such as photos, multimedia, manuscripts, has become common. Access to and the use of resources in these diverse formats is facilitated by descriptive metadata records conforming to metadata standards other than MARC (Veve and Feltner-Reichert 2010). These alternative metadata semantics are more appropriate to the characteristics of the resources being described and the context in which these resources are housed and accessed. Additionally, libraries need to capture technical and preservation metadata for these resources in order to ensure long-term access. This process also requires the use of metadata semantics that go beyond the semantics of MARC. XML provides a common, hierarchically based syntactical structure onto which these different semantic sets can be layered.

Levels of access: As libraries commit to providing their resources in a digital format to improve accessibility and usefulness, they are digitizing not only books but also photographs, papers, and manuscripts held by archives and special collections units. Until now, these resources often have been described only at the collection, box, or folder level, not at the item level, limiting item-level access to these resources. User studies, such as in connection with next-generation library catalog design studies, confirm that users want more granular levels of access. This requires libraries to find ways to create or provide more granular metadata (Denton and Coysh 2011; Yang and Hofmann 2011). In order to meet expectations and make digitized resources accessible to users more granularly, libraries must modify cataloging and metadata work flows and must adopt non-MARC metadata standards that better support different levels and combinations of granularity. While some newer electronic books and electronic journals may include publisher-furnished metadata that provide users with chapter-level or article-level access, new approaches are required to create item-level metadata for resources previously described only at the folder level and for book resources digitized by the library now needing to be accessible more granularly (see Case Study 13.1). With its intrinsically ordered hierarchical approach to structured information, XML is a good carrier for metadata records that need to support multiple levels of granularity.

Increasing volume of resources to catalog: The number of digital resources that need to be cataloged and processed has increased as the number of resources that libraries purchase in digital format and digitize locally grows. This influx of resources to catalog requires catalogers and metadata librarians to modify existing work flows or create entirely new work flows to keep up. Metadata must be created for resources that are only available virtually to catalogers. The information needed for cataloging now comes in varied forms and from varied sources. In some cases, information provided by the publishers, vendors, or archives and special collection units, often in Microsoft Excel spreadsheet or FileMaker Pro format, must be used to create catalog records. The trick is to develop work flows and implement applications that can transform and merge different streams of digital data arriving from multiple sources into MARC format (or other metadata standards) and that can do so efficiently, with minimal oversight or human intervention, and in a timely manner. The use of XML can facilitate this.

Tools and systems: The integrated library system (ILS) on which many libraries have relied for the past few decades were designed with a traditional library setting in mind, that is, metadata described in MARC format and the online public access catalog (OPAC) as the single point of access to the bulk of a library's holdings. Already by 2007, according to the ACRL Kit *Metadata* (2007), locally developed resource management tools and other non-ILS applications were used more than turnkey ILS applications when it came to managing digital content held by academic and research libraries. This finding can be attributed to the fact that most ILS applications work only with metadata in MARC format and make it hard to provide access at multiple levels of granularity. This limitation of ILS applications explains why many newly created digital collections are represented only at the collection level in OPACs, not at the item level. Non-ILS applications designed with today's digital resources in mind enable varied levels of access and are better suited for searching and browsing digital library holdings. However, these systems require metadata descriptions conforming to metadata grammars other than MARC and therefore make it more difficult to search for traditional print and new digital resources simultaneously. Some digital resource management applications provide tools to amend the disjunction between traditional library finding tools and new digital content management systems. CONTENTdm®,[4] for example, makes it possible to export all item-level metadata to WorldCat[5] in Simple or Qualified Dublin Core format via its WorldCat Digital Collection Gateway.[6] On ingestion, metadata are transformed to MARC, which then allows item-level access to resources held in CONTENTdm via WorldCat. However, the Dublin Core to MARC transformation is not entirely satisfactory, and CONTENTdm-derived item-level cataloging metadata available in WorldCat are not ingested into local ILS applications. Recently, many libraries have successfully provided more integrated, granular levels of access to both print and digital holdings using a next-generation catalog application or Web-scale discovery system implemented on top of their existing ILS and non-ILS applications. (Serializing digital resource metadata in XML is sometimes a requirement to use these systems.) Even in these cases, however, metadata crosswalks are required, and to date, the ultimate results of such efforts vary widely in quality.

Need for having interoperable metadata: Increasingly, library resources can be discovered today through multiple methods of search. Library digital resources are found not only by using the library OPAC but also through search engines and portals such as Google, Flickr, Bing, Yahoo!, or similar services. Advanced technologies also make it easy to share or harvest XML-serialized metadata across library tools and other systems using protocols such as Open Archives Initiative Protocol for Metadata Harvesting (OAI-PMH),[7] Z39.50,[8] Search/Retrieve via URL,[9] or Really Simple Syndication feeds.[10] In order to make library resources more discoverable by users in aggregated environments, catalogers and metadata librarians must create shareable and interoperable metadata. Creating shareable and interoperable metadata implies the adoption and correct use of both metadata standards (schemas) that define how to organize and label metadata and data content standards that define how to format metadata values and use controlled vocabularies to populate the semantic elements of a metadata standard as discussed in Chapter 6. Although MARC has been used as a metadata standard for rich and structured descriptive metadata, it is not an ideal metadata standard for the Web environment. Libraries have to find a better way to create shareable and interoperable metadata using different, more Web-friendly metadata formats (Tennant 2004). Serializing metadata in XML is one way to help make metadata more Web friendly, and the use of XSLT to implement metadata crosswalks also can facilitate metadata interoperability.

User-generated metadata: Catalogers and metadata librarians are not the only people who create metadata today. Some Web services allow users to add tags or comments to metadata about resources. Many emerging next-generation cataloging applications, such as VuFind,[11] have features that enable users to add comments to descriptions of resources with which they are familiar. The photo management and sharing application Flicker[12] also allows users to add tags to and augment image descriptions. The Library of Congress has incorporated user-generated metadata from digital images it has posted to Flickr Commons[13] as a way to enhance its image metadata (Springer et al. 2008). Research projects, such as the Institute of Museum and Library Services Digital Content and Collections project,[14] and many individual libraries and cultural heritage institutions upload subsets of their digital images onto Flickr, in part to experiment with incorporating user-generated metadata into their regular metadata editing work flow to enhance and enrich resource descriptions. Although there is as yet no clear consensus as to the single best way to evaluate user-contributed metadata quality and integrate such metadata into established library cataloging work flows, it has become clear that it needs to be done. Technologies intrinsic to XML, like XML Namespaces, XML Schema, and XSLT, can facilitate metadata modularity, that is, the creation of XML metadata records that can contain both original and user-added metadata values while maintaining the provenance and source of all metadata values.

Challenges for Catalogers and Metadata Librarians

Changes in expectations and environments such as those described above translate into new challenges in bibliographic control that must be met by libraries. These changes have reshaped job descriptions in library technical services and cataloging units. The breadth and scope of work done by catalogers and metadata librarians are expanding, as are knowledge requirements for these positions. Catalogers and metadata librarians today are:

Catalogers and metadata librarians are becoming conversant with more than MARC: The MARC standard remains an important metadata grammar, but it is no longer as dominant in the library universe as it once was; it is now one metadata standard among many in the library domain. Metadata records for many newly created and purchased digital resources are still authored in accord with the MARC standard. However, MARC is not suitable for all digital resources curated by libraries. As discussed in Chapters 5 and 6, libraries have begun using other metadata standards, such as Simple and Qualified Dublin Core, MODS, VRA Core, and EAD, to describe digital resources. Metadata and data content standards for description are now selected in accordance with the characteristics of the resources being described. The tools and content management systems from which the resources being described are expected to be accessed are also a consideration. MARC and the *Anglo-American Cataloguing Rules*, Second Edition[15] have long been dominant in library contexts, but today, use of different metadata standards and different data content standards is rapidly increasing. Catalogers and metadata librarians must make decisions about which metadata standard and data content standard to use for authoring metadata about specific collections and resources. In order to make informed decisions, catalogers and metadata librarians must have working knowledge of multiple data content standards, emerging non-MARC metadata standards, and trends regarding the use of these standards.

Catalogers and metadata librarians are learning how to author other types of metadata: Traditionally, the focus of most library catalogers and metadata librarians has been on bibliographic description. With increasingly diverse formats of digital resources, libraries today also need to create and maintain technical, administrative, and preservation metadata, as well as descriptive metadata, to ensure long-term resource access and to maintain resource provenance. Recently, the National Science Foundation (NSF) required that proposals it receives include a supplementary document describing the project's long-term Data Management Plans (DMP). The NSF anticipates an expanding role for academic libraries in preserving and managing data created by NSF-funded projects (NSF 2011). To meet these expectations and to be in a position to contribute to DMPs developed by campus faculty, catalogers and metadata librarians in academic libraries must be prepared to work with library information technology units and subject specialists to develop appropriate descriptive, technical, administrative, and preservation metadata guidelines for both traditional and nontraditional categories of information resources.

Catalogers and metadata librarians are describing resources at multiple levels of granularity: In approaching the creation of descriptive metadata records for digital resources, catalogers and metadata librarians now also need to decide what granularity of description is best to meet users' needs. The levels of access that libraries provide to information resources have changed. The granularity of resource description is an important consideration if a goal of a project is to integrate well with emerging Library Linked Open Data standards and best practices.[16] Users want access to resources discoverable in a library's OPAC or next-generation catalog system that spans more than just the book and journal title levels of granularity ("Redefining the Academic Library" 2011). While a collection of digital resources needs a collection-level metadata to increase the discoverability of the collection as a whole, item-level metadata enabling each item in the collection to be discovered and accessed is also desirable. As described in Case Study 9-1, the *Emblematica Online* project uses a metadata standard called SPINE[17] to describe digitized emblem books at two different levels of granularity: book and emblem. SPINE is a good example of an application profile that mixes multiple metadata standards to describe digitized resources at multiple levels of granularity. Depending on the project and resources, catalogers and metadata librarians must know what metadata standards are most appropriate for the resources and levels of description.

Catalogers and metadata librarians are collaborating more broadly: Cataloging is becoming an increasingly collaborative activity. While collaborative cataloging is well established (e.g., cooperative cataloging through the Online Computer Library Center), user expectations and the capability of technology to facilitate the collaborative authoring of XML metadata records is prompting even more collaboration, including with collaborators outside library technical services. Catalogers and metadata librarians must now work closely with other units, such as with information technology units providing support for authoring and editing software and systems, with special collections units for subject knowledge and collection development, or with users outside the library altogether who have expertise in contributing useful metadata. Catalogers and metadata librarians actively share their experiences and institution- or consortium-wide best practices with others through vehicles such as the *Digital Library Federation/Aquifer Implementation Guidelines for Shareable MODS Records*,[18] *Best Practices for OAI Data Provider Implementations*,[19] and *Best Practices for the CONTENTdm Users*.[20] In addition, as more libraries develop joint projects to share as well as expand their resources, cataloging records are created and managed in shared environments in systems such as CONTENTdm that intrinsically support distributed cataloging and collection development.

EXPLOITING XML IN LIBRARY WORK FLOWS

In order to respond to challenges and changes such as described above, libraries need to exploit technologies such as XML. The availability of powerful, general purpose XML tools and associated standards such as XSLT and the *W3C XML*

Schema Definition Language[21] can make library metadata work flows more efficient and more scalable while at the same time allowing catalogers to create better, more reusable, and more interoperable, enriched, and enhanced metadata. Ultimately, this improves the experience of library users. As described in Chapters 1 and 3, XML is not a metadata standard but rather a meta-markup language into which metadata records may be serialized. By design, XML is capable of facilitating the creation, use, and sharing of structured information. When metadata are serialized as XML, it becomes easier to implement metadata crosswalks, validate metadata records, and extract and reuse substructures and values contained in metadata records. XML provides a common syntactic base that spans metadata standards and data content standards, making it easier to support and adapt work flows that span multiple metadata formats.

XML facilitates metadata interoperability: Metadata interoperability requires both syntactic interoperability, the basic ability to recognize and exchange metadata records, and semantic interoperability, the ability to understand the meaning in whole or in part of metadata records exchanged. In the library domain, syntactic and semantic interoperability have often been conflated. Thus, traditional MARC specifies both semantics (Main Entry, Added Entries, Imprint, and so on) and syntax (a specific magnetic tape streaming serialization format). The use of XML for syntactic interoperability allows libraries to decouple syntax and semantics. For example, OAI-PMH (which is today routinely used by libraries to exchange XML metadata records) is an XML-based protocol focused primarily on syntactic metadata interoperability. OAI-PMH can be used to exchange XML metadata records conforming to many different metadata grammars. The job of OAI-PMH is to get the XML metadata records to the service provider. Once that is achieved, XML namespaces and the ordered hierarchy of content objects approach of serializing metadata inherent to XML facilitate semantic interoperability. XML applications that understand one specific set of metadata semantics (i.e., one namespace) can easily extract only those values it considers actionable and ignore the rest (i.e., the values of elements associated with other namespaces). This allows XML metadata records to be created that can be exchanged with multiple metadata-consuming applications. Each metadata-consuming application extracts values of interest from the XML records provided and ignores the rest. Finally, the availability of XML DTDs, XML schemas, and Resource Description Format (RDF) schemas allows implementers to share descriptions of metadata semantics in a standard way, further facilitating interoperability. In particular, the association of unique namespace identifiers with an XML Schema Definition (XSD), a set of metadata semantics (e.g., http://purl.org/dc/elements/1.1/ is the namespace identifier for Simple Dublin Core), facilitates universal recognition of the semantics used in XML metadata records exchanged.

XML improves the efficiency of metadata creation: XML facilitates the design of metadata creation work flows. As discussed in Case Study 11.2 in Chapter 11, the University of Illinois Library uses XSLT style sheets in its work flow to create catalog records for books from its collection digitized by the Open Content Alliance (OCA). The starting point for this work flow is MARCXML records for the print volumes being digitized. Similarly, the University of Michigan Library uses XML and related technologies in its metadata creation work flow for digital resources (Powell 2008). These two examples illustrate how XML and its auxiliary technologies can help make the metadata creation work flow more efficient, especially important as libraries need to deal with an increasing number of resources requiring cataloging.

XML facilitates reuse and repurposing of metadata: As discussed in Chapter 11, XPath and XSLT style sheets can be used to transform XML metadata records into other formats and to extract values from XML metadata records. Metadata values for specific attributes can be extracted and combined with metadata values from other sources. The work flow described in Case Study 13.1 (see also Case Study 9.1 in Chapter 9) illustrates how XML metadata records conforming to the SPINE metadata schema can be created by combining elements and attributes from multiple sources (e.g., a MARC catalog record and a spreadsheet) and then manipulated in multiple ways for new functions (e.g., disseminated via OAI-PMH, transformed with XSLT to create multiple views of the metadata, and transformed with XSLT to populate a relational database). Metadata reuse and repurposing using XML and XSLT is at once powerful and efficient.

CASE STUDY 13.1
Emblematica Online

Synopsis: SPINE is a metadata grammar developed for describing emblem books and emblems contained in emblem books. The XSD for SPINE was introduced and discussed in Case Study 9.1. The University of Illinois Library creates and uses SPINE XML metadata records for emblem books as part of the *Emblematica Online* project.[22] Since SPINE XML metadata records contain both book- and emblem-level metadata, creating these records requires merging metadata from multiple sources. Once created, SPINE XML metadata records are enriched using a locally developed XML-based application. This application adds links to several additional digital derivatives of original page image scans. Subsequently, added Iconclass[23] subject entries link to machine-actionable RDF-XML heading descriptions, enabling users to use the Iconclass hierarchy to discover resources. Enriched metadata records are used in multiple ways to support end-user access to digitized emblem resources. Individual volume-level SPINE XML metadata records are dynamically transformed to XHTML for viewing by library users. XSLT also is used to transform SPINE records into Structured Query Language (SQL[24]) insert statements in order to populate a relational database with metadata values and portions of XML metadata records. This database is then used to support discovery of digitized emblem resources at multiple levels of granularity.
Illustrates: Combining metadata from multiple sources using an XSLT style sheet; creating XHTML using an XSLT style sheet; using XML metadata records to support end-user search and discovery.

FIGURE 13.1 Example of a book-published emblem (Murer 1622), courtesy of the Rare Book and Manuscript Library at the University of Illinois at Urbana-Champaign and the *Emblematica Online* Project.

Renaissance and Baroque emblem books flourished in Europe as a popular literary genre from the mid-sixteenth to the early eighteenth century. Emblems (Figure 13.1) are compound (integrating text and graphics) and highly contextual, often influenced by contemporaneous events, such as the Reformation and the Thirty Years' War. Emblem creators drew inspiration from such diverse sources as the Bible, classical antiquity, fables, mythology, science, and medicine. As objects of research, emblems straddle multiple scholarly domains, such as art and cultural history, literature, semiotics, religious studies, and political science.

Today, the Herzog August Bibliothek (HAB) in Wolfenbüttel, Germany, and the University of Illinois at Urbana-Champaign have two of the largest collections of emblem books in the world. In 2009, the University of Illinois and HAB received a grant from the U.S. National Endowment for the Humanities and the German *Deutsche Forschungsgemeinschaft* for the *Emblematica Online* project. With these resources, the two libraries have digitized nearly 730 emblem books and created a prototype for a community-based next-generation OpenEmblem portal to provide multicollection access to digitized emblem resources. XML technologies have been essential to implementing the project's metadata strategy and this new prototype portal.

When the University of Illinois Library began working with the OCA to digitize emblem books housed in its Rare Book and Manuscript Library, the library's OPAC system already contained book-level MARC catalog records for these items. However, book-level records alone are not sufficient to support all facets of emblem scholarship. Many individual emblem books contain more than 100 emblems, and a few contain more than 1,000. While emblem books as a whole are studied by scholars and while the bibliographic context of an emblem is important, individual emblems and components of individual emblems are also objects of scholarly inquiry. Emblem scholars want to take advantage of the fact that digitization makes it easier to discover and retrieve individual components of a digitized resource. *Picturae*, the graphic elements of emblems, are important examples of Renaissance and Baroque imagery and symbolism. The textual components of emblems play specific roles in analyzing and interpreting emblems and can be targets of research on their own. Therefore, subbook levels of descriptive metadata are needed. As described in Case Study 9.1, the SPINE metadata schema supports description at two levels of granularity (the book and the emblem) that support three levels of access (the book, the emblem, and the Iconclass).

Creating SPINE Metadata Records for Each Emblem Using XSLT

The overall *Emblematica Online* metadata work flow as implemented at the University of Illinois (depicted in Figure 13.2) involves multiple XSLT transformations and the integration of metadata from two sources. Basic emblem descriptive properties—emblem number (in its book), starting page number for each emblem (a single emblem may span as many as 10 pages), emblem

FIGURE 13.2 *Emblematica Online* Project metadata work flow.

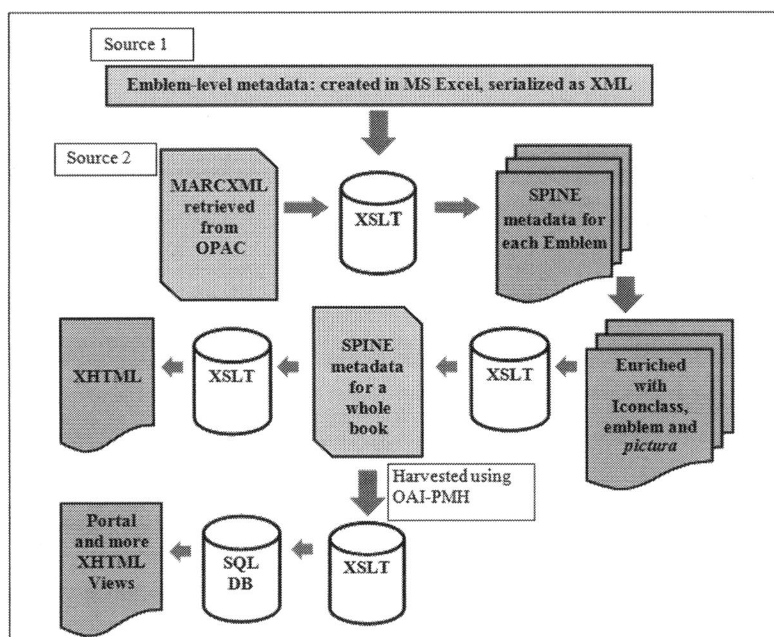

FIGURE 13.3 Excerpt of a spreadsheet containing emblem-level descriptive metadata.

	B	C	D	E	F	G	H
1	Book Title:	Emblemata miscella nova...					
2	Author:	Murer, Christoph					
3		Bib ID:	2895515			Last Update:	10/25/2010 20:29
4		OCA ID:	xliequadragintae00mure				Unregistered
5							
6	Page No.	Emblem No.	Motto (Early German)	Motto (Latin)	Motto (Other)	Other Language	Motto (Normalised German)
7		I.	Alchimisterey:	Alchimia.			Alchemie:
8		II.	Ampt eines Speiszmeisters:	Officium probi oeconomi.			Amt eines Speisemeisters:
9		III.	Bilgerschafft der Christen.	Peregrinatio Christianorum.			Pilgerschaft der Christen.
10		IV.	Brunn desz Lebens.	Fons vitae.			Brunn des Lebens.
11		V.	Burgerliche einigkeit die beste Rinckm	Concordia civium tutissimum praesidium.			Bürgerliche Einigkeit, die beste Ringmauer.
12		VI.	Comoedi.	Comoedia.			Komödie.

motto transcription(s), and so on—are recorded in a Microsoft Excel spreadsheet (Figure 13.3). This spreadsheet is populated not by metadata librarians but rather by emblem scholars and their graduate research assistants using a template created by librarians. The spreadsheet is saved in a Microsoft-specific XML format (Figure 13.4) to facilitate subsequent work flow steps. Volume-level bibliographic information is retrieved from the University of Illinois OPAC via a service (built using generic XML programming libraries) that dynamically transforms traditional MARC records to MARCXML. These two sources of metadata are merged using XSLT to create a SPINE metadata record for each individual emblem in a volume.

The XSLT that merges spreadsheet and MARCXML metadata and creates SPINE XML metadata records for each individual emblem in an emblem book has three main functions:

1. Fetch the MARCXML record for the book containing the emblem (using the XSL `document` function) and transform this record into a `<teiheader>` node in the result-tree to create the book-level bibliographic part of the SPINE XML metadata record.
2. Create a `<copyDesc>` node to contain copy-specific information (owning library, which copy, and so on) about the print volume actually digitized and add this element to the result-tree (this part of the transform relies on a combination of MARCXML values and input parameters).
3. Create an `<emblem>` node in the result-tree to contain emblem-specific metadata from the Microsoft Excel spreadsheet.

The XSLT that creates the individual emblem SPINE XML metadata records conforms to XSLT version 2.0.[25] XSLT version 2.0 was developed in parallel with XPATH 2.0. XSLT version 2.0 allows one style sheet that generates multiple result-trees, each serialized as a separate XML file. This allows the XSLT to create an entire book's worth of SPINE XML metadata records at one time, which is feasible since each individual spreadsheet provides all the emblem-level metadata (one emblem per row) for an entire book. Each individual emblem SPINE XML metadata record is saved to a book-level folder. The XSLT includes a global parameter, `<xsl:param name="first EmbRegNo" select="first_emblem_id"/>`. This parameter is passed into the XSLT and used to seed construction of individual emblem identifiers. Each

FIGURE 13.4 A row from spreadsheet in Figure 12.3 serialized as XML.

```
...
<Row ss:AutoFitHeight="0">
  <Cell ss:Formula="=NOT(AND(ISBLANK(RC[3]),ISBLANK(RC[4]),ISBLANK(RC[5]),
                      ISBLANK(RC[7])))">
    <Data ss:Type="Boolean">1</Data><NamedCell ss:Name="EmblemYesNo"/></Cell>
  <Cell ss:Index="3"><Data ss:Type="String">I.</Data>
    <NamedCell ss:Name="Print_Area"/><NamedCell ss:Name="citeNo"/></Cell>
  <Cell><Data ss:Type="String">Alchimisterey:</Data>
    <NamedCell ss:Name="Print_Area"/><NamedCell ss:Name="Motto_EarlyGerman"/></Cell>
  <Cell><Data ss:Type="String">Alchimia.</Data>
    <NamedCell ss:Name="Print_Area"/><NamedCell ss:Name="Motto_Latin"/></Cell>
  <Cell ss:StyleID="s33"><NamedCell ss:Name="Print_Area"/>
    <NamedCell ss:Name="Motto_Other"/></Cell>
  <Cell ss:Index="8"><Data ss:Type="String">Alchemie:</Data>
    <NamedCell ss:Name="Print_Area"/><NamedCell ss:Name="Motto_NormGerman"/></Cell>
  <Cell ss:StyleID="s34"><NamedCell ss:Name="Print_Area"/>
    <NamedCell ss:Name="EmblemID"/></Cell>
  <Cell ss:StyleID="s34"><NamedCell ss:Name="Print_Area"/>
    <NamedCell ss:Name="EmblemURL"/></Cell>
  <Cell ss:StyleID="s34"><NamedCell ss:Name="Print_Area"/>
    <NamedCell ss:Name="PicturaURL"/></Cell>
...
</Row>
...
```

emblem identifier is registered in an emblem registry maintained by the University of Illinois Library at Urbana–Champaign. The XSLT includes an element (`<xsl:output name="emblemLevel" method="xml" indent="yes"/>`) that specifies the result-document model (`"emblemLevel"`) to be used when saving each result-tree to a file.

The style sheet uses XSLT templates to simplify the implementation of the transform. The top-level template, which matches on the root of the source-tree, works as a master plan for the transform. As shown in Figure 13.5, this template invokes the other two templates using the `<xsl:call-template>` element. Notice that these templates are called with parameters. For convenience, the master template instantiates and makes use of six variables: `<bibID>`, `<uiuHdl>`, `<OCAId>`, `<marcURL>`, `<marcFile>`, and `<tHd>`. Note that the value of one of these variables (`$tHd`) is the result of calling the "`tHd`" template. Another of the variables (`$marcFile`) is the complete MARCXML record for the emblem book being described.

Figure 13.6 shows the top part of the template that adds emblem-level information to the book-level metadata and then saves the complete result-tree to the file system. Emblem-level values retrieved from the XML copy of the Excel spreadsheet are passed to this template each time it is invoked in the form of template-specific parameters. An incomplete example of the emblem node of the resulting single-emblem SPINE XML metadata record is shown in Figure 13.7. Note that the XML shown in Figure 13.7 has been

FIGURE 13.5 A top-level XSLT template (calls two other templates).

```
<xsl:template match="/">
  <xsl:variable name="bibID"
                 select="normalize
space(/ss:Workbook/ss:Worksheet[@ss:Name='TheBook']/ss:Table/ss:Row[3]/
ss:Cell[./ss:NamedCell[@ss:Name='Motto_EarlyGerman']]/ss:Data)"/>
  <xsl:variable name="uiuHdl"
            select="normalize-
space(/ss:Workbook/ss:Worksheet[@ss:Name='TheBook']/ss:Table/ss:Row[4]/
ss:Cell[./ss:NamedCell[@ss:Name='Motto_EarlyGerman']]/@ss:HRef)"/>
  <xsl:variable name="OCAId"
       select="normalize-
space(/ss:Workbook/ss:Worksheet[@ss:Name='TheBook']/ss:Table/ss:Row[4]/
ss:Cell[./ss:NamedCell[@ss:Name='Motto_EarlyGerman']]/ss:Data)"/>
  <xsl:variable name="marcURL"
select="concat('http://dli.grainger.uiuc.edu/GetMARC/one.aspx/',$bibID,'.xml')"/>
   <xsl:variable name="marcFile" select="document($marcURL)"/>
   <xsl:variable name="tHd">
     <xsl:call-template name="teiHead">
       <xsl:with-param name="marcRec" select="$marcFile"/>
       <xsl:with-param name="bidID" select="$bibID"/>
     </xsl:call-template>
   </xsl:variable>
   <xsl:for-each
select="/ss:Workbook/ss:Worksheet[@ss:Name='TheBook']/ss:Table/ss:Row[position()>6]
[ss:Cell[ss:NamedCell[@ss:Name='EmblemYesNo']]!=0]">
    <xsl:call-template name="makeEmblem">
        <xsl:with-param name="eNO" select="position()"/>
        <xsl:with-param name="wID" select="concat('uiu',$bibID)"/>
        <xsl:with-param name="hdl" select="$uiuHdl"/>
        <xsl:with-param name="tHdr" select="$tHd"/>
        <xsl:with-param name="OCAfolder" select="$OCAId"/>
    </xsl:call-template>
  </xsl:for-each>
</xsl:template>
```

FIGURE 13.6 A part of the "makeEmblem" XSLT template.

```
<xsl:template name="makeEmblem" xmlns="http://diglib.hab.de/rules/schema/emblem">
         <xsl:param name="eNO"/>
         <xsl:param name="wID"/>
         <xsl:param name="hdl"/>
         <xsl:param name="tHdr"/>
         <xsl:param name="OCAfolder"/>
         <xsl:variable name="eID"
             select="format-number(number($eNO)+number($firstEmbRegNo)-1, '000000')"/>
         <xsl:result-document
 href="file://///libgrvaruna/emblemimages/{$OCAfolder}/emblem{$eID}.xml"
             format="emblemLevel">
...
```

FIGURE 13.7 Emblem-level SPINE metadata record.

```
...
<emblem xmlns:xlink="http://www.w3.org/1999/xlink" xml:id="E000944" citeNo="I."
        xlink:href="http://djatoka.grainger.illinois.edu/index.html?url=http://
emblemimages.grainger.illinois.edu/xliequadragintae00mure/JP2Processed/
xliequadrag intae00mure_0013.jp2&amp;amp;crop=false"
        globalID="http://hdl.handle.net/10111/EmblemRegistry:E000944">
        <motto>
             <transcription xml:lang="de">Alchimisterey:<normalisation
xml:lang="de">Alchemie:</normalisation>
             </transcription>
             <transcription xml:lang="la">Alchimia.</transcription>
        </motto>
        <pictura xml:id="E000944_P1"
               xlink:href="http://djatoka.grainger.illinois.edu/
adore-djatoka/resolver?url_ver=Z39.88-
2004&amp;rft_id=http://emblemimages.grainger.illinois.edu/xliequadragintae00mure/JP2Pro-
cessed/xliequadragintae00mure_0013.jp2&amp;svc_id=info:lanl-repo/svc/getRegio-
n&amp;svc_val_fmt=info:ofi/fmt:kev:mtx:jpeg2000&amp;svc.format=image/jpeg&amp;
svc.level=5&amp;svc.rotate=0&amp;svc.region=564,180,1492,1968">
        <iconclass rdf:about="http://www.iconclass.org/rkd/31A247">
               <skos:notation>31A247</skos:notation>
               <skos:prefLabel>looking over the shoulder</skos:prefLabel>
        </iconclass>
        <iconclass
rdf:about="http://www.iconclass.org/rkd/31A2531(+9161)">
               <skos:notation>31A2531(+9161)</skos:notation>
               <skos:prefLabel>hand(s) bent towards the head (+
protecting)</skos:prefLabel>
        </iconclass>
...
```

enriched by adding subject headings from the Iconclass thesaurus to each emblem's *pictura* (graphic element). Iconclass is a vocabulary designed for classifying images, that is, works of art, book illustrations, reproductions, photographs, and so on, and is used by museums and art institutions around the world. Links to derivative views of each emblem and each emblem's *pictura* have also been added.

Conditional Transformation by Proxy

With a second XSLT style sheet, the individual emblem SPINE XML metadata records are combined to create a SPINE XML metadata record for a complete emblem book. The XSLT style sheet used for this process embeds fragments of an XSLT style sheet created by the Digital Library Federation Aquifer project[26] to convert MARCXML to MODS XML. Consistent with a recent agreement between HAB and the University of Illinois, the MODS XML is used in the complete book SPINE XML metadata record instead of the book-level bibliographic description (<teiHeader>) used in the single-emblem SPINE metadata records. After fetching and converting the emblem book's MARCXML record to a MODS node in the result-tree and then adding a <copyDesc> node (which is copied intact from the first single-emblem SPINE metadata record), the XSLT style sheet grabs the <emblem> element of each single-emblem SPINE metadata record associated with the book, adding each to the result-tree.

Complete book SPINE metadata records are used in multiple ways in the *Emblematica Online* project. As discussed in Case Study 11.2 in Chapter 11, an XHTML page can be generated from an XML metadata record by embedding an `xml-stylesheet` processing instruction at the top of the record specifying an XSLT style sheet for transforming the XML metadata record into XHTML. When project staff use a Web browser to retrieve a single-emblem or a complete book-level SPINE metadata record from one Library Web server, the XSLT style sheet on that Web server allows the Web browser to transform the SPINE XML metadata record into an XHTML view of the book and emblem metadata, as referenced by the processing instruction in the XML metadata record (see Figure 13.8).

The link to the XSLT style sheet specified in an `xml-stylesheet` processing instruction can be absolute or relative to the root of the Web server or relative to the location of the SPINE metadata record. The SPINE metadata records created for the Emblematica Online project include `xml-stylesheet` processing instructions that specify the location of an XSLT style sheet using an address relative to the Web server root. This allows conditional transformation by proxy. The same SPINE metadata records behind the

FIGURE 13.8 XHTML page created from SPINE metadata record.

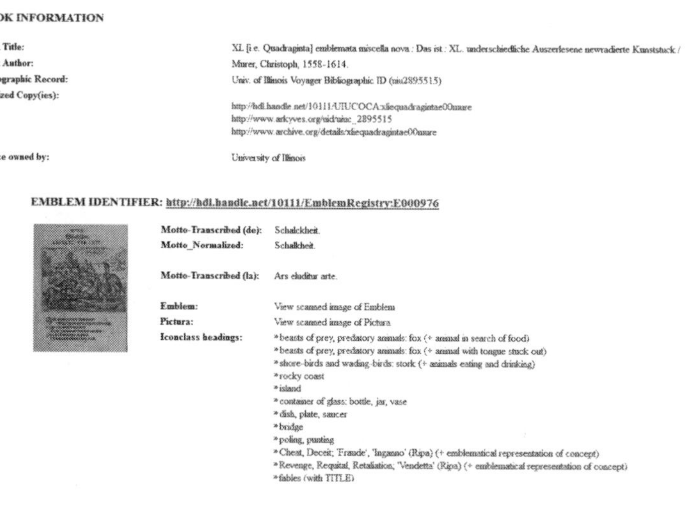

XHTML view shown in Figure 13.8 also are made available by a proxy Web service from a second Library Web server. The XSLT style sheet on this Web server also transforms the SPINE metadata record into an XHTML page; however, this second XSLT style sheet adds JavaScript that allows the SPINE metadata record to be annotated. In this way, by making the XML metadata records available by proxy from another Web server hosting a different XSLT style sheet, the same XML metadata records can be used both by staff needing to review emblem book descriptions and by end users involved in digitized emblematica annotation.

The OpenEmblem Portal

Once digitization and metadata creation for the *Emblematica Online* project were under way, researchers at the University of Illinois and HAB turned their attention to the design and execution of a shared portal to provide enhanced discovery and access over their combined digital emblem holdings. Complete book SPINE XML metadata records also are used to support this browse-and-discovery portal. Behind the scenes, the *Emblematica Online* prototype OpenEmblem Portal relies on metadata residing in an SQL-conformant relational database. This database is populated by harvesting University of Illinois and HAB complete book SPINE XML metadata records from OAI-PMH data providers maintained by or on behalf of these institutions. Harvested SPINE XML metadata records are then transformed by yet another XSLT style sheet. This XSLT style sheet transforms each complete book SPINE XML metadata record into a series of SQL insert statements that are then executed to load the book-level and emblem-level metadata into the SQL database. This database is then used to support end-user search and discovery over the combined digital emblem book holdings of HAB and the University of Illinois.

Figures 13.9 through 13.11 are screen shots of an early prototype version of the *Emblematica Online* OpenEmblem Portal. As illustrated in these three screen shots, the design of this portal takes advantage of the SPINE schema design to support user access to digitized content at both the book and the emblem level. A tabbed motif is used. Default search is by keyword, but options are provided also to search over book metadata only, over emblem metadata only, or over both book and emblem metadata simultaneously. When displaying book-level search results, basic bibliographic metadata for matching titles are displayed in the first tab, labeled "Book Results." If an item from the book result list is selected, a complete display of all book-level metadata for that item is presented in this same tab, relabeled "Book Details" (Figure 13.9). This display includes a link to the digitized volume at the University of Illinois or HAB, a link to the catalog record (at the owning institution) for the print volume digitized, and links to views of digital derivatives held at other locations when applicable.

FIGURE 13.9 Presentation of book-level bibliographic description as viewed in the prototype portal's "Book Details" tab.

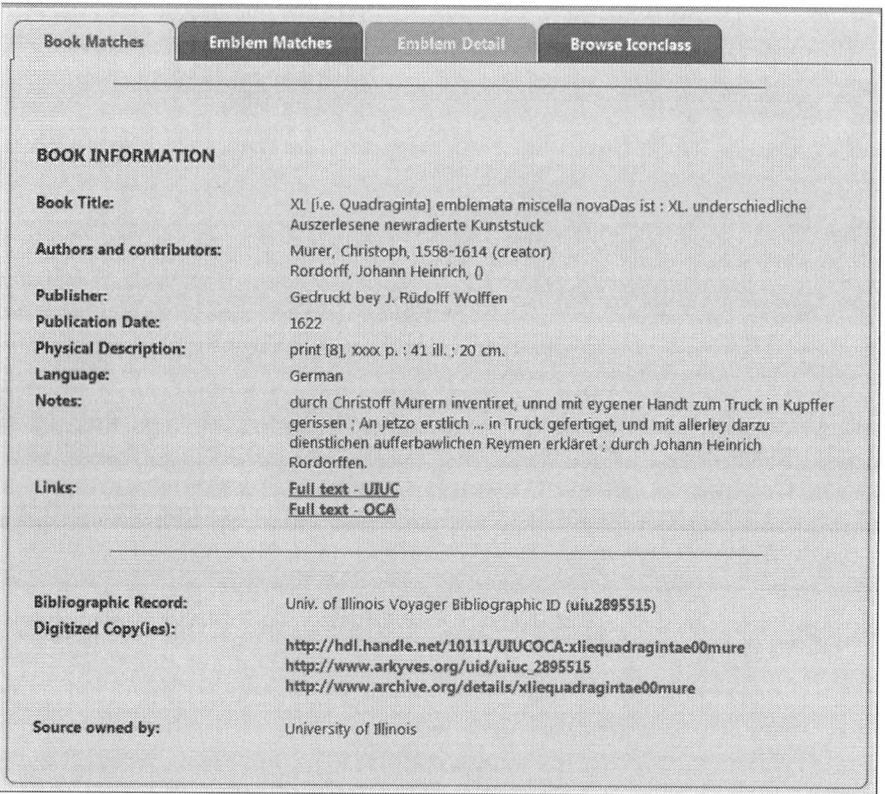

When browsing emblem-level search results or the list of all emblems in a book, a second tab, labeled "Emblem Matches," provides thumbnail representations of emblem *picturae* (Figure 13.10). Selecting an item from this display will activate a third tab, labeled "Emblem Detail" (Figure 13.11). This tab displays complete emblem-level metadata. The detailed display of an emblem metadata record includes a transcribed motto and potentially other transcribed or normalized text associated with the emblem (*subscriptio*, *commentatio*, and so on), a link to the description of the emblem book containing that emblem, the globally unique identifier of the emblem, links to the first page of the emblem on the HAB Web site or to a single-image complete view of the emblem on the University of Illinois Web site, links to additional component views of the emblem when available (e.g., to the emblem's *pictura*), and links to Iconclass headings that have been assigned to the emblem.

The tabbed interface approach is designed to allow users to switch between granularities of emblem-related resources easily and quickly. For example, a user can search for emblems by key word, view detailed metadata for one of

FIGURE 13.10 In the "Emblem Matches" tab, the prototype portal displays emblem *picturae* and mottos.

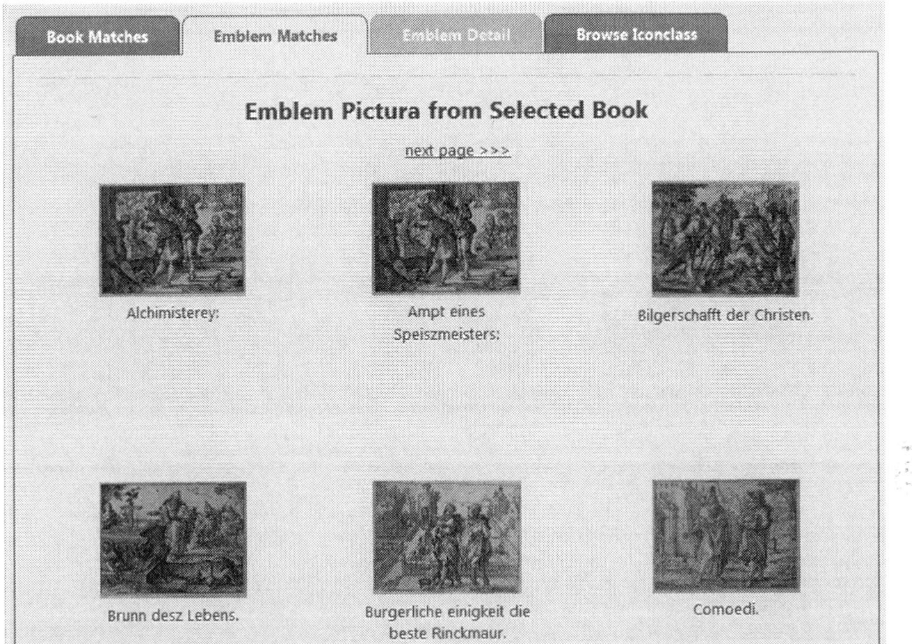

the emblems discovered, link to the detailed record for the book containing that emblem, see the *pictura* and motto for each of the other emblems contained in that book, select a different emblem to view in detail, and so on. A fourth tab is provided for browsing Iconclass subject headings. This tab is activated by selecting an Iconclass heading from the detailed view of an emblem. RDF-XML descriptions of each Iconclass heading can be fetched from a Web service at the Iconclass site (Figure 13.12).

Note that preferred labels in multiple languages are provided for each Iconclass heading. The Iconclass thesaurus is hierarchical, so narrower terms (immediate children) and a broader term (immediate parent) are also provided in each heading's RDF-XML description. The portal processes these XML elements to create a display of the user selected heading in the context of the Iconclass hierarchy. Users can then navigate the Iconclass hierarchy from that point to find another Iconclass heading on which to search.

Figure 13.13 shows one way the OpenEmblem Portal uses the RDF-XML Iconclass heading descriptions to facilitate end-user browsing of digitized emblem resources. In the scenario illustrated, a user has found an emblem of interest (Vogel 1649, 56–57). One of the Iconclass headings assigned to the *pictura* of this emblem is 25F33(EAGLE)(+5245), "predatory birds: eagle (+ animal(s) holding something)." As illustrated in Figure 13.13, the user can move from the display of detailed emblem metadata to a view of the Iconclass

FIGURE 13.11 In the "Emblem Details" tab, the prototype portal displays emblem-level description, including motto and Iconclass headings assigned to the emblem's *pictura*.

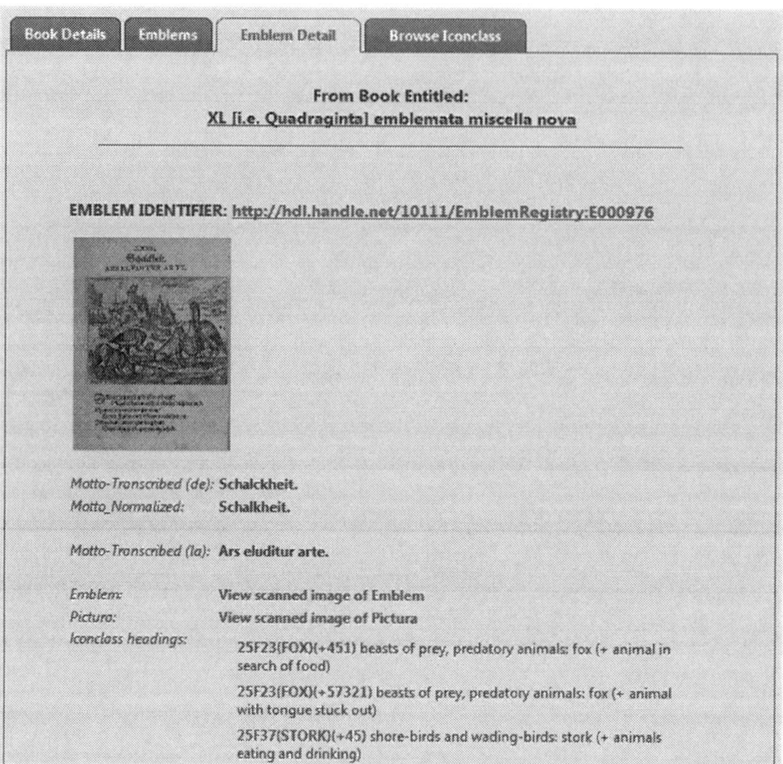

hierarchy centered on this particular Iconclass heading (i.e., under the fourth tab of the interface). The user may then browse up or down the hierarchy (in any of the languages supported by Iconclass), at any point selecting a heading for a new search of the portal. In this instance, the user browses up the hierarchy to 25F, "animals," then down the hierarchy to search on 25F23(. . .), "beasts of prey, predatory animals (with NAME)." This search retrieves several *picturae* and associated emblems, including the *picturae* shown in Figure 13.13. Iconclass headings assigned to emblem *picturae* are indexed locally in English and in the modern version of the language of the emblem. Notation codes are also indexed to take advantage of the hierarchical structure of Iconclass codes such that searches retrieve *picturae* having exactly matching headings and any *picturae* having a heading below the requested heading in the Iconclass hierarchy.

CLOSING THOUGHTS

Cataloging and metadata work flows in libraries continue to evolve. The advent of the Web and dramatic increases in digital content curated by libraries have helped to drive this evolution. Emerging technologies and tight budgets are also factors. By exploiting technologies like XML, catalogers and metadata librarians are learning to do more with less.

FIGURE 13.12 Iconclass heading 25F33 (EAGLE) described in RDF-XML.

```
<rdf:RDF>
  <rdf:Description rdf:about="http://iconclass.org/25F33%28EAGLE%29">
    <rdf:type rdf:resource="http://www.w3.org/2004/02/skos/core#Concept"/>
       <skos:prefLabel xml:lang="fr">oiseaux de proie : aigle</skos:prefLabel>
       <skos:prefLabel xml:lang="en">predatory birds: eagle</skos:prefLabel>
       <skos:prefLabel xml:lang="cn">predatory birds: eagle</skos:prefLabel>
       <skos:prefLabel xml:lang="de">Greifvögel: Adler</skos:prefLabel>
       <skos:prefLabel xml:lang="it">uccelli rapaci: aquila</skos:prefLabel>
       <skos:prefLabel xml:lang="fi">petolinnut: kotka</skos:prefLabel>
       <skos:inScheme rdf:resource="http://iconclass.org/rdf/2011/09/"/>
       <skos:notation>25F33(EAGLE)</skos:notation>
       <skos:narrower rdf:resource="http://iconclass.org/25F33%28EAGLE%29%28%2B0%29"/>
       <skos:narrower rdf:resource="http://iconclass.org/25F33%28EAGLE%29%28%2B1%29"/>
       <skos:narrower rdf:resource="http://iconclass.org/25F33%28EAGLE%29%28%2B2%29"/>
       <skos:narrower rdf:resource="http://iconclass.org/25F33%28EAGLE%29%28%2B3%29"/>
       <skos:narrower rdf:resource="http://iconclass.org/25F33%28EAGLE%29%28%2B4%29"/>
<skos:narrower rdf:resource="http://iconclass.org/25F33%28EAGLE%29%28%2B5%29"/>
<skos:narrower rdf:resource="http://iconclass.org/25F33%28EAGLE%29%28%2B6%29"/>
<skos:narrower rdf:resource="http://iconclass.org/25F33%28EAGLE%29%28%2B7%29"/>
<skos:narrower rdf:resource="http://iconclass.org/25F33%28EAGLE%29%28%2B8%29"/>
<skos:narrower rdf:resource="http://iconclass.org/25F33%28EAGLE%29%28%2B9%29"/>
<skos:narrower rdf:resource="http://iconclass.org/25FF33%28EAGLE%29"/>
<skos:related rdf:resource="http://iconclass.org/25Fk12"/>
<skos:broader rdf:resource="http://iconclass.org/25F33%28...%29"/>
  </rdf:Description>
</rdf:RDF>
```

FIGURE 13.13 Starting from a display of emblem details, scholars can link to and browse the Iconclass subject hierarchy to find other emblems with related Iconclass headings.

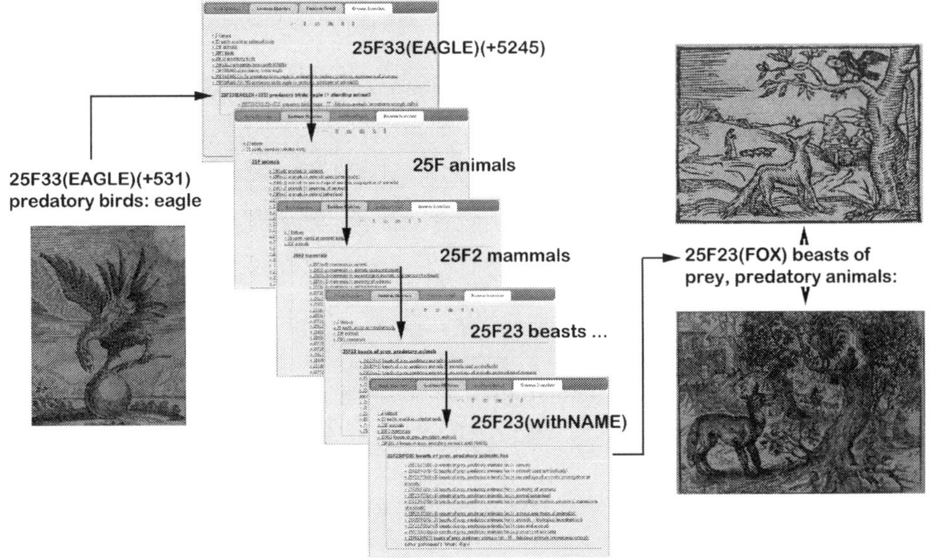

Evolving user expectations are also driving change. The ways librarians create and use metadata must keep up with user requirements. Users expect to find more and more library resources in digital format and expect immediate access to these resources. Semantic Web technologies and models of information in combination with initiatives such as Library Linked Open Data and Library 2.0 make it possible to collaborate more closely with domain scholars and other users when creating and curating resource metadata (Davidson 2008). Emerging technologies and approaches to knowledge management are prompting catalogers and metadata librarians to consider new paradigms. Catalogers and metadata librarians no longer rely exclusively on MARC or a single, monolithic ILS. When it comes to describing many kinds of digital resources, MARC is neither economical nor efficient. As Tennant (2004) suggests in "A Bibliographic Metadata Infrastructure for the Twenty-First Century," creating MARC catalog records for every digital resource can be expensive and makes it hard to create individual item-level metadata for a growing number of digital collections. In order to improve efficiency and efficacy of cataloging and metadata work flows, catalogers and metadata librarians need to be able to select from a range of metadata standards the most appropriate for the content at hand.

Given such a requirement, practical considerations dictate the separation of the syntactic and semantic facets of metadata. XML provides a strong syntactic foundation for metadata work flows and can be used to help make these work flows more robust and scalable while at the same time supporting a diversity of metadata semantic options. In XML, metadata can easily be migrated, segmented, and reused. Exploiting XML, DTDs, XSD, XSLT, and RDF in cataloging work flows makes it possible to meet library users' increasingly more sophisticated expectations. Ultimately, of course, XML is not a solution by itself. Rather, it can be a component of solutions implemented by catalogers and metadata librarians. XML is a useful tool but only in the hands of skilled and well-informed librarians.

QUESTIONS AND TOPICS FOR DISCUSSION

1. Think about changes and challenges for catalogers and metadata librarians that are not listed in this chapter but that also may have an impact on the future of bibliographic control.
2. Discuss the best way to provide staff members with training for XML. What is needed, and what ought to be considered?
3. The information included in library cataloging records, as well as the way it is delivered to users, has changed over time. What, in your opinion, are the most important changes that have affected the user experience?
4. As discussed, cataloging work flows are still evolving. Think about how XML and XML-related technologies can contribute positively to the evolution of cataloging work flows.

SUGGESTIONS FOR EXERCISES

1. The SPINE metadata for individual emblems has the book-level information in the <teiHeader> element created from MARCXML. Create an XSLT style sheet for transforming MARCXML to <teiHeader>.
2. Starting with the emblem metadata shown in Figure 13-7, create an XSLT style sheet that can generate the XHTML view of this metadata as shown in Figure 13.8. The XML schema for SPINE is publicly available on the Web at http://diglib.hab.de/rules/schema/emblem/emblem-1-2.xsd.

NOTES

1. http://www.w3.org/2001/sw.
2. http://www.w3.org/2005/Incubator/lld/XGR-lld-20111025.
3. http://www.w3.org/TR/rdfa-core/.
4. http://www.contentdm.org.
5. http://www.worldcat.org.
6. http://www.oclc.org/gateway/works/default.htm.
7. http://www.openarchives.org.
8. http://www.niso.org/standards/resources/Z39.50_Resources.
9. http://www.loc.gov/standards/sru.
10. http://www.rssboard.org.
11. http://vufind.org.
12. http://www.flickr.com.
13. http://www.flickr.com/commons.
14. http://imlsdcc.grainger.uiuc.edu.
15. http://www.aacr2.org.
16. http://www.w3.org/2005/Incubator/lld/wiki/Library_standards_and_linked_data.
17. http://diglib.hab.de/rules/schema/emblem/emblem-1-2.xsd.
18. https://wiki.dlib.indiana.edu/download/attachments/24288/DLFMODS_ImplementationGuidelines.pdf.
19. http://webservices.itcs.umich.edu/mediawiki/oaibp/index.php/DataProviderPractices.
20. http://contentdmmwg.wikispaces.com/file/view/BPG1.9.pdf.
21. http://www.w3.org/TR/xmlschema-0.
22. http://emblematica.grainger.illinois.edu.
23. http://www.iconclass.nl/home.
24. http://www.iso.org/iso/iso_catalogue/catalogue_tc/catalogue_detail.htm?csnumber=53681.
25. http://www.w3.org/TR/xslt20.
26. https://wiki.dlib.indiana.edu/download/attachments/1081387/DLF_MARC2MODS.xsl?version=1&modificationDate=1211391748000.

REFERENCES

Davidson, Cathy N. 2008. "Humanities 2.0: Promise, Perils, Predictions." *PMLA* 123, no. 3: 707–17.

Denton, William, and Sarah Coysh. 2011. "Usability Testing of VuFind at an Academic Library." *Library Hi Tech* 29, no. 2: 301–19. DOI: 10.1108/07378831111138189

Murer, Christoph. 1622. *XL [i.e. Quadraginta] emblemata miscella nova: Das ist: XL. underschiedliche Auszerlesene newradierte Kunststuck*. Zürych: Gedruckt bey J. Rüdolff Wolffen.

National Science Foundation. 2011. "NSF Data Management Plan Requirements." Available at: http://www.nsf.gov/eng/general/dmp.jsp

Powell, Christina Kelleher. 2008. "OPAC Integration in the Era of Mass Digitization: The MBooks Experience." *Library Hi Tech* 26, no. 1: 24–32.

"Redefining the Academic Library: Managing the Migration to Digital Information Services." 2011. Available at: http://www.theconferencecircuit.com/wp-content/uploads/Provosts-Report-on-Academic-Libraries2.pdf

Springer, Michelle, Beth Dulabahn, Phil Michel, Barbara Natanson, David Reser, David Woodward, and Helena Zinkham. 2008. "For the Common Good: The Library of Congress Flickr Pilot Project." Available at: http://www.loc.gov/rr/print/flickr_report_final.pdf

Tennant, Roy. 2004. "A Bibliographic Metadata Infrastructure for the Twenty-First Century." *Library Hi Tech* 22, no. 2: 175–81.

Veve, Marielle, and Melanie Feltner-Reichert. 2010. "Integrating Non-MARC Metadata Duties into the Workflow of Traditional Catalogers: A Survey of Trends and Perceptions among Cataloger in Four Discussion Lists." *Technical Services Quarterly* 27, no. 2: 194–213.

Vogel, Johann. 1649. *Meditationes emblematicae de restaurata pace Germaniae*. Francofurti: Apud Joh. Dav. Zunnerum.

Yang, Sharon Q., and Melissa A. Hofmann. 2011. "Next Generation or Current Generation? A Study of the OPACs of 260 Academic Libraries in the USA and Canada." *Library Hi Tech* 29, no. 2: 266–300. DOI: 10.1108/07378831111138170

Glossary of XML Terms

Attribute A class of XML markup objects used to associate with an element a named value that elaborates, augments, or functions as the content of the element. Syntactically, an attribute is a name-quoted value pair appearing in an element start-tag or as part of an empty-element-tag.

CDATA XML applications parse XML metadata records in order to distinguish content from markup. CDATA (Character Data) is content that is not meant to be parsed. Segments of a metadata record designated as CDATA can include characters such as "<" and "&" without causing confusion between markup and content.

Comments Markup used to insert a comment into an XML metadata record. Syntactically, XML Comments begin with "<!--" and end with "-->". The text of the comment is contained between these character sequences.

Content object In an XML metadata record each discrete unit of information can be modeled as a *content object*. For example, the title of a book is a common content object in a bibliographic record. XML is a way to organize a metadata record into an Ordered Hierarchy of Content Objects.

Document Object Model (DOM) The World Wide Web Consortium (W3C) has formally defined a generic Document Object Model (DOM) application programming interface for accessing and manipulating the content and markup of XML and HTML documents. The DOM approach models such documents as trees of nodes. The DOM is similar to but not identical with the ways that schemas, DTDs, XPath, and XSLT model XML documents. The term "DOM" is often used imprecisely. The W3C DOM is primarily of interest to programmers.

DTD A Document Type Definition is used to define the names of and relationships between markup objects (elements, attributes, and entities) allowed in XML metadata records conforming to a specific metadata standard. XML metadata records can be automatically validated for conformity to a DTD as a way to ensure record correctness.

Element A core class of XML markup objects used in delineating the structure and hierarchy of an XML metadata record. Syntactically, elements are delimited by a start-tag and paired end-tag or by an empty-element-tag. An element may contain a content object value or other elements (children) or be empty.

Empty-element-tag In XML, empty elements are sometimes used as structural tokens (e.g., to indicate a chapter break) or to show the absence of information (e.g., an empty title element for an untitled work). Empty elements can be represented by a start-tag immediately followed by an end-tag but more typically are represented by a single empty-element-tag, such as `<title />`.

End-tag Markup denoting the end of an element. Always paired with a start-tag and always begins "</". The name immediately following the slash must match the element name of the corresponding start-tag, such as `<title></title>`.

General entities and character references Classes of XML markup objects used as placeholders in content or attribute values. Syntactically, these begin with an ampersand character ("&") and end with a semicolon (";"), for example, "`<`" for "<". They stand in for special characters (e.g., the copyright symbol, "©"), for sequences of characters and/or markup used in multiple places in a record (e.g., a date), or for nontextual content.

Markup Everything in an XML metadata record that is not part of the metadata (i.e., content) is markup. XML markup begins and ends with left- and right-hand angle brackets ("< >") and exposes the structure and content objects of an XML metadata record, facilitating record use and reuse.

Namespace XML Namespaces provide a means to associate element and attribute names used in XML metadata records with a particular metadata grammar (standard) and a specific DTD or Schema (for validation). Namespaces are globally identified by Uniform Resource Identifiers.

Node XML metadata records are often represented as tree structures. In tree data model views of XML, each part of the tree—each element, attribute, entity, segment of text, and so on—is called a node.

PCDATA Unlike CDATA, Parsed Character Data are meant to be parsed and interpreted by XML parsers. For example, the character reference "`>`" in PCDATA will be recognized as a stand-in for ">", and the string `<title>` will be recognized as a start-tag.

Processing instructions Markup used to insert an application-specific instruction into an XML metadata record. XML parsers are allowed to ignore these instructions, but certain processing instructions are widely recognized, such as the one for associating an XSLT style sheet with an XML document. Syntactically, XML processing instructions begin with "<?" (but not "`<?xml`") and end with "?>".

Schema An XML schema (like a DTD) is used to define names of and relationships between markup objects (element, attribute, and entity) allowed in a class of XML metadata records. Records can be automatically validated for conformity to a schema (or schemas). As compared to DTDs, schemas can be used in combination and better specify constraints on the type of data an element may contain.

SGML XML was derived from Standard Generalized Markup Language, an international standard meta-markup language that predates the World Wide Web. XML is largely a restricted subset of SGML that is better optimized for use on the Web.

Start-tag Markup denoting the beginning of an element. Always paired with an end-tag and always begins with "<" followed immediately by the name of the element, such as `<creator></creator>`. Start-tags may also include attributes.

Style sheet Used to process the contents of an XML metadata record for presentation. XSL style sheets also can be used to analyze, manipulate, and transform XML metadata records in order to reuse or repurpose their information.

Valid XML A valid XML metadata record meets all the syntactic requirements of the XML specifications, such as for element naming, attribute and general entity syntax, and so on. Additionally, a valid XML metadata record also conforms to the constraints on semantics specified in a DTD or schema.

Well-formed XML A well-formed XML metadata record meets all the syntactic requirements of XML, such as for element naming and attribute and general entity syntax, but has not been validated against a DTD or schema. A well-formed XML metadata record becomes valid XML when it is validated against a DTD or schema.

XHTML Extensible HTML (XHTML) is a version of HTML that conforms to the syntactic requirements of XML (which are generally stricter and cleaner than the syntactic requirements of HTML).

XInclude XML Inclusion provides syntax and a processing model for merging together segments of separate XML documents.

Xlink XML Linking Language is used to define links between XML metadata records and between XML metadata records and other kinds of content. Analogous to HTML anchor elements but more expressive.

XML Extensible Markup Language (XML) is an open standard that is used to serialize (i.e., encode and describe) structured data and to facilitate the maintenance, organization, sharing, and reuse of these data by computer applications. (See additional definitions in Chapter 1.)

XML Declaration Every XML version 1.0 metadata record should start—and every XML version 1.1 metadata record must start—with an XML Declaration. Syntactically, an XML Declaration starts with "`<?xml`" and ends

with "?>". An XML Declaration specifies the version of XML to which the record conforms syntactically and may declare character encoding and other similar information about the record.

XPath XML Path language is used to navigate, analyze, and retrieve specific information from XML metadata records. XPath is an expression-based language that includes a set of built-in core operators and functions to give the language additional intrinsic programming power. It is meant to be embedded within a host language such as XSLT.

XPointer XML Pointer allows direct citing of individual components of an XML document (based on the component's XPath location path expression).

XQuery XML Query Language is a language for searching an XML document directly. It relies on XPath and shares the same underlying data model.

XSD Schemas conforming to the W3C XML Schema Definition Language are commonly given the file extension ".xsd" and referred to as "XSDs."

XSL The Extensible Stylesheet Language (XSL) family of specifications defines the semantics that enable XML metadata record transformation and presentation. The main components of XSL are XPath, XSLT, and XSL-FO.

XSL-FO The Extensible Style Sheet Language for Formatting Objects is an expression-based language for formatting XML. XSL-FO borrows concepts from the Cascading Stylesheet (CSS) language, extending this model to support more complex formatting, such as the creation of a PDF from XML.

XSLT XSL Transformations is a declarative, functional programming language for manipulating XML. XSLT can be used to selectively transform, reuse, and repurpose components of XML metadata records, typically saving generated results in other XML formats, such as XHTML, or other metadata standards. XSLT depends on XPath.

Index

About the Authors

TIMOTHY W. COLE is professor of library administration, professor of library and information science, and head of the Mathematics Library at the University of Illinois at Urbana-Champaign. A member of the faculty at Illinois since 1989, he has held prior administrative appointments as head of library digital services and development, systems librarian for digital projects, and assistant engineering librarian for information services. He researches and teaches on metadata work flows and digital library interoperability and is a principal investigator (PI) for the *Open Annotation Collaboration*, a co-PI for the *Emblematica Online* project and a co-PI/past PI for the *IMLS Digital Collections and Content* project. He is a member of the *Library Hi Tech* Editorial Board, past chair of the National Science Digital Library Technology Standing Committee, and a former member of the Open Archives Initiative Protocol for Metadata Harvesting (OAI-PMH) Technical Committee. He has published and presented widely on metadata best practices, OAI-PMH, digital library interoperability, and the use of XML and SGML for encoding metadata and digitized scholarly resources in science, mathematics, and literature. He has more than 50 published authored or coauthored papers in such diverse venues as *IEEE Computer*, *RQ*, *Reference Services Review*, *Lecture Notes in Computer Science*, *Library Hi Tech*, *Early Modern Literary Studies*, and the *Journal of Library Metadata*. He has presented research findings at the Institute of Museum and Library Service (IMLS) WebWise Conference, the American Library Association annual meeting, the American Society for Information Science and Technology annual meeting, the American Association of Law Libraries annual meeting, the Joint Conference on Digital Libraries, the Society for Emblem Studies International Conference, and elsewhere. In 2007, he coauthored *Using the Open Archives Initiative Protocol for Metadata Harvesting*, a previously published volume in the Third Millennium Cataloging series.

MYUNG-JA ("MJ") K. HAN is a metadata librarian and assistant professor of library administration at the University of Illinois at Urbana-Champaign. Prior to this position, she worked for the Illinois Harvest Project as a visiting metadata librarian. Her main responsibilities consist of developing application profiles for digital collections, creating metadata for digital resources, and evaluating and enhancing cataloging and metadata work flows. Her research interests include interoperability of metadata, especially using OAI-PMH and semantic web technologies, relationships between collection description and item-level metadata, and issues on bibliographic control in the digital library environment. She has published papers in *Library Trends*, *Library Resources and Technical Services*, and the *Journal of Library Metadata* on metadata quality and bibliographic control. She has presented her research findings at the American Library Association conferences, the International Conference on Dublin Core and Metadata Applications, and CONTENTdm User Group meetings.

Made in the USA
Middletown, DE
21 July 2018